WOMEN AND LITERATURE IN BRITAIN,
1800–1900

These new essays by leading scholars explore nineteenth-century women's writing across a spectrum of genres. The book's focus is on women's role in and access to literary culture in the broadest sense, as consumers and interpreters as well as practitioners of that culture. Individual chapters consider women as journalists, editors, translators, scholars, actresses, playwrights, autobiographers, biographers, writers for children and religious writers, as well as novelists and poets. The impact of women in the literary marketplace, women's role in public debate, the cultural power of women readers, women writers' construction of gender and sexuality, and the formation of a female canon are central concerns in a century which saw the emergence of a mass audience for literature. A unique chronology offers a woman-centred perspective on literary and historical events and there is a guide to further reading.

JOANNE SHATTOCK is Professor of Victorian Literature and Director of the Victorian Studies Centre at the University of Leicester. She has recently edited volume IV (*1800–1900*) of *The Cambridge Bibliography of English Literature*, 3rd edn (1999), and is the author of *The Oxford Guide to British Women Writers* (1993). She has published on women's writing, the nineteenth-century periodical press, nineteenth-century literary reviewing and on autobiography. Other books include *Politics and Reviewers* (1989), *Dickens and other Victorians* (1988) and *The Victorian Periodical Press* (with M. Wolff; 1982). She co-edits a monograph series, The Nineteenth Century, and is an associate editor of the *New DNB*. She is President of the British Association for Victorian Studies.

WOMEN AND LITERATURE IN BRITAIN 1800–1900

EDITED BY

JOANNE SHATTOCK

University of Leicester

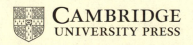

CAMBRIDGE
UNIVERSITY PRESS

PUBLISHED BY THE PRESS SYNDICATE OF THE UNIVERSITY OF CAMBRIDGE
The Pitt Building, Trumpington Street, Cambridge, United Kingdom

CAMBRIDGE UNIVERSITY PRESS
The Edinburgh Building, Cambridge CB2 2RU, UK
40 West 20th Street, New York, NY 10011–4211, USA
10 Stamford Road, Oakleigh, VIC 3166, Australia
Ruiz de Alarcón 13, 28014 Madrid, Spain
Dock House, The Waterfront, Cape Town 8001, South Africa

http://www.cambridge.org

First published 2001

Printed in the United Kingdom at the University Press, Cambridge

Typeface Baskerville MT 11/12.5 pt. *System* QuarkXPress™ [SE]

A catalogue record for this book is available from the British Library

Library of Congress Cataloguing in Publication data

Women and literature in Britain, 1800–1900 / edited by Joanne Shattock.
p.   cm.
Includes bibliographical references and index.
ISBN 0 521 65055 0 (hardback) – ISBN 0 521 65957 4 (paperback)
1. English literature – Women authors – History and criticism.   2. Women and
literature – Great Britain – History – 19th century.   3. English literature – 19th
century – History and criticism.   I. Shattock, Joanne.
PR115.W58   2001
820.9′9287′09034–dc21   2001025136

ISBN 0 521 65055 0 hardback
ISBN 0 521 65957 4 paperback

Contents

Contributors

MARGARET BEETHAM is Reader in the Department of English at Manchester Metropolitan University. She is the author of *A Magazine of Her Own? Domesticity and Desire in the Woman's Magazine 1800–1914* (1996), and of a number of articles on popular print and feminist theory. She is co-editor with Kay Boardman of the forthcoming *Victorian Women's Magazines: an Anthology* (2001).

VIRGINIA BLAIN is a Professorial Fellow in English at Macquarie University in Sydney. She is a co-author, with Patricia Clements and Isobel Grundy, of *The Feminist Companion to Literature in English* (1990) and an associate editor of the *New DNB*. Her recent publications include *Caroline Bowles Southey: the Making of a Woman Writer* (1998), *Victorian Women Poets: a New Annotated Anthology* (2000) and two collections of essays on women's poetry, edited with Isobel Armstrong, *Women's Poetry in the Enlightenment* and *Women's Poetry, Late Romantic to Late Victorian* (both 1999). She is currently writing a book on gender anxieties in Victorian poetry.

BARBARA CAINE is Professor of History at Monash University. She has written extensively on nineteenth-century English feminism. Her books include *Destined to be Wives: the Sisters of Beatrice Webb* (1986), *Victorian Feminists* (1992) and *English Feminism 1780–1980* (1997). She is general editor of *Australian Feminism: a Companion* (1998) and is currently working on a collective biography of the Strachey family.

HILARY FRASER, Professor of English at the University of Western Australia, is the author of *The Victorians and Renaissance Italy* (1992) and *English Prose of the Nineteenth Century* (with Daniel Brown, 1997). She is currently working on Victorian women art historians and, with Judith Johnston and Stephanie Green, a project on women, gender and the Victorian periodical press, entitled *Gender Divides*.

ELISABETH JAY is Professor of English and Associate Head of the School of Humanities at Oxford Brookes University. She has published on a wide range of nineteenth-century topics and genres, including women's writing, autobiography and biography, Victorian poetry and fiction. Her publications include *The Religion of the Heart: Anglican Evangelicalism and the Nineteenth-Century Novel* (1979), *Faith and Doubt in Victorian Britain* (1986) and *Mrs Oliphant: 'A Fiction to Herself'. A Literary Life* (1995). She co-edits a series on Religion and Culture for Macmillan and is an editor of the journal *Literature and Theology*.

JUDITH JOHNSTON teaches in the Department of English at the University of Western Australia. She is the author of *Anna Jameson: Victorian, Feminist, Woman of Letters* (1997) and, with Margaret Harris, edited *The Journals of George Eliot* (1998). She is currently completing a book on Victorian journalism, entitled *Gender Divides*, with Hilary Fraser and Stephanie Green, and developing another project on Australia and the British periodical press in 1800–1900.

ELIZABETH LANGLAND, Dean of Humanities and Professor of English at the University of California at Davis, is the author of *Nobody's Angels: Middle-Class Women and Domestic Ideology in Victorian Culture* (1995), *Anne Brontë: the Other One* (1989), and *Society in the Novel* (1984). She has co-edited *A Feminist Perspective in the Academy: the Difference It Makes* (1981), *The Voyage In: Fictions of Female Development* (1983) and *Out of Bounds: Male Writers and Gender(ed) Criticism* (1990). She has also published numerous articles on women in literature, feminist theory, Victorian literature and culture, cultural studies and narrative theory.

KATHERINE NEWEY is a theatre historian and senior lecturer in Theatre Studies at Lancaster University. She has published on early nineteenth-century fiction, Victorian melodrama, Australian and British popular theatre, and women playwrights of the nineteenth century. She is currently writing a full-length study of women's writing for the theatre from 1780 to 1915.

LINDA H. PETERSON is Professor of English and Director of the Bass Writing Programme at Yale University. She is the author of *Victorian Autobiography: the Tradition of Self-Interpretation* (1986) and *Traditions of Victorian Women's Autobiography: the Poetics and Politics of Life Writing* (1999). Her current project investigates the myths and material conditions of British women's authorship in the nineteenth century.

LYN PYKETT is Professor of English at the University of Wales Aberystwyth. She has written widely on nineteenth-century literature and culture. Her books include *Emily Bronte* (1989), *The 'Improper' Feminine: the Women's Sensation Novel and the New Woman Writing* (1992), *The Sensation Novel* (1994), and *Engendering Fictions: the English Novel in the early Twentieth Century* (1995). She is currently working on Dickens and Wilkie Collins.

VALERIE SANDERS is Professor of English Literature at the University of Hull and taught previously at the Universities of Sunderland and Buckingham. Her books include *The Private Lives of Victorian Women: Autobiography in Nineteenth-Century England* (1989) and *Eve's Renegades: Victorian Anti-feminist Women Novelists* (1996). She has also edited Harriet Martineau's letters (1990) and recently published *Records of Girlhood: An Anthology of Nineteenth-Century Women's Childhoods* (1999). Her current project is a study of brother/sister relationships in nineteenth-century literature and culture.

JOANNE SHATTOCK is Professor of Victorian Literature and Director of the Victorian Studies Centre at the University of Leicester. She has recently edited volume IV *(1800–1900)* of *The Cambridge Bibliography of English Literature* 3rd edn (1999). Her books include *The Oxford Guide to British Women Writers* (1993) and *Politics and Reviewers* (1989). She has edited *Dickens and other Victorians* (1988) and with Michael Wolff, *The Victorian Periodical Press: Samplings and Soundings* (1982). She is an associate editor of the *New DNB* and co-editor of The Nineteenth Century monograph series for Ashgate. She is currently working on a study of biographies of nineteenth-century women writers.

LYNNE VALLONE is Associate Professor of English at Texas A & M University. She is the author of *Disciplines of Virtue: Girls' Culture in the Eighteenth and Nineteenth Centuries* (1995), co-editor with Claudia Nelson of *The Girl's Own: Cultural Histories of the Anglo-American Girl, 1830–1915* (1994) and co-editor with Mary Ann O'Farrell of *Virtual Gender: Fantasies of Subjectivity and Embodiment* (1999). Her book on Queen Victoria's girlhood, *Becoming Victoria*, is forthcoming from Yale University Press.

JOANNE WILKES is a Senior Lecturer in English at the University of Auckland, New Zealand. Her publications include a study of the reception-history of Jane Austen's *Persuasion* and an edition for the World's Classics of Geraldine Jewsbury's novel *The Half Sisters* (1995). Her recent book, *Lord Byron and Madame de Staël: Born for Opposition* (1999), has received the Rose Mary Crawshay Prize from the British Academy and the Elma Dangerfield Award from the International Byron Society. She is currently working on nineteenth-century women as literary critics.

Acknowledgments

First and foremost I wish to thank my fellow contributors for sharing their expertise and enthusiasm for their subjects, and for their professionalism at all times, but particularly during the protracted process of turning thirteen individualistic essays into a coherent book. At Cambridge University Press Josie Dixon first proposed the project, and with her customary drive and knowledge of the subject made it a reality. Linda Bree has been a sympathetic, knowledgeable and astute reader and has also guided the manuscript through the press. I am also grateful for specialist advice from Alison Yarrington, Suzanne Fagence and Caroline Arscott.

Joanne Shattock

Chronology

The names of writers are given in the form most commonly used, eg. Elizabeth Barrett Browning, Anne Thackeray Ritchie. The dates of individual works are those of the first publication in volume form, rather than the serial version.

	Contexts	Texts
1800		Maria Edgeworth, *Castle Rackrent*
1801		Maria Edgeworth, *Moral Tales For Young People*, *Early Lessons*, *Belinda*; Elizabeth Hamilton, *Letters on Education*; Amelia Opie, *Father and Daughter*
1802	*Edinburgh Review* founded	Joanna Baillie, *Plays on the Passions* vol. II; Mary Meeke, *Midnight Weddings*; Jane West, *The Infidel Father*
1803		Mary Hays, *Female Biography*; Jane Porter, *Thaddeus of Warsaw*; Joanna Southcott, *Song of Moses and the Lamb*
1804		Joanna Baillie, *Plays on the Passions* vol. III; Maria Edgeworth, *Popular Tales*
1805	Battle of Trafalgar	Amelia Opie, *Adeline Mowbray*; Ann Taylor and Jane Taylor, *Original Poems for Infant Minds*
1806	*Monthly Repository* founded	Charlotte Dacre, *Zofloya: or The Moor*; Maria Edgeworth, *Leonora*; Sydney Owenson, Lady Morgan, *The Wild Irish Girl*; Ann Taylor and Jane Taylor, *Rhymes for the Nursery*

	Contexts	Texts
1807		Anne Grant, *Letters from the Mountains*; Charles Lamb and Mary Anne Lamb, *Tales from Shakespear*, Anna Maria Porter, *The Hungarian Brothers*; Charlotte Smith (d. 1806), *Beachy Head with other Poems*; Madame de Staël, *Corinne*
1808	Peninsular War begins	Miss Byron, *The English-woman*; Elizabeth Hamilton, *The Cottagers of Glenburnie*; Hannah More, *Coelebs in Search of a Wife*
1809	*Quarterly Review* founded	Felicia Hemans, *Poems*; Charles and Mary Anne Lamb, *Mrs Leicester's School*; Anna Seward (d. 1809), *Poetical Works*, ed. Walter Scott
1810		Lucy Aikin, *Epistles on Women*; Anna Laetitia Barbauld, The British Novelists (series begun); Mary Russell Mitford, *Miscellaneous Poems*; Jane Porter, *The Scottish Chiefs*; Ann Taylor and Jane Taylor, *Hymns for Infant Minds*
1811		Jane Austen, *Sense and Sensibility*; Anna Laetitia Barbauld, *The Female Speaker*, *'Eighteen Hundred and Eleven'*; Mary Brunton, *Self Control*; Mary Tighe, *Psyche, with other Poems* (priv. ptd 1805)
1812		Lady Charlotte Bury, *Self Indulgence*; Miss Byron, *The English-man*; Felicia Hemans, *Domestic Affections and other Poems*; Barbara Hofland, *The Son of a Genius*; Jane West, *The Loyalists*
1813	Southey becomes Poet Laureate	Jane Austen, *Pride and Prejudice*; Mary Russell Mitford, *Poems on the Female Character*
1814	Napoleon abdicates Colburn's *New Monthly Magazine* founded	Jane Austen, *Mansfield Park*; Mary Brunton, *Discipline*; Fanny Burney, *The Wanderer*; Maria Edgeworth, *Patronage*; Mary Martha Sherwood, *Little Henry and his Bearer*
1815	Battle of Waterloo 18 June	Christian Johnstone, *Clan Albin*; Helen Maria Williams, *A Narrative of the Events which have taken Place in France*
1816		Jane Austen, *Emma*; Lady Caroline Lamb, *Glenarvon*
1817	*Blackwood's Magazine*, *Literary Gazette* founded	Elizabeth Carter, ed., *Letters to Mrs Montagu*

Year	Events	Literary works
1818		Lucy Aikin, *Memoirs of the Court of Queen Elizabeth I*; Jane Austen, *Northanger Abbey*, *Persuasion*; Susan Ferrier, *Marriage*; Mary Shelley, *Frankenstein*; Mary Martha Sherwood, *The History of the Fairchild Family* pt 1 (pt 2 1842, pt 3 1847)
1819	Peterloo Massacre	Mary Brunton, *Emmeline*; Hannah More, *Moral Sketches*; Mary Shelley, *Matilda* (pbd 1959); Helen Maria Williams, *Letters on the Events which have Passed in France*
1820	Accession of George IV; Trial of Queen Caroline	Elizabeth Barrett Browning, *The Battle of Marathon*; Felicia Hemans, *The Sceptic*
1821		Joanna Baillie, *Metrical Legends*; Letitia Landon, *The Fate of Adelaide*
1822		Lucy Aikin, *Memoirs of the Court of King James I*; Amelia Opie, *Madeline*
1823	*Forget-Me-Not* (annual) founded	Caroline Bowles, *Tales of the Factories*; Barbara Hofland, *The Daughter of a Genius*; Mary Russell Mitford, *Julian*; Mary Shelley, *Valperga*
1824	*Westminster Review* and *Friendship's Offering* (annual) founded	Susan Ferrier, *The Inheritance*; Catherine Gore, *Theresa Marchmont*; Letitia Landon, *The Improvisatrice*; Mary Russell Mitford, *Our Village* (5 vols. 1824–37)
1825	Establishment of Ladies Society for the Relief of Negro Slaves	Alexander Dyce, *Specimens of British Poetesses*; Felicia Hemans, *The Forest Sanctuary and other Poems* (enlarged 1829); Letitia Landon, *The Troubadour*; Wm Thompson, *Appeal of One-Half of the Human Race, Women, against the Pretensions of the other Half, Men*
1826		Elizabeth Barrett Browning, *Essay on Mind*; Anna Jameson, *The Diary of an Ennuyée*; Mary Russell Mitford, *Foscari*; Anna and Jane Porter, *Tales round a Winter Hearth*; Ann Radcliffe, *Gaston de Blondville*; Mary Shelley, *The Last Man*
1827		Lady Charlotte Bury, *Flirtation*; Letitia Landon, *The Golden Violet*
1828	Duke of Wellington Prime Minister; *The Keepsake* (annual), the *Athenaeum*, the *Spectator* founded	Felicia Hemans, *Records of Women*; Mary Russell Mitford, *Rienzi*
1829		Anna Jameson, *The Loves of the Poets*; Letitia Landon, *The Venetian Bracelet*; Caroline Bowles Southey, *Chapters on Churchyards*

	Contexts	Texts
1830	Earl Grey Prime Minister; July Revolution, France; *Fraser's Magazine* founded	Catherine Gore, *Women as they are, or The Manners of the Day*; Maria Jane Jewsbury, *The Three Histories*; Mary Shelley, *The Fortunes of Perkin Warbeck*
1831		Susan Ferrier, *Destiny*; Catherine Gore, *Mothers and Daughters*; Mary Somerville, *The Mechanism of the Heavens*
1832	Great Reform Bill *Chambers's Edinburgh Journal*, *Tait's Edinburgh Magazine* founded	Anna Jameson, *Characteristics of Women*; Harriet Martineau, *Illustrations of Political Economy* (9 vols. 1832–4); George Sand, *Indiana* (tr. 1850); Frances Trollope, *Domestic Manners of the Americans*
1833	*Heath's Book of Beauty* (annual) founded	Lucy Aikin, *Memoirs of the Court of King Charles I*; Isabel Hill, trans of Mme de Staël's *Corinne*; Anne Manning, *Village Belles*; Harriet Martineau, *Poor Laws and Paupers Illustrated* (1833–4); George Sand, *Lelia*
1834	Lord Melbourne Prime Minister; Christian Johnstone edits *Tait's Edinburgh Magazine* (to 1846)	Lady Blessington, *Conversations with Lord Byron*; Maria Edgeworth, *Helen*; Harriet Martineau, *Illustrations of Taxation*; Mary Russell Mitford, *Charles the First*; Mary Somerville, *On the Connection of the Physical Sciences*
1835		Fanny Kemble, *Journal of a Residence in America*; Mary Russell Mitford, *Belford Regis*; Mary Shelley, *Lodore*
1836		Catharine Gore, *Mrs Armytage*; Mary Howitt, *Wood Leighton*; Caroline Norton, *A Voice from the Factories*; Caroline Bowles Southey, *The Birth-day*
1837	Accession of Queen Victoria *Bentley's Miscellany* founded	Anna Bray, *Trelawny of Trelawne*; Sara Coleridge, *Phantasmion*; Letitia Landon, *Ethel Churchill, or The Two Brides*; Harriet Martineau, *Society in America*; George Sand, *Mauprat*; Mary Shelley, *Falkner*; Frances Trollope, *The Vicar of Wrexhill*
1838		Lady Charlotte Guest, trans of *The Mabinogion*; Anna Jameson, *Winter Studies and Summer Rambles in Canada*; Harriet Martineau, *Retrospect of Western Travel*
1839	An Act to Amend the Law relating to the Custody of Infants	Rosina Bulwer Lytton, *Cheveley; or The Man of Honour*; Sarah Stickney Ellis, *The Women of England*; Letitia Landon, *The Zenana and Minor Poems*; Sarah Lewis, *Woman's Mission*; Harriet Martineau, *Deerbrook*; Catherine Sinclair, *Holiday House*; Frances Trollope, *The Widow Barnaby*

1840	Marriage of Victoria and Albert	Caroline Clive, *IX Poems by V*; Agnes and Elizabeth Strickland, *Lives of the Queens of England* (1840–8); Flora Tristan, *Promenades dans Londres*; Frances Trollope, *Michael Armstrong, the Factory Boy*
1841	Sir Robert Peel Prime Minister	Catherine Crowe, *The Adventures of Susan Hopley*; Catherine Gore, *Cecil*; Charlotte Elizabeth Tonna, *Helen Fleetwood*
1842	*Illustrated London News* started	*Diary and Letters of Fanny Burney 1778–1840*; Sarah Stickney Ellis, *The Daughters of England*; George Sand, *Consuelo* (trans. 1846)
1843	Wordsworth becomes Poet Laureate	Sarah Stickney Ellis, *The Wives of England*; *The Mothers of England*; Anna Katherine Elwood, *Memoirs of the Literary Ladies of England*; Charlotte Elizabeth Tonna, *The Wrongs of Woman* (1843–4); Frances Trollope, *Jessie Phillips*; *The Barnabys in America*
1844		Elizabeth Barrett Browning, *Poems*; Mary Cowden Clarke, *Concordance to Shakespeare* (1844–5); Lady Georgina Fullerton, *Ellen Middleton*; Elizabeth Sewell, *Amy Herbert*
1845		Eliza Acton, *Modern Cookery*; Sarah Flower Adams, *The Flock at the Fountain*; Margaret Fuller, *Woman in the Nineteenth Century*; Anne Marsh, *Mount Sorel*; Harriet Martineau, *Forest and Game Law Tales* (1845–6); Carolina, Baroness Nairne, *Lays from Strathearn*
1846	Lord John Russell Prime Minister	Charlotte Brontë, Emily Brontë and Anne Brontë, *Poems by Currer, Ellis and Acton Bell*; Marian Evans (George Eliot), trans. of *Das Leben Jesu* by J. F. Strauss; Elizabeth Sewell, *Laneton Parsonage*; Anne Marsh, *Emilia Wyndham*
1847	*Howitt's Journal* founded	Anne Brontë, *Agnes Grey*; Charlotte Brontë, *Jane Eyre*; Emily Brontë, *Wuthering Heights*; Lady Georgina Fullerton, *Grantley Manor*; Elizabeth Gaskell, 'Libby Marsh's Three Eras', 'The Sexton's Hero', in *Howitt's Journal*; Mary Howitt, *The Hero of West-Waylan*; *The Works of George Sand*, ed. M. M. Hays; Elizabeth Sewell, *Margaret Percival*
1848	Revolution in France	George W. Bethune, *The British Female Poets*; Anne Brontë, *The Tenant of Wildfell Hall*; Catherine Crowe, *The Night Side of Nature*; Elizabeth Gaskell, *Mary Barton*; Geraldine Jewsbury, *The Half-Sisters*; Anna Jameson, *Sacred and Legendary Art* (1848–52); Frederick Rowton, *The Female Poets of Great Britain*; Mary Somerville, *Physical Geography*
1849	*Household Words, Eliza Cook's Journal* founded	Charlotte Brontë, *Shirley*; Anne Manning, *The Maiden and Married Life of Mary Powell*; Harriet Martineau, *History of England during the Thirty Years' Peace* (1849–50); Margaret Oliphant, *Passages in the Life of Mrs Margaret Maitland*

	Contexts	Texts
1850	Tennyson Poet Laureate	Elizabeth Barrett Browning, *Poems*; Elizabeth Gaskell, *Lizzie Leigh*, *The Moorland Cottage*; Agnes and Elizabeth Strickland, *Lives of the Queens of Scotland* (1850–9)
1851	The *Monthly Packet* founded and edited by Charlotte Yonge (1851–90)	Elizabeth Barrett Browning, *Casa Guidi Windows*; Mary Cowden Clarke, *The Girlhood of Shakespeare's Heroines* (1851–2); Geraldine Jewsbury, *Marian Withers*; Anne Manning, *The Household of Sir Thomas More*; Anne Marsh, *Lettice Arnold*
1852		Dinah Mulock Craik, *The Head of the Family*; Mary Russell Mitford, *Recollections of a Literary Life*; Florence Nightingale, 'Cassandra' (pbd in Ray Strachey, *The Cause*, 1928); Harriet Beecher Stowe, *Uncle Tom's Cabin*
1853	Crimean War 1853–6	Charlotte Brontë, *Villette*; Elizabeth Gaskell, *Cranford*, *Ruth*; Elizabeth Sewell, *The Experience of Life*; Charlotte Yonge, *The Heir of Redclyffe*
1854		Barbara Bodichon, *A Brief Summary of the Laws Concerning Women*; Marian Evans (George Eliot) trans. of Ludwig Feuerbach's *Essence of Christianity*; Caroline Norton, *English Laws for Women in the Nineteenth Century*; George Sand, *Histoire de ma Vie* (1854–5)
1855	Lord Palmerston Prime Minister; *Saturday Review* founded	Caroline Clive, *Paul Ferroll*; Elizabeth Gaskell, *North and South*; Anna Jameson, *Sisters of Charity*; Bessie Rayner Parkes, *Remarks on the Education of Girls*; Catherine Winkworth, *Lyra Germanica*
1856		Isabella Bird, *The Englishwoman in America*; Dinah Mulock Craik, *John Halifax Gentleman*; Anna Jameson, *The Communion of Labour*; Charlotte Yonge, *The Daisy Chain*
1857	Matrimonial Causes Act Indian Mutiny	Eliza Acton, *The English Bread Book*; Charlotte Brontë (d. 1855), *The Professor*; Elizabeth Barrett Browning, *Aurora Leigh*; Elizabeth Gaskell, *The Life of Charlotte Brontë*; Emily Pfeiffer, *Valisneria; or A Midsummer Night's Dream*
1858	*English Woman's Journal* (1858–64) begun	George Eliot, *Scenes of Clerical Life*; Adelaide Procter, *Legends and Lyrics*; Anne Manning, *Deborah's Diary*; Dinah Mulock Craik, *A Woman's Thoughts about Women*

1859	Langham Place circle and Society for Promoting the Employment of Women founded; *All the Year Round* and *Macmillan's Magazine* established	George Eliot, *Adam Bede*, 'The Lifted Veil' (in *Blackwood's Magazine*); Dinah Mulock Craik, *A Life for a Life*; Emily Eden, *The Semi-Detached House*; Mary Sewell, *Children of Summerbrook*
1860	*Cornhill Magazine* founded; Emily Faithfull starts the Victoria Press	Elizabeth Barrett Browning, *Poems before Congress*; Emily Eden, *The Semi-attached Couple*; George Eliot, *The Mill on the Floss*; Florence Nightingale, *Notes on Nursing*; Mary Sewell, *Mother's Last Words*; Charlotte Yonge, *Pigeon Pie*
1861	American Civil War 1861–5	Isabella Beeton, *The Book of Household Management*; George Eliot, *Silas Marner*; Adelaide Procter, ed., *The Victoria Regia*; Jane Williams, ed., *The Literary Women of England*; Mrs Henry Wood, *East Lynne*
1862		Mary Elizabeth Braddon, *Lady Audley's Secret*; Elizabeth Barrett Browning, *Last Poems*; Frances Power Cobbe, *Female Education*; Christina Rossetti, *Goblin Market and other Poems*
1863	Emily Faithfull founds the *Victoria Magazine*	M. E. Braddon, *Aurora Floyd*, *Eleanor's Victory*, *John Marchmont's Legacy*; George Eliot, *Romola*; Elizabeth Gaskell, *Sylvia's Lovers*; Julia Kavanagh, *English Women of Letters*; Caroline Norton, *Lost and Saved*; Margaret Oliphant, *Salem Chapel*, *The Rector and the Doctor's Family*; Ouida, *Held in Bondage*; Anne Thackeray Ritchie, *The Story of Elizabeth*
1864	Contagious Diseases Acts	Frances Power Cobbe, *Broken Lights*; George Eliot, 'Brother Jacob' (in *Cornhill Magazine*); Elizabeth Gaskell, *Cousin Phillis*; Margaret Oliphant, *The Perpetual Curate*; Lady Wilde, *Poems by Speranza*
1865		Lucy Duff Gordon, *Letters from Egypt*; Eliza Lynn Linton, *Grasp your Nettle*; Florence Marryat, *Love's Conflict*; Bessie Rayner Parkes, *Essays on Woman's Work*; John Ruskin, 'Of Queens' Gardens' in *Sesame and Lilies*; Charlotte Yonge, *The Clever Woman of the Family*

	Contexts	Texts
1866	*Aunt Judy's Magazine*, *Englishwoman's Review* founded; M. E. Braddon editor of *Belgravia* 1866–76; Second Reform Bill;	George Eliot, *Felix Holt*; Elizabeth Gaskell, *Wives and Daughters*; Margaret Oliphant, *Miss Marjoribanks*; Christina Rossetti, *The Prince's Progress and other Poems*; Augusta Webster, *Dramatic Studies*
1867	Women's Suffrage petition presented to Parliament; Mrs Henry Wood buys and edits the *Argosy*	Rhoda Broughton, *Cometh up as a Flower*; Jean Ingelow, *The Story of Doom*; Eliza Lynn Linton, *Sowing the Wind*; Ouida, *Under Two Flags*; Anne Thackeray Ritchie, *The Village on the Cliff*; Hesba Stretton, *Jessica's First Prayer*; Augusta Webster, *A Woman Sold and other poems*
1868	Gladstone Prime Minister (December)	Louisa May Alcott, *Little Women*; Frances Power Cobbe, *Criminals, Idiots, Women and Minors*; George Eliot, *The Spanish Gypsy*; Frances Cashel Hoey, *A House of Cards*; Eliza Lynn Linton, 'The Girl of the Period' (in *Saturday Review* 14 March); Queen Victoria, *Leaves from a Journal of our Life in the Highlands*
1869	Oxford and Cambridge local examinations made available to women; Elizabeth Garrett Anderson qualifies as a doctor	Josephine Butler, ed., *Women's Work and Women's Culture*; Harriet Martineau, *Biographical Sketches*; Juliana Horatia Ewing, *Mrs Overtheway's Remembrances*; Jean Ingelow, *Mopsa the Fairy*; John Stuart Mill, *The Subjection of Women*; Mary Somerville, *On Molecular and Microscopic Science*
1870	Franco-Prussian War (1870–1); Education Act; Married Women's Property Act gives women right to their own earnings; *Women's Suffrage Journal* begun	James Austen-Leigh, *Memoir of Jane Austen*; Rhoda Broughton, *Red as a Rose is She*; Augusta Webster, *Portraits*
1871	Women eligible for election to Local School Boards	Jane Austen, *Lady Susan, The Watsons* (in 2nd edn of J. Austen-Leigh's *Memoir*); George Eliot, *Middlemarch* (in 8 parts 1871–2); Ouida, *Folle-Farine*

Year	Events	Publications
1872		Emily Eden, *Letters from India*; Jean Ingelow, *Off the Skelligs*; Eliza Lynn Linton, *Joshua Davidson*; Christina Rossetti, *Sing-Song: a Nursery Rhyme Book*
1873	Girton College, Cambridge, opened	Juliana Horatia Ewing, *A Flatiron for a Farthing*; Anne Thackeray Ritchie, *Old Kensington*; Charlotte Yonge, *The Pillars of the House*
1874	Disraeli Prime Minister	George Eliot, *The Legend of Jubal*; Christina Rossetti, *Speaking Likenesses*; Ouida, *Two Little Wooden Shoes*; Dorothy Wordsworth, *Recollections of a Tour in Scotland* (written 1803)
1875		Dinah Mulock Craik, *The Little Lame Prince*; Alice Meynell, *Preludes*; Helen Mathers Reeves, *Comin' thro' the Rye*; Christina Rossetti, *Goblin Market, The Prince's Progress and other Poems*
1876	Women gain right to register as physicians	Isabella Banks, *The Manchester Man*; George Eliot, *Daniel Deronda*; Mary Louisa Molesworth, *Carrots*; Margaret Oliphant, *Phoebe Junior*
1877	The *Nineteenth Century* started	Frances Hodgson Burnett, *That Lass o' Lowrie's*; Amelia Edwards, *A Thousand Miles up the Nile*; Jessie Fothergill, *The First Violin*; Harriet Martineau's *Autobiography*; Mary Louisa Molesworth, *The Cuckoo Clock*; Anna Sewell, *Black Beauty*
1878	Women admitted to degrees at University of London	Kate Greenaway, *Under the Window*; Fanny Kemble, *Records of a Girlhood*; Helen Mathers Reeves, *Cherry Ripe!*; Augusta Webster, *A Housewife's Opinions*
1879		Isabella Bird, *A Lady's Life in the Rocky Mountains*; George Eliot, *Theophrastus Such*; Mary Louisa Molesworth, *The Tapestry Room*
1880	Gladstone's Second Cabinet	Isabella Bird, *Unbeaten Tracks in Japan*; Lady Florence Dixie, *Across Patagonia*; Eliza Lynn Linton, *The Rebel of the Family*; Margaret Oliphant, *A Beleaguered City*; Ouida, *Moths*; Augusta Webster, *Disguises*
1881		Mathilde Blind, *The Prophecy of St Oran*; Frances Power Cobbe, *The Duties of Women*; Christina Rossetti, *A Pageant and other Poems*
1882	Married Women's Property Act	Lady Caroline Fox, *Journals*; Frances Cashel Hoey, *The Question of Cain*; Emily Pfeiffer, *Under the Aspens*; Margaret Oliphant, *A Little Pilgrim in the Unseen*; Edith Simcox, *Episodes in the Lives of Men, Women and Lovers*

Year	Event	Works
1891		Wollstonecraft's *Vindication of the Rights of Woman*, ed. Millicent Garrett Fawcett, 'John Oliver Hobbes' (Pearl Craigie), *Some Emotions and a Moral*; Eliza Lynn Linton, 'The Wild Women: as Politicians', 'The Wild Women: as Social Insurgents', both in the *Nineteenth Century*; 'Lucas Malet', *The Wages of Sin*; Florence Marryatt, *There is no Death*; Olive Schreiner, *Dreams*; Somerville and Ross, *Naboth's Vineyard*; Beatrice Webb, *The Co-operative Movement in Britain*
1892	Gladstone forms Fourth Cabinet	Mary Coleridge, *The Seven Sleepers of Ephesus*; 'Michael Field', *Sight and Song*; Emily Lawless, *Grania*; Eliza Lynn Linton, 'The Partisans of the Wild Women'; Christina Rossetti, *The Face of the Deep*; Mary Ward, *The History of David Grieve*
1893		Annie Besant, *An Autobiography*; Helen C. Black, *Notable Women Authors of the Day*; Marie Corelli, *Barabbas*; George Egerton, *Keynotes*; Sarah Grand, *The Heavenly Twins*; Alice Meynell, *Poems*
1894	Formation of National Union of Women's Suffrage Societies	Gertrude Bell, *Persian Pictures*; Mona Caird, *The Daughters of Danaus*; *The Life of Frances Power Cobbe by herself*; George Egerton, *Discords*; Elizabeth Robins, *George Mandeville's Husband*; Somerville and Ross, *The Real Charlotte*; Flora Annie Steel, *The Potter's Thumb*; Mary Ward, *Marcella*
1895	Lord Salisbury Prime Minister; the *Woman's Signal* established	Marie Corelli, *The Sorrows of Satan*; Ella d'Arcy, *Monochromes*; Isabella Ford, *On the Threshold*; Augusta Webster, *Mother and Daughter*
1896	Alfred Austin becomes Poet Laureate	Marie Corelli, *The Mighty Atom*; Mary Coleridge, *Fancy's Following*; 'Lucas Malet', *The Carissima*; Alice Meynell, *The Colour of Life, Other Poems*; Christina Rossetti, *Poems*, ed. W. M. Rossetti
1897		Mona Caird, *The Morality of Marriage and other Essays*; George Egerton, *Symphonies*; Sarah Grand, *The Beth Book*; Mary Kingsley, *Travels in West Africa*; *Women Novelists of Queen Victoria's Reign*; May Sinclair, *Audrey Craven*; E. L. Voynich, *The Gadfly*; Dorothy Wordsworth, *Journals*, ed. W. Knight
1898		'Elizabeth' (Elizabeth Von Arnim), *Elizabeth and her German Garden*; Alice Meynell, *The Spirit of Place*; May Sinclair, *Mr and Mrs Nevill Tyson*; Mary Ward, *Helbeck of Bannisdale*

Introduction

Joanne Shattock

No group of women, undistinguished by rank, unendowed by beauty, and known to but a limited circle of friends as unimportant as themselves have ever, I think, in the course of history – certainly never in this century – come to such universal recognition. The effect is quite unique, unprecedented, and difficult to account for; but there cannot be the least doubt that it is a matter of absolute fact which nobody can deny.[1]

Margaret Oliphant's assessment of the Brontë 'phenomenon', written in 1897, was accurate. The sisters' reputation was as high fifty years after their deaths as it had been during their brief lives. The occasion of her tribute, a collection of essays by living women novelists writing on their deceased sisters, was a public recognition of an equivalent phenomenon. *Women Novelists of Queen Victoria's Reign: a Book of Appreciations*, commissioned by the fiction publishers Hurst and Blackett, celebrated nearly a century of achievement by women writers. Oliphant had heralded the achievement much earlier, famously declaring in 1855 that the nineteenth century, 'which is the age of so many things – of enlightenment, of science, of progress – is quite as distinctly the age of female novelists'.[2]

Her comment, and the Hurst and Blackett collection, told only part of the story. To a prolific novelist like Oliphant, and to many less partial observers, women appeared to have appropriated fiction as their particular genre. What the remark did not acknowledge was the extent and variety of women's contributions to nineteenth-century literary culture in its widest sense.

There was undoubtedly a heightened awareness, even a sense of excitement about women's increased presence on the literary scene. One of the ways in which this registered publicly was in the number of biographical dictionaries, anthologies and retrospective assessments of women writers which were published in the period. Early collections

I

such as Mary Hays's *Female Biography: or Memoirs of Illustrious and Celebrated Women of All Ages and Countries* (1803) and Mary Matilda Betham's *A Biographical Dictionary of the Celebrated Women of every Age and Country* (1804), while including few women writers, nevertheless established a model of female collective biography.[3] From them emerged a steady flow of publications concerned with women authors, which recycled biographical details and added a modicum of critical assessment. Mary Ann Stodart's *Female Writers, Thoughts on their Proper Sphere and their Powers of Usefulness* (1842), Anna Katherine Elwood's *Memoirs of the Literary Ladies of England* (1843), Jane Williams's *The Literary Women of England* (1861) and Julia Kavanagh's *English Women of Letters* (1863) promised, on the whole, more than they delivered in terms of critical acuity, or even factual accuracy, but collectively they conveyed the sense that at mid-century it was time to reassess, and to celebrate, women's place in literature. Inadvertently, of course, the collections also contributed to the creation of a literary canon.

Women poets were singled out for special treatment, often with the telling designation of 'poetesses'. Alexander Dyce's *Specimens of British Poetesses* (1825) and Leigh Hunt's 'Specimens of British Poetesses' 1847[4] were matched at the end of the century by E. S. Robertson's *English Poetesses* (1883), the last perfecting the art of damning with faint praise. George W. Bethune, *The British Female Poets* (1848) and Frederick Rowton's *The Female Poets of Great Britain* (1848) combined anthology with biographical notes. Elizabeth Sharp's *Women's Voices* (1877) and 'Sarah Tytler' [Henrietta Keddie] and J. L. Watson's *The Songstresses of Scotland* (1871) were two influential anthologies of women poets compiled by women. A. H. Miles in his ten-volume collection, *The Poets and Poetry of the Century* (1891–7) devoted one volume to women poets. Each of these publications, while outwardly celebratory, also separated the women poets from their male colleagues. As was the case with the other collections, they engaged in a process of canon formation.

What the biographical dictionaries, collections and anthologies did not register were the inroads women writers were making into a range of discourses outside the literary mainstream. Some of these were in traditionally masculine disciplines such as history, science and political economy. Women's contributions to children's literature, religious discourse and to the literature of domestic economy, traditionally feminine pursuits, increased in number and in profile in an age of mass publishing. Self-writing, which included autobiography and the domestic memoir, was another genre in which women made an impact, adding these forms to the letters and dairies they had always written. Often the dutiful assemblers of materials for biographies written by their male relations and colleagues, they now published biographies themselves, both individual and collective. Women's established presence in the theatre, as actresses, patrons and as playwrights, was reinforced in the nineteenth century. They became journalists, historians of art, literary critics, translators and editors. It is the extraordinary richness and variety of women's contributions to nineteenth-century literary culture, their forays into an expanding range of discourses, which forms the subject of this book.

Women writers have traditionally written across a spectrum of genres. The opening up of more avenues for a writing life in the nineteenth century meant that the practice became almost routine. For every women writer who was recognized as a poet or a novelist, there were as many who combined one of these genres with output in at least one other. Another important factor in this period was the necessity of employment for women of the middle class.

The polarization of the 'public' (male) and the 'private' (female) sphere is part of Victorian ideology, but, as historians remind us, it was a very real part of nineteenth-century experience. One of the ways in which women negotiated this seemingly rigid barrier was through writing. As work of all kinds gradually moved out of the home and into a public workplace, writing remained one means of employment which could be conducted from within the domestic sphere, 'with only the name and the product of the author being necessarily in the public domain' as Dorothy Thompson has pointed out.[5]

Valerie Sanders, in her study of the literary marketplace as it affected women writers of fiction (ch. 7), shows how they confronted an almost entirely masculine literary establishment, from editors and publishers' readers through to publishers and reviewers. She focuses on a number of significant relationships between women authors and male publishers, unique combinations of talent and temperament which had an impact on each partner. She shows too how women networked in a 'hit-and-miss' fashion to facilitate this particular rite of passage into a male world. Earnings were important to women authors, not least because they were the key to becoming professional, and few women remained long as innocents in the commercial world. In chapter 8, Virginia Blain identifies the poet Letitia Landon as a shrewd manipulator of the literary marketplace, and points out that, whereas in the 1830s poetry was a

profitable genre for poets like Landon and Felicia Hemans, this was not
the case for others like Augusta Webster and Mathilde Blind, writing
later in the century.

One vital arena for the woman writer in the nineteenth century, and
one of which her eighteenth-century predecessors had only a foretaste,
was the expanding periodical press. The role of journalism as an adjunct
of a literary career for women, and later a career in its own right, the
opportunities the press offered to the emerging woman writer, and the
impact of reviewing, on both the reviewer and the subject, are themes
which run through many of the chapters in this book. Virginia Blain sees
the press as a forum through which women poets could encounter each
other's work for the first time, and through which they could become
known to one another or at least begin a 'conversation' among themselves. Barbara Caine, in her discussion of women's contribution to
public debate (ch. 5), notes the extent to which women used journalism
and their access to the periodical press to 'shift the framework of discussion' about women, to give women the public forum they lacked, and
to make their voices 'a significant part of public culture'.

Joanne Wilkes (ch. 2) writes of the ways in which male reviewers
ascribed particular characteristics to writing on the basis of the author's
sex, and how insistently reviewers wrote with definite preconceptions of
the authors as women. Virginia Blain sees the advent of female reviewers, particularly of poetry, as decidedly helpful in improving the treatment of women poets. Hilary Fraser and Judith Johnston (ch. 11)
emphasize the crucial role of the press in the professionalization of
women's writing. However, they and Barbara Caine independently
make the point that, while the periodical press offered women opportunities to write on subjects from which they had hitherto been excluded,
such as political economy and science, they were regarded as populariz-
ers of those subjects, rather than the instigators of new ideas. The role
of writers like Harriet Martineau and Frances Power Cobbe, both of
them eminent 'women of letters', was to explain and distill the ideas of
(male) political economists and scientists, rather than writing on these
subjects in their capacity as professionals. Periodical writing, Johnston
and Fraser argue, thus became feminized.

Work and home, the domestic and the professional, were competing
pulls in the lives of nineteenth-century women writers in ways recogniz-
able to the modern woman. The power structures inherent in the
domestic household, and the codes of social conduct, on the other hand,
were aspects of life from which no nineteenth-century woman was

immune. Elizabeth Langland writes (ch. 6) of an extensive 'discourse of domesticity' in the form of household manuals and conduct books written by women, which regulated authority and established power networks within the domestic sphere. The 'social capital' generated by middle-class domestic managers was the equivalent of the economic capital earned by their husbands. She also demonstrates the ways in which novels by women from Oliphant and Gaskell to George Eliot 'inscribed and exposed' the dynamic of the domestic household.

Work is inscribed in a variety of ways in women's writing. In her chapter on self-writing (ch. 10), Linda Peterson shows how women autobiographers variously represented their writing lives, particularly in relation to their domestic lives. She identifies missionary autobiographies as important accounts of women engaged in serious work outside the home, undertaking heroic action. Katherine Newey (ch. 9), writing of nineteenth-century women's involvement in the theatre at several levels, sees this as a visible instance of 'women's increasing autonomy and self-definition through work' in the period. Judith Johnston and Hilary Fraser note a focus, in the biographies of some women writers, on the life only as it served the career, rather than the way in which the profession may have framed the life. Joanne Shattock on the other hand (ch. 1) sees biographers of women writers varying in their emphases, some deliberately presenting the writing life, others determined to reveal or to explain 'the woman behind the books' to a reading public eager for this revelation.

Margaret Beetham (ch. 3) focuses on the woman as reader, the consumer of a vast and increasing print culture directed to her. She identifies 'a set of cultural anxieties' around the figure of the female reader which were to do with class and race as well as gender and sexuality. The analogy of the consumption of food and the consumption of print was 'endemic' in nineteenth-century discourses of reading. She sees the growth in magazines addressed to women as consumers as one indication of the interconnectedness of the domestic and the public worlds, of production and consumption, 'whether of books, roast beef or Paris fashions'. Lyn Pykett (ch. 4) argues that women's participation in the cultural domain, and particularly writing, was one of the most significant ways in which nineteenth-century women could shape and change how they understood their own gender and sexuality. Her chapter examines the multiplicity of discourses, medical, legal and historical, which contributed to that process. One of her concerns is the way in which nineteenth-century constructions of gender and sexuality intersected with those of class.

Religion offered an alternative network to women who were excluded from masculine literary circles and contacts. The writing of tracts and the editing of Christian journals and magazines for women presented another point of entry into literary culture, as Elisabeth Jay suggests (ch. 12). She identifies translation, religious verse and the writing of religious biography as three additional genres through which women engaged with religious discourse and from which they sometimes moved into the literary mainstream. Both Jay and Lynne Vallone in her discussion of writers of children's literature (ch. 13) point to the Evangelical educational agenda for women which was such a formative influence on a number of women writers. Vallone notes a concern for separate, gendered fiction for girls and boys which emerged in children's literature from the mid-century.

The range of writers discussed in these chapters offer incontrovertible evidence of the growing professionalization of women's writing in the nineteenth century and their indelible presence in a variety of discourses. The women writers we have come to regard as canonical: Austen, Shelley, the Brontës, Elizabeth Gaskell, George Eliot, Elizabeth Barrett Browning, Christina Rossetti, are present in many of the essays. As biographical subjects they are discussed in chapter 1 where it is argued that biographies constructed the woman writer inherited by the next generation of writers and readers. They offer evidence in chapter 2 of the influence of reviewing and contemporary reception in the formation of a canon. They feature in discussions of the marketplace, women's poetry, women's reading, self-writing, and writing for children. By placing them in context with their less well-known colleagues, and by situating their literary production alongside an enormous body of non-canonical writing by women, their achievement is given a series of important new perspectives.

The scope and variety of women writers and texts discussed in this book, from the authors of household books, domestic memoirs, girls' stories, religious verse, to the writings of feminist campaigners, playwrights, journalists and historians of art, alter irrevocably our perception of the terrain of women's writing in the nineteenth century. No longer can we accept without qualification the assertion that this was *the age of female novelists*.

The essays in this volume are focussed, as the title suggests, on women and literature in *Britain*. It is a truism that the ramifications of women's contributions to literary culture in the nineteenth century extended far beyond these shores. Relationships with women writing in North America were strong. The influence of both major and minor figures extended to Australia and other colonial centres, and, as was the case with North America, the relationship was reciprocal. We have not attempted a study of what might be termed the centre and the periphery, nor of women's literary relations with the continent. These subjects are sufficiently complex and also vast as to warrant a study of their own. Nor have we considered in detail non-metropolitan literary cultures within the United Kingdom, although representative figures from centres outside London figure in many of the chapters. This subject too awaits an independent study.

As is the case with other volumes in the *Women and Literature* series, the essays are preceded by a woman-centred chronology of cultural and literary events, legislation and public debates affecting women in the nineteenth century. A Guide to Further Reading is organized according to the major themes and topics covered in the book.

NOTES

1 Mrs Oliphant, 'The Sisters Brontë', in *Women Novelists of Queen Victoria's Reign. A Book of Appreciations* (London: Hurst and Blackett, 1897), p. 6.

2 [Margaret Oliphant], 'Modern Novelists – Great and Small', *Blackwood's Magazine* 77 (May 1855), p. 555. Valerie Sanders discusses the implications of her remark in Ch. 7, p.142.

3 There had been earlier collections, such as George Ballard's *Memoirs of Several Ladies of Great Britain* (1752) and John Duncombe's *The Feminiad; or Female Genius: A Poem* (1751), but Hays's and Betham's collections appearing within a year of one another were important influences on what followed.

4 In his *Men, Women and Books: a Selection of Sketches, Essays and Critical Memoirs from his Uncollected Writings*, vol. II (London, 1847).

5 Dorothy Thompson, 'Women, Work and Politics in Nineteenth-Century England: the Problem of Authority in Jane Rendall, ed., *Equal or Different: Women's Politics 1800–1914* (Oxford: Blackwell, 1987), p. 69.

CHAPTER I

The construction of the woman writer

Joanne Shattock

'A woman and her book are identical' – or so Edgar Allen Poe reflected when reading an early collection of poems by Elizabeth Barrett Browning.[1] Remembering the autobiographical nature of much of Barrett Browning's early work, his comment is not surprising. But it has a more general relevance for nineteenth-century women writers. The charge that they could only write of what they knew, and that what they knew best was themselves, was made regularly by reviewers. The easy association of the life and the work, or, more accurately, a refusal to separate them, was crucial to the reading of these writers by their contemporaries. In this chapter I am concerned with the reading of Victorian women, how they were read in the nineteenth century, particularly how they read one another, and how we read them today. More specifically I am interested in the role that contemporary biography played in this process: how, in a number of celebrated instances, a biography constructed the woman writer inherited by the next generation of writers and readers of both sexes.

It was the feminist critic Ellen Moers who first made the point that nineteenth-century English women writers sought and created the sense of a literary community by reading one another's books. 'The personal give-and-take of the literary life was closed to them', she wrote, 'Without it they studied with a special closeness the works written by their own sex, and developed a sense of easy, almost rude familiarity with the women who wrote them.'[2] Of course these were highly intelligent women reading the work of other highly intelligent women. They knew better than to look only for self-representation in these texts. They were astute critics of one another's work and conveyed their views, sometimes in personal correspondence, sometimes in published reviews. But to these writers, reading one another's books made them feel that they knew the authors. It was an alternative to a female literary society.

This reading culture was not confined to women writers as readers. It extended to all women readers. In her study of attitudes to women's reading in the Victorian period, Kate Flint notes the sense of community felt by women readers of fiction and the emergence of female heroines as role models.[3] I am suggesting that both the seeking of role models, and the felt need for a personal knowledge of these women, governed the reading of biographies as well as the works of women writers by one another. To the wider reading public, both male and female, the biographies attracted the curious and the prurient as biographies have always done, but for this wider readership too there was a sense of wanting to know the woman behind the books.

Richard D. Altick in his *Lives and Letters: a History of Literary Biography in England and America* notes the post-Romantic enthusiasm for literary biography, a process driven by an instinctive 'quest for the creator behind the creation'. He suggests that the lives of writers, as distinct from other biographical subjects, acquire their appeal from the seeming remoteness of the literary life from ordinary experience, a sense derived from the Romantic poets that the writer was a person apart from society, and in some way 'special'.[4] In the case of nineteenth-century women writers, the search for the woman behind the books acquired a particular fascination because relatively few people knew these women personally. Although professional writers, they did not inhabit the public sphere. They were not members of the universities, they could not frequent the clubs and societies which were the haunts of male writers; they did not give readings or lectures; their connection with politics and the professions was tangential, through family connections; even opportunities for travel were circumscribed. Their increasing contribution to the world of journalism was conducted from home. Details of their lives were often the subject of gossip and speculation. And it was often to pre-empt further gossip and the circulation of erroneous material or to control the way their lives were presented to the public that biographies were commissioned. This was Patrick Brontë's reason for asking Elizabeth Gaskell to write the life of his daughter Charlotte. It was also one of William Godwin's reasons for writing a memoir of his wife Mary Wollstonecraft. And it was the reason why friends and supporters of Letitia Landon conducted a campaign to rescue her reputation after her premature death, a campaign conducted by writing and rewriting her life – and her death – for more than thirty years.

Most women writers, like many of their male colleagues, shunned biography and took steps to prevent any such posthumous publication, or their families did it for them. Cassandra Austen destroyed many of

Jane Austen's letters because she regarded them as too personal. Maria Edgeworth reacted against a proposed biographical preface to her works with the argument that 'as a woman, my life, wholly domestic, cannot afford anything interesting to the public'.[5] Elizabeth Gaskell secured her daughters' assurances that there would be no biography after her death. Margaret Oliphant extracted a deathbed promise from her literary executors that there would be no account of her life, a somewhat ironic injunction from the author of five biographies and numerous biographical sketches. Harriet Martineau recalled and destroyed her own letters. Yet Oliphant and Martineau were two of the few women writers in the nineteenth century who wrote autobiographies, possibly to pre-empt the biographies they so opposed. George Eliot resolutely refused to contribute personal biographical information to various collective biographical projects of the period. She expressed her opposition to biography on several occasions, the last on the death of her partner G. H. Lewes when she announced that there was to be no biography. 'The best history of a writer is contained in his writings: – Biographies generally are a disease of English literature', she wrote to a friend.[6] Yet, as their published correspondence reveals, both Lewes and Eliot were avid readers of contemporary biography.

Victorian biography, it is fair to say, has received a bad press of late. The burgeoning of literary biography both inside and outside the academy, as we are presently experiencing it, has brought with it a new self-consciousness, an interest in the development of the genre, although it trails behind the intense critical and theoretical focus on autobiography.[7] In these assessments the so called 'Victorian model', by which is meant the two- or three-volume 'Life and Letters', is regarded as a primitive form, representative of the dark days, before Freud's theories were common currency, and before Lytton Strachey's iconoclastic reworking of the genre. In other words it is a form which modern literary biography has left behind. I do not want to spend time defending the 'Victorian model', but I would caution against the assumption that there was a standard one, that they were always reverent, that there was 'no sex, no scandal, no self-doubt on the part of either subject or writer', as one modern practitioner has described them.[8]

Comparatively few women writers were memorialized by full-scale biographies. Collective biographies of women writers, on the other hand, were published in profusion. Alison Booth has written of the exemplary element inherent in collective biographies of historical figures.[9] Those devoted to women writers had the additional effect of contributing, however unofficially, to the creation of a canon. Works such as Anna Katherine Elwood's *Memoirs of the Literary Ladies of England* (1843), Jane Williams's *The Literary Women of England* (1861) and Julia Kavanagh's *English Women of Letters* (1863) recycled biographical information and offered some critical assessment of mainly novelists and prose writers. Frederick Rowton's *The Female Poets of Great Britain* (1848) and Eric S. Robertson's *English Poetesses* (1883) did the same for women poets. The impact of a magazine culture and the emergence of the personal interview were reflected in Helen C. Black's *Notable Women Authors of the Day* (1893), based on interviews conducted for the *Lady's Pictorial*. At the end of the century fiction publishers Hurst and Blackett produced *Women Novelists of Queen Victoria's Reign* (1897) in which living women novelists offered retrospective assessments of their elder and now deceased sisters.

The most ambitious biographical project of the period was undoubtedly John Morley's English Men of Letters, its title indicative of its focus. There were no female biographical subjects in the first series, projected in 1877, and only a handful in the second, begun in 1902: Leslie Stephen's *George Eliot* (1902), Austin Dobson's *Fanny Burney* (1903), Emily Lawless's *Maria Edgeworth* (1904) and Francis Warre Cornish's *Jane Austen* (1913).[10] In the wake of Morley's venture, and no doubt influenced by it, J. H. Ingram inaugurated the Eminent Women series, published by W. H. Allen.[11] The subjects ranged from English women writers of the period, through European figures such as George Sand, Madame de Staël, Madame Roland and the actress Rachel, to public figures like Elizabeth Fry and Susannah Wesley. Ingram was ambitious in the authors he sought to attract, and some of the biographer/subject pairings were intriguing: Charlotte Yonge on Hannah More (1888), the journalist and feminist Florence Fenwick Miller on Harriet Martineau (1884), the poets Matilde Blind and Mary Robinson on George Eliot (1883) and Emily Brontë (1883), Julia Ward Howe on Margaret Fuller (1883).

The volumes were uneven in quality. Elizabeth Robins Pennell's *Mary Wollstonecraft* (1885), Fenwick Miller's *Harriet Martineau*, and Robinson's *Emily Brontë*, stand out, the last two, along with Blind's *George Eliot* and Anne Gilchrist's *Mary Lamb* (1883), constituting the first full-length biographies of their subjects. One of the reasons for the flat quality of many of the biographies was their reliance on existing published sources, and the biographers' apparent reluctance to do more than reprocess material. The preface to Sarah Malden's *Jane Austen* (1889) acknowledged its reliance on James Austen-Leigh's 1870 *Memoir*, and Lord

Brabourne's recent edition of letters (1884). On the other hand,
Christina Rossetti, with characteristic scrupulousness, withdrew from
her agreement to write on Ann Radcliffe when she failed to locate sufficient material about her life.[12] Her sister-in-law Lucy Brown Rossetti
apparently found no such difficulty with her volume on Mary Shelley
(1890).

Several of the biographers went in search of unpublished correspondence as an obligatory first step, confident in the assumption that the
possession of private letters would enable them to present an 'authentic'
biography of their subjects, as Helen Zimmern insisted in the preface to
her volume on Maria Edgeworth (1883). To a reading public with little
personal knowledge of these biographical subjects, the impact of published correspondence was electric. A letter was the equivalent of an
overheard conversation, an intimate glimpse of the 'real' woman. Anne
Thackeray Ritchie, reviewing the first full-length biography of Jane
Austen, which contained some of her letters, exulted: 'For the first time
we seem to hear the echo of the voice, and to see the picture of the
unknown friend who has charmed us so long.'[13] Nina Kennard, pleased
that she could base her biography of Rachel on a cache of her letters,
wrote confidently in the preface: 'We fall back on her letters as the true
key to this extraordinary woman's character.'[14]

Rosemarie Bodenheimer, in *The Real Life of Mary Ann Evans*, has
emphasized the expectations which readers of published letters brought
to their reading – a scarcely disguised hope that the writer of the correspondence would emerge as the equivalent of the personality revealed
in her books. More significantly, Bodenheimer has argued that letters
can often be as much fictional constructs as the novels they are expected
to amplify, and that the 'small representation of myself', as Eliot once
referred to a letter she was composing, was as self-fashioning as any of
her fiction.[15] But readers of the standard Victorian 'Life and Letters',
seemingly unaware of these subtleties, sought from the letters the same
reassurance that they sought from the biographies, that by reading them
they were getting to know the woman behind the books. This same
uncritical belief that letters offered an unmediated view of character
was to hold as true for the published letters of Mary Wollstonecraft and
Charlotte Brontë as it did in the case of Jane Austen and Maria
Edgeworth. And it could be argued that John Walter Cross's selection
and presentation of George Eliot's letters – 'the sad soliloquy in which
Mr Cross condemned her to tell the story of her life',[16] as Virginia Woolf
described Cross's efforts – so coloured and distorted the portrait of Eliot

presented in her *Life*, that it determined her reputation for the next forty years.

In what follows I want to present four examples of biographies of women writers, each of which had an extraordinary impact when it was published, and has had an influence on the way we read these women today. Two of the biographical subjects, Mary Wollstonecraft and Jane Austen, are from the late eighteenth and early nineteenth centuries, but it is their Victorian biographies which are of importance. They were both, in a manner of speaking, read as Victorian women. The other writers, Charlotte Brontë and George Eliot, were each the subject of a controversial Victorian biography.

It is one of the paradoxes in the history of feminism that Mary Wollstonecraft is widely accepted as the founding figure in Anglo-American feminism, but that she was rarely even mentioned, let alone venerated, for most of the nineteenth century, the period in which active feminism took root. The reason for her ambiguous status in the hundred years following her death, it is generally accepted, was the haunting and powerful *Memoirs of the Author of 'The Rights of Woman'*, which her husband William Godwin began to write within a fortnight of her death and which he published in January 1798. His intention was to give an unvarnished version of his wife's life before a scandalous one could appear. The effect of his memoir, with its revelations of her sexual transgressions, her infatuation with the painter Fuseli, her liaison with the American trader Gilbert Imlay and the birth of an illegitimate daughter, and her subsequent liaison with – and later marriage to, Godwin – provoked a response, in the words of a modern biographer, of 'fascination and horror in more or less equal parts.'[17]

Godwin's portrait, is, in his words, of 'a woman with sentiments as pure, as refined, and as delicate as ever inhabited a human heart'; a woman who had 'trusted to the clearness of her spirit for the direction of her conduct', and to 'the integrity of her views for the vindication of her character'. There were no circumstances of her life 'that in the judgement of honour and reason could brand her with disgrace'.[18] The memoir is of a passionate, intelligent, courageous woman whose life was lived according to her principles. The outcome of the biography was the absolute reverse of what he had intended. Contemporary readers, it would appear, registered only the scandalous revelations. After a period in which she was subjected to a series of personal attacks,[19] Wollstonecraft's name disappeared for nearly fifty years.

Reading the *Memoirs* today it seems incredible that it was not read then, as it now comes across so clearly, as a tragedy. One of its most moving aspects is the conjunction of Wollstonecraft, beautiful, impulsive, by turns tough and vulnerable, with the reserved, pompous and yet adoring Godwin to whom love had come so late. Her childhood, her career as a governess, the period in France, the beginning of her writing, are all narrated, but the focus is on her unhappy relationships, particularly her 'unequal' (the word is Godwin's) one with Imlay, and her two attempts at suicide, followed by her relationship with Godwin. The trajectory of the narrative is that of a tragedy and Wollstonecraft becomes a tragic heroine, culminating in Godwin's agonized account of her death in childbirth. It is a memoir of a woman, not of a writer, or a feminist. There is no attempt to discuss her intellectual development, nor does Godwin consider her feminist ideas in any detail. At the end of the memoir he reflects on the way in which her mental faculties complemented his:

As long as I can remember, I have been discouraged, when I have endeavoured to cast the sum of my intellectual value, by finding that I did not possess, in the degree of some other men, an intuitive perception of intellectual beauty . . . What I wanted in this respect, Mary possessed, in a degree superior to any other person I ever knew. The strength of her mind lay in intuition. She was often right, by this means only, in matters of mere speculation. Her religion, her philosophy, (in both of which the errors were comparatively few, and the strain dignified and generous) were, as I have already said, the pure result of feeling and taste . . . And yet, though perhaps, in the strict sense of the term, she reasoned little, it is surprising what a degree of soundness is to be found in her determinations . . . In a robust and unwavering judgment of this sort, there is a kind of witchcraft.[20]

So the author of *A Vindication of the Rights of Woman* with its persuasive advocacy of equal education and meaningful work for women is turned into the intuitive feminine complement to the Man of Reason. This seems to have been lost on contemporary readers of Godwin's memoir, obsessed as they were by its personal revelations, but it has not been lost on Wollstonecraft's modern biographers or on the historians of feminism. In their view Godwin committed a double murder of Wollstonecraft's reputation, firstly by his misguided candour and secondly by his unwitting undermining of her intellectual credentials.

The memoir has received considerable attention from both Wollstonecraft and Godwin scholars, not all of whom have been so critical of Godwin. Mitzi Myers notes rightly that the memoir 'remains the

substratum on which even the newest lives erect their varying portrayals'. She sees the memoir as a double autobiography – 'as close to
Wollstonecraft's own version of her history as we are likely to get',
because of her propensity for confession and self-revelation, but also an
interpretation of that life 'which is very much a part of Godwin's intellectual – and – emotional autobiography'.[21]

Wollstonecraft's life story was retold and reformulated throughout the
nineteenth century. It was by means of biography, not a discussion of *A
Vindication of the Rights of Woman*, or of her fiction, that her rehabilitation
as a writer and thinker was negotiated and secured. The first discussion
of her life occured in 1843 in Anna Katherine Elwood's *Memoirs of the
Literary Ladies of England*, a sympathetic biographical sketch which recycled much of Godwin's memoir, even to his phrases, but then added a
cautionary note: Wollstonecraft, whom nature intended to be 'a bright
pattern of perfection to her sex' had by her erroneous theories and false
principles, rendered herself instead 'the beacon by which to warn the
woman of similar endowments with herself, of the rocks upon which
enthusiasm and imagination are too apt to wreck their possessor'.
Elwood looked forward to a possible republication of the *Vindication*. Her
comment proved proleptic. The publisher William Strange issued a
'third edition revised and re-edited' in 1844.[22]

In the 1850s there were signs of renewed interest and a subtle shift in
the response to her life. Eliza Lynn, the prickly, abrasive journalist and
novelist, celebrated Wollstonecraft in an article in an obscure periodical,
the *English Republic*, produced by her future husband, the engraver W. J.
Linton, in 1854. The main events of her life again were retold, but now
she was pronounced 'a name that shall live as long as women are loved
or as genius is honoured . . . one of our greatest women, because one of
the first who stormed the citadel of selfishness and ignorance'.[23] There
was much in Wollstonecraft's life which would have been attractive to
Eliza Lynn, then a radical by inclination, who had left her family and
moved to London in order to earn her living by writing, still not an easy
task for a woman at mid-century.

It is significant too that in the following year, in 1855, Marian Evans
compared the *Vindication of the Rights of Woman* to the work of Margaret
Fuller in an anonymous article for the *Leader* (13 October 1855). 'There
is in some quarters a vague prejudice against the *Rights of Woman* as in
some way a reprehensible book', she wrote. But she found it 'eminently
serious, severely moral, and withal rather heavy – the true reason,
perhaps, that no edition has been published since 1796'.[24]

Historians of feminism insist that Wollstonecraft was not forgotten in the nineteenth century, that she is mentioned in memoirs and essays and private correspondence in ways which show clearly how much she was thought about. Barbara Caine argues that Wollstonecraft was not so much unknown to mid-Victorian feminists as carefully and consciously avoided in their published and public work, an avoidance which offers 'revealing insights' into the importance of sexual transgression within Victorian feminism itself. She sees Eliot's article as written on the assumption that the details of Wollstonecraft's life were widely known, and written moreover with the intention of showing that Wollstonecraft's text had not been contaminated by her private life, that her scandalous life had no effect on the reception of the text – a point which, she suggests, was important to Marian Evans, writing the article within the first year of her liaison with Lewes.[25]

References to Wollstonecraft in women's texts in the mid-nineteenth century are sparse. Harriet Martineau, writing her *Autobiography* in the 1850s, distanced herself from her as 'with all her powers, a poor victim of passion with no control over her own peace', but acknowledged that every allowance must be made for her, 'from the constitution and singular environment which determined her course'.[26] There is a single mention of her in Eliot's letters in 1871,[27] a reference to one of her suicide attempts, the details of which she could only have got from Godwin's memoir. Margaret Oliphant referred to her briefly in her *Literary History of England in the end of the Eighteenth and beginning of the Nineteenth Century* (1882). Barbara Caine is right in noting that her name crops up in the correspondence of figures like Bessie Parkes and Barbara Bodichon,[28] and Adele Ernstrom has shown how how often male writers referred to her work in the first half of the century, not always flatteringly.[29]

The public recognition of Wollstonecraft was slow in coming. It was only in the 1880s and 1890s that she was fully reinstated, by a process which renegotiated the details of her life in biographies and through the publication of her letters. In the early 1870s the writer and publisher Charles Kegan Paul obtained access to Sir Percy Shelley's extensive collection of the papers of his maternal grandparents for a projected biography of William Godwin. The result, *William Godwin: His Friends and Contemporaries* (1876), was as much a biography of Wollstonecraft as of Godwin. The major portion of the first volume focussed on their relationship, narrated by extensive quotation from their letters. Wollstonecraft's letters to her lover Gilbert Imlay had been published in full by Godwin in the third and fourth volumes of her *Posthumous Works* in 1798. What had never before been in the public domain were her letters to Godwin written in the brief period of their life together – detailed, affectionate, daily letters; 'They are really little informal conversations on paper', as Kegan Paul described them, 'To read them is like listening to someone talking'.[30]

The impact of these published letters in humanizing both Wollstonecraft and Godwin is incalculable. Kegan Paul made use in whole or in part of approximately a third of Sir Percy Shelley's collection in his life of Godwin. Three years later, he drew on the same materials for a memoir of Wollstonecraft prefixed to an edition of the *Letters to Imlay*. Reinstatement and restitution were his aims, and he began cautiously. Only eighty years after her death 'has any serious attempt been made to set her right in the eyes of those who will choose to see her as she was'. Wollstonecraft's opinions, 'save on one point, were those which most cultivated women now hold'.[31] He dealt carefully with her personal relationships, failing to find any confirmation of a sexual attachment to Fuseli, despite the 'preposterous' claims of his biographer. On the relationship with Imlay he adopted a line which was to become the orthodox view, adopted by subsequent biographers – that an official or public marriage in the Paris of that day would have put her life at risk, and that they were 'married' in all save a ceremony.

Kegan Paul's effective whitewash of Wollstonecraft's sexual transgressions, and his argument that her opinions were now generally accepted, were carefully designed, according to a modern critic, to 'prove her worthy of serious consideration as a writer by re-establishing her respectability as a woman'.[32] Wollstonecraft's writing, in other words, gets short shrift as her biographer concerns himself with re-establishing her womanly qualities.

It is arguable whether Kegan Paul's memoir or the republished letters to Imlay made the greater impact on Victorian readers – letters, as Alice Meynell commented in her review, which were 'too intimate for good taste, perhaps too intimate for good feeling, to accept', but written, as with all Wollstonecraft's work, 'quick with the feelings of the personal and intense woman, who took her life so greatly to heart'.[33] Kegan Paul's line on her personal relationships and his blunting of the radicalism of her views was next taken up by Elizabeth Robins Pennell in her biography of Wollstonecraft, published in Boston in 1884 and revised for the Eminent Women series the following year.[34] Pennell presented Wollstonecraft in a wholly attractive light, as the victim of undeserved censure, explained away her sexual transgressions by embracing Kegan Paul's 'explanations', and endorsed her views on women's rights.

One indication of the way in which these later biographies were constructing Wollstonecraft was an anecdote which Kegan Paul related in the life of Godwin and repeated in his memoir, which was then quoted in the reviews of the memoir, retold by Pennell in her biography, and quoted by her reviewers, so that it quickly gained authority. It was a story told at Godwin's expense, which picked up the contrast between the stuffy, emotionally underdeveloped philosopher and the impulsive, passionate woman by whom he was enthralled. It originated with Godwin's friend Basil Montagu, one of the few intimates who were in the house during Wollstonecraft's last days. As the story goes, Mary had been in great pain and was suffering from a high fever: 'At the sudden cessation of great pain she cried to her husband, "Oh, Godwin, I am in heaven!" and he replied, "You mean, my dear, that your physical sensations are somewhat easier."'[35]

The Wollstonecraft which these later biographies construct is, ironically, the one which Godwin had attempted to project all along, the woman whose life was lived according to her principles. But the image in all of them is of the woman, not of a writer. The woman and her books were, for her nineteenth-century readers, as Poe had said of Barrett Browning, identical. There were, however, two editions of *A Vindication of the Rights of Woman* at the end of the century,[36] one with an introduction by Millicent Garrett Fawcett in 1891 and a second by Elizabeth Pennell in 1892, both of which positioned Wollstonecraft's ideas in relation to the current debate on women. By virtue of the biographies and these belated editions, Wollstonecraft's rehabilitation, nearly a hundred years after Godwin's memoir, can be said to have been accomplished.

In contrast to Wollstonecraft, references to Elizabeth Gaskell's *Life of Charlotte Brontë*, published in 1857, proliferate in the letters and diaries of women writers on both sides of the Atlantic. The *Life* is the most celebrated biography of a woman writer in the nineteenth century, a biography written by a novelist of her friend, a greater novelist, a friend whom she had met only five times. Their friendship was based almost entirely on correspondence. The story of the lives of the Brontës is well known and the writing of Gaskell's biography has been well documented.[37] What is of importance to this discussion is the impact the *Life* had on contemporary readers, and how it affected the way in which Charlotte Brontë and also her sisters were read subsequently.

By the time of her death in 1855 the main facts about the Brontës were in the public domain. Charlotte's biographical preface to the 1850 edition of *Wuthering Heights* and *Agnes Grey* had revealed the identity of Currer, Ellis and Acton Bell. Harriet Martineau wrote a sympathetic obituary in the *Daily News*, an obituary which traded on her personal knowledge, and hinted that the novels had their basis in the life of Charlotte Brontë and her sisters.[38] This of course was what most readers had suspected. What they wanted to know from a biography was more precise: what kind of a woman could have produced those books, with their strange settings, their portraits of passionate, rebellious heroines with an undisguised desire to be loved. What they read in Gaskell's *Life* was a story, a tragedy, as moving, as disturbing as any of the novels. It became another text, the last work by Charlotte Brontë.

'Tell me when you have read the life of Currer Bell', George Eliot wrote to Sara Hennell, 'Some people think its revelations in bad taste – making money out of the dead, wounding feelings of the living. We thought it admirable, cried over it, and felt the better for it'. 'The book . . . makes us familiar inmates of an interior so strange, so original in its individual elements and so picturesque in its externals . . . that fiction has nothing more wild, touching and heart-strengthening to place above it,' Lewes had written earlier to Elizabeth Gaskell – 'The early part is a triumph for you; the rest a monument for your friend.'[39] Anna Jameson commented on the 'truth of that wonderful infinite life – in which there seems to have been so little of external fact or circumstance – and such a boundless sphere of feeling and intellect crammed into a silent existence'.[40] Lady Caroline Fox wrote in her journal: 'She is like her books, and her life explains much in them which needs explanation'.[41] Most readers would have agreed.

This biography is concerned with the woman rather than her books. There is little in it about Charlotte Brontë's writing or about its development. Gaskell missed, for example, the significance of the juvenilia. Her attitude to her subject is not uncomplicated. She both pitied and admired her. She acknowledged Charlotte's superior talents and the differences between them as novelists but there is a sense too in which, despite her gifts of observation and sympathy, she did not fully understand her subject.

What Gaskell's *Life* did was to increase the interest in the lives of all the Brontës and to legitimize speculation about the relationship between the life and the work. She had after all encouraged this herself in her implication of the Revd Carus Wilson as the original of Mr Brocklehurst in *Jane Eyre*, in one of the two lawsuits which threatened her after publication. Astute readers read Gaskell's *Life* in conjunction with the novels, moving easily between the two, making assumptions about the real-life originals of the various characters. Another result of the *Life* was a vast increase in the number of biographies of individual Brontës and of the family, along with books with titles like *Haworth Past and Present* (1879), *The Birthplace of Charlotte Brontë* (1884) and *Brontëana* (1898). Its culmination was the foundation of the Brontë Society, and the establishment of Haworth as a place of literary pilgrimage.

The number of new biographies from the 1870s prompted Margaret Oliphant to declare that the Brontës were 'the first victims of that ruthless art of biography which is one of the features of our time'.[42] One of the results of this was the reconstruction of Emily Brontë, who had been given a secondary role in Gaskell's *Life*. The picture she presented of Emily was a partial one, filtered through Charlotte. The stories she relates, particularly those which convey her ruthlessness, punishing her dog Keeper, and her stoicism, branding her arm with a hot iron, and her courage when facing death, were responsible for the image of a grim, humourless and somewhat unearthly creature, which later biographers sought to correct. The renegotiation of the sisters' positions *vis-à-vis* one another also began, with the result that, by the end of the century, Emily was seen as the more original of the two.

One of the first to attempt this repositioning was the poet A. Mary F. Robinson in the Eminent Women series in 1883 in which she makes full use of Gaskell's *Life*, T. Wemyss Reid's 1877 biography of Charlotte and other material supplied by Reid, manuscript notes received from Charlotte's school friend Ellen Nussey, unpublished letters of Charlotte and her brother Branwell, and a range of contemporary sources. In what was one of the best-written of the Eminent Women series, Robinson retold the Brontë story with Emily, and to a lesser extent Branwell, as the central foci. The fact that it was Emily and not Charlotte who was chosen as the biographical subject in the series reinforces Miriam Allott's assertion that by the 1880s Emily had begun to replace Charlotte in critical attention.[43]

Gaskell's *Life of Charlotte Brontë* had a profound impact on the way all three sisters were read in the decades following Charlotte's death. Readers today are more sceptical of Gaskell's achievement. Margot

Peters has argued that Gaskell saw it as her duty to create 'a noble Charlotte Brontë who was first of all a lady', and as a result ignored the anger and sexuality she saw in the novels, and emphasized instead Brontë's femininity and fragility.[44] Lyndall Gordon has urged that we need to 'open up the gaps in her life', gaps left by Gaskell and other Victorian biographers.[45] Deirdre D'Albertis sees Gaskell not as the self-effacing loyal friend who regarded her own talents as decidedly secondary, and who was proud, as she puts it, to 'bask in the luminous rays of Brontë's genius', but as a fellow novelist entering into a disguised form of literary competition with Brontë, a competition which turned on their anti-thetical notions of duty and how, if at all, this could be balanced with the demands of art.[46] Her argument is intricate, and, I confess, persuasive.

Despite the force of these new readings, Gaskell's *Life of Charlotte Brontë* is still the biography with which every new biographer takes issue. If we wanted an example of its potency for nineteenth-century readers, we need only read the autobiography of the late nineteenth-century novelist Mary Cholmondeley, the daughter of a vicar of a remote parish in Shropshire, whose mother died when she was very young, who suffered from ill health much of her life, spent most of her time in the company of her father helping with parochial duties, had an unhappy love affair and never married, had a younger sister who wrote poetry and died young, and had other siblings who were talented. Linda Peterson has demonstrated how her family memoir, entitled *Under One Roof: a Family Record* (1918) bears uncanny echoes of Gaskell's *Life of Charlotte Brontë*.[47]

Both the *Memoirs of the Author of 'The Rights of Woman'* and the *Life of Charlotte Brontë*, by virtue of their enduring legacies, have secured for themselves near-mythic status. I want to turn now to two less distinguished biographies of women writers, biographies which have long been superseded, but which were, when they were published, equally influential in constructing the writer inherited by the next generation of readers and writers: a memoir of Jane Austen, the first biography of her to be published, in 1870, and John Walter Cross's *George Eliot's Life*, which was published in 1885.

One of the readers on whom Gaskell's *Life* made an impression was the Reverend James Austen-Leigh, Vicar of Bray, and the nephew of Jane Austen. In the biography Gaskell quoted the now famous correspondence between Charlotte Brontë and G. H. Lewes, in which he had suggested that Charlotte might do well to read *Pride and Prejudice*, and she had responded giving her reservations about Austen's methods.[48] What is remarkable is not her frequently quoted response to the novel but the fact that she had not until then read it. The history of Jane Austen's reputation in the fifty years following her death in 1817 has yet to be written. Looking back from our position today, it is difficult to realize that for most of the nineteenth century she was a minority interest. Edith Simcox, writing in the *Academy* in 1870, observed that she 'has always been . . . the favourite author of literary men',[49] but even that cannot be taken for granted. When Dickens's friend and biographer John Forster first read the dialogue between Mrs Nickleby and the dressmaker Miss Knag in *Nicholas Nickleby*, he told Dickens that he must have been reading Miss Bates in *Emma*, but to his surprise, he found that 'he had not at this time made the acquaintance of that fine writer'.[50] Jane Austen had her champions, among them Scott, Richard Whately, the philosopher and churchman, and G. H. Lewes. The historian T. B. Macaulay, another admirer, once indicated that he intended to write a memoir as well as introductions to a new edition of her novels. Had he done so, her reputation in the nineteenth century might have been quite different. As it was, when she died, very little was known about her. Her brother Henry wrote a short biographical notice which was prefixed to the posthumous edition of *Northanger Abbey* and *Persuasion* in 1817. There was a cheap edition of her work published in 1833 in Bentley's Standard Novels, but after that there was nothing by way of a literary event to bring her to the mind of the public.

The event which began the process of turning Jane Austen into a more popular author was a memoir published in 1870 by her nephew, James Austen-Leigh, a man in his sixties who had never published anything before in his life, whose sole qualification for the task was that Jane Austen was his aunt, and that he had attended her funeral. Jane Austen, as is well known, had lived her entire life in the bosom of her family, and the family in turn regarded her reputation as a family matter. Moreover, various branches had differing views on what, if anything, the public should know about her. It was probably the death of her last surviving brother, Francis, in 1865 that removed the opposition to making more details of her life available.

Austen-Leigh's memoir is the story of 'dear aunt Jane', as he calls her, the nicest of spinster aunts, who was never too busy to have an encouraging chat about a story one was writing, or to play a game; who avoided literary society; dressed in middle-aged clothes before her time; hid her writing under the blotter if anyone came into the room. 'We did not think of her as being clever, still less as being famous; but we valued her as one always kind, sympathizing and amusing', he wrote.[51] The picture prompted William Dean Howells to remark that 'we might wish her now to have had a niece or a nephew or two less, if we might so have had a book or two more from her'.[52] We learn how adept she was at spillikins, how skilful at cup and ball, how neatly folded her letters were, that she rarely spilled the wax.

Looking back from the high point of mid-Victorian prosperity Jane Austen's nephew was anxious that his aunt's life might not appear as grand as he would have liked. He explained that gentry at that time often dined at four o'clock to save candles, that dinner tables were not as splendid as they were now, that ladies were even known to wash the breakfast china. He also exercised a certain amount of censorship. He did not mention Jane Austen's mentally defective brother George, her brother Henry's bankruptcy, or her two short-lived romantic attachments. He stressed too the remoteness of her life, from national events and from society. In her writing she was 'always very careful not to meddle with matters of which she did not throughly understand. She never touched upon politics, law or medicine.' She was not highly accomplished 'according to the present standard'. Her talents did not introduce her to the notice of other writers or connect her with the literary world. Her life 'was passed in the performance of home duties and the cultivation of domestic affections, without any self-seeking or craving after applause'.[53]

That last sentence is in fact the family 'line' on Jane Austen begun by Henry's memoir, and carried on by Austen-Leigh. His *Memoir* is an affectionate tribute from an elderly nephew. The portrait of his aunt is of a lady-like amateur for whom writing was a polite accomplishment. As with Gaskell's biography of Brontë, the emphasis is on the woman, not on the writing. There is no mention of what we now know of Austen the perfectionist, constantly revising her texts. There is no sense either of the sharp eye, the shrewdness, the sense of irony, the biting wit. 'Aunt Jane' is too nice, and too limited in her perspective on her world, in contrast to the Jane Austen we read today.

What the *Memoir* accomplished was the awakening of public interest in an author virtually forgotten. It generated a large number of reviews and appreciative essays, written by devoted enthusiasts who wanted to share their enthusiasm. It did not immediately create a new readership; that came later. The reviews of the various editions of the *Memoir*, which remained constantly in print until the end of the century, were written for readers who were familiar with the texts. On the other hand, the *Memoir* was well timed. It came after a decade of the so-called 'sensation' fiction of Dickens, Wilkie Collins, of Miss Braddon and Mrs Henry Wood. It came too at the point when enthusiasm for George Eliot had begun to wane. It made this Jane Austen ripe for rediscovery.

It was her unsensationalism, her wholesomeness, the seemingly non-intellectual quality of the novels, and their evocation of a more tranquil past age which made them attractive. All of this was promoted by the focus of the *Memoir*. 'Dear books!' Anne Thackeray Ritchie wrote, 'bright, sparkling with wit and animation, in which the homely heroines charm, the dull hours fly, and the very bores are enchanting'.[54] This sentimentalized view of Austen, which was not, to be fair to Ritchie, her only perspective – (she saw clearly Austen's strengths), the view of an Austen who could provide an escape from the stresses of the present day – domestic comedy in period costume – was one which caught the public mood. So too did the small scale of her work, its miniaturism, summed up by the somewhat patronizing epithet of her next biographer, Goldwin Smith, as the work of that 'wonderful little woman'.[55] Another strand of enthusiasm for Austen at the end of the nineteenth century was that of connoisseurship, the view that an appreciation of her was a mark of the highest literary taste. Its subscribers swapped quotations and anecdotes, dropped the names of her characters into their normal conversation, and so on. That approach to Austen has continued up to the present day.

Finally, in 1900 an article entitled 'The Renascence of Jane Austen' published in the *Westminster Review* by Janet Harper explained why all those men and women currently in their forties, in other words born after 1860, who had not read Jane Austen because she was not fashionable in their youth, were now clamouring to do so, and why there was a sudden demand for popular editions of the novels. It was her Englishness, her 'thoroughly English, realistic and moral solidity' which made her attractive, for the home market and as a cultural export: 'Now the Saxon can introduce Miss Austen's novels to our colonists in Australia, or to the Americans, or to any foreigners with a glow of patriotism, for he knows he is presenting something entirely English.'[56]

It cannot be said that the women writers who read Austen-Leigh's *Memoir* were more sensitive or more astute critics than the male reviewers. Mary Ward, Margaret Oliphant and Anne Thackeray Ritchie all wrote intelligently about her, all saw her greatness, and their criticism stands up well today. But so too did an important article by Richard

Simpson.[57] Austen had many biographers in the decades following the *Memoir*, including those by Goldwin Smith (1887) and by Sarah Malden in the Eminent Women series. Another member of the family, Lord Brabourne, published the first edition of her letters in 1884, and there was yet another biography by two more family members in 1913.[58]

The real growth in readers of Jane Austen came after 1900. Those new readers inherited Austen-Leigh's Jane Austen, and the vestiges of 'Aunt Jane' are with us still. It helps to explain why modern critics of Austen persist in their interrogation of the historical and cultural assumptions behind her novels: 'Is she a feminist in the Wollstonecraft tradition?' 'Why in an age which saw so much of war, revolution and social upheaval does she not mention any of it? Did she acknowledge that Sir Thomas Bertram's Antiguan estates were maintained on the proceeds of the slave trade?' All of these questions, which we currently debate at length, are indirectly the result of a Victorian biography and the novelist it constructed.

When George Eliot died in 1880 Leslie Stephen wrote that the world had probably lost 'the greatest woman who ever won literary fame, and one of the very few writers of our day to whom the name "great" could be conceded with any plausibility'. Ten years later she was being ridiculed by W. E. Henley in a series of epigrams as 'an apotheosis of Pupil-Teachery' and 'George Sand *plus* Science and *minus* Sex'.[59] Why had her reputation experienced so swift a decline? The process had probably begun before her death, in the years following the publication of *Middlemarch* in 1871–2. Samuel Butler's friend and correspondent Miss Savage, writing to him in 1878 complaining that there were a great many difficult words in the book of his she was currently reading, added 'But I don't mind them, for I have a dictionary which I bought two years ago, as I wished to read *Daniel Deronda* in the original'.[60] Her witticism was probably more indicative of public opinion than she realized. The height of Eliot's popularity as a novelist was reached with *Adam Bede*, not *Middlemarch*. *The Times* reviewer said of the latter that it 'has not the live-liness, variety and picturesqueness of its great predecessor [Adam Bede]'.[61] In place of these it had 'a philosophical power' and, for her Victorian readers, therein lay the problem.

Her reputation as an intellectual, among a smaller, self-selecting section of the public, on the other hand, had never been greater. The picture of Eliot as a sage, a woman of 'masculine intellect', as was fre-quently said of her, was one which women readers and women writers found offputting. There are many accounts of her famous Sunday afternoons at The Priory, her Highgate home. The recollections of women writers who met her are strikingly similar in their ambivalence. They were ushered into her presence by the genial G. H. Lewes. They found themselves sitting beside her, often on a footstool, looking up at her, 'she talking and I listening' as one of them, Lucy Clifford, reported.[62] They commented on her wonderful silk dresses, her large head and her horse-like face, which became almost beautiful when animated, and her grave smile. Many, like Lucy Walford, endeavoured to link the woman with the books:

She had meant to be civil and kind. But how heavily drove the wheels of her chariot! How interminably dragged that interview! Could it be possible that this was the creator of 'Mrs Poyser', and 'Hetty'? 'Dinah', yes; and 'Adam Bede', and 'Maggie Tulliver', and any number more of serious, thoughtful people – I could picture the heavy brow bent in weighty cogitation over such, – but little frivolous, selfish Hetty?[63]

The image was inspiring but a little too awesome; it was also a role model almost impossible of emulation.

The writing of Eliot's 'official' biography after her death was undertaken by her husband of eight months, John Walter Cross. It was not the first biography. Mathilde Blind published a brief one in the Eminent Women series in 1883. Eliot's devoted disciple Edith Simcox had hoped to write the authorized Life herself, but had been pre-empted by Cross who took the decision to write it in order to prevent anyone else from publishing one.[64] His three-volume *Life* was over five years in the making. Among the many tributes in the press in the months following her death were two extensive obituaries, one in *Blackwood's* (February 1881) and another in the *Westminster* (July 1881) which made public for the first time some of the details of Eliot's writing life.[65] The *Blackwood's* article used the archive of her correspondence with John Blackwood to relate the now familiar details of their partnership and her connections with the firm. That in the *Westminster* recounted her connection with the Brays, the Hennells and Dr Brabant; and her association with Chapman and the *Westminster* circle, including the philosopher Herbert Spencer. The article made no reference to Marian Evans's more personal involvement with any of these figures, but collectively the two obituaries told the story of the making of 'George Eliot'.

But it was Cross's three-volume *Life* published four years later, in 1885, which became the focus of posthumous reassessment and in effect determined her reputation for the next four decades. The significance of the title page would not have been lost on her friends and acquaintances:

'George Eliot's Life as related in her letters and journals, arranged and edited by her husband J. W. Cross'.

The reading public, as opposed to the smaller circle who had come into contact with her, knew at least two things about George Eliot: that she had lived with Lewes, who was not her husband, for nearly twenty-five years, and that she had been an 'advanced thinker', if not an atheist. They were agog for more details of this woman's life. What they got, as Gladstone rightly said, was 'a reticence in three volumes'. 'If it is true that the most interesting of George Eliot's characters is her own, it may be said also that the most interesting of her books is her Life', the historian Lord Acton, a confidant of Cross, wrote at the beginning of his review.[66] It was a good opening, but it was not true. 'We see the heroine, not reflected from other minds, but nearly as she saw herself, and cared to be known', he continued. That was partly true. Margaret Oliphant claimed that George Eliot out of her own mouth had been 'made to prove herself a dull woman'.[67]

As Cross organized it, the biography was a series of letters and extracts from journals, three volumes of 500 pages each, with dates in marginal glosses and occasional short paragraphs of connecting narrative. Cross wrote well in the sketch he provided of Eliot's childhood up to the time the letters began but the narrative was not continued. For a husband of only eight months he is nonetheless an insistent presence. There is much of 'in fact my wife told me', 'one of the books we read together at Cheyne Walk' and 'as she was always fond of referring to, in our talks', and so on.

The *Life* presents precisely what Austen-Leigh and Gaskell left out of their biographies, an account of a writing life. They had concentrated on the woman, not the writer. Cross did the reverse. Eliot's reading and her views on her contemporaries are here; the important relationship with John Blackwood; the genesis of each novel and the aftermath of publication – all are documented in her letters. So too are her travels, which were extensive, and her headaches, which were frequent. But two of the great crises of her life are scarcely mentioned. Her religious deconversion gets swept aside in an account of her translations of the German biblical criticism of David Friedrich Strauss and Ludwig Feuerbach; and the estrangement from her brother Isaac, which occurred in 1854 when she took the decision to live with Lewes and continued until her marriage in 1880, is simply not referred to, presumably to spare Isaac's feelings. The objects of two of her celebrated infatuations, John Chapman and Herbert Spencer, are glossed in a note. It is just conceivable that Cross did not know of these relationships. His handling of Lewes is decorous, and at times even generous, but there is no recognition of their crucial partnership, or of Lewes's role in the creation and sustaining of 'George Eliot'. In his introduction Cross argued that by letting George Eliot tell her own story through her letters, it would better demonstrate her intellect and character. By virtue of his selections and 'prunings' as he termed them, he was constructing a version of George Eliot as carefully as if he had written the narrative himself.

Gordon Haight, the modern editor of the letters, has convincingly demonstrated Cross's smaller sins of omission, showing the ways in which he stripped the correspondence of wit, spontaneity, gaiety and humour and left a ponderous, ultra-serious Eliot. 'Even in an invitation to dinner' as John Morley remarked, 'the words imply a grave sense of responsibility on both sides.'[68] 'She took herself with tremendous seriousness', Margaret Oliphant observed, 'and was always on duty, never relaxing.'[69] 'Before she wrote a tale at all', said Frederic Harrison, 'George Eliot in mental equipment, stood side by side with Mill, Spencer, Lewes and Carlyle.'[70] For the readers of her novels that was precisely the problem with the central character of the biography. 'Is this the woman who wrote Adam Bede?'[71] Margaret Oliphant asked in her review, echoing Lucy Walford's reaction when meeting George Eliot. 'They wear *me* out – I know that. After a day at the Lewises [*sic*] I am worn to a thread', the actress and diarist Fanny Kemble once commented to a friend, reporting the non-stop intellectual conversation at The Priory.[72] Most readers of Cross's *Life* felt similarly worn out.

Women writers as readers of *George Eliot's Life* saw something else – a masculine model of the writing life, a model which their own circumstances made impossible. Lewes had kept George Eliot in what Margaret Oliphant called a 'mental greenhouse' and had taken care of her. Few if any women could hope for such working conditions. There was, after her death, among women writers a kind of collective resentment of George Eliot, a resentment of her success, her predominance. 'No one will ever mention me in the same breath with George Eliot',[73] Margaret Oliphant wrote in her autobiography, an autobiography which she was prompted to write after reading Cross's *Life*.

At least one other woman writer was prompted by *George Eliot's Life* to write the story of her own. Eliza Lynn Linton, whose career paralleled George Eliot's, resented her success and probably her personal happiness and what she saw as the betrayal of Eliot's early radicalism for the '"made" and articial pose which was her distinguishing characteristic in later years'[74]: 'She was so consciously "George Eliot" – so interpenetrated, head and heel, inside and out, with the sense of her importance as the great novelist and profound thinker of her generation, as to make her society a little overwhelming, leaving us baser creatures the impression of having been rolled very flat indeed.'[75]

Cross's 'lifeless silhouette', as David Carroll has commented, intervened between the novels and the reading public and set the seal on her reputation for many years.[76] 'Women writers no longer looked to her as a role model. She was the butt of jokes like Henley's. Yet the gradual reversal of her reputation began with a woman writer's reading of Cross's *Life*. Virginia Woolf, in preparation for an article in the *Times Literary Supplement* to mark the anniversary of George Eliot's birth, in 1919, began with the biography. 'I am reading through the whole of George Eliot, in order to sum her up once and for all, upon her anniversary', she wrote to a friend; 'So far, I have only made way with her life, which is a book of the greatest fascination, and I can see already that no one else has ever known her as I know her.'[77]

Woolf's essay began the slow process of revaluation, a process which took another thirty years, and was contributed to by Lord David Cecil, by Joan Bennett, and by F. R. Leavis, who paved the way for the modern critics of George Eliot. Like Jane Austen, the George Eliot we read today has come only comparatively recently into the Pantheon. And, as with Austen, a Victorian biography constructed the writer which the twentieth century inherited, and the next generation of readers had to renegotiate.

Am I, I wonder, indulging in special pleading for these biographies which I find so crucial to the way in which we read these Victorian women? I have been concerned so far only about women novelists. A cursory look at the lives of nineteenth-century women poets suggests yet more evidence of the impact of biography on their after-lives. One example is that most self-fashioning of women poets, Letitia Landon or L. E. L., as she styled herself, who was so successful in constructing a poetic identity that she, or rather L. E. L., became of more interest to her readers than her work. The notoriety which surrounded Landon during her brief life, largely the result of gossip about her romantic attachments, as well as her conscious attempts at self-presentation, was exceeded only by the rumour and innuendo which followed her unexpected death in 1838 in suspicious circumstances.

Her friend Laman Blanchard published the authorized biography in 1841, having agreed to undertake the task before her death. There the matter might have rested, had not various of her friends objected to Blanchard's attempts to present a balanced account of the circumstances surrounding her death, and to support a verdict of accidental death. A war of words ensued, conducted in the form of biographical articles which challenged aspects of Blanchard's interpretation, arguing variously for suicide, and even murder. The full story has yet to be written.[78] What is interesting in the case of Landon is the potency of biography, the intensity and longevity of the dispute, which was still raging in the 1860s, and the way in which aspects of her life and her death completely subsumed any posthumous interest in her poetry. Linda Peterson has recently demonstrated, for example, how Elizabeth Barrett Browning drew on details of Landon's life as presented in Blanchard's biography, in her portrait of the writing life of a woman poet in *Aurora Leigh*.[79]

It was Robert Browning, in his *Essay on Shelley*, who remarked that 'we covet . . . biography'.[80] He was speaking of a certain kind of contemporary poet for whom, as he said, 'readers of his poetry must be readers of his biography also'. The comment has a particular resonance for the readers of nineteenth-century women writers who have always found it difficult to separate the life from the work. The energy of modern biographers looks set to ensure that this remains the case.

NOTES

1 E. A. Poe, review of *The Drama of Exile and other Poems* by Elizabeth Barrett Barrett, *The Broadway Journal* 1 (1845), pp. 4–5. Quoted by Glennis Stephenson, 'Letitia Landon and the Victorian Improvisatrice: the Construction of L. E. L.', *Victorian Poetry* 30 (1992), p. 2.
2 Ellen Moers, *Literary Women* (London: Women's Press, 1978), p. 43
3 See Kate Flint, *The Woman Reader 1837–1914* (Oxford: Clarendon Press, 1993), especially ch. 8 'Reading Practices' and ch. 9 'Fictional Reading'.
4 Richard D. Altick, *Lives and Letters: a History of Literary Biography in England and America* (New York: Knopf, 1966), p.xi.
5 Marilyn Butler, *Maria Edgeworth, a Literary Biography* (Oxford University Press, 1972), p. 9.
6 *The George Eliot Letters*, ed. Gordon S. Haight, 9 vols. (New Haven: Yale University Press, 1954–79), vol. VI, p. 230.
7 See the Guide to Further Reading for recent discussions.
8 Martin Stannard, 'The Necrophiliac Art?' in Dale Salwak, ed., *The Literary Biography: Problems and Solutions* (Basingstoke: Macmillan, 1996), p. 32.
9 Alison Booth, 'The Lessons of the Medusa: Anna Jameson and Collective Biographies of Women', *Victorian Studies* 2 (Winter 1999/2000), pp. 257–88.

10 George Eliot, however, was invited to write the volume on Shakespeare in the first series, after Matthew Arnold and J. F. Seeley had declined (*Letters*, VI, pp. 416–17).

11 The series, or some volumes, were published in the United States as the Famous Women series, by Roberts Brothers, Boston.

12 See Jan Marsh, *Christina Rossetti: a Literary Biography* (London: Jonathan Cape, 1994), pp. 495–6. According to Marsh, Rossetti declined the 'two Georges' (Sand and Eliot) as well as Harriet Martineau because she found their views unsympathetic, expressed an interest in Elizabeth Fry and Mary Lamb, agreed to consider Elizabeth Barrett Browning, and eventually attempted Ann Radcliffe.

13 A. T. Ritchie, 'Jane Austen', *Cornhill Magazine* 24 (August 1871), p. 159.

14 Mrs Arthur Kennard, preface to *Rachel*, Eminent Women series (London: W. H. Allen, 1885). Helen Zimmern, in the preface to her biography of Maria Edgeworth in the same series, emphasized her access to an unpublished memoir by Edgeworth's mother, and to a large number of her private letters through which she was able to present 'what I hope is at least an authentic biography'.

15 Rosemarie Bodenheimer, *The Real Life of Mary Ann Evans: George Eliot, Her Letters and Fiction* (Ithaca: Cornell University Press, 1994), p. xiv.

16 Virginia Woolf, 'George Eliot', in *Collected Essays* vol. 1, (London: Hogarth Press, 1966), p. 198.

17 Claire Tomalin, *The Life and Death of Mary Wollstonecraft* (London: Weidenfeld and Nicolson, 1974), p. 233.

18 William Godwin, *Memoirs of Mary Wollstonecraft*, with a preface by John Middleton Murry (London: Constable, 1928), p. 106.

19 W. Clark Durant's edition of the *Memoirs* (London: Constable, 1927) reprints most of the contemporary reviews, pp. 337–47.

20 *Memoirs*, ch. 9, pp. 124–5.

21   Mitzi Myers, 'Godwin's Memoirs of Wollstonecraft: the Shaping of Self and Subject', *Studies in Romanticism* 20 (Fall 1981), pp. 299–300.

22 A. K. Elwood, *Memoirs of the Literary Ladies of England*, 2 vols. (London: Henry Colburn, 1843), vol. II, pp. 152–3. Elwood noted that the late Maria Jane Jewsbury had intended to 'remodel' the 'Rights of Woman', to make it 'attractive and useful' but had given up the project after her marriage. Strange's reprint was in a cheap format which advertised a number of self-help manuals on the end papers, including *The Domestic Dictionary and Housekeeper's Manual, Emigration and Colonization Considered, The Nuptial Pocket-book; or, The Philosophy of Reproduction*, a *Handbook for Married Women* and *Every Family's Book of Health and Domestic Economy*.

23 [Eliza Lynn], 'Mary Wollstonecraft', *The English Republic* 3 (1854), pp. 422, 424.

24 'Mary Wollstonecraft and Margaret Fuller', *Essays of George Eliot*, ed. T. Pinney (London: Routledge, 1963), p. 201. She was obviously unaware of William Strange's 1844 reprint.

25 Barbara Caine, 'Victorian Feminism and the Ghost of Mary
    Wollstonecraft', *Women's Writing* 4:2 (1997), pp. 261–73.
26 *Harriet Martineau's Autobiography*, 3 vols. (London: Smith Elder, 1877), vol. I,
    pp. 400, 402.
27 *The George Eliot Letters*, V, pp. 160–1.
28 See Barbara Caine, *English Feminism 1780–1980* (Oxford University Press,
    1997), pp. 23–42, 93–101.
29 Adele M. Ernstrom, 'The Afterlife of Mary Wollstonecraft and Anna
    Jameson's *Winter Studies and Summer Rambles in Canada*', *Women's Writing* 4:2
    (1997), pp. 277–98.
30 Charles Kegan Paul, *Biographical Sketches* (London: Kegan Paul, Trench,
    1881), p. 319.
31 *Mary Wollstonecraft: Letters to Imlay*, with a prefatory memoir by C. Kegan Paul
    (London: Kegan Paul and Co., 1879), p. v. See also Kegan Paul's signed
    article which previewed the contents of the memoir, 'Mary Wollstonecraft:
    a Vindication', *Fraser's Magazine* n.s.17 (June 1878), pp. 748–62.
32 Margot Peters, 'Biographies of Women', *Biography: an Interdisciplinary
    Quarterly* 2 (Summer 1979), p. 206.
33 Alice Meynell, *Essays of Yesterday and Today* (London: George G. Harrap,
    1926), p. 39.
34 The 1885 version in the Eminent Women series is substantially shorter than
    the edition in the Boston Famous Women series, due to extensive cuts in the
    quotations from Wollstonecraft's letters, undertaken presumably to fit
    Ingram's 200-page format.
35 *Mary Wollstonecraft: Letters to Imlay* (1879), pp. lix–lx; C. Kegan Paul, *William
    Godwin: his Friends and Contemporaries*, 2 vols. (London: Kegan Paul, Trench,
    Trubner, 1876), vol. I, p. 323.
36 *A Vindication of the Rights of Woman* with an introduction by Mrs Henry
    Fawcett (London: T. Fisher Unwin, 1891), and *A Vindication of the Rights of
    Woman by Mary Wollstonecraft* with an introduction by Elizabeth Robins
    Pennell (London: Walter Scott, 1892).
37 See Angus Easson, *Elizabeth Gaskell* (London: Routledge, 1979), ch. 5, and
    Jenny Uglow, *Elizabeth Gaskell: a Habit of Stories* (London: Faber and Faber,
    1993), ch. 19.
38 'Charlotte Brontë', reprinted in Martineau, *Biographical Sketches* (London:
    Macmillan, 1869).
39 *The George Eliot Letters*, II, pp. 315, 330.
40 Judith Johnston, *Anna Jameson: Victorian, Feminist, Woman of Letters* (Aldershot:
    Scolar Press, 1997), p. 19.
41 Miriam Allott, ed., *The Brontës: the Critical Heritage* (London: Routledge, 1971),
    p. 371.
42 Mrs Oliphant, 'The Sisters *Brontë*', in *Women Novelists of Queen Victoria's Reign.
    A Book of Appreciations* (London: Hurst and Blackett, 1897), p. 56.
43 See Allott, ed., *The Brontës: The Critical Heritage*, p. 44.
44 Peters, 'Biographies of Women', *Biography* 2 (Summer 1979), p. 205.

45 Lyndall Gordon, 'Women's Lives: The Unmapped Country', in John Batchelor, ed., *The Art of Literary Biography* (Oxford: Clarendon Press, 1995), p. 88.

46 Deirdre D'Albertis, '"Bookmaking out of the Remains of the Dead": Elizabeth Gaskell's *The Life of Charlotte Brontë*', *Victorian Studies* 37 (Autumn 1995), p. 1.

47 See Linda Peterson, *Traditions of Victorian Women's Autobiography: the Poetics and Politics of Life Writing* (London: University Press of Virginia, 1999), ch. 6.

48 Her comments, in a letter of 12 January 1848, are quoted by B. C. Southam, *Jane Austen: the Critical Heritage*, vol. 1 (London: Routledge, 1968), p. 126: 'Why do you like Miss Austen so very much? . . . I had not seen *Pride and Prejudice* until I read that sentence of yours, and then I got the book. And what did I find? An accurate daguerreotyped portrait of a commonplace face; a carefully fenced, highly cultivated garden, with neat borders and delicate flowers; but no glance of a bright, vivid physiognomy, no open country, no fresh air, no blue hill, no bonny beck. I should hardly like to live with her ladies and gentlemen, in their elegant but confined houses.'

49 Edith Simcox, *The Academy* (12 February 1870), p. 118.

50 John Forster, *The Life of Dickens*, ed. J. W. T. Ley (London: Cecil Palmer, 1928), p. 121.

51 J. E. Austen-Leigh, *A Memoir of Jane Austen by her Nephew* (London, 1870), intro. by Fay Weldon (London: Folio Society, 1989), p. 2.

52 Quoted by B. C. Southam, *Jane Austen: the Critical Heritage*, vol. II (London: Routledge, 1987), p. 3.

53 Austen-Leigh, *Memoir*, pp. 13, 77–8, 1.

54 Anne Thackeray Ritchie, 'Jane Austen', *Cornhill Magazine* 24 (August 1871), p. 158.

55 Quoted by B. C. Southam, *Jane Austen: the Critical Heritage*, vol. II, p. 14.

56 Janet Harper, 'The Renascence of Jane Austen', *Westminster Review* 153 (April 1900), p. 444.

57 See B. C. Southam, *Jane Austen: the Critical Heritage*, vol. I, pp. 241–65.

58 *Letters of Jane Austen*, ed. Edward, Lord Brabourne, 2 vols. (London: Richard Bentley, 1884); W. Austen-Leigh and R. A. Austen-Leigh, *Jane Austen: Her Life and Letters. A Family Record* (London: Smith Elder, 1913).

59 Gordon S. Haight, ed., *A Century of George Eliot Criticism* (London: Methuen, 1966), pp. 136, 162.

60 *Letters between Samuel Butler and Miss E. M. A. Savage 1871–1885*, ed. G. L. Keynes and B. Hill (London: Jonathan Cape, 1935), p. 168.

61 David Carroll, ed., *George Eliot: the Critical Heritage* (London: Routledge, 1971), p. 28.

62 Quoted by Elaine Showalter, 'The Greening of Sister George', *Nineteenth-Century Fiction* 35 (1980–1), p. 294.

63 L. B. Walford, *Memories of Victorian London* (London: Edward Arnold, 1912), p. 140.

64 Barbara Bodichon expressed the view that Cross neither could nor would

write the biography, and that the task should fall to Simcox. See K. A. Mackenzie, *Edith Simcox and George Eliot* (Oxford University Press, 1961), p. 121.

65 W. Allardyce, 'George Eliot', *Blackwood's Magazine* 129 (February 1881), pp. 255–68; W. W. Call, 'George Eliot: Her Life and Writings', *Westminster Review* n.s. 9 (July 1881), pp. 154–98. I am indebted to Margaret Harris for drawing these articles to my attention.

66 Quoted by Haight, *A Century of George Eliot Criticism*, p. 151.

67 [M. O. W. Oliphant], *Edinburgh Review* 161 (April 1885), p. 517.

68 John Morley, 'The Life of George Eliot', *Macmillan's Magazine* 51 (Feb 1885), p. 242.

69 *Autobiography and Letters of Mrs Oliphant*, ed. Mrs Harry Coghill (1899), reprinted with an introduction by Q. D. Leavis (Leicester University Press, 1974), p. 7.

70 Frederic Harrison, *Fortnightly Review* 37 (1 March 1885), quoted by Carroll, ed., *Critical Heritage*, p. 38.

71 [Oliphant], *Edinburgh Review* 161, p. 519.

72 Walford, *Memories of Victorian London*, p. 145.

73 Oliphant, *Autobiography*, pp. 5–8.

74 E. Lynn Linton, 'George Eliot', in *Women Novelists of Queen Victoria's Reign*, p. 72.

75 E. Lynn Linton, *My Literary Life* (London: Hodder and Stoughton, 1899), pp. 86–7.

76 Carroll, ed., *Critical Heritage*, p. 40.

77 *The Letters of Virginia Woolf*, ed. Nigel Nicholson and Joanne Trautmann, 6 vols. (New York: Harcourt, 1975–80), vol. II, p. 321.

78 Glennis Stephenson, in *Letitia Landon: the Woman Behind L. E. L.* (Manchester University Press, 1995) outlines the main areas of dispute. Blanchard took pains to emphasize that the lovelorn heroines of Landon's poetry who often died for love were totally unlike Landon herself. This was to dissuade readers from the conclusion that a hasty marriage and emigration to West Africa as the wife of a colonial governor had driven Landon to suicide. Others of her friends preferred to blacken Governor Maclean, and hinted at a West African mistress who was displaced upon Landon's arrival.

79 See Peterson, *Traditions of Victorian Women's Autobiography*, ch. 4.

80 *Browning's Essay on Shelley*, ed. Richard Garnett (London: Alexander Moring, 1903), p. 35.

CHAPTER TWO

Remaking the canon

Joanne Wilkes

In January 1870, a respected British weekly, the *Athenaeum*, discussed several now-forgotten novels, and gave them short shrift. These included *Lady Betty*, by Christabel Coleridge, and *Herbert Tresham*, by the Revd J. M. Neale. Christabel Coleridge's novel is criticised mainly for its plot, which the anonymous reviewer finds badly constructed, tedious and implausible, while the Revd Neale's book is faulted both for being 'pedantically written', and for telling an 'insignificant' tale which the reviewer believes is 'a mere pretext for thrusting the author's opinions down the reader's throat'.[1] The review identifies no redeeming features in *Herbert Tresham*, but acknowledges that *Lady Betty* does contain 'some pleasing writing', and therefore suggests that Christabel Coleridge is 'capable of something better'. What is notable, however, is that *Lady Betty*'s faults are ascribed to the writer's sex, while this is not the case with the Revd Neale's novel. The review of Christabel Coleridge's text begins: 'It scarcely needed the author's name affixed to the title page of "Lady Betty", to tell us it was the work of a lady' – and goes on to call the novel's story 'feeble and badly designed', as if this were the natural corollary of female authorship. By contrast, the pedantry and offensive didacticism of *Herbert Tresham* are not linked to the Revd Neale's sex, or even to his clerical status.

These reviews represent a minor instance of a practice endemic to nineteenth-century literary criticism – the ascription of particular characteristics to writing on the basis of its author's sex. Although this happened to texts by writers of both sexes, the practice was more common in discussions of women's publications. In general, such a habit fostered a reductive approach to women's writing, since the capacities attributed to women meant that their writings were considered less substantial and significant than men's.[2]

To some extent, women writers' works which, by the end of the nineteenth century, had come to be esteemed as of lasting importance had escaped from the kinds of judgments about women's writing which served to trivialize it. These writers are also those who enjoy the highest critical reputation today – Jane Austen, Charlotte and Emily Brontë, and George Eliot among novelists, and Elizabeth Barrett Browning and Christina Rossetti among poets. But the process by which the oeuvre of these writers came to be valued more highly than those of their female contemporaries did not involve simply a kind of 'transcendence' of contemporary assumptions based on the authors' sex. Rather, genuine responsiveness to these authors' writing was often inflected by definite preconceptions about them as women.

The reasons why some nineteenth-century authors entered the literary canon, and thus benefitted from the increasing attention given to English (rather than Greek and Roman) literature at schools and universities from the late nineteenth century, are complex. They relate to the characteristics of the authors' works themselves, of course, but also entail such factors as the readers' (varying) horizons of expectations, the vagaries of publishing history, and the images conveyed by biographical accounts. Needless to say, certain male writers also came to be seen as more significant than contemporaries of their own sex – Wordsworth, Coleridge, Keats, Shelley, Byron, Scott, Dickens, Thackeray, Tennyson, Robert Browning. There were also literary histories which sought to recuperate the achievements of women writers, such as Jane Williams's *The Literary Women of England* (1861), focussed on poetry, and Julia Kavanagh's *English Women of Letters* (1862), concentrating on novelists. Here I aim to suggest, by drawing on nineteenth-century commentaries on nineteenth-century women novelists, some of the factors affecting the perceptions of those who achieved the highest reputations. By contrast, I will trace the very different fate of a woman writer who was habitually invoked in nineteenth-century literary discourse, but whose works were constantly dismissed as insignificant – Anne Brontë.[3]

The issue of the *Athenaeum* which criticises the novels by Christabel Coleridge and the Revd J. M. Neale reviews more enthusiastically another publication of 1870, James Edward Austen-Leigh's *Memoir* of his aunt Jane Austen. According to this review, Austen's novels, which had first appeared over fifty years earlier, have now 'become classics'[4] – a view borne out by literary histories like David Masson's *British Novelists and Their Styles* (1859) and Kavanagh's *English Women of Letters*, which both present Austen's novels as superior to those of her contemporaries.[5] Both

Austen's popularity and her critical reputation continued to rise: critical discourse in the late nineteenth and early twentieth centuries is full of encomiums on her novels, and multiple editions of them appeared.[6] But conceptions of her writing were strongly affected by assumptions about her personality.

Austen-Leigh's *Memoir* of 1870 is one of several texts about women writers produced by family members or close friends that strongly influenced the reception of their work. As chapter 1 has suggested, such biographical material is best seen, not as efforts to reveal the 'truth' about the writers concerned, but, rather, as attempts to present versions of them which would make a favourable impression on nineteenth-century readers. Biographers were aware that, in venturing into the public domain via their fiction or poetry, women writers were going outside the realm of private domestic life to which many contemporaries thought they should confine themselves. Hence biographical accounts often compensated for such perceptions by emphasizing their subjects' devotion to home-life and lack of self-orientated ambition for public recognition. In the case of Jane Austen, her relatives' versions of her extended this emphasis to highlight the apparent modesty of her literary claims, in a way which dovetailed with nineteenth-century assumptions about literary traits characteristic of women writers.

The 1870 *Memoir* reinforces the view of Austen which had already gained wide currency through the 'Biographical Notice of the Author' which Jane Austen's brother Henry had appended to the first edition of *Northanger Abbey* and *Persuasion* published late in 1817, soon after her death. The notice was reproduced in slightly altered form in the first (*Sense and Sensibility*) volume of the edition of Austen brought out in Bentley's Standard Novels (1833 –), and in many subsequent reprints and new editions of this volume, up to the 1880s.[7] Although Henry Austen does acknowledge his sister's intelligence and indeed her 'genius', he also claims that she was reluctant to venture into print, and that, when she did, 'no accumulation of fame would have induced her, had she lived, to affix her name to any productions of her pen'.[8] Furthermore, as if he feared that Jane Austen's novels might themselves imply that her attitude to society was more critical and satirical than was in keeping with the forbearance and modesty expected of the nineteenth-century woman, Henry Austen assured her readers that 'she always sought, in the faults of others, something to excuse, to forgive or forget', and that she was never guilty of a 'severe expression'.

The representation of Jane Austen offered by her nephew in the 1870 *Memoir* is very similar. According to Austen-Leigh, she was happy to spend her time 'in the performance of home duties, and the cultivation of domestic affections, without any self-seeking or craving after applause'. In addition she was 'as far as possible from being censorious or satirical', and the 'most delightful characters' in her novels reflected 'her own sweet temper and loving heart'.[9] Much commentary on Austen, particularly after the *Memoir*, celebrated the woman as well as the work, highlighting her devotion to home life and lack of literary ambition. By contrast, the gradual decline of Fanny Burney's reputation was probably related to the fact that she was seen as living 'in a blaze of social recognition, a petted darling of the town'.[10] Moreover, a belief in her contented and unsatirical disposition began to inflect attitudes to the novels, so that her humour was characterized as quiet and kindly, her irony (if identified at all) presented as gentle or good-natured, her fiction overall seen as 'perfectly finished' and 'exquisite', like the women's work of embroidery in which – Austen-Leigh assured his readers – she had excelled.

Most importantly, however, Austen was thought to be a woman whose writings had definite limitations – and limitations many commentators found easy to associate with women writers as such. Perceived as a writer who based her novels on the character-types and social groups with which she was personally familiar, together with their circumscribed concerns and overall lack of strong passions, she was assumed to have little knowledge of life outside this narrow milieu, nor any grasp either of abstract ideas or of 'major' issues like warfare or political unrest. But this was only to be expected of a woman: as a critic in the *London Review* opined in 1860, 'the most successful female novelists are those who have drawn upon the topics that lay closest to hand', because they draw on women's capacity for 'quiet and vivid surface observation' – but their works would not contain any 'generalisation, or reasoning, of a practical kind'.[11]

Such fiction could not, this critic goes on to say, be 'of the highest order', since artistic greatness involves going beyond transcription of one's surroundings to demonstrate creative power. And given that creativity was strongly linked to mental capacities, notions about women's intellectual inferiority to men meant that women writers were seen as inferior in the creative sense, as less capable of original thinking. Men, according to a critic writing in 1883, are given to speculation, to constant questioning, whereas women are more trustful and accepting, and therefore lack imagination; as a corollary, the man 'has excelled the woman as an artist'.[12]

Jane Austen owed much of her nineteenth-century prestige as a woman writer, however, not simply to her characteristically female limitations, but also to her own supposed awareness of these limitations, especially as implied by a letter quoted in her relatives' biographical accounts. Addressed to J. E. Austen-Leigh as a boy, it first saw the light in Henry Austen's 'Biographical Notice', and was probably cited more often in nineteenth-century discussion of Austen than any passage from her novels. Referring to her young nephew's mislaying of some of his own fictional efforts, Jane Austen disclaims having appropriated them herself: 'What should I do, my dearest E. with your manly vigorous sketches, so full of life and spirit? How could I possibly join them on to a little bit of ivory, two inches wide, on which I work with a brush so fine as to produce little effect after much labour?' Numerous commentators, ignoring the likelihood that the experienced novelist's self-deprecation here was a gesture of kindness to a younger relative, took literally her characterization of her own fiction's scope as 'a little bit of ivory, two inches wide', and cited it approvingly as showing Jane Austen's admirable consciousness of her own limitations. So eventually, in the *Dictionary of National Biography* entry on Austen, written near the end of the century by prominent literary critic Leslie Stephen, the letter is quoted to demonstrate that 'No writer ever understood better the precise limits of her own powers.' (In the vein of much criticism in this ilk, the article suggests that Austen's novels are characterized by 'unconscious charm' and 'delicate subsatirical humour'.)

If the consensus had been that Austen could do no more than transcribe the foibles of the narrow social circle she knew from personal experience, then her reputation would probably not have endured to the end of the century and beyond. Tricia Lootens argues that there are no reputations so vulnerable to eclipse as those of women writers who come to be perceived as representing 'universal' feminine traits, since their canonicity depends on 'the fleeting authority of their canonizers' sexual politics'.[13] Austen's near-contemporary, the poet Felicia Hemans, is a notable case in point: she is presented as ultra-feminine in both Frederic Rowton's *The Female Poets of Great Britain* of 1848 and Eric S. Robertson's *English Poetesses* of 1883, but the later text puts far greater emphasis on her alleged limitations. As far as fiction is concerned, Nicola Diane Thompson suggests similar reasons for the fading of the novelist Charlotte Yonge's reputation by the end of the nineteenth century: her fiction seemed to incarnate traditional feminine traits, and nothing else.[14]

In Austen's case, however, the durability of her fiction was often insisted on. For example, W. J. Dawson in 1905 calls her 'one of the true immortals of English literature' whose novels are 'likely to endure to quite unprophesied generations', while Edmund Gosse, in his history of modern English literature, invokes 'that impeccable JANE AUSTEN, whose fame becomes ever more inaccessible to the devastating forces of time and shifting fashion' (Gosse's emphasis).[15] What many commentators recognized was that Austen's achievement did, after all, require a creative gift.

The novelist Margaret Oliphant, for example, averred that Austen could 'turn . . . commonplace events into things more interesting than passion', and that *Pride and Prejudice* 'might have been the outcome of the profoundest prolonged observation and study of mankind'. And for Gosse, Austen's characters are creations, not transcriptions: she is 'among the creators of the world'. Mary Ward, meanwhile, suggests that the circumscription of Austen's material is a matter of choice, not personal limitation: she possesses a 'capacity for isolating from the vast mass of detail which goes to make up human life just those details and no others which will produce a desired effect and blend into one clear and harmonious whole'.[16]

A couple of astute nineteenth-century critics went further in questioning the pervasive image of dear Aunt Jane and her modest miniature-painting. Oliphant argued that the novels themselves expressed a kind of 'feminine cynicism' arising from Austen's position as a woman intelligent enough to perceive people's selfishness, meanness and stupidity, but unable, partly because of her sex, to do anything to mitigate them.[17] Richard Simpson, in the best nineteenth-century commentary on Austen, argued that the realism of her works arose, not from 'direct imitation of nature', but from 'looking through, and amusing herself with, the aberrations of pretended imitators' – that is, she trained herself into 'an artist' less through observation than through reading other fiction which purported to represent 'life'.[18] Yet the 'little bit of ivory' and the unambitious woman contented with her domestic round were seldom far away. The overall consensus was that, however brilliantly and even creatively Austen handled her material, that material still had its limitations, and she never demonstrated a capacity to move beyond it. Hers was a self-effacing, restricted – and therefore unthreatening – kind of genius. Like a Victorian woman who attracted a proposal of marriage through modestly refraining from seeking one, Jane Austen was admitted into the canon.

Whether or not nineteenth-century readers consciously compared Charlotte Brontë's novels with those of Jane Austen, the evidence suggests that they valued *Jane Eyre* and its successors for very different qualities. Moreover, the impact of *Jane Eyre* on first publication (in 1847) was more strong and immediate than that of any of Austen's novels, and the curious quasi-male pseudonyms adopted by the three Brontë sisters (Currer, Ellis and Acton Bell) aroused much speculation. The situation was complicated too when the publisher T. C. Newby, who had accepted Emily's *Wuthering Heights* (by 'Ellis Bell') and Anne Brontë's *Agnes Grey* (by 'Acton Bell'), cashed in on the popularity of Charlotte's novel by representing her sisters' novels as 'by the author of *Jane Eyre*'. Then, after the deaths of Emily (December 1848) and Anne (May 1849), Charlotte wrote for the new editions of *Wuthering Heights* and *Agnes Grey* a 'Biographical Notice' (1850) which offered impressions of their personalities and focussed attention on the isolation and brevity of their lives. Charlotte herself consolidated her reputation during her lifetime with two more novels, *Shirley* and *Villette*, but survived only till March 1855, dying in her thirty-eighth year. Soon afterwards, a commentator could declare that

while the giant of war [in the Crimea] is trampling down lives by thousands, and shouting in trumpet-tongued fury, the 'smallest of women,' from a grave in a village which is only a dot on the largest map, sits a queen in the memory of more millions than the Macedonian [Alexander the Great] dreamed of when he looked wistfully over the sea for another world to conquer.[19]

Thus the legend of the Brontës had begun to take shape: the mysterious, closely bonded sisters, producing works of literary genius in a wild and lonely Yorkshire village, but with lives tragically cut short in their prime. Gaskell's biography of Charlotte would fix this image in the public mind, with the pathos very much to the fore. Like Jane Austen's, the Brontës' novels were interpreted in relation to their lives – but there were notable differences in the ways each of the three sisters and her novel(s) were perceived.

Throughout the nineteenth century, Charlotte Brontë was written about more often than either of her sisters, and her novels went into more editions, *Jane Eyre* remaining the most popular. This novel was adapted for the stage in several versions, and therefore became familiar beyond the (mainly middle-class) novel-reading public.[20] There was also more information available about Charlotte's life, since she survived longer, had more links with the world outside Haworth, and left more personal papers.

Commentators late in the century recalled *Jane Eyre* as something new in fiction – a view borne out by the initial responses to the novel as well. According to Margaret Oliphant, after the 'old-fashioned' novels of Catherine Gore and Anne Marsh in earlier decades, *Jane Eyre* 'took the world by storm' in 1847, such that the advent of Charlotte Brontë was that of 'a new and startling claimant of the highest honours', who made 'a kind of revolution in fiction' which had a profound effect on the next generation of women novelists.[21] A few years later, Clement Shorter would agree, declaring that 'after the current novels of her day, *Jane Eyre* was a model of outspokenness, a veritable volcano', since it was 'as original a novel as was ever submitted to the judgment of the reading public'.[22]

Charlotte Brontë's fiction was often praised for its emotional power, its passion. This passion might be identified with its treatment of love – what Shorter calls the 'ideal' of a 'passionate devotion of one human being to another, growing more intense with time, based partly on intellectual sympathy, partly on spiritual affinity, and yet again upon absorbing passion'.[23] But the passion might also be the 'outspokenness' he attributes to *Jane Eyre* – the novels' challenges to social convention, their attacks on social and religious hypocrisy. Mary Ward says of Charlotte's (and Emily's) works at the end of the century that they possess 'power and vitality', the sisters' personalities 'challenge no less than they attract', such that 'their vigorous effect upon the reader's sympathies and judgement has been always part of their ascendancy, and one great secret of their enduring fame'. Of Charlotte, she observes that, in each novel, she 'touches the shield of the reader; she does not woo or persuade him; she attacks him'.[24] In a speech written for the opening of the Haworth Parsonage Museum in 1895, T. Wemyss Reid lauded Charlotte for breaking the 'bonds of a narrow conventionalism'.[25]

Offering challenges, and attacking 'narrow conventionalism' and 'social limitations' were not ventures which all nineteenth-century readers and critics accepted unambiguously in women writers, betraying as they might qualities of aggression and independent thinking. Elizabeth Gaskell's representation of Charlotte Brontë, however, eventually disarmed this kind of criticism: as well as a person of great gifts whose life was brief and scarred by tragedy, she was portrayed as a woman whose directness and forthrightness were signs of both her Yorkshire background and her ardent, serious-minded sincerity. In addition, she had devoted much of her life to her family, as a dedicated daughter and sister.

Hence Wemyss Reid's speech, although acknowledging that Haworth Parsonage is known as 'the home of a wonderful genius', also claims that 'we love and reverence it still more as having been the scene of the life of patient endurance, unmurmuring submission, and steadfast devotion to duty of one of the noblest of her sex'.[26]

Whether Haworth Parsonage was the home of more than one 'wonderful genius' was doubtful to Victorian commentators. Neither Emily nor Anne attracted the widespread admiration accorded their sister. Of the two, however, it was clearly Emily and her works which aroused the greater fascination.

When *Wuthering Heights* appeared in 1848, it was received with some hostility (albeit not as much hostility as is often assumed). Reviewers were bewildered, even horrified, by what they saw as the ferocity and the improbability of the characters, the coarseness of the language, and the author's apparent lack of a clear moral viewpoint. But there was some acknowledgment of the sheer power of the writing – and this would have been one reason why the novelist was universally assumed to be male.[27]

The actual identity of the author was of course disclosed in Charlotte Brontë's posthumous 'Biographical Notice' of her sisters, plus her 'Editor's Preface to the New [1850] Edition of *Wuthering Heights*' and her Prefatory Note to her selections from Emily's poems.[28] Charlotte was very concerned to explain her sister's novel with reference to the physical and social locale of its setting, and especially to her sister's strong emotional bond with this area. For, she asserts, the many readers to whom the West-Riding of Yorkshire is 'alien and unfamiliar', and who possess calm manners and moderate feelings, 'will hardly know what to make of the rough, strong utterance, the harshly manifested passions, the unbridled aversions, and headlong partialities of unlettered moorland hinds and rugged moorland squires, who have grown up untaught and unchecked, except by mentors as harsh as themselves'. And if the novel is 'rustic', and 'moorish, and wild, and knotty as a root of heath', then this was only 'natural' since its author was 'a native and nursling of the moors'. For Emily, 'her native hills were far more to her than a spectacle; they were what she lived in, and by, as much as the wild birds, their tenants, or as the heather, their produce'.[29]

Charlotte also tried to disarm criticism of the novel's fiercer characters by pointing to the particular restrictions of Emily's experience: since she knew West Yorkshire rustics and their family legends from observation and hearsay rather than through direct conversation with them, 'what her mind had gathered of the real concerning them, was too exclusively confined to those tragic and terrible traits of which, in listening to the secret annals of every rude vicinage, the memory is sometimes compelled to receive the impress'. Hence Emily did not understand the implications of her creations, how they would impact on others.[30]

Drawing attention to the limitations of a woman writer's experience could, as the nineteenth-century commentary on Jane Austen shows, generate patronizing responses. But although *Wuthering Heights* never attained the critical or popular success of Charlotte's novels in the nineteenth century, it was often praised, and did go into many editions, both separately and collected with the other Brontë novels. Indeed commentators sometimes implied that appreciation of *Wuthering Heights* required a wider comprehension and a more discriminating taste on the part of the reader. For 'J. F-' in 1887, for example, Emily's novel is 'undoubtedly too grim and terrific' ever to attain the popularity of Charlotte's novels, but 'it has far more power, even far more originality'.[31] As noted in chapter 1, too, it was Emily rather than Charlotte Brontë who was chosen in the 1880s for inclusion in J. H. Ingram's Eminent Women series.

It is notable too that Victorian responses to *Wuthering Heights* are largely free of preconceptions based on the author's sex, and Charlotte's representation of her sister contributed to this circumstance as well. For Charlotte's Emily was a strange and (in Victorian terms) androgynous creature. She had an 'unpretending outside' and 'powers . . . unadapted to the practical business of life', but an inflexible will and an 'altogether unbending' spirit. She was 'unobtrusive', with 'retiring manners and habits', but, within, 'lay a secret power and fire that might have informed the brain and kindled the veins of a hero'. She was both 'stronger than a man' and 'simpler than a child' – unique in fact, 'her nature stood alone'.[32] The impression that Emily possessed 'masculine' qualities was reinforced by the views of M. Héger (Charlotte and Emily's schoolmaster in Brussels), as quoted by Gaskell: he felt that Emily's 'powerful reason' and her 'strong, imperious will' meant that 'she should have been a man – a great navigator'.[33]

Emily emerges, then, as a figure too little a woman to be patronized as a writer, but, although she may be man-like, she is not completely so. Moreover, her unusual personality and her unusually solitary life, amidst the fierce Yorkshire people and the wild Yorkshire moors make her, if a literary genius, a one-off phenomenon. As a unique case, she did not threaten contemporary preconceptions about women's writing as such.

So Matthew Arnold, in 'Haworth Churchyard, April, 1855', a poem commemorating Charlotte's death, evoked Emily in some of its better lines – lines which became well known:

> and She -
> (How shall I sing her?) – whose soul
> Knew no fellow for might,
> Passion, vehemence, grief,
> Daring, since Byron died,
> That world-fam'd Son of Fire, who sank
> Baffled, unknown, self-consum'd;
> Whose too-bold dying song
> Shook, like a clarion-blast, my soul.[34]

Two years later John Skelton calls Emily 'a Titan' with a 'stern, taciturn, untameable' nature, and goes on to relate her personality to the protagonists of her novel:

A volcano is beneath the flowers where we stand, and we cannot tell where it may burst. There is a refrain of fierce poetry in the men and women she draws – gleams of the gipsy savageness and of the gipsy tenderness. A strange fire, inherited from an Eastern kindred, lighted among Norland moors, burns in their eyes. They flutter on the confines between our love and our hate.[35]

As this last example suggests, praise of Emily Brontë's writing could verge on the rhapsodic. Later reactions could be (but were not always) more focussed on the novel itself, as in the 1887 article by 'J. F.', which strives to deal with the complexity of Heathcliff: 'within the sphere of English fiction', this writer declares, 'Heathcliff stands alone'. Therefore, if we 'do not understand him', then 'it is highly probable we were never intended to do so', so that we should 'try to realise and accept the fact that there may be just one or two things yet left in heaven and earth not dreamt of by our philosophy'.[36]

Finally, *Wuthering Heights* was praised for its impersonality, its demonstration of Emily's power to create rather than simply transcribe. Although the novel's provenance could supposedly be accounted for by her character and by her peculiar interaction with her surroundings, it was not perceived as autobiographical. This was partly the result of the novel's narrative structure – but it was also another by-product of Charlotte's portrayal of her sister. For that 'secret power and fire' of Emily's were mysterious and inaccessible, as she was someone who protected 'the recesses of [her] mind and feelings' even from her sisters, and she had no other intimates.[37] So Shorter would declare that 'Emily was never more aloof than in her great novel', since 'it is dramatic, it is vivid and passionate, but it is never self-revealing'.[38]

By contrast, the novels of Anne Brontë could be criticized for being *too* autobiographical, and for failing to demonstrate imaginative power. According to Shorter in 1905, both of Anne's novels are 'transcripts of the life [Anne] knew and little more'. That they are still published – and he acknowledges that new editions of them came out once their copyrights had expired by 1890 – is a tribute to the 'glamour' of the Brontë name rather than to their own value or popularity.[39] Mary Ward, who wrote the introductions to the new Haworth edition of the complete Brontë novels in 1899–1900, also disparaged Anne, claiming that she 'was not strong enough, her gift not rigorous enough, to enable her to transmute experience and grief', so that her second novel, *The Tenant of Wildfell Hall*, possesses 'the truth of a tract, or a report', but not the 'truth of imagination'.[40]

Like Emily's, Anne's reputation had much to do with Charlotte's representation of her in the 'Biographical Notice', but the outcome was very different. The problem confronting Charlotte in discussing *The Tenant* was that the novel dealt with subject matter not considered proper for women writers to handle – marital breakdown brought on by the husband's alcoholism and adultery – and contained scenes of drunkenness, violence and swearing. Charlotte accounted for Anne's use of such material by presenting her as conscience-driven, forcing herself to portray the evils of alcoholism because of her bitter and very personal experience (of their brother Branwell's decline): Anne persuaded herself that it was 'a duty to reproduce every detail . . . as a warning to others'.[41] Charlotte's account, then, actually encouraged readers to respond to the text as 'a report' rather than as an imaginative creation. Meanwhile Anne herself emerges from Charlotte's description as a much more feminine creature than Emily: she was equally reserved and taciturn, but she lacked 'the power, the fire, the originality' of Emily. 'Milder and more subdued', she possessed only the 'quiet virtues'.

Charlotte's version of Anne's life and writing invited interpretations of her novels as simple transcriptions of her experience, and readings of her character which made her seem like an Austen minus the wit. Responses to Anne and her writing were much affected too by what commentators expected to find in a Brontë – for her novels lacked the passion associated with those of her sisters. A constant refrain of commentary is that Anne would not be remembered at all, if it were not for her more brilliant sisters. According to Mary Ward, 'it is not as the writer of *Wildfell Hall*, but as the sister of Charlotte and Emily Brontë, that Anne Brontë escapes oblivion'; Margaret Oliphant claims that Anne 'need scarcely have been mentioned except for her relationship to the other two', and that she had only been induced to become a writer through their 'vehemence and strong impulse'.[42] Even when she is granted talent, it is a lesser talent: Matthew Arnold's 'Haworth Churchyard', for example, pays tribute to Anne too, but lukewarmly, as 'She, whose genius, though not / Puissant like [Charlotte's], was yet / Sweet and graceful'.

Nineteenth-century commentators often treated Anne Brontë as an embarrassment, as a figure who had to be mentioned because she was there, but one to be dismissed as quickly as possible, while she has been largely ignored in twentieth-century criticism until the 1980s. She has suffered, rather than benefitted, from her sisters' 'glamour': as well as seeming more limited in personality, she has written novels which lack *Jane Eyre*'s outspoken quasi-personal voice, or the compelling larger-than-life characters in a wild natural and social setting which have drawn readers to *Wuthering Heights*.

That Anne suffered from being a different kind of novelist from her sisters is brought out most starkly in the comments by 'J. W. E.' on *The Tenant* in 1859. This commentator criticizes the novel for lacking 'the unity of design, the glowing imagination, the over-ruling genius of Emily Brontë', and the 'brutality of [Anne's] characters' is 'more repulsive' too, since they lack 'the charm of sympathy with outward nature' of their counterparts in *Wuthering Heights*. On the other hand, like Emily Brontë's novel, *The Tenant* does reveal 'the rugged natures that inhabit the Yorkshire uplands, the dreary mansions and monotony of savage isolation'.[43] *The Tenant* is thus recalled here as a much inferior version of *Wuthering Heights* – although Anne Brontë's novel is not set explicitly in Yorkshire, and does not focus on 'the dreary mansions and monotony of savage isolation' at all. For this commentator, if *The Tenant* is a Brontë novel, it must resemble *Wuthering Heights*, but as it is only by Anne, it must be second-rate. Even a more sympathetic critic, 'J. A.', can only appreciate *The Tenant* insofar as it possesses the strengths of the other sisters' novels: it 'decidedly claims kindred with *Wuthering Heights* and *Jane Eyre*' because it contains 'forcible descriptions in it which none out of the Brontë family could have written'.[44] That Anne Brontë has not even yet escaped from her sisters' long shadows is suggested by the way the recent television adaptation of *The Tenant of Wildfell Hall* (BBC, 1996) not only gave the novel a recognizably Yorkshire setting, but altered the ending so as to make the man the heroine eventually weds, Gilbert Markham, more like a recognizably 'Brontë' hero. In the novel, Gilbert makes a fool of himself after Arthur Huntingdon's death, pursuing his widow Helen while constantly misconstruing her motives and feelings, and even crediting a rumour that she has married someone else. In the television version, *Helen* assumes *Gilbert* has wed an old flame, and is only rescued from a disconsolate state when he intervenes, having charged across the moors to her in a Heathcliff-like manner.

It is difficult to judge whether Anne Brontë's works would have gained a higher reputation – or, alternatively, have been lost to sight – had she not always been compared with her sisters. But response to her work in the nineteenth century was skewed by her failure to conform to either of the models of woman novelist which proved to have the most long-lasting appeal: the modest and delicately witty miniaturist, and the impassioned daughter of the Yorkshire moors.

The woman novelist with the greatest claim for intellectual stature in the nineteenth century was undoubtedly George Eliot – but the course of her reputation during the period bears witness to the precariousness of female intellectual pretensions. During her lifetime, her works were seldom given the condescending treatment often accorded women's fiction. But after her death in 1880, Eliot's reputation suffered a long-lasting decline – a change which had much to do with contemporary response to her widower J. W. Cross's *Life*.

George Eliot achieved a major critical and popular success with her first full-length novel, *Adam Bede*, in 1859. There was much speculation about the person behind the pseudonym, but the novelist was generally assumed to be male, and possibly a clergyman. So the review in *The Times* declared: 'There can be no mistake about *Adam Bede*. It is a first-rate novel, and its author takes rank at once among the masters of the art.'[45] By the time *The Mill on the Floss* appeared in 1860, many knew that the pseudonym concealed not only a woman, but a woman living with a man out of wedlock, and the translator of significant German works (D. F. Strauss's *Life of Jesus* and Ludwig Feuerbach's *Essence of Christianity*) which had challenged contemporary Christian beliefs. These revelations caused some disquiet, but the praise could not be gainsaid, and Eliot's novels continued to be well received – for their representation of rural provincial life, their humour, their psychological insight and their intellectual grasp.

The success of *Adam Bede* was never surpassed by the reception of any of Eliot's subsequent novels. The response to *Middlemarch* twelve years later (1871–2) is illuminating: although the novel was recognized as ambitious and wide-ranging in scope, and as penetrating in its insights, the failures of its idealist protagonists Dorothea Brooke and Tertius Lydgate conveyed a melancholy which could be attributed to Eliot's lack of belief in any power transcending humanity, while, as chapter 1 has suggested, readers also began to find the narrator's complex speculations heavy-going. Strictures on what was seen as the growing predominance of reflective passages in Eliot's fiction became more pronounced with her last novel, *Daniel Deronda* – especially as commentators were less interested in the personalities and aspirations of the Jewish characters prominent in this novel, than they had been in the more familiar predicaments of Eliot's earlier protagonists. So A. V. Dicey in the *Nation*, for example, complained that now 'reflection prevails over description, and the moral purpose always discernible in George Eliot's works threatens to throw into the shade the author's creative power . . . instead of the action of a drama telling its own tale, you have the reflective comment of a chorus of moralists'.[46]

What starts to happen is that commentators increasingly divide Eliot's output into her earlier and later novels, and express a preference for the earlier ones – with *Romola* (1863) forming the dividing line. Leslie Stephen's obituary article on Eliot is interesting in this context, since he expresses more enthusiasm for the 'works of her first period' (*Scenes of Clerical Life, Adam Bede, The Mill on the Floss, Silas Marner*) than for their successors. He perceives in her later books a 'growing tendency to substitute elaborate analysis for direct presentation' of character, while the novels' increasing concentration on their protagonists' inability to fulfil their aspirations gives the later books a 'tone of melancholy'. Moreover, Stephen's preference is expressed in terms of the earlier novels' 'charm', and implies nostalgia for a simpler kind of novel-writing which is linked for him with the (comfortably) simpler way of life of the past that he believes the earlier novels to embody: 'the sphere which she has made specially her own is that quiet English country life which she knew in early youth', so that for most readers Eliot is primarily the creator of 'the exquisite series of scenes so lovingly and vividly presented in the earlier stage'. Although reading *Romola* or *Middlemarch* exposes readers to 'a comprehensive and vigorous intellect', they miss the 'charm' and 'magic' of *Adam Bede*.[47]

Stephen's emphasis on the 'charm' of her early fiction hints that he is thinking of George Eliot's sex, an impression borne out by his criticizing some of her male characters as too 'feminine', on the grounds that Eliot was 'a true woman'. (Stephen's *DNB* article on Jane Austen, we recall, had praised her novels' 'unconscious charm'.) But he does acknowledge the calibre of Eliot's mind. What happens with the publication of Cross's *Life* in 1885, however, is that, despite the biography's concentration on Eliot's mental life, her intellect actually comes to be taken less seriously. In giving much space to the male thinkers who influenced her intellectual development, the biography unwittingly encouraged some commentators to belittle Eliot's intellectual brilliance and claims to creativity.[48]

So for the critic in the *Saturday Review*, Cross's book shows 'how impressionable, how emotional, how illogical' and therefore 'how feminine' George Eliot was.[49] The corollary was that her intellectual ideas were adopted from the various male thinkers with whom she happened to come into contact, whether personally, or through their works. That is, Eliot, like ostensibly less impressive women writers, was not really an original creative talent. For example, novelist Eliza Lynn Linton asserted that Eliot's works were 'eminently the result of other men's teaching; throughout her life she bore the impress of one, now of another, of various masters'.[50] When Stephen came to write the *DNB* entry on Eliot after the advent of Cross's *Life*, he did mention her 'mind of extraordinary grasp and perceptive faculty', but can now bolster his earlier view of her as 'a true woman', by pointing to her 'feminine tendency . . . to accept philosophers at their own valuation'.

Accordingly, the assumption that Eliot's earlier, less overtly cerebral fiction is much superior to the later becomes a critical orthodoxy, and the second group of novels is presented as stodgily didactic and verbose. Critical orthodoxy affects general perceptions too, to judge from the publication history: from the late nineteenth century the latter group of novels ceases to be published outside collected editions, whereas there are several new editions of *Adam Bede*, *The Mill on the Floss* and *Silas Marner*, once these fall out of copyright in 1901–3. So Hugh Walker, echoing contemporary assumptions about women's personal traits and capacities, observes a gradual fading of 'the fresh, easy grace, the flexibility of language, the lightness of touch' from Eliot's fiction, to be replaced by too many 'leaden paragraphs wherein the author seems to be struggling under a burden too great for her strength'.[51] Gender-based assumptions are also evident in late nineteenth-century literary histories. George Saintsbury declares in 1896 that her 'docility' induced Eliot to alter her religious outlook under the influence of her friends Charles Bray and Charles Hennell, and to become a novelist at the prompting of G. H. Lewes. Her later works, he argues, betray her lack of 'invention', and, rather than demonstrating a fine intellect, evince a 'pseudo-scientific spirit' and 'most portentous jargon'. Finally Edmund Gosse, who had attributed creative genius to Jane Austen, found none in George Eliot: the latter lacked 'imaginative invention', and succeeded only when she reproduced what she had seen and heard. She had triumphed in her earlier fiction as a (feminine) 'close observer of nature, mistress of laughter and tears, exquisite in the intensity of cumulative emotion', but in her later work, as if foolishly aping men, she had become 'the mechanician [*sic*], overloading her page with pretentious matter, working out her scheme as if she were building a steam-engine'.[52]

Late nineteenth-century critics, then, could be uncomfortable with a woman writer's intellectual claims, and anxious to assimilate them to still-powerful assumptions about women's capacities. In being construed as a quite conventional woman, and as a writer who apparently lacked either Jane Austen's light touch or the forthrightness earned by suffering which was attributed to Charlotte Brontë, Eliot risked being depreciated and neglected. And so it proved, until well into the twentieth century.

NOTES

1 'Novels of the Week', *Athenaeum* no. 2202, (8 January 1870), p. 54.
2 The most recent detailed study on this topic is Nicola Diane Thompson, *Reviewing Sex: Gender and the Reception of Victorian Novels* (London: Macmillan, 1996).
3 The factors affecting the reputations of the most prominent nineteenth-century women poets, Elizabeth Barrett Browning and Christina Rossetti, have been studied in detail by Tricia Lootens in her *Lost Saints: Silence, Gender, and Victorian Literary Canonization* (Charlottesville and London: University Press of Virginia, 1996).
4 *Athenaeum* (8 January 1870), p. 55.
5 David Masson, *British Novelists and Their Styles. Being a Critical Sketch of the History of British Prose Fiction* (Cambridge: Macmillan, 1859), pp. 180ff.; Julia Kavanagh in her *English Women of Letters: Biographical Sketches*, 2 vols. (London: Hurst and Blackett, 1862; 2nd edn, 1863), vol. II, pp. 191, 352–3.
6 See David Gilson, 'Editions and Publishing History', in J. David Grey ed., *The Jane Austen Handbook* (London: Athlone Press, 1986), pp. 135–9.
7 See David Gilson, 'Henry Austen's "Memoir of Jane Austen"', *Persuasions* 19 (1997), p. 12.

8 Henry Austen, 'Biographical Notice', rptd in B. C. Southam, ed., *Jane Austen: The Critical Heritage* (London: Routledge, 1968), pp. 73–7. The two volumes edited by Southam (the other is *Jane Austen: the Critical Heritage*, vol. II (1987)) contain a wide selection of critical material on Austen, from the earliest reviews to 1940. The first volume of Ian Littlewood, ed., *Jane Austen: Critical Assessments*, 4 vols. (Robertsbridge: Helm International, 1996), also covers nineteenth-century responses to Austen and her novels.

9 J. E. Austen-Leigh, *Memoir of Jane Austen* (2nd edn, 1870), ed. R. W. Chapman (Oxford: Clarendon Press, 1951), pp. 175, 93, 2.

10 Richard Burton, *Masters of the English Novel* (1909); rptd Freeport, New York: Books for Libraries Press, 1969), p. 103.

11 'Female Novelists', *London Review* 1 (1860), p. 137, rptd in Elizabeth K. Helsinger et al., eds., *The Woman Question: Society and Literature in Britain and America, 1837–1883*, vol. III: *Literary Issues* (Chicago and London: University of Chicago Press, 1983), p. 53.

12 Eric S. Robertson, *English Poetesses: A Series of Critical Biographies, with Illustrative Extracts* (London, Paris, New York: Cassell, 1883), pp. xii–xiii.

13 Lootens, *Lost Saints*, p. 74.

14 Thompson, *Reviewing Sex*, pp. 103ff.

15 W. J. Dawson, *Makers of English Fiction* (London: Hodder and Stoughton, 1905), pp. 31ff.; Edmund Gosse, *Modern English Literature: A Short History* (London: William Heinemann, 1897; revised edn, 1905), p. 295.

16 Margaret Oliphant, *The Literary History of England in the End of the Eighteenth and Beginning of the Nineteenth Century*, 3 vols. (London: Macmillan, 1886), vol. III, pp. 171ff.; Gosse, *Modern English Literature*, pp. 195–6; [Mary Humphry Ward], 'Style and Miss Austen', *Macmillan's Magazine* 51 (December 1884), pp. 84–7, rptd in *Jane Austen: The Critical Heritage*, vol. II, pp. 180–7.

17 See her *Literary History of England*, vol. III, pp. 222, 226, and her review of Austen-Leigh's *Memoir* in *Blackwood's Edinburgh Magazine* 107 (March 1870), pp. 294–5, partly rptd in Littlewood, ed., *Jane Austen: Critical Assessments*, vol. I, pp. 375–86.

18 See his review of Austen-Leigh's *Memoir* in *North British Review* 53 (April 1870), pp. 129–52, rptd in *Jane Austen: The Critical Heritage*, vol. I, pp. 241–65, and Littlewood, ed., *Jane Austen: Critical Assessments*, vol. I, pp. 387–408.

19 'Reading Raids, No. VI. Currer, Ellis, and Acton Bell', *Tait's Edinburgh Magazine* 22 (1855), pp. 416–23, rptd in Eleanor McNees, ed., *The Brontë Sisters: Critical Assessments*, 4 vols. (Robertsbridge: Helm Information, 1996), vol. I, pp. 159–60. This collection draws together articles on the Brontës and their works, from early reviews to recent studies. Also useful is Miriam Allott, ed., *The Brontës: the Critical Heritage* (London: Routledge, 1974).

20 Patsy Stoneman's *Brontë Transformations* (Brighton: Harvester Wheatsheaf, 1995) deals with creative and critical responses to *Jane Eyre* and *Wuthering Heights* from the novels' first appearance to the early 1990s.

21 Margaret Oliphant and F. R. Oliphant, *The Victorian Age of English Literature*, 2 vols. (London: Percival, 1892), vol. I, pp. 318–21; Stoneman's *Brontë*

Transformations discusses later nineteenth-century women writers' adaptations of the *Jane Eyre* plot.

22 Clement Shorter, *Charlotte Brontë and Her Sisters* (London: Hodder and Stoughton, 1905), pp. 173, 170.

23 Ibid., p. 239.

24 Introduction to Haworth edition of *Wuthering Heights* (1900), pp. xi–xli, rptd in McNees, ed., *The Brontë Sisters: Critical Assessments*, vol. II, p. 41.

25 Reid, *Brontë Society Transactions*, 1:3 (December 1895), pp. 19–32; rptd in McNees, ed., *The Brontë Sisters: Critical Assessments*, vol. I, p. 265.

26 McNees, ed., *The Brontë Sisters: Critical Assessments*, vol. I, p. 265.

27 *Wuthering Heights* is one of the novels whose reception is discussed in detail by Thompson in *Reviewing Sex*.

28 These texts are all reprinted in 'Biographical Notice of Ellis and Acton Bell', the Appendix to the World's Classics edition of *Wuthering Heights*, ed. Ian Jack (Oxford University Press, 1976), pp. 361–70.

29 Ibid. (Preface to the novel), pp. 365–6.

30 Ibid., p. 367.

31 '*Wuthering Heights*', *Temple Bar* 81 (December 1887), pp. 562–8, quoted in McNees, ed., *The Brontë Sisters: Critical Assessments*, vol. II, p. 40.

32 'Biographical Notice of Ellis and Acton Bell', pp. 363–4.

33 Gaskell, *Life of Charlotte Brontë*, p. 230.

34 *Fraser's Magazine* 51 (May 1855), pp. 527–30, rptd in McNees, ed., *The Brontë Sisters: Critical Assessments*, vol. I p. 608. Arnold, and others responding to Emily's writings, were sometimes thinking of her poetry as well, notably her last lines, beginning 'No coward soul is mine'.

35 'Charlotte Brontë', *Fraser's Magazine* 55 (May 1857), pp. 569–82, quoted in McNees, ed., *The Brontë Sisters: Critical Assessments*, vol. I, pp. 200–1.

36 '*Wuthering Heights*', quoted in McNees, ed., *The Brontë Sisters: Critical Assessments*, vol. II, p. 37.

37 'Biographical Notice of Ellis and Acton Bell', p. 360.

38 Shorter, *Charlotte Brontë and Her Sisters*, p. 139.

39 Ibid., p. 139.

40 Quoted in Allott, ed., *The Brontës: The Critical Heritage*, p. 459.

41 'Biographical Notice of Ellis and Acton Bell', p. 363.

42 Ward, quoted in Allott, ed., *The Brontës: The Critical Heritage*, p. 460; Margaret Oliphant and F. R. Oliphant, *The Victorian Age of English Literature*, vol. I, p. 320.

43 'Emily Brontë ("Ellis Bell")', quoted in McNees, ed., *The Brontë Sisters: Critical Assessments*, vol. I, p. 79.

44 'The Three Sisters', quoted in McNees, ed., *The Brontë Sisters: Critical Assessments*, vol. I, pp. 223–4.

45 Review by E. S. Dallas, *The Times* (12 April 1859), p. 5, rptd in David R. Carroll, ed., *George Eliot: the Critical Heritage* (London: Routledge & Kegan Paul, 1971), p. 77. Nineteenth-century commentary on Eliot and her writings is also collected in the first volume of Stuart Hutchinson, ed., *George*

Eliot: Critical Assessments, 4 vols. (Robertsbridge: Helm Information, 1996). See also J. Russell Perkin, *A Reception-History of George Eliot's Fiction* (Rochester, N.Y.: University of Rochester Press, 1995).

46 [A. V. Dicey], *Nation* (19 October 1876), pp. 245–6, rptd in Carroll, ed., *George Eliot: the Critical Heritage*, p. 399.

47 Leslie Stephen, *Cornhill Magazine* 43 (February 1881), pp. 152–68, rptd in Carroll, ed., *George Eliot: the Critical Heritage*, pp. 464–84.

48 J. W. Cross, Preface to *George Eliot's Life, as Related in her Letters and Journals*. 3 vols. (Edinburgh and London: William Blackwood and Sons, 1885), vol. I, p. vi.

49 *Saturday Review* (7 February 1885), p. 181, quoted in *George Eliot: the Critical Heritage*, p. 487.

50 Eliza Lynn Linton, *Temple Bar* 73 (January–April 1885), p. 516, quoted in Teresa Mangum, 'George Eliot and the Journalists: Making the Mistress Moral', in Kristine Ottesen Garrigan, ed., *Victorian Scandals: Representations of Gender and Class* (Athens, GA: Ohio University Press, 1992), pp. 167–8.

51 Hugh Walker, *The Age of Tennyson* (1897; rptd Freeport, N.Y.: Books for Libraries Press, 1969), p. 267.

52 George Saintsbury, *A History of Nineteenth-Century Literature (1780–1895)* (London: Macmillan, 1896), pp. 321–4; Gosse, *Modern English Literature*, pp. 371–2.

CHAPTER THREE

Women and the consumption of print

Margaret Beetham

Charlotte Brontë's *Jane Eyre*, published in the middle of the nineteenth century (1847), opens with a scene in which the child Jane has retreated into 'a double retirement'; a window seat with drawn curtains provides a safe physical space, the book she holds on her crossed knees provides a psychological space distinct from, though resonating with, the harsh reality of her situation. In this opening scene, reading gives the female child pleasure and also provides a way of understanding herself and her place in the world. Called from her book by the bullying John Reed, she names him a tyrant 'like the Roman slave drivers' she has read about in Goldsmith's *History of Rome*.[1] It is no wonder that John Reed forbids her the book and reminds her that it is *his* property, since he is the man of the house. From this moment to the end of the novel, in which Jane reads the world and books to the blind Rochester, *Jane Eyre* implicitly invokes other experiences of reading and explicitly invites 'The Reader' into the text.[2]

This moment from *Jane Eyre* suggests some of the themes I want to address in considering the topic of nineteenth-century women as consumers of print. These include questions of access to print; print as property – in other words its circulation in the form of commodities in the most advanced capitalist economy of the nineteenth century; reading in relation to physical and psychological space, for – as this passage emphasizes – books are both material objects and texts to be read; reading as a source of pleasure for women and a way of making sense of themselves and the world; its potential power, and the anxieties which reading (especially the reading of young women) produced in those with authority over them.

However, there is a problem about making generalizations about women and reading on the basis of *Jane Eyre*. After all this is fiction and, besides, a fiction by an exceptional woman and one whose work was condemned by many contemporaries as unwomanly and unfit itself for

55

female reading. Though the opening of *Jane Eyre* gives us a powerful representation of female reading, it is not 'representative' in the sense of typical. Would it not be better to look at literacy statistics or sales figures of books or library lendings? What kind of evidence is there about women's consumption of print in nineteenth-century Britain?[3]

THEORIES, STATISTICS AND OTHER TEXTS ABOUT READING

For anyone embarking on such a study there is a vast range of resources, including statistical and other kinds of quantitative data such as sales figures for books and newspapers, contemporary surveys of reading habits, and evidence of literacy levels.[4] However, these documents are themselves texts which need careful reading. If we take the most basic example, levels of literacy, the way this is usually calculated for the nineteenth century is by analysis of who could sign their names in the marriage register, which is a rough measure of who could *write*. But at the start of the century children might well learn to read but not to write, some literate brides of illiterate husbands might choose not to sign, and so on.[5] Though it may be the best we have, the evidence of marriage registers needs to be treated cautiously.

There are analogous problems with much of the other surviving statistical and survey data. Membership of libraries, for example, like book purchases or subscriptions, was framed by the legal doctrine that the wife's interest and existence was subsumed in the husband's. It was the husband's name which appeared on subscription lists or library registers. So even where we have a list of borrowings, as we do for example for the Portico Library in Manchester, it was the Revd William, not Mrs Gaskell, who was a member and we cannot be sure which of the books he took out were for her reading and which for his or both. Nineteenth-century social investigators invented 'modern' methods of social survey and statistical analysis and the surveys of reading or book ownership they left us are invaluable, but from this distance we can see how they were shaped by anxiety about the dangers of popular reading.[6]

As well as these contemporary lists, surveys and statistics, there survives a large body of material from the nineteenth century about reading and specifically about women's reading which was either concerned with theories of reading or attempted to offer practical guidance on what and how to read. Much of this work of examining the role of reading and the reader went on in the pages of periodicals (reviews, magazines and newspapers). The big reviews, the quarterly journals, which dominated the start of the century, focused on the discussion of books and other periodicals, and this remained a major element of much of the general periodical press. Magazines addressed specifically to women, which were in most respects quite unlike the weighty literary reviews, from mid-century onwards included not only fiction and poetry but also book reviews and advice on reading alongside advice on dress or household management. By the 1890s this crucial ingredient of the magazine had typically become 'Chats about Books'. This was the title which Arnold Bennett, writing under the name 'Barbara', gave to his weekly column for the magazine *Woman*, which he edited.[7] Though reviews do not tell us what women were reading, they offer powerful indications not only of what was available but of what was likely to be read and they indicate how reading was related to contemporary ideas of gender.[8]

With all this mass of material evidence to draw on, questions of who was reading and what they read still remain difficult to answer. If we ask about the *how* of reading this problem is compounded. By this I mean both the material 'how' (the relation between reading in a public library, reading aloud in the family and solitary reading – like Jane's in the window seat) and how the reader made sense of the text. Sally Mitchell in her work on nineteenth-century working women's reading and Lynne Pearce in her discussion of late twentieth-century reading argue that if we assume that reading always means interpretation we miss the impor-tant ways in which fiction may arouse feelings or give expression to fantasy.[9] Janice Radway, in her late twentieth-century ethnographic research on women readers of popular romance, found that they saw it as a way of asserting their own needs and giving attention to themselves rather than others – almost regardless of the content of the book.[10] We cannot simply extrapolate such research back to the nineteenth century but it is suggestive of the complex meanings of the act of reading.

This links to the final set of texts which we need to draw on in this dis-cussion, that is late twentieth-century critical debate on reading and in particular feminist theoretical work on the relationship of reading and gender. Critics as different as Roland Barthes, Jonathan Culler, Stanley Fish and Wolfgang Iser have made the reader or the process of reading central to their theory.[11] Much of this theorizing, as feminist critics have pointed out, assumes a universalized and abstract reader who looks uncannily like the rational, white, male intellectuals who elevated him to the centre of scholarly study.

Ever since Kate Millet argued angrily in *Sexual Politics* that women have been taught to read like men and must learn to read like women and Judith Fetterley suggested that women should be 'resisting readers', refusing the positions offered them by the text, the relation of gender to reading has occupied feminist critics in both theory and practice.[12]

In what follows I assume that these are important resources for understanding the ways women in the nineteenth century consumed, that is read, texts. There is no single model of the woman as consumer of texts. Indeed, I argue that the woman reader is not a fixed entity but rather is herself in process and may be becoming a different self or subject through the process of reading. Reading constitutes the reader at the same time as the reader constitutes her own version of the text. Just as Jane Eyre used her reading of Goldsmith to understand herself in the world and to speak out from that understanding, so women reading *Jane Eyre*, or the cheap romances condemned by serious critics, could articulate themselves through that text, whether by identification, by resistance or simply by the act of withdrawing into the world of the book.

QUESTIONS OF ACCESS

Access to print depends at the most basic level on being able to read. Despite the difficulties of assessing literacy levels, we can be certain that in the last decade of the nineteenth century for the first time the vast majority of women in Britain could read and had some kind of access, however limited, to print.[13] The increases both in general literacy and in that of women as a proportion of the population continued to be patchy. Women in rural areas were less likely to be able to read than their city sisters or rural men, and women in the south were more literate than women in the north. However, David Vincent has argued that in the 1880s and 1890s for the first time ever women's levels of literacy had not only caught up with male rates but in two out of three English counties literate women outnumbered literate men: 'In terms of basic attainments the progress of Victorian England had caused a widespread subversion of the established hierarchy of the sexes.'[14] Cautious though we need to be about generalization on 'the woman reader', we can say with confidence that it was in the nineteenth century that the mass of British women entered the world of literacy, even if they did so in a rather piecemeal and ragged fashion.

Of course this did not necessarily mean that working-class women actually read very much, beyond the occasional personal letter – though these were an important element in the working-class desire for, and practice of, literacy. The first systematic attempts to measure the scale of poverty in London and York revealed that at the end of Victoria's reign a third of people were living in poverty so absolute that they could not afford basic food, and adequate lodging.[15] This made acquiring even cheap papers very difficult, and space, time or light for reading did not come easily. In a survey carried out in Middlesbrough over a number of years and published in 1907 (six years after Victoria's death), Lady Bell found that few working-class women had the leisure to read, even though most of the households visited did have cheap books or papers.[16] One of the most important ways in which working men had access to print was through membership of Reading Rooms and Mechanics' Institutes but these public spaces were not available to women.[17]

However, access to print did not absolutely depend on personal levels of literacy. In working-class households and communities it was common practice until well into the twentieth century for the literate to read to and for others.[18] Nor was purchase the only way women could get hold of books and papers. Print circulated through borrowing, exchanges and shared copies, a point to which I shall return. For those who chose to spend pennies on print, there was a huge expansion in the number and variety of penny and half-penny papers in the 1880s and 1890s and these provided the most readily available form of reading for working-class women to buy. As a result, middle-class critics often castigated working women for reading only the cheapest serialized novelettes. But such evidence as we have suggests a far more complex picture of working-class reading, including that of women, some of whom read widely when they had the chance. This was particularly true of domestic servants who were the largest single occupational group and who often had access to their employers' books and magazines, either because they were passed on or, perhaps more often, because they were read secretly as the servant went about her work.[19]

However, few would dispute the claim made by the romantic novelist, Annie S. Swan, in 1892 that 'it is the middle-class woman who is the reader of today among her sex'.[20] She was introducing a new magazine, *Woman at Home*, one of many launched in the 1890s aimed at precisely this group. Annie Swan was contrasting the middle-class woman not only with the working-class but also with aristocratic ladies who, she argued, were too taken up with society life to be interested in reading. Though she produced no evidence for her claims she was almost certainly right. Middle-class women read more books and periodicals than any other group.

For these women, who had more than basic literacy and some

material comfort, access to print was greater than it had ever been before. They could go to branches of Mudie's or other circulating libraries where a guinea ticket enabled them to get the next volume of *Adam Bede* by the George Eliot everyone was talking about or Mrs Braddon's wonderfully exciting *Lady Audley's Secret*. If they could not get to the library, they could arrange to have books delivered.[21] There were more and more magazines and newspapers available by subscription, which lay on the table in the middle-class drawing room to be taken up and glanced at or read by family members and guests.

Though the public coffee house or gentlemen's club remained, like the working-class reading rooms, as crucial sites for access to print from which women were barred, there was a counter-vailing tug towards defining the feminized space of home as a site for family reading. Even the morning newspaper was now available for the man of the house to read at breakfast.[22] When Dickens called his periodical *Household Words* he signalled his acknowledgment of this trend. In doing so he was well aware of such rival journals as the *Family Friend* with its frontispiece illustration of a family gathered together as the father read to them.[23] The father might read to the family, but it was the mother, the 'woman at home', who was the enabler and manager of the domestic sphere.

Though their freedom from paid labour was a privilege, the position of these middle-class women was still based on their legal and economic dependence on men and this constrained their access to print. Probably those who fared best were 'the daughters of educated men', in Virginia Woolf's phrase.[24] Some fathers, both real and fictional, gave their daughters the run of their libraries.[25] Elizabeth Barrett's autocratic father ensured she had access to all the books she wanted whether in English or Greek. More often it was mothers who dictated daughters' reading and, for reasons I return to below, they were less likely than fathers to encourage the avid reader. Even in homes with well-stocked book shelves there was no guarantee that reading by girls would be regarded as anything but a distraction from proper feminine tasks like sewing.

For those women whose fathers, husbands or brothers might not be so well read, access to print could be spasmodic and contingent. When George Eliot wrote *The Mill on the Floss*, her novel about a woman's hunger for (book) knowledge, she understood this precisely. Maggie Tulliver's only access to books was through the men in her life: first her father, who had bought a row of nicely bound volumes entirely for their appearance; secondly, the devoted Luke, the pedlar who bought her a ragbag of books he had picked up; and thirdly, Philip Wakem whose loan of books was at once dangerous and keenly pleasurable.

Eliot was looking back to the period of her own childhood in the 1830s. By the time *The Mill on the Floss* came out in 1860, the first free civic public libraries were being founded and by the 1890s they were spreading slowly.[26] Though the appearance of women in these libraries remained controversial, they were a promise of wider access for all, including those who did not have educated fathers and who were not themselves able to enter as purchasers into the burgeoning market in print.

PRINT AS COMMODITY: PRINT AS TEXT

The market is central to any account of reading in the nineteenth century. Although older methods of publication lingered on, this century saw the completion of the process begun in eighteenth-century Grub Street, so that buying and selling (rather than patronage or sub-scription) became the engine which drove the production of print. Yet, as I have already suggested, books circulated also in a whole range of other economies than the market and women as consumers participated in all these economies. This section explores what this might mean.

Primarily, books were (and are) commodities, and publishing was a major industry at the heart of the Industrial Revolution. We are used to the idea that we, at the turn of the second millennium, are living through an 'information' revolution. However, that first industrial revolution in the late eighteenth / early nineteenth century was as much about infor-mation as about manufacture, and its media were print-based. Transformations in the market in print were fuelled by and fuelled the processes of industrialization and imperialism which made Britain the first industrial nation and the centre of a world wide Empire. The enor-mous expansion of print was in part made possible by new processes of production, first in the mechanics of printing and then in paper making. Publishers were also quick to exploit new ways of marketing and new places and times which could be used for reading. The railway boom of the mid-century led to the development of 'railway reading' and new outlets on station platforms. When commuting into cities to go to work became more common, publishers developed journals characterized by the short paragraph and the 'Tit-bit' for these shorter journeys.[27] At every level, the expansion in print depended on publishers identifying new groups of potential customers, first in the domestic market and then overseas in the Empire and North America, and then evolving new kinds of publication for them. A crucial part of this process was the targeting of women as readers, first those in the middle class and then, as the century went on, girls and working-class women.

New or newly important genres addressed to women included manuals of instruction on how to be a woman by writers like Sarah Ellis, who in the 1840s wrote *The Women of England*, *The Wives of England* and *The Daughters of England*; exemplary biographies like Samuel Smiles's mid-century *Clever Girls and How they Became Famous Women*, or *Heroines of the Household* by 'The Author of the Heavenward Path', which were produced as Sunday school or school prize books; in the 1880s and 1890s there were beautifully produced, gilt-edged gift books with titles like *Happy Homes and How to Make Them* by J. W. Kirton, which claimed to be in its ninety-second thousand when it was reprinted in 1882. There was a growing number of books and magazines which gave recipes, advice on housework, on nursing the sick at home and child-care, as well as advice on education, including reading. By the end of the century there were scores of magazines addressed to women, some of them claiming sales in the hundreds of thousands and distribution across the world.

However, we cannot assume that the publisher's target reader ever matches the historical reader exactly. The consumer is not necessarily the purchaser. Some books were bought for show or to give as gifts and may not have been read at all. The Religious Tract Society and other such groups produced literature for middle-class women to distribute to their working-class neighbours and Dickens at least was well aware that such reading matter was likely to be rejected by those it was intended to uplift.[28] Nineteenth-century gift books turn up still in second-hand book shops with pages so clean that they have clearly been kept for show, like Mr Tulliver's books in *The Mill on the Floss*. Even more important, perhaps, is the obverse of this, that many books and even journals and magazines had multiple readers. In this period when reading matter of any kind was relatively expensive, readers borrowing from circulating, commercial and eventually the public libraries, shared books and journals in and between households, sent them to friends overseas in the colonies, and regularly swapped current numbers of magazines, swaps which were sometimes arranged through advertising in the magazines themselves but more often were informal.[29] Clearly publications addressed to 'women' were likely to be read by whole households including men and children. There is evidence, for example from letters pages, that men read women's magazines just as women read works which assumed their readers' masculinity.

Though we cannot therefore simply equate the woman consumer with the publisher's target purchaser or even with the historical purchaser, we can assume that much of this specially targeted material was bought either by or for women and was also read by them. No wonder that, as Kate Flint has shown, representations of women reading appeared regularly in the frontispieces of books and magazines and also on the visiting cards which middle-class women left when they were engaged in the formalities of making social calls.[30] Middle-class women were defining themselves as 'readers'.

Such definition works with a different kind of economy than the market, namely the circulation of meanings, ideas and identities. The commodities produced by the print industry were also texts which were crucial to the spread of 'modern' knowledge, to the development of new forms of education, a more democratic politics, new forms of work and entertainment. These publishing genres addressed to women offered their readers new ways of understanding themselves and the world, new kinds of identity.

Such an idea would have been familiar in the nineteenth century when the enormous power of print to transform individuals and societies was axiomatic. When the young Mary Shelley wrote her novel, *Frankenstein*, in 1818, she imagined that the monster would learn what it was to be a subject through reading. This representation, even down to the contents of the monster's library, would not have seemed strange to contemporary radical campaigners who believed that reading, whether of weekly papers or the works of Milton, was a crucial part of their struggle for rights as political and social subjects. Nor was this belief confined to radicals. From the 1830s, alongside overtly radical periodicals with slogans like 'Knowledge is Power', a series of relatively cheap magazines and papers aimed to spread non-political or 'useful knowledge'. The men and women who produced these early popular journals were entrepreneurs who also had faith in the transformative power of print.[31] Religious groups like the Religious Tract Society, inspired by the Evangelical writer, Hannah More, likewise believed that print was the crucial medium for spreading the word and religious publishers continued throughout the century to produce tracts, 'Sunday reading' for middle-class homes and prize or gift books.

However, the kind of reading which was most often associated with

women was none of these but rather the novel. Twentieth-century literary history has tended to agree with nineteenth-century assumptions
that the rise to literary importance of the novel was linked to the increasing importance of women as readers.[32] As Terry Lovell has argued, it is
likely that middle-class men were also novel readers but their activities
were less constrained than women's, for whom reading was one of the
few legitimated forms of leisure.[33] Nevertheless, the link between novel
reading and women remained. It was a major cause of anxiety about
female reading which the nineteenth century inherited from the eighteenth and which it carried forward into the economics and politics of
reading in the new century.

ANXIETIES ABOUT WOMEN'S READING

The confidence in the power of print both as commodity and as text produced its own anxieties. In the first half of the century successive governments tried to control access to print and particularly to newspapers by
a system of penal taxation. These 'Taxes on Knowledge', as the campaigners for a free press called them, were designed to control what the
authorities saw as dangerous anti-government and irreligious publications.[34] Though aimed especially at newspapers, their effect was to raise
the price and therefore restrict access to all forms of print for the first
half of the century. The last of these taxes, the one on paper, was not
lifted until 1861. Their lifting signalled an enormous expansion in what
contemporaries described as the 'free trade' in print. The assumption
that women would not be interested in 'news', that is political affairs,
means that much of the discussion of this up to the late twentieth
century has assumed a gender-blind stance which presupposes a purely
male readership. However, the imposition and eventual lifting of the
'taxes on knowledge' affected women's reading as much as men's,
though perhaps in different ways.[35]

In the second half of the century anxiety about increasing access to
print took a slightly different form. Rather than concern about overtly
political writing, there were waves of public anxiety about the trivializ-
ing of culture and the spread of sensational writing. It was taste rather
than social stability which seemed to be at risk. Although this was an
endemic anxiety – there was, for example, a furious debate in the serious
periodicals during the 1860s – it rose to a crescendo at the end of the
century when the foundations of the modern mass press were laid.[36] The
huge increase in cheap (that is, affordable) papers which this brought

about was condemned as dragging the whole of English print culture down to the level of 'the quarter educated'.[37] Such formulations explicitly linked fears about the debasement of literature with the introduction of universal elementary education in 1870. Like earlier anxiety about political writings, this anxiety was class-based but the terms used to describe it (emotional, sensational and feather-brained) carried connotations of femininity.[38]

These anxieties surrounding taste and morality tended to take print culture as the ground on which was played out the decline of the English middle class, perceived as under threat from an expanding working class on one hand and cultural 'invasion' from America and Europe on the other. Such fears were informed by Social Darwinist theories of the struggle between societies and by fashionable talk of decadence at the end of the century. Central to such fears of the decline of Britain were the increasing public visibility and audibility – some said 'stridency' – of women as writers and readers and a related fear, therefore, of the increasing feminization of a culture perceived as having been characterized by its masculine vigour.[39]

The figure of 'The New Woman', who emerged in the 1890s, was only the last in a series of representations of the rebellious woman thrown up in the nineteenth-century press. However, she was significant because her arrival, or invention, was linked to these other anxieties and because it worked at the level both of the popular press and of the literary elite. Round the figure of this 'new' woman as reader and/or writer crystallized a whole set of cultural anxieties which were to do with class and race, as well as gender and sexuality. To understand these end of the century debates, we need to explore how the woman reader figured at the centre of anxieties about print culture from earlier in the century.

In *Northanger Abbey*, published in 1818 but written earlier, Jane Austen wittily satirized early nineteenth-century anxiety about female reading. Her novel dealt with the 'horrid' Gothic romances so popular at the end of the previous century and which Austen herself clearly read and enjoyed – as she assumed her readers did. Equally she assumed a readership familiar with some long-established concerns about the deficiencies of female reading, in terms of both what and how women read. Central to these, as I have already suggested, was the belief that, if women read at all, they read novels rather than the more serious genres like history, which Austen's heroine, Catherine, found so tedious. Novels encouraged in women, it was believed, certain kinds of inappropriate reading to which women were prone, especially a tendency to mis-identify with female heroines or take for fact what should be understood as fiction. So Catherine in *Northanger Abbey* is gently mocked by the hero because she assumes a direct correspondence between the fantasy Italy of Mrs Radcliffe's romances and the home counties of England. Austen neatly dissected and countered such anxieties even as she seemed to invoke them.

These concerns were wide-spread across all western European cultures and pre-dated Jane Austen as well as continuing after her death.[40] In the seventeenth century the typical reader of romance had been characterized as a maid servant in whom such reading induced ridiculous and false expectations.[41] Because the working-class woman reader posed a double threat to middle-class male rationality, such representations persisted. Long-standing and wide-spread though they were, however, these anxieties about novel reading were given a new force in nineteenth-century Britain, partly because of the Evangelical movement, which began in the late eighteenth century. For Evangelicals and those influenced by them, novels were dangerous mainly because they were not true. The belief that reading should be primarily a way of gaining access to spiritual truths remained a powerful one. In the Evangelical 'Mother's Magazines' of the 1840s, reading fiction was denounced as ungodly and – a slightly different but also powerful argument – a distraction from women's serious vocation as wives and mothers.[42] The influence of Evangelicalism waned as the century wore on, but it continued to shape the weekly pattern of reading in many middle-class homes. Here novels and other 'frivolous' forms of print enjoyed in the week were put away on Saturday night, and volumes of sermons, devotional works or moral 'true stories' took their place as designated Sunday reading.

The propensity of women to read novels, however, was a concern for other reasons than these. The central subject matter of nineteenth-century fiction was romantic love, the discovery of a sexual partner, for, as Anthony Trollope put it succinctly, 'There must be love in a novel.'[43] This, combined with the tradition of narrative closure, made the wedding the favoured trope for novel endings. Though finding a suitable husband was defined as women's work, the danger of such reading for young, unmarried girls was that it might give them knowledge about sexuality which was unsuitable for them. Even more dangerous were the feelings such texts were likely to arouse in untutored girls. Since the argument was that women were likely to be governed by feeling rather than intellect, their reading was shaped by their lack of rationality and the romantic plot of the novel could only exacerbate this.

Indeed, since fiction was deemed easy reading, women's preference for novels was taken as a sign of their intellectual weakness and their tendency to read in a desultory or unsystematic way. Women were 'quick but shallow' according to Tom Tulliver's schoolmaster in *The Mill on the Floss*. It was the feminine delight in both writing and reading 'silly novels' which concerned many men and women – both those who believed this was evidence of innate inferiority and those who wanted to raise the intellectual level of 'the sex'.[44]

These assumptions meant, as Maggie Tulliver the quick and shallow heroine of Eliot's novel found to her cost, that women readers were caught in a double bind. Scolded for frivolous delight in novel reading on one hand, on the other they were barred from serious reading or from the study of subjects deemed beyond their powers of intellect or judgment. Evidence of and desire for this kind of knowledge was regarded as unfeminine. Elizabeth Gaskell prefaced her novel, *Mary Barton*, which dealt with the social problems of industrial Manchester, with a disclaimer that she knew 'nothing of political economy'.[45] George Eliot's fictional Maggie Tulliver is denied the chance to learn Latin like her brother and her desire to do so is evidence of her failure to be a good girl. The growth of public schools for middle-class boys from the 1840s further institutionalized the capacity to read Latin and Greek as a crucial marker of both class and gender, since neither the working-class nor middle-class girls had access to such schools or to the traditional universities with their classical curricula. Even at the end of the century when middle-class girls' schooling had improved enormously and some women were admitted to lectures at the universities, the argument about whether women could 'read', in other words study, the same academic subjects as men persisted. Much of the prolific literature in periodicals and books addressed to women and girls on what they ought to read was caught up in this dilemma. In *Sesame and Lilies*, perhaps the most influential of all mid-Victorian discussions of what boys and girls should read, John Ruskin made an eloquent argument for allowing girls to read the same books as boys, including novels, as long as they were good ones. But he drew the line at women reading theology.

However, for Ruskin, as for many of his contemporaries, what women read was less a cause of anxiety than how they read. In 'Of Queens' Gardens', the section of the book on girls' reading, Ruskin started from the premise that reading is about power and laid out his argument about

men's and women's very different, though complementary, powers. He
argued that the absolute difference between them meant that, even when
young women read exactly what men did, they must read it differently
and for a different purpose. A woman's reading must give her 'All such
knowledge . . . as may enable her to understand, and even aid, the work
of men.'[46] She must read not for knowledge or self-development but to
enable her as wife and mother, the one whose task it was to protect her
home from the harsh knowledge of the world which was man's lot.
Ruskin's concern to direct women's reading was the product of his sense
of their domestic and sexual power; the woman reader was the queen in
the walled garden which represented both her body and the domestic
space of Home.

THE DOMESTIC BODY: WOMEN AND THE CONSUMPTION OF PRINT

The assumption of an intimate relationship between reading, the
woman's body and domestic space is central to the discourses of
nineteenth-century print culture. It shaped the material reality of the
publishing houses and the lending libraries as well as the organization of
objects, space and time in the bourgeois home. Isabella Beeton's
immensely popular and much re-printed *Book of Household Management*
was not only an example of the way print now entered into the most
private domestic relationships as a shaping force, it made explicit the
assumption that managing reading was a crucial part of the mistress's
duties in respect of her household. Among other advice on servants and
running the house, Beeton instructs her readers on 'the Manner of
Passing Evenings at Home':

Where there are young people forming a part of the evening circle, interesting
and agreeable pastimes should especially be promoted . . . It has often been
remarked that nothing is more agreeable to the feminine members of a family
than the reading aloud of some good standard work or amusing publication. A
knowledge of polite literature may be thus obtained by the whole family especially if the reader is able and willing to explain the more difficult passages.[47]

For Beeton, providing the right publications and managing household
reading was exactly analogous to the provision of pleasant meals and
managing the consumption of food which occupied most of the pages
of *The Book of Household Management*. Just as providing good food was
crucial if the wife was to keep her husband away from the dangerously
attractive public eating houses or clubs, so the provision of pleasant

reading must keep the younger members of the family away from the even more dangerous world of pernicious publications and the streets, which were the implicit alternative to the domestic circle.

The mistress's management of the consumption of print worked on a number of levels, both material and symbolic. In the separation of the masculine sphere of public life and the feminized sphere of home which had become the organizing principle of bourgeois society by the mid-century, economic activity was divided between production, situated in the masculine world of work, and consumption, which was situated in the domestic and for which women were largely responsible. The privileging of production in theorizing the social extended across the spectrum of thinkers from the liberal defenders of capitalism, the followers of Adam Smith, to capitalism's most thorough-going critic, Karl Marx.[48]

In the late twentieth century the importance of consumption both in the market and in the symbolic creation of identities and communities has become central to both economic and cultural theory. However, it is a mistake to locate the politics of consumption in the late twentieth century, or only in post-modernity. The household, the 'oikumene' from which the word economy itself is derived, was throughout the nineteenth century perceived as crucial to consumption – and this was women's sphere. Mrs Beeton was joined by a host of others eager to instruct women in how to wield the power this gave them. In particular, as the century went on, magazines addressed to women were increasingly taken up with advice on shopping and increasingly financed by advertisements, not least by publishers. As this makes clear, consumption, whether of books, roast beef or Paris fashions, though it might take place in the private, was absolutely linked to the public. Production and consumption were and are interconnected. Separating the private from the public world was simultaneously necessary and impossible, a dilemma which provided the dynamic for writers as different as Beeton and Ruskin.

What follows from this is, firstly, that the paradigm in which production figures as active and masculine, while consumption is passive and feminine, will not do. Domestic consumption was always active and had its own cycles of activity. In relation to food the mistress must first choose and buy carefully but then she must work to create the meals for the household to consume. What follows from this, also, is that consumption was and is both material and symbolic; it is about the production of identities and meanings as much as material wealth – or rather the two are intertwined. Serving meals as Beeton instructed was both the product and the creator of the family's social standing, evidence of its material and its cultural capital. Similarly, pleasure in the 'good standard work or amusing publication' was a signifier of the family's capital (the reading woman was the leisured woman who did not have to work). Such reading also gave that 'knowledge of polite literature' which was part of the cultural capital needed by the middle-class girl (along with playing the piano or painting) to ensure her a suitable husband.

The analogy of the consumption of food and the consumption of print which I have been pursuing was endemic in nineteenth-century discourses of reading, particularly female reading. The contrast between 'healthy' or wholesome reading and texts which were 'garbage' or even 'poisonous' recurs again and again. It was linked to another persistent metaphor of reading, particularly the reading of novels, as addictive. The trope of reading as digestion is deeply rooted in Western European cultures which have been shaped by Christianity, whose central symbol works through an equation of word and bread. However, in the mid-Victorian period it took on particular urgency and was mobilized specifically in relation to women.[49]

Both eating and reading involve the taking in of external substances which then become part of us, so they are potentially life-giving and also dangerous transgressions of the barriers between outside and inside, not-self and self. In the nineteenth century the discursive separation of a dangerous outside world from the safety of the domestic circle which I have been discussing emphasized the need to control both eating and reading. However, it was not all reading or all readers who were perceived as equally at risk. It was women, and within that category particularly young and working-class women, who were in danger, because these groups were the primary focus of cultural anxiety about the female body and female sexuality.

Throughout the century theories of reading assumed that, while men might read intellectually, women felt their reading in their bodies. At the moment when Beeton's *Book of Household Management* came out in volume form in 1861 it was the particular relationship of 'sensation fiction' to women's reading which occupied the reviewers and magazine writers.[50] The term 'sensation' suggests the way these novels were thought to work directly on the body, a trope for which appetite became the most obvious but not the only metaphor. Readers were also represented as flushed and hectic, or abandoned to their reading in a state of erotic arousal.

The figure of the woman reading was thus itself read or understood in relation to discourses of the female body as essentially sexual. The link between reading and the sexualized female body can be traced back to Christian interpretations of the Garden of Eden story, in which woman's desire to consume the fruits of knowledge was explicitly linked to the acquisition of sexual knowledge and blamed for the ills of mankind. That late nineteenth-century thinker, Freud, took up these embedded assumptions of the link between eating and the sexualized body and theorized them in terms of oral and genital phases, a theoretical framework which persists today. Maud Ellman has argued, in *The Hunger Artists*, that in Freud it is eating which is the repressed. Rather than eating standing in for genital sex, she suggests that sexual activity is always an attempt to return to the earliest delight of the infant in the satisfaction of the breast.[51] Certainly the cultural anxiety about female reading, the ingestion of knowledge, was linked in the nineteenth century to anxiety about (female) sexuality.

Linked to this also was the prevalence of the romantic plot in the novel and the assumptions, firstly, that women read novels and, secondly, that it was particularly the young unmarried women who would be affected by such works. It is significant that in Beeton's account the general term 'young people' slides into 'the feminine'. Some middle-class families jokingly referred to the 'J. P.', which stood for 'Jeune Personne', the French making clear grammatically that 'young' here equalled 'female'. It was 'the young person' (female) whose cheek was likely to blush at reading something unsuitable and it was the young woman who was likely to respond with racing pulse and flushed face to the seductions of sensational reading. The nubile bodies of young women most clearly represented the contradictions of a femininity which was both sexual and innocent. In relation to consumption these bodies were, as Patricia Ingham has argued, consistently represented in fiction as themselves to be consumed.[52] Consumption in the sense of gobbling up sweets or fiction carried buried in it that older meaning of being oneself eaten up by desire, or by disease. Reading in the family circle not only ensured that suitable reading was provided but also ensured the monitoring of bodily reactions to reading and prevented that vice of solitary reading which was so often depicted visually.[53] The unspoken in all this was pornography, that kind of reading which works most directly on the body.

The sexual body of the reading woman was not only youthful. It was also a classed body. Working-class women, as I have suggested, were presumed to be even more susceptible to sensationalist kinds of reading than their middle-class counterparts because their sexuality was more uncontrolled. Middle-class women who were concerned about the condition of the working class were routinely encouraged not only to give them reading matter but also to arrange reading circles. Here the domestic scene of reading could be replicated with the women sitting doing their needlework while being read to and this was the pattern of much early social intervention work with women and girls.[54] It is not surprising that in much of the literature addressed to mistresses of middle-class households, those women who controlled the reading of other women, there were detailed instructions about the kind of books to give to domestic servants. The main concern was to ensure servants did not waste their time on 'silly sensational stories in poisonous publications which are brought to the back door in gentlemen's houses'.[55] Instead the mistress should provide a Bible and Prayer Book, a dictionary, some cheap domestic weekly or monthly packet, and recipe books.[56]

These discourses had a profound effect on the whole of the print industry. Libraries and booksellers, in particular Mudie's and W. H. Smith's, proclaimed that they vetted books to ensure that they could be read aloud in the family circle without bringing a blush to the cheek of the young person.[57] This not only constrained the access of many readers to what was published but at a more profound level shaped what publishers and editors were prepared to print and even what writers felt able to write. It was only in the ferment of the 1890s to which I have alluded that the dominance of this discourse was ended, through a rebellion by writers and readers who argued that English publishing must become once again addressed to grown-up men.[58] It was in this context that the New Woman sought to re-define her femininity in terms of print culture.

CONCLUSION

These anxieties about and attempts to control women's reading were certainly powerful. But they are not the whole story. Indeed their very prevalence may be taken as evidence that the models of control so energetically preached in domestic manuals and articles on reading had constantly to be reinforced. Florence Nightingale described being read aloud to in the family circle as a form of torture; it was 'like lying on one's back with one's hand tied and having liquid poured down one's throat', an intellectual force-feeding felt almost literally on the body. But she still managed to sustain a rigorous course of private reading.[59] In this she was like Harriet Martineau and countless others who used reading as a way of resisting the forms of femininity into which society tried to fit them. Nor was this confined to middle-class women. As I suggested above, even domestic servants sometimes found ways of reading what they wanted. Amy Cruse reports that Mary Howitt, the editor, writer and translator, found her cook in the kitchen one day reading *Essays and Reviews*, and Burnett recorded accounts from one servant who regularly read her master's local history books and another who read *Uncle Tom's Cabin* when she should have been working, even though she was beaten for doing so.[60]

Charting the pleasures of reading – both individual and shared – is difficult. However, there is evidence that for many women reading was a source of delight as well as inspiration. They recorded this in autobiographies, diaries, reviews for journals, and in magazine interviews with women writers. However, it is most evident in the flowering of women's writing in this period. Many of the women writers whose work this volume explores made clear that their writing grew out of their reading. Sometimes this was implicit, sometimes explicit, as in Jane Austen's witty reworking of her Gothic foremothers, Elizabeth Barrett Browning's poems to her predecessor poets L. E. L., Felicia Hemans and George Sand, or in the new woman novelists' use of the plot device of reading as a means of transformation for the heroine, as in Sarah Grand's *The Heavenly Twins*. Such writings show the importance of reading both as a source of pleasure for nineteenth-century women and as a source of the power to question their world and create new ways of being in it.

NOTES

1 Charlotte Brontë, *Jane Eyre* (Harmondsworth: Penguin, 1966; rptd 1977), p. 43.

2 This invitation is most famously enacted in the sentence in ch. 38 where Jane declares, 'Reader, I married him.'

3 This article focuses on England. Along with other scholars in this area I owe an intellectual debt to Kate Flint's *The Woman Reader, 1837–1914* (Oxford University Press, 1993). Other parts of the English-speaking world, notably America, had related but different histories – as did Britain's European neighbours. For an account of one other European country see Berry Dongelmans and Doudien de Vries, 'Reading, Class and Gender: the Sources for Research on Nineteenth-Century Readers in the Netherlands', in *SPIEL (Siegener Periodicum zur Internationalen Empirischen Literaturwissenschaft)* 19 Jg. H.1. (Frankfurt: Peter Lang, 2000). For a fuller discussion of sources and methodology see Margaret Beetham, 'In Search of the Historical Reader', in the same volume.

4   There are no independently audited circulation figures for periodicals or
    book sales in the nineteenth century, though some research on publishers'
    archives has found print runs. Surveys of and articles on reading were fre-
    quent in the press but most did not deal specifically with women, though see
    Salmon (below). Among these general articles are: Helen Bosanquet,
    'Cheap Literature' *Contemporary Review* 79 (1901), pp. 671–81; R. W.
    Chapman, 'Cheap Literature', *British Quarterly Review* 29 (1859), pp. 313–45;
    W. M. Gattie, 'What English People Read', *Fortnightly Review* 46 (1889) pp.
    306–21; J. G. Leigh, 'What do the Masses Read?' *Economic Review* 14.2 (1904),
    pp. 166–77; T. C. Phillips, 'The Reading of the Working Classes', *Literature*
    6 (1900), pp. 359–60; and three articles by E. G. Salmon: 'What Boys Read',
    Fortnightly Review n.s. 39 (1886), pp. 248–59; 'What Girls Read', *Nineteenth
    Century* 20 (1886), pp. 515–29; 'What the Working Class Read', *Nineteenth
    Century* 20 (1886), pp. 108–17.

5   David Vincent, *Literacy and Popular Culture; England 1750–1914* (Cambridge
    University Press, 1989), especially pp. 1–52; see also R. D. Altick, *The English
    Common Reader; A Social History of the Mass Reading Public* (University of
    Chicago Press, 1957), esp. pp. 141–72.

6   For example, one of the first Reports to the Manchester Statistical Society,
    founded in 1833, was on 'Immoral and Irreligious Works sold in
    Manchester' (T. S. Ashton, *Economic and Social Investigations in Manchester
    1833–1933* (Hassocks: Harvester Press, 1934), p. 141).

7   Bennett also ran competitions in which readers voted for their favourite
    books of the previous year and explained why they liked them. See
    Margaret Beetham, *A Magazine of Her Own? Domesticity and Desire in the
    Woman's Magazine, 1800–1914* (London: Routledge, 1996) pp. 177–89.

8   See Nicola Thompson, *Reviewing Sex: Gender and the Reception of Victorian Novels*
    (London: Macmillan, 1996).

9   Sally Mitchell, 'Sentiment and Suffering: Women's Recreational Reading in
    the 1860s', *Victorian Studies* 21 (1977), pp. 29–45, and *The Fallen Angel: Chastity,
    Class and Women's Reading 1835–1880* (Bowling Green, Ohio: Bowling Green
    University Popular Press, 1981); Lynne Pearce, *Feminism and the Politics of
    Reading* (London: Edward Arnold, 1997).

10 Janice Radway, *Reading the Romance: Women, Patriarchy and Popular Culture* (New
    York: Chapel Hill, 1984).

11 Roland Barthes's argument that the author was dead moved the reader
    centre stage and made the study of the pleasures of reading the main task
    for the critic; see Roland Barthes, *S/Z* trans. R. Miller (New York: Hill and
    Wang, 1974), and *The Pleasure of the Text*, trans. R. Miller (New York: Hill and
    Wang, 1975). Jonathan Culler made 'reading' and indeed 'reading as a
    woman' the starting point for his account of deconstruction for English
    readers (see Jonathan Culler, *On Deconstruction; Theory and Criticism after
    Structuralism* (London: Routledge and Kegan Paul, 1982)). Reader-response
    theory, Stanley Fish's idea of reading communities, Iser's interest in the way
    aesthetics relate to particular historical situations, all have in common a

stress on the reader (Stanley Fish, *Is There a Text in This Class? The Authority of Interpretive Communities* (Cambridge, MA: Harvard University Press, 1980); Wolfgang Iser, *The Act of Reading: A Theory of Aesthetic Response* (Baltimore: Johns Hopkins University Press, 1978); Jane Tompkins, *Reader-Response Criticism: From Formalism to Poststructuralism* (Baltimore: Johns Hopkins University Press, 1980)).

12 Kate Millett, *Sexual Politics* (London: Abacus, 1970); Judith Fetterley, *The Resisting Reader: a Feminist Approach to American Fiction* (Bloomington: Indiana University Press, 1978).

13 Vincent, *Literacy and Popular Culture*, esp. pp. 1–52.

14 Ibid., p. 26.

15 Charles Booth's survey of London, *Life and Labour of the People in London* (London, 1902–4), came out in seventeen volumes; B. S. Rowntree, *A Study in Town Life* (London, 1901).

16 Lady Bell (Mrs. Hugh Bell), *At the Works; A Study of a Manufacturing Town* (London: Thomas Nelson, 1907; 2nd edn, 1911), pp. 203–41. She noted that the workman read more than his wife (p. 207) and, if the wife read, it was only on Sunday (p. 211).

17 Alan Lee, *The Origins of the Popular Press 1855–1914* (London: Croom Helm, 1976), pp. 35–41; Altick, *English Common Reader*, pp. 188–212.

18 Bell, *At the Works*, pp. 203–14.

19 Though much of the material on working-class reading assumes all members of the class were male, it is still useful for this study. See Jonathan Rose, 'Rereading "The English Common Reader": a Preface to the History of Audiences', *Journal of History of Ideas* 53 (1992), pp. 150–68; Theresa Gerrard, 'New Methods in the History of Reading', *Publishing History* 43 (1998). On domestic servants, see E. Higgs, *Domestic Servants and Households in Rochdale 1851–1871* (New York and London: Garland, 1986), and J. Burnett, *Useful Toil: Autobiographies of Working People from the 1820s to the 1920s* (Harmondsworth: Penguin, 1974), pp. 135–234.

20 *Woman at Home* 1 (1893), p. 62.

21 Guinevere Griest, *Mudie's Circulating Library and the Victorian Novel* (Bloomington: Indiana University Press, 1970), esp. pp. 27–30.

22 Lee, *Origins of the Popular Press*, p. 37.

23 *Family Friend* (1849–50) 2 (Front plate).

24 Virginia Woolf, *Three Guineas* (1938; Harmondsworth: Penguin, 1977), p. 6.

25 Flint, *The Woman Reader* pp. 200–1; a fictional example is Dr Gibson in Gaskell's *Wives and Daughters* but Gibson at first does not think Molly needs to learn to read or write at all.

26 Altick, *English Common Reader*, pp. 213–39.

27 W. H. Smith built up his business through the station book-stall. The 'New Journalism' of the 1880s and 1890s, especially *Tit-Bits*, was aimed in part at the new commuters including the women 'typewriters'.

28 The bricklayer in Dickens's *Bleak House* rejects Mrs Pardiggle's tract as only fit for 'babbies'.

29 Advertisements for swapping magazines appeared regularly in such magazines as *The Queen*. See *The Queen* 68 (28 March, 1885), p. 338. All historians
of reading agree that magazines and newspapers were read by multiple
readers.

30 Flint, *The Woman Reader*, pp. 319–30.

31 These editors included Mary Howitt, who with her husband, William,
edited *Howitts' Journal* and, most remarkably, Eliza Cook, who edited *Eliza
Cook's Journal*. Though readership is impossible to judge, Cook did address
women's concerns specifically.

32 Ian Watt's *The Rise of the Novel* (1957; rptd Harmondsworth: Penguin, 1985)
laid the ground for this.

33 Terry Lovell, *Consuming Fiction* (London: Verso, 1987), p. 39.

34 Taxes were levied on rags, which were the raw material for making paper,
on advertisements and, until 1842, on any paper which printed 'news'. See
Joel Wiener, *The War of the Unstamped; the Movement to Repeal the British
Newspaper Tax 1830–1836* (Ithaca: Cornell University Press, 1969).

35 For example, in 1860, Samuel and Isabella Beeton expanded their publishing of women's journals with a new weekly, *The Queen,* and an enlarged
version of their monthly *English Woman's Domestic Magazine.* Beeton linked
this explicitly with the expectation of the repeal of the tax on paper
('Preface', *Englishwoman's Domestic Magazine* n.s. 3 (1861)).

36 For a discussion of the 1860s see Kelly J. Mays, 'The Disease of Reading
and Victorian Periodicals', in John Jordan and Robert L. Patten, eds.,
*Literature in the Marketplace: Nineteenth-Century British Publishing and Reading
Practices* (Cambridge University Press, 1995), pp. 165–94.

37 George Gissing's *New Grub Street* (1891) was the most bitter book-length
exploration of this.

38 Matthew Arnold coined the phrase 'New Journalism' and described it in
these terms. Arnold, 'Up to Easter', *Nineteenth Century* 21 (1887), pp. 629–43.

39 Sally Ledger, *The New Woman: Fiction and Feminism at the Fin de Siècle*
(Manchester University Press, 1997).

40 Gustave Flaubert's *Madame Bovary* (1857), though much later than Austen, is
the most famous exploration of this theme.

41 J. Pearson, 'Women Reading, Reading Women', in Helen Wilcox ed., *Women
and Literature in Britain 1500–1700* (Cambridge University Press, 1996), pp.
92–3.

42 See the *Christian Lady's Magazine* 1 (1836), p. 328 and the *Mother's Magazine* 60
(1840), which concluded 'If you want to be weak-headed, nervous and good
for nothing, read novels.' See Beetham, *A Magazine of her Own?* pp. 48–56.

43 Quoted in Peter Gay, *The Bourgeois Experience: Victoria to Freud.* vol. II: *The
Tender Passion* (Oxford University Press, 1986) p. 136; see this entire section
in Gay.

44 George Eliot, *The Mill on the Floss* (1860; World's Classics Edition, Oxford
University Press, 1980), p. 150; [Eliot] 'Silly Novels by Silly Lady Novelists',
Westminster Review (October 1856), rptd in T. Pinney, ed. *Essays of George Eliot*
(London and New York: Routledge, Kegan Paul, 1963), pp. 300–24.

45 [Elizabeth Gaskell], 'Preface', *Mary Barton* (1848; Harmondsworth: Penguin, 1977) p. 38.

46 John Ruskin's *Sesame and Lilies* was his most popular book. It consisted of two lectures, 'Of Kings' Treasuries' on boys' education and 'Of Queens' Gardens' on girls' (*Sesame and Lilies* (London: George Allen, 1864), p. 113).

47 [Isabella Beeton], *The Book of Household Management* (London: S. O. Beeton, 1861), p. 17.

48 It was only in 1899 with Thorstein Veblen's influential *Theory of the Leisure Class* that a theory focusing on consumption developed. For this section see A. Bermingham, 'The Consumption of Culture; Image, Object, Text', in A. Bermingham and J. Brewer, eds. *The Consumption of Culture 1600–1800* (London: Routledge, 1995), pp. 1–20.

49 This has been well documented by Flint in *The Woman Reader* but also by other recent critics, e.g. Pamela Gilbert, *Disease, Desire and the Body in Victorian Women's Popular Novels* (Cambridge University Press,1997), esp. pp. 15–57.

50 See, e.g., 'Sensation Literature', in Beeton's *The English Woman's Domestic Magazine* n.s. 6 (1863), pp. 14–19 which consistently describes the reading of these novels in terms of addiction and a diseased appetite and advises mothers to lock them away from their daughters.

51 Maud Ellman, *The Hunger Artists: Starving, Writing and Imprisonment* (London: Virago, 1993).

52 Patricia Ingham, *Dickens, Women and Language* (Hassocks: Harvester Wheatsheaf, 1992), esp. pp. 28–35; see also Helena Mitchie, *The Flesh made Word: Female Figures and Women's Bodies* (Oxford University Press, 1987).

53 Flint, *The Woman Reader*, pp. 319–30.

54 See, for example, Mrs Bayly, *Ragged Homes and How to Mend Them* (London: James Nesbit, 1860), esp. pp. 122–36.

55 'A Mistress's Council' (Society for the Promotion of Christian Knowledge) quoted in Frank Huggett, *Life below Stairs* (Stevenage: Robin Clarke, 1977), pp. 52–3.

56 See *Employers and Female Domestic Servants: Their Rights and Responsibilities* (1896).

57 Griest, *Mudie's Circulating Library*, ch. 6 (pp. 120–55)

58 George Moore's (1885) *Literature at Nurse or Circulating Morals* is perhaps the best-known example of this.

59 Florence Nightingale, 'Cassandra', extracts published in Ray Strachey, *The Cause* (1928; rptd Bath: Cedric Chivers, 1970), p. 402.

60 Amy Cruse, *The Victorians and their Reading* (London: Unwin, 1935) p. 101 and John Burnett, *Useful Toil*, pp. 224, 231; see also Lee, *Origins of the Popular Press*, p. 38: 'The Morning Post was read by gentlemen and by gentlemen's gentlemen, by ladies and by ladies' maids.'

CHAPTER FOUR

Women writing woman: nineteenth-century representations of gender and sexuality

Lyn Pykett

[M]any of the saddest and deepest truths in the strange science of sexual affection are to [the female novelist] mysteriously and mercifully veiled . . . She is describing a country of which she knows only the more frequented and the safer roads.[1]

[S]exuality [is] a contested site for other struggles and social divisions, particularly those of class, gender, and race.[2]

In a much-quoted episode towards the end of Jane Austen's *Persuasion* (1818), the heroine, Anne Elliot, discusses with Captain Harville a contentious aspect of gender and sexuality: the relative constancy in love of men and women. Captain Harville, who, like many of his Victorian successors, slips easily from the subject of women to that of 'woman', declares: ' "I do not think I ever opened a book in my life which had not something to say upon woman's inconstancy." ' Anne Elliot, all too familiar with the pains of being a constant woman, replies: 'if you please, no reference to examples in books. Men have had every advantage of us in telling their own story. Education has been theirs in so much higher a degree; the pen has been in their hands' (chapter 23).

Austen wrote these words at a time when women had already taken the pen into their own hands, following what Virginia Woolf described as the most important change in British history: the period of 'extreme activity of mind . . . among women' when middle-class women began to write for money.[3] What kinds of narratives about women, gender and sexuality did women write once they had the advantage of telling their own story in fiction, poetry, magazine articles, conduct books, pamphlets, biographies and autobiographies? Were these stories in fact their own, or did the women writers of the nineteenth century still write to a male or masculinist script? These are two of the questions this chapter will address in its attempt to consider how women's writing contributed to the way nineteenth-century culture represented women and related issues of gender and sexuality.

Nineteenth-century writing, by both men and women, was the site of a vigorous contest over who could represent Woman or women, and how Woman and women could be represented aesthetically, culturally and politically.[4] Given their lack of political representation, and their inequitable legal and social position, participation in the cultural domain – and particularly writing – was one of the most significant ways in which nineteenth-century women could shape and change how they understood their own gender and sexuality, and how these were understood more generally. Of course, cultural representation is not simply a 'source of identity', it is also a 'site of power and regulation',[5] and women's writing was, to a great extent, shaped by male-controlled or masculinist institutions of publishing and by a gendered critical discourse which was fairly comprehensively internalized by female writers and reviewers.[6] Women writers' representations of women, Woman, the feminine, and female sexuality were also shaped by the unstable, contradictory and 'uneven'[7] conceptualizations of feminine gender and female sexuality which proliferated in the male-controlled domains of the law, social analysis, medicine, science and the emerging field of psychoanalysis, in all of which Woman was constructed as a 'relative creature',[8] who was defined through biological, affective and legal relationships to others.

Biomedical discourse defined the female in terms of her reproductive function as 'a biological entity, a sexed body':[9] Woman's nature and her social role were said to be controlled by her womb and her ovaries, and were the inevitable and indivisible consequences of her reproductive function. As Henry Maudsley put it in 1874, 'the male organisation is one, and the female organisation another . . . [Woman] will retain her special sphere of development and activity determined by the performance of those [reproductive] functions'.[10] This view, together with arguments about Woman's inferior evolutionary development,[11] became part of the rhetoric of the separate spheres, and was used as an argument against women being admitted to the public world of work and politics, and to the same education as men. It was held that the taxing of the brain would use up resources of energy which should be conserved for reproductive activity: women, it was argued, 'cannot choose but to be women; cannot rebel successfully against the tyranny of their organisation'.[12] Women who sought to rewrite the script on female education had to engage with the medical and evolutionary discourses on Woman's inferior physical development, and her special adaptation for reproduction. Thus, in an article in the *Fortnightly Review* (April 1874), Elizabeth Garrett Anderson reversed the standard medical case on the supposedly harmful effects of study on women's health, arguing that the cases brought forward by Henry Maudsley and others:

> could be outnumbered . . . by those in which the break-down of nervous and physical health seems . . . to be distinctly traceable to want of adequate mental interest and occupation in the years immediately succeeding school life. Thousands of young women, strong and blooming at eighteen, become gradually languid and feeble under the depressing influence of dulness . . . till in a few years they are morbid and self-absorbed, or even hysterical.[13]

The sexed body was also a classed and racial body, since normative, 'respectable', 'domestic' femininity was white and middle-class. Woman was constructed as different from, and inferior to, man, but, by virtue of her class and racial identity, she was also different from (and usually superior to) working-class and aristocratic women, and African and Oriental women. On the other hand nineteenth-century biomedical and socio-medical investigations repeatedly linked Woman's inferiority to man to her similarities to children, the subordinate classes, and to 'inferior' or 'primitive' races. Most nineteenth-century scientists who wrote on sex difference agreed that 'in the evolutionary development of the race, women had lagged behind men, much as "primitive people" had lagged behind Europeans',[14] and they cited as evidence such shared characteristics as earlier puberty, smaller skull and brain size, and lower pain threshold than white men. In fact, in the age of empire it is difficult to detach ideas about gender from those about race, as each seems to have been developed in relation to the other. As Susan Meyer has demonstrated, the idea that white women were like people of other races, and that 'events within the English home had a certain parallel with events in the colonies' recurs frequently in nineteenth-century writing, not least in writing by women – for example, Charlotte Brontë, Emily Brontë and George Eliot – who use race metaphorically to explore issues of gender, transmuting the idea of a shared inferiority into a 'shared experience of frustration, limitation and subordination'.[15]

Women's supposed developmental or evolutionary proximity to children, primitives and animals was at the centre of a contradictory construction of femininity as both pre-sexual and entirely sexual. Theodor von Bischoff's observation of spontaneous ovulation in a mammal in 1843 provided a scientific explanation for the widely held biomedical theory that women, like other mammals, were 'dominated by the involuntary periodicity of the reproductive system'.[16] One consequence of this theory was to deny or marginalize the role of women's pleasure in sexual intercourse and construct Woman as passionless. Another was to make the self-sacrificing maternal instinct Woman's defining characteristic. This view of 'normal femininity', propounded (for example) by William Acton in his frequently reissued (and increasingly populist) *The Functions and Disorders of the Reproductive System* (1857), was both reproduced and resisted in the domestic and romantic plots of novels by women throughout the period, and appropriated and redeployed by both conservative and reforming women who sought to redefine socio-sexual relations. On the other hand, there was also an important counter-discourse of female sexuality, which defined both female sexual health and feminine purity in terms of sexual knowledge and activity, rather than of ignorant passionlessness. George Drysdale, for example, recommended sexual activity, vigorous physical exercise, a change in 'female education, and the cramping views as to female decorum', and 'solid and real knowledge . . . of the human body and the human mind'.[17] It is this latter perception of female sexuality, and of the damaging effects of both prevailing definitions of femininity and the social structures which they support and reproduce, which is found in a great deal of the fiction written by women in this period; for example, in novels by the Brontë sisters and George Eliot, in a range of sensation novels in the 1860s, and in the New Woman fiction at the end of the century. This view was also espoused by female activists, pamphleteers and journalists who wrote about and campaigned for wider educational and employment opportunities for women, a more open approach to women's sexuality, and rational dress; it was developed further by the female associates of turn-of-the-century proponents of the new sexual science, such as Havelock Ellis and Edward Carpenter.

Although the concepts of instinctive maternal feeling and passionlessness were central to nineteenth-century representations of Woman, these representations were also haunted by the spectre of an unruly, disruptive female sexuality. From the 1850s onwards the figures of the prostitute, the mad or bad mother, and the degenerate or hysterical female who is unable to marry, refuses marriage or, having married, refuses maternity or rejects her children feature prominently in medical treatises, works of popular science and the newspaper and periodical press, as well as in novels and poems. These figures of disruptive female sexuality in turn were productive of both a discourse and a practice of surveillance and control, involving the moral, medical and legal management of Woman (and women). Such disruptive figures were not simply alternatives to normal, respectable femininity; rather normative maternal Woman was constructed in relation to her deviant others. The figure of the prostitute is particularly interesting. For some social commentators, such as William Rathbone Greg, the prostitute was the counterpart of passionless maternal Woman; she was produced by middle-class marriage customs, middle-class definitions of maternal femininity and by the economic vulnerability of all women.[18] While many social commentators focused on prostitution as a social and moral contagion, medical men such as William Acton,[19] focused on it as physical contagion. They represented prostitutes as threatening the future of the race by spreading venereal disease, either by infecting middle-class men who subsequently infected their wives and children, or, in cases where prostitution was simply a temporary stage of economic activity followed by marriage (quite often to a social superior), by spreading disease to their husbands and offspring.

The prostitute who infected her own children was just one of the bad mothers who figured in the medical discourse of maternal deviance. Another such figure is the mad mother, or victim of puerperal insanity, a much-discussed female disorder during a period in which the female condition became increasingly pathologized, and in which 'the predominance of women among the institutionalized insane first becomes a statistically verifiable fact'.[20] Its symptoms, which were an inversion of the maternal feminine ideal, included: 'a total negligence of, and often a very strong aversion to, her child and husband . . . explosions of anger . . . with vociferations and violent gesticulations', and the abandonment of previously 'correct, modest demeanour'.[21] The medical discourse on puerperal insanity intersected with the legal discourse on infanticide as nineteenth-century society struggled to reconcile the actuality of murderous mothers with its own mythology of the self-sacrificial maternal instinct, by representing infanticide as an unfortunate by-product of female biology and attributing it to an abnormal weakness in a woman's mind immediately following childbirth. Mary Elizabeth Braddon's Lady Audley is perhaps the most famous fictional example of this condition. However, in *Lady Audley's Secret* (1862), Braddon treats satirically both her heroine's self-diagnosis of hereditary madness passed on through the mother and activated by childbirth, and the diagnosis of Dr Alwyn Mosgrave (a specialist in women's illnesses) which leads to Lady Audley's incarceration in a Belgian sanatorium: the first is treated equivocally as a possible subterfuge which is used to avoid legal sanction, and the second as an equivocation, an example of the way in which medical discourse, male medical practitioners and male relatives combined to label deviant female behaviour as 'mad'.

The hysteric was another important figure of deviant femininity. Nineteenth-century medical practitioners tended to equate hysteria with that mutability, duplicity, concealment and penchant for histrionics which some saw as 'natural' female propensies, some as the product of women's social conditioning, and others, such as the anti-feminist writer Eliza Lynn Linton, attributed specifically to *modern* 'unwomanly' Woman.[22] Edward Tilt, for example, argued that 'mutability is characteristic of hysteria, because it is characteristic of women', while Robert Brudenell Carter attributed female hysteria to the fact that 'the woman is more often [than the man] under the necessity of endeavouring to conceal her feelings'. H. B. Donkin acknowledged a number of possible social causes of female hysteria, but saw its main cause as women's unsatisfied sexual and maternal drives.[23] In the latter part of the century, especially in the clamour about 'Revolting Daughters' and 'Wild Women' in the pages of the *Nineteenth Century*,[24] and in the debates about the New Woman and the New Woman writing in the newspaper and periodical press, hysteria came to be associated, both positively and negatively with female resistance or aberrance: with feminism and with women's defiance of, and frustration with, socially imposed roles, as well as with the frustration of their 'true' maternal 'nature'. Like the prostitute, the hysteric was represented as imperilling the future of the race, by passing her 'disease' on to her children.

Biomedical discourse was instrumental in constructing and maintaining the domestic ideal and the rhetoric of the separate spheres, both of which were predicated on a view of Woman as inherently different from and complementary to (rather than competitive with) man: 'The man to work, the woman to love; the man to earn, the woman to distribute; the man to protect, the woman to cling'.[25] The instability or fragility of this rhetoric is also conveyed by the words that follow those just quoted: '–ah! that is the ideal life, which, unhappily, so few ever attain'. Defenders of complementarity, including numerous women writers, such as Sarah Ellis (the author of conduct or advice books addressed to the mothers, daughters and wives of England), argued that women (and particularly wives and mothers) exercised a special kind of power through the emotional, moral and spiritual influence they wielded in the domestic sphere.[26] This concept of feminine influence and the power attaching to women's supposedly superior morality and spirituality (deriving in large part from their sexual purity) was espoused by conservatives and also by some advocates of the woman's cause throughout the century. Others refused to trade 'equal rights, equal admission to all social privileges' for 'a position apart' as 'a sort of sentimental priesthood'.[27]

No matter how it was perceived or deployed, female dependence was constructed and perpetuated by a legal system which infantilized women and equated them with 'Criminals, idiots, . . . and minors', as Frances Power Cobbe put it in her essay in *Fraser's Magazine* (December 1868), which asked 'Is the classification sound?' As Barbara Bodichon (a founder member of the Langham Place group of proto-feminists which published the *Englishwoman's Journal*) pointed out, a single woman of twenty-one was independent: 'But if she unites herself to a man, the law immediately steps in, and she finds herself legislated for, and her condition of life suddenly and entirely changed. Whatever age she may be of, she is again considered as an infant.'[28] Bodichon is referring here to the legal practice of couverture, as defined by William Blackstone in 1765: 'By marriage, the very being or legal existence of a woman is suspended, or at least incorporated or consolidated into that of the husband, under whose wing, protection, or cover she performs everything, and she is therefore called in our law a *femme covert*.'[29]

Although the law of couverture meant that married women were not legal subjects, women generally were the subject (or object) of a proliferation of legal discussion and legislation throughout the nineteenth century. As Barbara Bodichon observed in her concluding remarks to *A Brief Summary*: 'Women, more than any other members of the community, suffer from over-legislation.' From the 1830s onwards there was vigorous contestation over the legal control (or, conversely, the empowerment) of women in matters of marital rights and rights over their children; their ownership and control of property; their ownership and control of their bodies; and their civil and political rights. The contest over women's status as legal and civic subjects was played out in a number of controversies and campaigns, for example: campaigns about the laws governing marriage, separation, divorce and child custody which came to prominence with the Caroline Norton Case in the 1830s, and which remained a source of agitation throughout the period; successive attempts to reform the Married Women's Property laws; controversies in the 1860s about the rights of husbands and other male kin to incarcerate their supposedly mad female relatives in sanatoria or lunatic asylums; debates from the 1860s onwards about the policing of female sexuality via the Contagious Diseases Acts (under which women suspected of prostitution were subjected to forced medical examination and detention without trial for up to three – and later six – months), and campaigns to halt what the opponents of these Acts saw as the statutory rape involved in the invasive medical examination of prostitutes; late-nineteenth-century debates about marital rape and the domestic imprisonment of women by husbands seeking the 'restitution of conjugal rights'; debates and campaigns throughout the century about women's political (dis)enfranchisement. These issues and the contemporary debates about them were also a persistent theme of fiction by women, and played an important part in shaping the nineteenth-century novel.

The Caroline Norton affair, which reads like the plot of a Gothic novel from the 1790s or a sensation novel of the 1860s, offers an interesting perspective on the ways in which biomedical and legal discourses intersected in the control of women and in the shaping of their self-representation. Caroline Norton's legal battles and her attempts to gain access to her three sons, her earnings from her writing and property inherited from her parents, following the breakdown of her marriage to the violent and drunken George Norton, served as a painful illustration of married women's legal disabilities. Norton published a successful volume of poems (*The Sorrows of Rosalie*, 1829) and the less successful *The Wife and Woman's Reward* (1835) – two stories treating of unrequited first love and the marital difficulties of their heroines – before taking up her pen in earnest in response to the lack of legal redress of married women. She intervened in debates on the Infant Custody Bill, which became law in 1839, with a privately circulated pamphlet *The Separation of Mother and Child by the Law of 'Custody of Infants', Considered* (1838) and *A Plain Letter to the Lord Chancellor on the Infant Custody Bill* (1839), using the pseudonym of 'Pearce Stevenson Esquire'. Subsequently she joined battle over the Matrimonial Causes Bill (introduced into Parliament in 1854), publishing *English Laws for Women in the Nineteenth Century* (1854) and the *Letter to the Queen on Lord Chancellor Cranworth's Marriage and Divorce Bill* (1855).

Norton also dramatized the travails of mistreated married women in novels which drew on her own experience. *Stuart of Dunleath* (1851) recounts the marital travails of the penniless Eleanor Raymond, who marries a man she does not love (Sir Stephen Penrhyn) following the apparent suicide of the man she does love (her guardian, David Stuart, whose speculations with her fortune have led to her financial ruin). Norton's own maternal melodrama is mirrored in her heroine's loss of her children (they are drowned when Eleanor's scheming sister-in-law compels her to take them on an ill-advised excursion), in Sir Stephen's ill treatment of her and in his subsequent sequestration of her fortune, which is restored to her when Stuart (who had faked his own suicide) reappears. Unlike the resourceful Norton, Eleanor dies alone, abandoned by her husband and forsaken by Stuart, who has married someone else. The most notorious of her novels, *Lost and Saved* (1863), was published at the height of the debate about sensation fiction and was reviewed alongside *East Lynne*, *Lady Audley's Secret* and *Aurora Floyd* as an example of the work of 'Our Female Sensationalists'.[30] *Lost and Saved* focuses on the double standard of sexual morality through the standard sensation plot device of the false matrimonial situation of its protagonist, Beatrice Brooke. Beatrice, who believes herself to be legally married to Montague Treherne after a mock ceremony, becomes estranged from her family as a result of concealing her 'marriage' (at her 'husband's' behest), and bears an illegitimate child who subsequently dies. Throughout the novel Beatrice's lonely and defenceless state is juxtaposed with the social success and power of the selfish, worldly and hypocritical figures of Lady Nesdale and the Marchioness of Updown. The novel offended some readers and reviewers because (like Elizabeth Gaskell's *Ruth*, 1853) it presented its fallen-woman heroine as the sexually innocent victim of male duplicity, and also as noble and resourceful when she is shunned by society. It also caused offence because (unlike *Ruth*) its heroine survives social calumny, is restored to her family and, instead of dying (the more usual end of fallen women in nineteenth-century fiction), marries a widower who had previously been deserted by his unfaithful wife. Even 'Mrs Norton's best friends', the *Christian Remembrancer*'s reviewer averred:

are obliged to admit that her story . . . is unfit for the drawing-room table, and ought to be kept out of the way of young ladies. She fights the battle of her sex by showing the injustice of the world, in its severity towards a certain class of errors, if committed by the helpless and the weak, and the tolerance of the same and much worse when perpetrated by the powerful and strong. Its highest morality . . . is that to sin with feeling is better than to sin without. (223)

Norton's attacks on the unreformed child custody laws anticipated Harriet Taylor Mill's assertion that 'the division of mankind into two castes [men and women], one born to rule over the other, is . . . a source of perversion and demoralization',[31] but they also invoked (or, perhaps, mobilized for rhetorical effect) the theory of Woman's natural maternal propensities:

There are other laws besides those made by men – what says the holier law, the law of nature?

Does nature say that the woman, who endures for nearly a year a tedious suffering, ending in an agony which perils her life, has no claim to the children she bears? . . . that the woman who has watched patiently through the very many feverish and anxious nights which occur even in the healthiest infancy, has no claim to the children she has tended? And that the . . . sole claim rests with him, who has slept while she watched. . . ? No! the voice of nature cries out against the inhuman cruelty of such a separation.[32]

This representation of the mother can be read in various ways. On the one hand it represents motherhood both as a biological imperative and as womanly fulfilment through self-abnegation. On the other hand, motherhood is represented as melodrama, through the spectacle of a mother's suffering, either for her child, or as a result of the actual or threatened removal or loss of the child. This maternal melodrama is enacted (with differing inflections) in numerous novels by women throughout the nineteenth century: from Anne Brontë's *The Tenant of Wildfell Hall* (1848), whose heroine is involved in a struggle with her violent and drunken husband for the custody and education of their son; through Mrs Henry Wood's *East Lynne* (1861), whose sympathetically presented heroine, separated from her children as a consequence of her adultery, returns disguised as their governess only to watch the lingering death of one of them without being able to acknowledge her maternity; to George Eliot's *Daniel Deronda* (1876) and Mona Caird's *The Daughters of Danaus* (1894), in which a female character is faced with a choice between her child(ren) and a musical vocation. In *Daniel Deronda* this dilemma is rehearsed in the retrospective narrative that the singer Alcharisi tells to Daniel, the son whom she abandoned for her art. It is central to the narrative of *The Daughters of Danaus*, which focuses on its heroine's struggles with social convention and gender stereotypes in her efforts to pursue her ambition of becoming a composer: Hadria leaves her husband and children in order to further her musical studies in Paris, but, unlike Alcharisi, she is eventually 'boomeranged' back into a more conventional wifely and motherly role. Equally prominent is the obverse fantasy of maternal deprivation, the child's loss of the mother. As Carolyn Dever has observed, the ideal mother 'is the ghost that haunts' the nineteenth-century novel, since, despite their preoccupation with women's influence and power in the domestic sphere, Victorian novels very rarely embody that power in actual mothers, but 'invariably feature protagonists whose mothers are dead or lost, swept away by menacing and often mysterious outside forces'. This absent or dead mother is central to the construction and reproduction of the good mother as a cultural ideal; it negotiates contradictory representations of female sexuality, by subsuming 'the eroticized adult female' in the 'disguise of a dead – and therefore virtuous, pure, noble, and true – mother'.[33]

Florence Nightingale's reading of the absent mother in fiction adds yet another dimension to the complexities and contradictions of nineteenth-century representations of mothers and other women. For Nightingale, fiction is the space of fantasy in which the daughter can escape from the coercive model of 'Woman's mission' and feminine behaviour which was embodied in, and policed by, middle-class society's 'good mother.' The 'main charm of reading novels', Nightingale writes in her autobiographical fragment 'Cassandra', 'is that the heroine has generally no family ties (almost invariably no mother), or, if she has, these do not interfere with her entire independence'.[34] 'Cassandra' is a thoroughgoing critique of the lot of domestic maternal Woman. Nightingale's middle-class women have 'passion, intellect, [and] moral activity', but a 'place in society where no one of [these] three can be exercised' (p. 396). Woman's '"domestic duties"', much vaunted by the female authors of conduct books (as Nightingale bitterly points out), are, in this account, merely 'high-sounding words, which, for the most part, are bad habits (which she has not the courage . . . the strength to break through)' (p. 404). The domestic hearth is a place of confinement and torpor, where women's lives are broken into fragments and their time stolen from them by social obligations. Nightingale's *cri de coeur* offers a social explanation for the female hysteria which doctors, on the whole, attributed to biological causes. It also constitutes a kind of case study of the hysteric: 'What [domestic women] suffer – even physically – from the want of . . . work no one can tell. The accumulation of nervous energy, which has had nothing to do during the day, makes them feel every night when they go to bed, as if they were going mad' (p. 508).

The frustrations of the woman sacrificed on the altar of family and prevented by the 'claim of social life', or prevailing conceptions of the woman's role, from becoming a writer or painter, or from achieving anything of substance, are a constant theme of women's writing (particularly the novel) throughout the period from Charlotte Brontë's ventriloquizing of Jane Eyre's impassioned address to the reader:

Women are supposed to be very calm generally: but women feel just as men feel; they need exercise for their faculties, and a field for their efforts as much as their brothers do; they suffer from too rigid a restraint, too absolute a stagnation, precisely as men would suffer; and it is narrow-minded in their more privileged fellow-creatures to say that they ought to confine themselves to making puddings and knitting stockings, or to playing on the piano and embroidering bags. It is thoughtless to condemn them, or laugh at them, if they seek to do more or learn more than custom has pronounced necessary for their sex. (chapter 12)

The theme was taken up by George Eliot in her depiction of Maggie Tulliver's thirst for knowledge and her 'eager passionate longings for all that was beautiful and glad' (*The Mill on the Floss*, Book III, chapter 5) and Dorothea Brooke's ardent yearning for 'some lofty conception of the world which might frankly include the parish of Tipton and her own rule of conduct there' (*Middlemarch*, chapter 1). It reaches a crescendo in the New Woman writing of the 1880s and 1890s in such novels as Mona Caird's *The Daughters of Danaus* (1894), Isabella Ford's *On the Threshold* (1895) and Mary Cholmondeley's *Red Pottage* (1899), all of which deal specifically with the aspirations of female characters to become writers, painters or musicians, and more generally with women's aspirations for a social role and/or a form of subjective validation and self-fulfilment which was denied to them by conventional stereotypes of femininity.

The writing of 'Cassandra' coincided with a flurry of writing by women on the limitations of the conception of the maternal woman and the constraints of the domestic life. Harriet Taylor Mill, for example, asserted in 1851 that 'it is neither necessary nor just to make imperative on women that they shall be either mothers or nothing'.[35] Others railed against some of the awful consequences for women of a conception of femininity based on love, marriage and the claims of social life. Prominent among Dinah Mulock Craik's *A Woman's Thoughts about Woman* was the view that 'the chief canker at the root of women's lives, is the want of something to do', while Barbara Bodichon argued that a woman who does not wish to marry, or who fails to secure a husband 'will surely be ill, miserable, or go mad, if she has no occupation'.[36] The frustrations of the constraints of the female lot are graphically represented in fiction by women throughout the period, from Jane Eyre's restless pacing on the roof of Thornfield Hall longing for 'more of practical experience than I possessed' and listening to 'a tale my imagination created, and narrated continuously; quickened with all of incident, life, fire, feeling, that I had not in my actual existence' (chapter 24), to the New Woman heroine's attempts to escape the role of dutiful daughter or wife by seeking self-fulfilment in a career, and by refusing or redefining marriage.

The subject of women's duties and women's work was fiercely debated throughout the period, and virtually all perspectives on this issue involved addressing the question of whether work outside the home could be reconciled with the domestic, maternal ideal. The debates about women and work also demonstrate very vividly the inter-dependence of nineteenth-century constructions of gender and sexual-ity with those of class. In the 1830s and 1840s the debate focused mainly on the conditions of women factory workers, and the relation of those conditions to the moral and physical condition of the working class. As dominant definitions of femininity in the early part of the century increasingly equated it with middle-class domesticity, so working-class women, who were required by the industrialized economy to work outside the home in factories, became defined almost as a separate species, differentiated from (middle-class) Woman by their supposed 'early maturation and menstruation, reduced fertility, perversions of maternal instinct, and the assumption of masculine form through mus-cular development'.[37] Philanthropic reformers, many of whom were women, based their reform programmes on the (re)domestication of the working-class, either by restoring women factory workers to the home, or making industrial relations more familial. This is particularly evident in industrial novels by women in the first half of the century, for example Frances Elizabeth Trollope's *Michael Armstrong, the Factory Boy* (1840), Charlotte Elizabeth Tonna's *Helen Fleetwood: Tale of the Factories* (1841), and Elizabeth Gaskell's *Mary Barton* (1848) and *North and South* (1854–5). It can also be seen in Bessie Rayner Parkes's *Essays on Woman's Work* (1865):

Do we wish to see the majority of women getting their own livelihood . . . are we trying to assist the female population . . . over a time of difficulty; or are we trying to develop a new state and theory of social life? I feel bound to say that I regard the industrial question from a temporary point of view . . . we are passing through a stage of civilization which is to be regretted and that her house and not the factory is a woman's happy and healthful sphere.[38]

From mid-century much of the debate about women and work focused on the predicament of the middle-class woman, and specifically on work as the means of avoiding the problem of female dependence, and of solving what W. R. Greg described as the surplus woman problem. More contentiously, some women writers pressed for education leading to meaningful work outside the home as a form of self-fulfilment for women. All arguments for women's work, but particularly the last-mentioned, had to engage with the construct of selfless, self-sacrificing maternal Woman. Many women writers sought to accommodate their conception of women's employment to this construct. Anna Jameson, for example, answered the question as to '[w]hether a more enlarged sphere of social work may not be allowed to woman in perfect accordance with the truest feminine instincts?' by transforming the Angel in the House into the Angel out of the House, for whom 'the domestic affections and the domestic duties . . . must be taken as the basis of all the more complicated social relations, and . . . carried out and developed in all the forms and duties of social existence'.[39] Others, such as Barbara Bodichon in *Women and Work* (1856) represented fulfilling work for women as a way of escaping the confinement of the role of the domestic Angel, the slave, the servant or the prostitute.

The debate about women and work also intersected with the debate about prostitution in the 1850s and the debates about the Contagious Diseases Acts in the 1870s. Josephine Butler, for example, deplored the fact that the 'absolute dependence on men to which so many women are reduced, means either beggary or *shame*'.[40] However, other campaigners against the Acts and against prostitution saw its primary cause as male lust and depravity rather than women's economic vulnerability, and throughout the 1870s and 1880s campaigners against the Contagious Diseases Acts mobilized the discourses of female passionlessness and woman's influence to effect a moral reform of society through the reform of male sexuality: 'the root is there . . . so long as you leave MEN as they are'.[41] Both the practice of prostitution and the social, medical and legal discourses on the subject were seen by many women writers and activists as having implications for all women, as is evident in this extract from the *Eighth Annual Report of the Ladies National Association for the Repeal of the Contagious Diseases Acts* (1877):

[T]he Acts were but the expression of the spirit of the time about women; . . . they could not have been planned, carried or maintained, if there had not been amongst us, amongst women as well as men, an acceptance of the doctrine that women are inferior to men, that men's interests are paramount, and that, where necessary, women must be entirely sacrificed to those interests, that women are unfit and unentitled to regulate their own lives, which must be ordered by men in the interests of men.[42]

Throughout the latter half of the century the interdependence of attitudes to prostitution and 'the spirit of the time about women' was emphasized by women writers, and especially by those who sought to reform, or even abolish, marriage. Of course the plots of novels, since the eighteenth century, had often turned on the buying and selling of middle- and upper-middle-class women in the marriage market, a practice which Jane Austen subjected to intense satiric scrutiny. Victorian women novelists, social commentators and reformers were more outspoken, often

linking middle-class marriage to sex slavery and prostitution. Charlotte
Brontë made this connection in her representation of Jane Eyre's unease
about Rochester's behaviour during their engagement: in an example of
that metaphorical use of race referred to earlier in this chapter, Jane
compares Rochester's attempts to buy dresses and jewels for her to a
sultan purchasing gold and gems for his slave (chapter 24). In the 1860s
the women's sensation novel often focused on the situation of the pur-
chased wife, sometimes dwelling minutely on her physical response to her
predicament: '[H]as he not bought me? . . . he has paid a handsome price
on the nail . . . [t]hat accursed arm is still around me – my buyer's arm –
that arm which seems to be burning into my flesh like a brand.'[43] New
Woman writers, such as George Egerton, were even more explicit, representing marriage as a form of legalized prostitution: 'As long as a man
demands from a wife what he must sue from a mistress as a favour . . .
marriage becomes for many a legal prostitution, a nightly degradation, a
hateful yoke under which they age, mere bearers of children conceived
in a sense of duty, not love.'[44]

From the 1850s onward articles and pamphlets by campaigners for a
married woman's rights over her own person and property frequently
represented marriage as a form of economic and sexual slavery akin to
prostitution. In 1888 this view of marriage was given a very wide public
exposure when Mona Caird's article 'Marriage' in the August issue of
the *Westminster Review* was used by the *Daily Telegraph* to solicit readers'
letters on the subject 'Is Marriage a Failure?' (27,000 letters had been
received when the correspondence closed at the end of September).
Caird claimed that 'the origin of our modern idea of possession in marriage' lay in the ancient customs of woman capture and wife purchase:
'the woman became the property of man, his own by right of conquest.
Now the wife is his by right of law.' Caird attributed the division of
women into two discrete categories – the married woman and the prostitute – to puritan conceptions of marriage as an institution designed to
curb sensuality. Marriage and prostitution, she argued, 'are the two sides
of the same shield . . . The same idea – the purchase of womanhood . . .
rules from the base to the summit of the social body.'[45]

Some late-nineteenth-century women writers and activists on the
marriage question, adopting the rhetoric used by the campaigners
against the Contagious Diseases Acts, sought the moral reform of marriage though the moral reform of men. Reform campaigns focused on
the double standard of sexual morality, the problem of venereal disease,

male violence within marriage and the concept of marital rape. To the scandal of some reviewers, these issues were also explored in graphic detail in fiction, for example in Sarah Grand's *The Heavenly Twins* (1893) and *The Beth Book* (1897). Caird's strategy for reforming marriage was to construct an alternative to the current institution, a new ideal, a 'free contract' based on equality, the economic independence of women, love and sympathy. Other *fin-de-siècle* women sought alternatives to marriage. Those who wished to see women as sexually autonomous as well as economically independent (Eleanor Marx, for example) advocated the Free Union. However, such a concept was anathema to many (perhaps most) women, and even its supporters, for the most part, saw it as an ideal goal which might be attained when women achieved true economic and sexual equality. Other alternatives to marriage advocated at this time were freely chosen spinsterhood, or companionship or romantic friendship with another woman, such as that between Hester Gresley and Rachel West in Cholmondeley's *Red Pottage*.

It was only at the end of the century, in the writings of male sexologists that same-sex love between women was explicitly recognized. Havelock Ellis's *Sexual Inversion* (1897) contains one of the earliest British discussions of lesbianism, albeit one that pathologized lesbian (and indeed other) sexualities. Ellis distinguished two types of lesbian: the 'invert', whose same-sex attraction was an innate abnormality, and who was herself physically mannish; and the 'pervert' (sometimes described as the 'pseudohomosexual'), for whom same-sex attraction was an acquired rather than an innate characteristic. Girls' schools, female colleges, clubs and settlement houses were all seen as breeding grounds of passionate friendships between women and of lesbian sexual practice. The new sexology, anti-feminist novelists (both male and female), and reviewers and journalists all linked lesbianism to feminism and the New Woman. *The Rebel of the Family* (1880), a novel by the anti-feminist Eliza Lynn Linton, anticipated the sexologists in its representation of the relationship of Mrs Bell Blount, the 'Lady President of the West Hill Society for Women's Rights', with some of her followers. Separated from her husband, Mrs Blount lives with her 'little wife', Connie Taylor. She recruits the novel's rebel-heroine, Perdita, for the movement by 'suddenly taking her in her arms and kissing her with strange warmth'. This behaviour, and the passionate letters with which she subsequently bombards Perdita, leave the heroine 'Half-attracted and half-repelled – fascinated by the woman's mental power and revolted by something too vague to

name yet too real to ignore.'[46] Later, Ellis's description of the female
invert, as Sheila Jeffreys notes, in *The Spinster and Her Enemies* (1985), classified as 'homosexual' many of the forms of behaviour, advocated by the
New Women of the 1890s (and criticized by antifeminists), which sought
to escape conventional feminine stereotypes:

When they still retain female garments, these usually show some traits of masculine simplicity . . . The brusque energetic movements . . . the direct speech,
the inflexion of the voice, the masculine straightforwardness and sense of
honour, and especially the attitude towards men, free from any suggestion either
of shyness or audacity, will often suggest the underlying psychic abnormality to
a keen observer.
      . . . There is also a dislike and sometimes incapacity for needlework and other
domestic occupations, while there is some capacity for athletics.[47]

This chapter began with the passionless woman of the domestic ideal
and her counterpart, the prostitute, and it ends with the rebellious,
mannish (or in some other versions *femme fatale*) New Woman. There are,
of course, numerous other ways of tracing the history of the stories that
nineteenth-century women writers told about women, gender and sexuality. For example, one could begin with the passionate, rebellious Jane
Eyre, whose revolutionary arrival, according to Margaret Oliphant,
transformed the English novel's representation of women, and one
could end with one of those heroines of the 'boomerang' novels of the
1880s and 1890s, who break down under the pressure of trying to redefine conventional sex–gender roles, and/or are boomeranged back into
them via marriage and motherhood. Whichever way one narrates this
history, one might trace, *en route*, a range of fictional and journalistic feminine stereotypes: the womanly woman; the fallen woman; the domestically imprisoned wife; the self-sacrificing maternal angel; the histrionic,
non-maternal, 'fast' 'Girl of the Period'; the scheming, assertive, often
sexually exploitative sensation heroine; the 'revolting daughters' of the
1880s and 1890s who rejected the models of femininity espoused by their
mothers, sought independence, education and entry to the professions,
and (depending on who is telling the story) were anti-men and anti-sex,
or sought for themselves the sexual freedom enjoyed by men in order to
pursue affairs with men or women (or both). However one plots this
history, wherever one touches down, one encounters women writers
reacting and responding to the confident-sounding, but often deeply
contradictory stories that their culture told them about themselves.
Some women writers (and it is important to remember that, on the

whole, this chapter deals with middle- or upper-middle-class women) espoused the domestic ideal of femininity (to use an imprecise but useful shorthand term) because they believed in it implicitly, and/or because it offered them and their class a kind of power. Others sought to rework and redeploy this ideal for a changing world. Yet others openly challenged it, rejecting it as outmoded and seeking another way of representing women or Woman. This is not a simple narrative of progress. Each of these positions or strategies can be found in writers at every point in the period. Moreover, notwithstanding its own instabilities and contradictions, the normative concept of the domestic feminine ideal continued to set the terms of debate and, to a great extent, to define the parameters of representation, even for those women writers who sought new ways of representing their gender.

NOTES

1 W. R. Greg, 'The False Morality of Lady Novelists', *National Review* 8 (1859), pp. 144–67, 149.
2 Judith Walkowitz, *City of Dreadful Delight: Narratives of Sexual Danger in Late-Victorian London* (London: Virago, 1992), p. 8.
3 *A Room of One's Own*, World's Classics, Oxford University Press 1992, p. 84.
4 Since it is a term which has a clear, if shifting and contested historical valency, I shall use the capitalized 'Woman' when invoking the nineteenth-century conception or construct of the essential, transcendent feminine subject.
5 The phrases are Angela McRobbie's, from 'Post-Marxism and Cultural Studies: a Post-script', in Lawrence Grossberg, Cary Nelson and Paula Treichler, eds., *Cultural Studies* (London: Routledge, 1992), p. 726.
6 See Lyn Pykett, *The 'Improper' Feminine: the Women's Sensation Novel and the New Woman Writing* (London: Routledge, 1992).
7 Mary Poovey, *Uneven Developments: the Ideological Work of Gender in Mid-Victorian England* (London: Virago, 1988), p. 4.
8 See Francoise Basch, *Relative Creatures: Victorian Women in Society and the Novel* (London: Allen Lane, 1974).
9 Susan Kingsley Kent, *Sex and Suffrage in Britain, 1860–1914* (London: Routledge, 1990), p. 30.
10 Henry Maudsley, 'Sex in Mind and Education', *Fortnightly Review*, 15 (1874), pp. 466–83, 466.
11 See Thomas Laycock, *A Treatise on the Nervous Diseases of Women: Comprising an Inquiry into the Nature, Causes and Treatments of Spinal and Hysterical Disorders* (London: Longman, 1840), and Patrick Geddes and J. Arthur Thompson, *The Evolution of Sex* (1889).
12 Maudsley, 'Sex in Mind and Education', 267.

13 Elizabeth Garrett Anderson, 'Sex in Mind and Education: a Reply', *Fortnightly Review* 15 (1874), pp. 582–94, 584.

14 Cynthia Eagle Russett, *Sexual Science: the Victorian Construction of Womanhood* (Cambridge, MA: Harvard University Press, 1989), pp. 55–6.

15 Susan Meyer, *Imperialism at Home: Race and Victorian Women's Fiction* (Ithaca, NY: Cornell University Press, 1996), p. 7.

16 Poovey, *Uneven Developments*, p. 7. See also Jill Matus, *Unstable Bodies: Victorian Representations of Sexuality and Maternity* (Manchester University Press, 1995), p. 122.

17 George Drysdale, *The Elements of Social Science* (1860), p. 172. (First published as *Physical, Sexual and Natural Religion* (London: John Churchill, 1854)).

18 W. R. Greg, 'Prostitution', *Wesminster Review* 53 (1850), pp. 238–68.

19 See W. Acton, *Prostitution Considered in its Moral, Social and Sanitary Aspects, in London and Other Large Cities, with Proposals for the Mitigation and Prevention of its Attendant Evils* (London: John Churchill, 1857).

20 Elaine Showalter, *The Female Malady: Women, Madness and English Culture, 1830–1980* (London: Virago, 1987), p. 52.

21 J. C. Bucknill and Daniel Hack Tuke, *A Manual of Psychological Medicine* (London: John Churchill, 1858), pp. 238–9.

22 See Linton's satirical portraits of modern female types in the *Saturday Review* in 1868 most famously 'The Girl of the Period', *Saturday Review* (14 March 1868), pp. 339–40.

23 Edward Tilt, *A Handbook of Uterine Therapeutics and of Diseases of Women* (London: Henry G. Bohn, 1853); R. B. Carter, *On the Pathology and Treatment of Hysteria* (London: John Churchill, 1853), p. 32; H. B. Donkin, entry on 'Hysteria' for the *Dictionary of Psychological Medicine* (London: J. and A. Churchill, 1892), vol. I.

24 See Eliza Lynn Linton, 'The Wild Women (Part I) as Politicians', *Nineteenth Century* 30 (1891), pp. 79–88, 'The Wild Women (Part II: Conclusion)', *Nineteenth Century* 30 (1891), pp. 596–605' and 'The Partisans of the Wild Women', *Nineteenth Century* 31 (1892), pp. 455–64; Mona Caird, 'A Defence of the So-called "Wild Woman"', *Nineteenth Century* 31 (1892), pp. 811–29; Blanche A. Crackanthorpe, 'The Revolt of the Daughters', *Nineteenth Century*, 35 (1894), pp. 23–31, 'The Revolt of the Daughters: a Last Word on the Revolt', *Nineteenth Century* 35 (1894), pp. 424–9; Mary E. Haweis, 'The Revolt of the Daughters: Daughters and Mothers', *Nineteenth Century* 35 (1894), pp. 430–6; Kathleen Cuffe, 'A Reply from the Daughters (no. I)', *Nineteenth Century* 35 (1894), pp. 437–42; Alys W. Pearsall Smith Russell, 'A Reply from the Daughters (no. II)', *Nineteenth Century* 35 (1894), pp. 443–50. I discuss these controversies briefly in *The 'Improper' Feminine*, pp. 139–40, and *passim*.

25 Eliza Lynn Linton, 'Loops and Parentheses', *Temple Bar* 6 (1862), pp. 52–60, 56.

26 Sarah Stickney Ellis was an educationalist and temperance activist as well as a writer. Her publications include a collection of stories with moral

themes, *Pictures of Private Life* (three series, 1833–7); *The Poetry of Life* (1835), a domestic novel; *Home or the Iron Rule* (1836), which foregrounded the role of the mother within the middle-class family; and *Family Secrets, or Hints to Those Who Would Make Home Happy* (3 vols., 1841–2). Today she is best remembered for her conduct books which went through numerous editions in the nineteenth century: *The Women of England, Their Social Duties and Domestic Habits* (1839); *The Daughters of England, Their Position in Society, Character and Responsibilities* (1842); *The Wives of England, Their Relative Duties, Domestic Influence, and Social Obligations* (1843) and *The Mothers of England, Their Influence and Responsibility* (1843).

27 Harriet Taylor Mill [with J. S. Mill] 'The Enfranchisement of Women', *Westminster Review* 109 (1851), pp. 289–311.

28 *A Brief Summary, in Plain Language of the Most Important Laws concerning Women; Together with a Few Observations Thereon* (1854), rptd in Tim Dolin, *Mistress of the House: Women of Property in the Victorian Novel* (Aldershot: Ashgate, 1997), p. 130.

29 Sir William Blackstone, *Commentaries on the Laws of England* (London, 1765), vol. I, p. xv.

30 'Our Female Sensationalists', *Christian Remembrancer* 46 (1863), pp. 209–36.

31 Harriet Taylor Mill, 'The Enfranchisement of Women', p. 295.

32 [Caroline Norton], *The Separation of Mother and Child by the Law of 'Custody of Infants', Considered* (1838), quoted in Susan G. Bell and Karen M. Offen, *Women, the Family and Freedom: the Debate in Documents* (Stanford University Press, 1983) p. 162.

33 Carolyn Dever, *Death and the Mother from Dickens to Freud* (Cambridge University Press, 1998), p. xi.

34 'Cassandra' (1859), rptd in Ray Strachey, *The Cause* (London: Virago, 1978), p. 397. For the history of the writing and publication of this fragment, see p. 395.

35 Harriet Taylor Mill, 'The Enfranchisement of Women', p. 293.

36 Dinah Mulock Craik, *A Woman's Thoughts About Woman* (1858), quoted in E. Helsinger, W. Veeder and R. Sheets, *The Woman Question: Society and Literature in Britain and America, 1837–1883*, 3 vols. (Manchester University Press, 1983), vol. III, p. 135; Bodichon, *Women and Work*, quoted in Helsinger *et al.* vol. II, p. 149.

37 Matus, *Unstable Bodies*, p. 58

38 Bessie Rayner Parkes, *Essays on Woman's Work*, quoted in Helsinger *et al.*, vol. II, p. 114.

39 Anna Jameson, 'The Communion of Labour' (1856), quoted in Helsinger *et al.* vol. II, p. 141.

40 Josephine Butler, *Sursum Corda* (Liverpool, 1871), p. 33.

41 Butler, *A Letter on the Subject of Mr Bruce's Bill Addressed to the Repealers of the Contagious Diseases Acts* (Liverpool, 1872), p. 16.

42 Quoted in Kingsley Kent, *Sex and Suffrage*, p. 77.

43 Rhoda Broughton, *Cometh up as a Flower* (London: Macmillan, 1867), p. 325.

44 George Egerton, 'Virgin Soil', in *Discords* (John Lane, 1894), p. 155.

45 Mona Caird, 'Marriage', *Westminster Review* 130 (1888), pp. 186–201, 189.

46 Eliza Lynn Linton, *The Rebel of the Family*, 3 vols. (London: Chatto and Windus,1880), vol. 1 p. 74.

47 Havelock Ellis, *Sexual Inversion*, vol. II [originally vol. I] of *Studies in the Psychology of Sex* (Philadelphia: F. A. Davies, 1927 [first published 1897), p. 250.

CHAPTER FIVE

Feminism, journalism and public debate

Barbara Caine

The extensive involvement of women writers in public debate through-out the nineteenth century has rarely been recognized, despite the fact that they addressed almost every imaginable social and political subject. In part, this is the result of a lack of any adequate language with which to describe or analyse either women's non-fictional writings or those who produced them. There were certainly lady novelists in the nineteenth century, but no terms emerged to describe women essayists or historians or journalists – and there was no broad recognition of the 'woman of letters'. The expansion of publishing in the late eighteenth and the nine-teenth centuries, like the rise of the periodical press and the emergence of journalism as an acceptable middle-class profession, provided oppor-tunities for women as well as for men, and significant numbers of women wrote and published pamphlets, tracts and books as well as literary reviews and essays. But, as Mary Poovey and Judith Johnston have argued, the very term 'man of letters', which accompanied and even cel-ebrated the rise of a new kind of writer, and the range of new forms of writing available to men, served quite explicitly to mask the rise of the woman of letters, and to render problematic the general category of the woman writer.[1]

Even when some of the ideas of women writers are acknowledged, in the many recent anthologies exploring nineteenth-century feminism, for example, there is little recognition of how extensive women's writings were even on these questions or of the important role that the 'woman question' played in giving women a voice in public debate.[2] Feminist writ-ings in the nineteenth century tend to be seen as part of feminist cam-paigns – rather than to fit within the broader framework of women's writing. It must be said that some feminist writers contributed to this per-ception. Frances Cobbe is a particular case in point. In her autobiogra-phy, Cobbe differentiated very clearly between her feminist and her other writings. She devoted a chapter entitled 'Journalism' to a discussion of her work for the daily paper, the *Echo*, and another entitled 'Literary Life' to her writings on theological and scientific questions. Her many widely read articles on women, however, were included in her chapter on 'The Claims of Women', effectively becoming an aspect of her involvement in the women's movement, rather than being seen as part of her literary output.[3]

Large numbers of women wrote pamphlets, periodicals and books on the broad question of women's emancipation. Many prominent feminist theorists and activists also wrote on other subjects of great public interest as well. This pattern was set by Mary Wollstonecraft whose *Vindication of the Rights of Woman* was preceded by an immense number of reviews and essays on contemporary literature and educational thought in the *Analytical Review*, and by a book on *The Rights of Man* written in reply to Edmund Burke's *Reflections on the Revolution in France*.[4] It was continued in the 1820s and 1830s by Harriet Martineau who covered a similarly wide range of subjects which began with essays on women's role in religion and on women's education, but soon expanded to include essays on contemporary social problems and developments in both Britain and the United States, illustrations of political economy, and then a number of essays on women's work and on their legal status.[5] Even Millicent Garrett Fawcett, best known as a suffrage leader in the later nineteenth century, was widely known for her writings on political economy long before she emerged as a suffrage leader. Indeed, by 1871, she was recognized as the most eminent female political economist in England and was suggested as a possible member of the Political Economy Club.[6] Fawcett also wrote on Irish Home Rule and on the Boer War. Her contemporary, Josephine Butler, the leader of the Contagious Diseases agitation, was another prominent woman writer. Butler wrote a great deal on her own campaign, but she also wrote on the nature of liberalism, on religion and on the justice of the British case in the Boer War.[7] All of these women contributed to the broad arguments surrounding the 'woman question', but they connected that question with other intellectual currents and they also brought women's voices to bear on many different social, political and cultural questions.[8]

In this chapter, I want to explore some of the reasons why women's written interventions into public debates gain so little recognition and to look at the ways in which feminist concerns and the 'woman question' involved women in a range of different kinds of writing. I want then to look at two prominent women writers, Harriet Martineau and Frances Power Cobbe, who combined their feminist interests with a wide range of other concerns – and who illustrate simultaneously the broad range of interventions women made into public debate and the ways in which these interests were brought to bear in their writings on feminism and on the woman question.

The vast increase in scholarship on nineteenth-century feminism evident in recent years has brought with it some important discussion of the journals and periodicals which the nineteenth-century English women's movement developed and used to organize and publicize their campaigns.[9] The succession of feminist periodicals, starting with the *English Woman's Review*, and followed by the *Victoria Magazine*, the *Englishwoman's Review of Social and Industrial Questions* and the *Women's Suffrage Journal*, demonstrate both the importance nineteenth-century feminists accorded to the setting up of their own journals – and the financial and ideological difficulties which made these ventures so short-lived.

There is no question of the importance of nineteenth-century feminist journals in the articulation of feminist ideas or in holding together the various campaigns which made up the movement. These specific journals were neither the only nor the most significant avenue for nineteenth-century feminist debate. The budgets and the financial difficulties which they faced made it hard for them to be able to afford professional writers – Frances Cobbe, for example, the best-known writer in the women's movement, was far too expensive for the *English Woman's Journal*. Hence these periodicals drew on the writing of a small number of enthusiasts and were unable to compete with successful journals in terms of the quality of their writing. George Eliot made it very clear that, in her view, the *English Woman's Journal* contained nothing that she would regard as serious from a literary point of view. 'For my own taste', she wrote to Bessie Parkes in 1857, 'I should say, the more business you can get into the journal – the more statements of philanthropic movements and social facts, and the less *literature*, the better. Not because I like philanthropy and hate literature, but because I want to *know* about philanthropy and don't care for second-rate literature.'[10]

Eliot may well have been expressing some prejudices here. But it is unquestionably the case that for those interested in following the development of ideas about women's nature, their legal and political disabilities, their interests, needs and capacities, it was quite possible to do so without these specifically feminist journals. Indeed, one of the things which is most striking about the nineteenth-century English popular and periodical press is the extent to which it simultaneously gave voice to debates about the nature of women which included feminist ideas and arguments – and gave women a voice in a range of matters of public concern. Comments from feminists themselves about the refusal of the commercial male-dominated press to allow 'the advocacy of any subject which would entail a breath of ridicule' or 'any thorough expression of opinion' and the insistence from some like Josephine Butler that there was a 'conspiracy of silence surrounding feminist campaigns'[11] is belied by the sheer volume of debate and discussion about the emancipation of women in mid-Victorian periodicals. It was in the pages of the *Westminster Review*, or *Fraser's Magazine*, the *Nineteenth Century* or the *Fortnightly Review* that the most significant feminist debates occurred – and in which women entered into debates and discussions about other political and social subjects.[12]

The 'woman question' was a staple of nineteenth-century serious journals. In the early part of the century, interest centred on women's nature and appropriate activities, and on the characteristics of women as writers. By the middle of the century, the issues covered were becoming more extensive as questions about women's work, their political and legal rights, the need for reform of the marriage laws and of girls' education assumed greater and greater prominence. The problems with marriage and the advantages of female celibacy, domestic violence, the iniquities of the sexual double standard and of prostitution, the desires of women for ever greater independence were all matters written about in major journals. Women writers had always participated in these debates, but in the first half of the century they mostly used male pseudonyms or published their work anonymously. In the mid-century, women writers became more and more visible as they published under their own names and thus brought an explicitly female voice to bear on these various debates.

It is worth pointing out here that the emergence of organized feminist campaigns in the mid nineteenth-century in itself owed much to the ways in which older women were entering into public debate on the woman question. The publication of Caroline Norton's *English Laws for Women in the Nineteenth Century* in 1854, detailing the ways women suffered through their loss of legal rights via marriage laws, was a major stimulus to the setting up of a campaign to reform those laws by Barbara Leigh Smith.[13] In a similar way, Harriet Martineau's ground-breaking discussion of women's work, her insistence on the range of work women did and of the importance of broad social recognition of women's need

for economic independence, played a significant part in the development of campaigns to extend the employment opportunities of
women.[14]

Women's voices were not only raised in support of the emancipation
of their sex. Particularly from the mid-century onwards, there were a
number of women, like Eliza Lynn Linton or Mrs Oliphant or Mrs
Humphrey Ward, who emerged as vocal opponents of women's emancipation. Eliza Lynn Linton's article 'The Girl of the Period', published
in the staunchly anti-feminist and even misogynist *Saturday Review* in
1868, set up a contrast between a traditional notion of 'a fair young
English girl', who was characterized by 'the innate purity and dignity of
her nature', and 'the girl of the period' who dyed her hair, painted her
face and lived a 'fast' and immoral life. Lynn Linton's article led to a
major controversy which engaged women writers and their male
counterparts and was carried on in other periodicals, particularly
Macmillan's Magazine, and in a number of novels.[15] It is hard, Nana
Rinehart argues, to see why this article caused quite such a stir – but it
certainly serves to demonstrate the extent of concern which surrounded
questions about women's activities and demands in the mid nineteenth-
century. It also establishes the pre-eminent place of women writers
within this debate. Thus, in 1869, a year after Lynn Linton had published her article, when a group of influential men led by the Positivist
lawyer, Frederick Harrison, decided that it was time to begin mounting
a campaign against the demand for women's suffrage, they saw it as necessary to have women write and sign articles opposing women's suffrage
rather than doing it themselves. Harrison tried to persuade Beatrice
Webb to organize a group of women to write 'The Ladies Appeal
against Female Suffrage', seeing this as likely to gain far more attention
than yet another article of his own insisting on the need for women to
confine their attention to family and home and extolling their domestic
virtues. The 'Ladies Appeal' did indeed set off an interesting debate
amongst women over the pros and cons of women's suffrage, which continued for a number of months and involved several major periodicals.[16]

By the 1860s, most major periodicals published work by women discussing feminism and women's emancipation. In the first half of the
century, however, it was radical journals which contained the most
extensive debate and provided the best outlet for women writers. There
was a scattering of articles in the *Edinburgh Review* and in *Blackwood's
Magazine* in the early nineteenth century discussing women writers and
presenting different views about women's intellectual capacities, but it

was the *Pioneer*, produced by the followers of the utopian socialist Robert Owen, along with the radical Unitarian journal, the *Monthly Repository*, which produced the first major debates in which women were actively engaged in the 1820s and 1830s.[17]

Barbara Taylor's classic study of Owenite feminism, *Eve and the New Jerusalem*, documents the important role of women lecturers like Emma Martin and Anna Wheeler in spreading Owenite views and in bringing questions about the status of women to the centre of the movement.[18] But women were also very prominent as writers, publishing letters, articles, petitions in the *Pioneer*, demanding recognition of their right to work and attacking male dominance and assumptions about male superiority both within the Owenite movement and in the wider social world.[19] The *Monthly Repository*, a radical periodical organized and edited first by Edward and then by William J. Fox, also gave a prominent place to discussion of the woman question. Edward Fox provided the first opportunities for Harriet Martineau to publish her writings on women in religious life and on women's education in the early 1820s. In the following decade, his brother William, a friend of J. S. Mill and Helen Taylor, and a man connected with Owenite as well as Unitarian circles, took over the *Monthly Repository* and made the woman question particularly prominent.[20] Fox and several of his male colleagues, including William Thompson, wrote several essays castigating male sexual promiscuity and the enslavement of women in marriage. More importantly, the *Monthly Repository* also included writings from many women, including Anna Wheeler and Mary Leman Grimstone, who set out very strongly – and in opposition to those of their male colleagues – their views on women and on the problems they faced. While Fox, Thompson and R. B. Adams bewailed women's victimization and misery, Wheeler and Grimstone argued for a view of women as capable and autonomous. They disputed the view that women were completely different from men in their intellectual and emotional attributes. Mary Leman Grimstone argued, for example, that the very idea that women were 'not capable of that self-abstraction – that concentration of the powers of the mind – that calm deliberate sobriety of contemplativeness, indispensable to statesmanship' was itself an illustration of male privilege and reflected the fact that men had far more opportunity to publish their views on women than women had to write about themselves. 'If lions and tigers ever learn to write', Grimstone commented,

what counterstatements we shall have to put against the descriptions of gallant hunts in which tigers turned tail and lions turned pale before the potent eyes of their human pursuer! Some such an effect will, I fear, follow when women come to fill the chair of oral anatomy; a different view will then be taken and given of some of the leviathans of fame, from Milton to Montgomery! How little was the conduct of the great Napoleon to Madame de Stael.[21]

While Owenite women and radical Unitarians made very important contributions to women's public writing, the most prominent and best-known woman writer of this period was undoubtedly the far more conservative Harriet Martineau. Martineau deserves considerable attention in any investigation of nineteenth-century women writers. Both the volume and the range of her writing is remarkable and she was unquestionably one of the best-known and most successful writers of the early nineteenth century. Her focus changed quite markedly in the course of her fifty-year writing career. In her early adult life in the 1820s, she concentrated primarily on prayer, devotion and the nature of faith. By the 1830s, these concerns were being replaced by new ones centring on social questions and by her writings on political economy. A visit to North America at this time led to essays and books on politics and society in America and she combined this interest with one on British history, particularly in relation to Ireland. In the 1850s, Martineau advocated some aspects of the positive philosophy of Auguste Comte and also became a convert to the new pseudo-science of mesmerism. In her final decade, the 1860s, she devoted most of her attention to English social questions including working-class life and work, to questions about education, to home life and domestic service. Martineau published in almost every major Victorian periodical including the *Athenaeum*, the *Edinburgh Review*, *Macmillan's Magazine*, the *Quarterly Review*, the *Pall Mall Gazette*, and the *London and Westminster Review*. She also published leader articles in the *Daily News*, producing a total of 1,642 of these between 1852 and 1866, plus a number of novels and a widely read autobiography.

The intensely unhappy childhood and family life, and the feeling of emotional and social isolation, exacerbated by her deafness, which Martineau depicted so clearly in her autobiography, led her to concentrate on a life of the mind in which writing and reading both provided her main occupation and took the place of other forms of social activity. In 1822, at the age of twenty, she published her first articles on women in religious life and on women's education in the *Monthly Repository*.

Martineau was fortunate in having established herself as a writer at an early age: in the mid 1820s a financial crisis in the family made it imperative that she support herself by her work – and writing was an easy way for her to do this. It was her writings on political economy which established Martineau as a popular writer – and through which she became financially independent. Like so many nineteenth-century women writers, Martineau found her own new direction through another woman writer: in 1827, she read Jane Marcet's extremely popular *Conversations on Political Economy*, a work intended primarily to introduce this new economic field to women readers. Martineau claimed that, in reading this book, she discovered that she had already written some stories which had been teaching political economy and decided that 'the principles of the whole science might be advantageously conveyed . . . [by] being exhibited in their natural workings in selected passages of social life'.[22] Martineau planned an ambitious series of *Illustrations of Political Economy*, and set about trying to find a publisher. No commercial publisher was prepared to undertake this venture and she was forced to seek support from her relatives, several of whom offered to subscribe to her work. The *Illustrations* were an immediate success: 1,500 copies of the first number were sold and within a few years, she was selling almost 10,000 copies of her tales and illustrations each month. Martineau's works on political economy were published in a variety of different forms: as individual tales in a series published by Charles Fox, or by the Society for the Diffusion of Useful Knowledge; in essays and articles published in the *Edinburgh Review*; and as novelettes welcomed by a variety of different publishers.[23]

In her *Illustrations of Political Economy*, Martineau sought, as she explained to her readers, to offer 'an explanation of the principles which regulate society' with 'pictures of what those principles are actually doing in the community'. She was an uncompromising individualist, rejecting any possibility of state intervention in the economy. The main emphasis in most of her illustrations was on the need for workers to take responsibility for their own lives and well being. In the most controversial of the *Illustrations*, a story entitled 'Weal and Woe in Garveloch', she addressed the question of poverty in terms of the Malthusian approach to population, arguing that it was necessary to limit population by late marriage and sexual abstinence.[24]

Martineau's writings on political economy illustrate very well both the opportunities – and the obstacles – which women faced when entering into public debate and taking up areas of thought in which they lacked formal training. Like her role model, Martineau emphasized the fact that her work popularized rather than initiated any aspect of political economy. She saw herself as writing for general readers, as instructing them in the importance of coming to terms with, and living according to the ideas set out by political economists concerning the nature of the market. She was particularly insistent on the need for general readers to understand Malthusian ideas about population increase – and how to limit or contain it. Martineau and Marcet were acknowledged as important by their own contemporaries, but not really seen as able to contribute to economic debates. In the mid nineteenth century, Millicent Garrett Fawcett faced a similar situation. Married young to the Cambridge Professor of Political Economy, Fawcett soon became very knowledgeable in this field – but was never deemed acceptable by the Political Economy Club. The capacities of these earlier women writers were completely denigrated at the end of the century when practitioners like Alfred Marshall were seeking to establish economics as a science and as a university-based discipline. For Marshall, who treated women's intellectual capacities with contempt, the success of Marcet and Martineau became a marker of the lack of precision and science within the field earlier in the century. Never again, he wrote in the 1890s, will 'a Mrs Marcet, or a Miss Martineau earn a goodly reputation' by throwing general economic principles 'into the form of a catechism or of simple tales by aid of which any intelligent governess might make clear to the children nestling around her where lies economic truth, and might send them forth ready to instruct statesmen and merchants how to choose the right path in economic policy, and how to avoid the wrong'.[25]

While Marshall's comments served to bury both Martineau and Marcet, their writings have recently become the subject of considerable interest amongst historians interested in establishing how the central tenets of political economy were disseminated amongst different social groups, and more broadly in the development of nineteenth-century social theory.[26] Deirdre David has argued moreover that, while Martineau always emphasized her own role as a popularizer rather than as contributing significantly to the theoretical framework of political economy, 'her female work of journalistic popularisation "made" Victorian England as much as did the male work of banking, business, and politics'.[27]

Alongside her other writings, Martineau constantly addressed the situation of women. Her earliest published articles were on 'Female Writers of Practical Divinity' and 'On Female Education' and she wrote a number of articles on women's social and legal disabilities in Britain and America, on women's work and wages, and finally on the threats posed to women by the sexual double standard and the regulation of prostitution. Martineau's writings on the situation of women gain immense cogency and strength from her capacity to combine them with broader analyses of economic developments or of political theory. Martineau's first discussion of women's suffrage occurred in her book *Society in America* which was published in 1837.[28] In this work, Martineau focussed her attention on two prominent liberal theorists, Thomas Jefferson and James Mill, castigating both for their failure to recognize that the democratic spirit by which governments derived their just power from the consent of the governed required that women be enfranchised. In their refusal to accept the need for women's suffrage, these two

most principled democratic writers on government have . . . sunk into fallacies, as disgraceful as any advocate of despotism has adduced. In fact, they have thus sunk from being, for the moment, advocates of despotism. Jefferson in America, and James Mill at home, subside, for the occasion, to the level of the author of the Emperor of Russia's catechism for the young Poles.[29]

In her view, governments could not make just laws, or laws which women should obey, concerning their taxation, their property or their legal status, without women's direct involvement through parliamentary representation. James Mill's well-known argument that the interests of most women were represented by their fathers or their husbands was completely unacceptable to her. Martineau castigated Mill for his complete failure to recognize that 'the interests of women who have fathers and husbands can never be identical with theirs'.[30] It was 'the principle of the equal rights of both halves of the human race' that had to be dealt with. This was 'the true democratic principle which can never be seriously controverted and only for a short time evaded'.[31]

In a similar way, Martineau's interest in economic questions and her skill in working with census data were of immense importance in her major article on women's work in the 1850s, which initiated a whole new debate on this question. Expressing her extreme irritation with 'the incessant repetition of the dreary story of spirit-broken governesses and starving needlewomen', she turned her attention to 'the full breadth of the area of female labour in Great Britain'.[32]

Martineau sought to break through the sentimentalizing of women and the popular, but completely erroneous, middle-class belief that most women were financially provided for within their own homes. Census results and major surveys revealed that, contrary to popular beliefs, 'a very large proportion of the women of England earn their own bread'. There was no saying, she argued ' how much misery may be saved by a timely recognition of this simple truth'.

We go on talking as if it were still true that every woman is, or ought to be supported by her father, brother, or husband: we are only beginning to think of the claim of all workers, – that their work should be paid for by its quality and its place in the market, irrespective of the status of the worker . . . We are (probably to a man) unaware of the amount of the business of life in England done by women; and if we do not attend to the fact in time, the knowledge will be forced on us in some disadvantageous or disagreeable way. A social organisation framed for a community of which half stayed at home, while the other half went out to work, cannot answer the purposes of a society of which a quarter remains at home while three-quarters goes out to work.[33]

The Census of 1851, she argued, showed the increase in the numbers of women involved in paid employment. Between 1841 and 1851, the female population increased in the ratio of 7 to 8, but the number of women engaged in independent industry increased in the far greater ratio of 3 to 4. Women were now employed in many forms of agriculture; in mining and extractive industries; in many industries concerned with 'the produce of the waters', including catching, curing and selling fish; in a wide variety of crafts and trades; and in domestic service. New occupations for women included manufacturing, especially the textile, lace and ribbon industries, as well as telegraphy and clerical work. Increasing numbers of women were also engaged in the keeping of lodging houses.[34]

Arguing strongly against prevailing ideas about the need for femininity to be nurtured within the home, Martineau would not accept that factory labour in itself brutalized women – or indeed men. Rather, she insisted, they were harmed by 'the state of ignorance in which they enter upon a life of bustle and publicity'.[35] Education was needed to enable girls both to work in factories and to carry out the traditional duties of women. The independence of women simply had to be accepted, she insisted, especially by men. Martineau saw one of the main problems of women to be the

jealousy of men in regard to the industrial independence of women: – it shows itself with every step gained in civilisation; and its immediate effect is to pauperise a large number of women who are willing to work for their bread; and, we need not add, to condemn to perdition many more who have no choice left but between starvation and vice.[36]

Martineau's feminist commitments became more and more pronounced in the course of the late 1850s and the 1860s. In the 1860s, Martineau was one of the first to oppose publicly the contagious diseases legislation aimed at regulating prostitution. In a series of letters in the *Daily News*, she voiced her fears about the ways in which the regulation of prostitution

stimulated vice and led to overall moral decay. The legislation which had
been passed in England, she argued, subjected women 'to the caprices of
police and the oppression of the law'.[37] It is interesting to note that it was
in these articles on the Contagious Diseases Acts where, for the first time,
Martineau dropped her male pseudonyms and signed herself 'An
Englishwoman'. It was a clear indication both of her new sense of connection with the emerging women's movement – and probably of her own
recognition that she would gain more attention writing on this subject as
a woman than as a man.

Martineau made her name writing on political economy, the new discipline which was coming to set the major framework for British economic
and political thought in the 1820s. By the mid century, the subjects which
were most important and of most general concern were not economics,
but rather questions about science and religion, and it was here that
Frances Cobbe, the best-known and most successful woman of letters in
the second half of the nineteenth century, made her mark. Like
Martineau, Cobbe had begun writing as a young woman living in her
parental home and seeking an intellectual outlet. Writing also provided
a way of dealing with her own personal religious crisis and her loss of
faith in the Evangelical Christianity embraced by her family. Her first
book, *The Theory of Intuitive Morals*, was written shortly after she had lost
her faith in Christianity and it was an exposition of her new religious
and philosophical beliefs and her ideas about a basis for morality which,
while it depended on moral intuition, was independent of Christian revelation.[38] Her moral and religious beliefs also provided a framework for
her feminism and especially for her insistence on the need to recognize
women's moral autonomy.

For Cobbe, as for Martineau, the early interest in writing was fortunate:
the death of her father in 1857 left in her mid-thirties free of familial
duties, but no longer mistress of the house which she had superintended
for many years and in straitened financial circumstances. Her father had
left her £200 per annum: generous by some standards, but certainly not
enough to allow her an independent life similar in comfort to that she had
known at the family home, Newbridge House. Within a very few years
Cobbe had begun to supplement this money by her writing.

Cobbe wrote for a number of different publications and on a vast
range of subjects. Her staple income came from journalism: first from
her contributions to the *Daily News* for which she acted as Italian correspondent on several occasions, and then from the regular leader columns

she produced three times each week for a daily paper, the *Echo*. In addition to the *Echo*, She wrote for *Fraser's Magazine*, *Macmillan's Magazine*, the *Quarterly Review*, the *Contemporary Review*, the *Fortnightly Review*, the *Theological Review* and the *New Quarterly Magazine*. Many of her essays were collected and re-published.

Although known now primarily because of her involvement in anti-vivisection and in the women's movement, in the nineteenth century Cobbe was equally well known for her religious writings. Her own religious position was very close to that of the American Transcendentalist, Theodore Parker, whose complete writings she edited and whose *Discourse of Religion* was an 'epoch-making book' for her. She had already come to most of Parker's conclusions before she read his work, but it 'helped me most importantly by teaching me to regard Divine Inspiration no longer as a miraculous and therefore incredible thing; but as normal and in accordance with the natural relations of the infinite and finite spirit'.[39] Parker's *Discourse on Religion* also contained a powerful critique of the masculine brutality evident in the Christian God.

This God was both King and Judge, but he showed in the exercise of his absolute power cruelty, jealousy, selfishness, vindictiveness and a complete lack of tenderness or compassion. In contrast to this, Parker put forward his own notion of a God who was 'not a king but a Father and Mother, infinite in power, wisdom and love'.[40] Parker's God combined both masculine and feminine qualities and thus incorporated reverence for women as well as for men. Parker thus aided Cobbe in establishing a framework for thinking about God and morality which allowed recognition of women's needs and established a framework for women's autonomy.

Working from this position, Cobbe believed profoundly in the importance of religion, but her understanding of religion was an ecumenical one which referred to 'a definite faith in a living and righteous God; and as a corollary therefrom, in the survival of the human soul after death . . . I mean by "Religion" that nucleus of simple Theism which is common to every form of Christianity and modern Judaism, and of course, in a measure also remote creeds.'[41] Cobbe's emphasis on the importance of religion and of a belief in a 'Power not ourselves which makes for righteousness' as the basis of morality brought her close to Unitarians and other advanced thinkers and her views on religious and moral questions were of interest, not only to feminist colleagues, but to a diverse group of male editors, writers and religious leaders including W. R. Greg, David Masson, John Morley and James Martineau.

Martineau indeed regarded Cobbe as one of the foremost English theological writers of the nineteenth century.[42] Cobbe's interests in religion
and ethics were very broad and she wrote extensively on the ethical
issues involved in science and in social questions as well as writing about
all forms of Christianity and about Judaism. But for all her apparent
breadth of vision, Cobbe ultimately believed that the only viable form
of religious belief was an enlightened and nonsectarian acceptance of
the wisdom of Christ – in other words her own position. This is made
very evident in her writings on Judaism. While opposing any form of
persecution of Jews or the denial to them of full legal and political rights,
Cobbe believed unquestioningly in the superiority of Christian ethics to
those of Judaism. If Judaism was to survive, she argued, it would have to
get rid of its excessive emphasis on ritual and ceremonial, its reliance on
tradition, and indeed of its Orthodox beliefs and practices and become:

A reformed, enlightened, world-wide creed, which a cultivated gentleman may
frankly avow and defend in the *salons* of London, Paris, Berlin or New York, and
in the progress of which he may feel some enthusiasm, – a creed which will
make him free to adopt from Christianity all that he recognises in it of the spir-
itually lofty and morally beautiful, – such a creed may have a future before it of
which no end need be foreseen. But for unreformed Judaism there can be
nothing in store but the gradual dropping away of the ablest, the most cultured,
the wealthiest, the men of the world and the men of the study – the Spinozas,
the Heines, the Disraelis – and the persistence only for a few generations of the
more ignorant, fanatical, obscure and poor.[43]

Cobbe's insistence on the superiority of Christianity to Judaism, and her
emphasis on the importance of the teachings of Christ, were closely
linked to her feminism. She felt that Christ's treatment of women was
admirable and exemplary. The story of the woman taken in adultery,
with its injunction 'Let him that is without sin amongst you first cast a
stone at her', was profoundly important to her. 'Would to God' she
wrote, 'that this Christ-like doctrine might ever become the received
Christian doctrine – that the sin of the man does not differ from that of
the woman – that all pretences of such differences should vanish before
the solemn appeal of conscience'.[44]

   Her religious ideas were also linked to her views on vivisectionism and
underlay her vociferous attack on the growing power of scientists and of
the medical profession. The lack of religious faith and the materialism
of scientists and medical men led in her view to their growing arrogance
and extreme disregard of the feelings of others. The brutal tendencies
which she saw as part of human nature and which 'have scarcely been

kept down while we believed ourselves to have immortal souls . . . will have it still more their own way when we feel assured we are only mortal bodies'. Cobbe believed that the practice of vivisection was not only appallingly cruel to the animals involved, but also served to brutalize those doctors and scientists who carried it out unmoved by the pain and suffering they inflicted. Indeed, she feared that they began to find excitement and even pleasure in their pursuit. Moreover, she shared with several other nineteenth-century feminists a sense that the torture of animals which was condoned by science was accompanied also by a brutal attitude to women over whose lives medical practitioners were taking greater and greater control. The parallels between the sufferings of women and those of animals was pronounced in Cobbe's writings, as she commented on medical experimentation and on the ways in which the needs of the patient are sacrificed to the doctor's desire to acquire either knowledge or manipulative skills.[45]

Like a number of mid twentieth-century feminists, Cobbe saw the medical profession as playing a major role in women's oppression. The Medical Council and the medical press in her view illustrated the growing arrogance of the profession. But even on the level of daily life, 'as medical officers in parishes and unions, factory and prison surgeons, public vaccinators, medical officers of health, inspectors of nuisances, and very commonly as coroners, the doctors are daily assuming authority which, at first, perhaps, legitimate and beneficial, has a prevailing tendency to become meddling and despotic'.[46] Cobbe regarded prevailing medical views about women, which saw them as constantly liable to ill-health, and defined female functioning as pathological, as false and self-serving. She was quite unable to accept that the rational deity in whom she believed could have 'designed a whole sex of Patients'.[47] She noted, with some sarcasm, that it was mainly middle-class women who were deemed to be victims of female valetudinarianism, women who have never been in want, nor suffered exposure to hardship or toil.[48] For this very reason, they were all able to pay the physicians who attended them handsomely. She wondered whether women would receive quite as much medical attention if England adopted the old Chinese custom whereby patients paid a salary so long as they were in health and ceased to pay when they were ill![49]

Cobbe's most powerful and effective writing on the situation of women, 'Wife Torture in England', brought together the issues involved in her writings on anti-vivisection and on the medical profession with her long-standing concern about the sufferings of married women.[50]

Written in the 1870s, when she was deeply engaged in the question of vivisection, 'Wife Torture', as Fanny Kemble noted, shifted Cobbe's attention away from other animals to write about the torture men inflicted on 'those dumb animals, their wives'.[51] The focus on the merits of celibacy and the avenues open to single women, evident in Cobbe's writings in the early 1860s, gave way to a more intense concern with their physical health and well-being in the late 1870s. 'Wife Torture in England' exemplifies this shift. Written when Cobbe was in the midst of the anti-vivisection campaign, it contains the fullest expression of her sense of the ultimate victimization of women. The problem, as Cobbe points out, is one not confined to the private realm of the home: individual acts of cruel behaviour were condoned and even encouraged by the wide-spread acceptance of domestic violence in society and in English culture generally. The popularity of Punch and Judy shows, as of *The Taming of the Shrew*, were of a piece with the fact that any mention of wife-beating tends 'to conduce rather than otherwise to the hilarity of a dinner party'. It was this general framework which allowed the further development of the aggravated or brutal assaults with which Cobbe was particularly concerned. She noted that some 1,500 of these cases in which women were not only beaten, but also kicked, burnt, blinded and maimed, came to the attention of the courts each year, and estimated that this made up about one-third of the total in number of cases.

On the basis of court records, Cobbe designated certain areas as the 'kicking districts'. These were usually ones with high population density, over-crowded housing and uncertain wages. She saw this behaviour as being closely linked to such living conditions and to drunkenness – especially that caused by adulterated drinks which 'literally sting the wretched drinkers into cruelty'. She saw the behaviour itself, and more especially the tolerance of it by successive governments, as being a direct result of women's lack of political rights, but she sought, as a remedy, the reform of the Matrimonial Causes Act so that such violence was accepted as grounds for granting to women a separation. Cobbe was one of the few people who, after taking up this question, rejected the flogging of the male perpetrators of such violence as a solution. The existence of such punishments would act as an additional disincentive to the women concerned to give testimony against their husbands. What they needed was to be released from the power of these men by being granted judicial separation. The impact of this article in terms of the immediate legal change brought by the Matrimonial Causes Act of 1878 has recently been questioned by James Hammerton, but, at the same time, he stresses the importance of Cobbe's writing in shifting the emphasis in discussion of wife-abuse away from a concern with punishment and reconciliation and towards her own feminist concern with the need for protection and financial independence for women.[52]

In choosing to focus on Martineau and Cobbe, I have looked at perhaps the two most successful women of letters in the nineteenth century. Both were widely published and very well known to editors and readers. Both women worked to establish their place by claiming expertise in a number of different areas extending across economics, religion, political developments and morality. Their claims were ones which were still acceptable in the second half of the nineteenth century, in the years before university degrees and specific professional status were requirements for anyone seeking to make public pronouncements. In their published writings, both Martineau and Cobbe entered into debate about many different issues, managing often to bring their concerns about the status of women to bear on a very broad range of social questions. Martineau and Cobbe were only two of the many women who published their ideas in the periodical press, and who made their ideas on the status of women a central part of public debate. It was not until the 1920s that feminists began explicitly to argue that their main task, once the vote was won, was that of changing the ways in which women were discussed and represented in literature and culture – but in their own individual ways, many nineteenth-century women used journalism and their access to the periodical press to shift the framework of discussion about women and to make women's voices a significant part of public culture.

NOTES

1 Mary Poovey, *The Proper Lady and the Woman Writer* (University of Chicago Press, 1984); Judith Johnston, *Anna Jameson: Victorian Feminist, Woman of Letters* (Aldershot: Ashgate, 1997) pp. 8–15.

2 See e.g. Jane Lewis, ed., *Before the Vote was Won: Arguments for and Against Women's Suffrage* (London: Routledge, 1987); Candida Lacey, *Barbara Bodichon and the Langham Place Group* (London: Routledge, 1987).

3 Frances Power Cobbe (1822–1904), *The Life of Frances Power Cobbe*, 2 vols. (London, 1894).

4 Wollstonecraft's writings have now been collected and run to nine volumes. See Janet Todd and Marilyn Butler, eds., *The Works of Mary Wollstonecraft* (London: Pickering and Chatto, 1989).

5 Harriet Martineau (1802–76). See Gillian Thomas, *Harriet Martineau*, (Boston: Twayne, 1980); Deirdre David, *Intellectual Women and Victorian*

Patriarchy: Harriet Martineau, Elizabeth Barrett Browning, George Eliot (London: Macmillan, 1987); Susan Hoecker-Drysdale, *Harriet Martineau: First Woman Sociologist* (Oxford and New York: Berg, 1992); Valerie K. Pichanick, *Harriet Martineau: the Woman and Her Work, 1802–76* (Ann Arbor: University of Michigan Press, 1980); and Gayle Yates, ed., *Harriet Martineau on Women* (New Brunswick, NJ: Rutgers University Press, 1985), Florence Fenwick-Miller, *Harriet Martineau* (Boston: Roberts Brothers, 1885), pp. 50–5.

6 Millicent Garrett Fawcett (1847–1929). For biographical details, see Millicent Fawcett, *What I Remember* (London: T. Fisher Unwin, 1925; rptd. Westport, CN, 1976); Ray Strachey, *Millicent Garrett Fawcett* (London: John Murray, 1931); David Rubinstein, *A Different World for Women: the Life of Millicent Garrett Fawcett* (London: Harvester Wheatsheaf, 1991); Barbara Caine, *Victorian Feminists* (Oxford University Press, 1992).

7 Josephine Elizabeth Butler (1828–1906). There is no recent biography of Butler. The fullest accounts of her life are still to be found in *Josephine E. Butler, An Autobiographical Memoir*, ed. G. Johnson and L. Johnson (Bristol: J. W. Arrowsmith, 1909) and A. S. G. Butler, *Portrait of Josephine Butler* (London: Faber, 1954). See also Judith Walkowitz, *Prostitution and Victorian Society: Women, Class and the State* (Cambridge University Press, 1980), and Caine, *Victorian Feminists*.

8 See Josephine E. Butler, *The Education and Employment of Women* (London: Macmillan, 1868); Butler ed., *Woman's Work and Woman's Culture* (London: Macmillan, 1869); *Personal Reminiscences of A Great Crusade* (London: H. Marshall and Son, 1896); *The Native Races and the War* (London: Gay and Bird, 1900).

9 See Pauline Nestor, 'A New Departure in Women's Publishing: the *English Woman's Journal* and *The Victoria Magazine*', *Victorian Periodicals Newsletter* 15 (1982), pp. 93–106; Sheila Herstein, 'The Langham Place Circle and Feminist Periodicals of the 1860s', *Victorian Periodicals Newsletter* 26 (1993), pp. 24–7; Philippa Levine, '"The Humanising Influence of Five o'clock Tea": Victorian Feminist Periodicals', *Victorian Studies* 33 (1990), pp. 293–306.

10 George Eliot to Bessie Parkes, 1 September 1857, in *The George Eliot Letters*, ed. Gordon S. Haight, 9 vols. (New Haven: Yale University Press, 1954–79), vol. II, p. 379.

11 See Levine, 'The Humanising Influence', p. 299.

12 See also Andrea Broomfield, 'Towards a more Tolerant Society: *Macmillan's Magazine* and the Women's Suffrage Question', *Victorian Periodicals Review* 23, (1990), pp. 120–6.

13 Pam Hirsch, *Barbara Leigh Smith Bodichon 1827–1898: Feminist, Artist and Rebel* (London: Chatto and Windus, 1998), pp. 184–206.

14 Bessie Rayner Parkes indicates the importance of these issues in her *Essays on Woman's Work* (London, 1865), pp. 55–62.

15 See Nana Rinehardt, '"The Girl of the Period" Controversy', *Victorian Periodicals Review* 13 (1980), pp. 3–9. See also Valerie Sanders, *Eve's Renegades: Victorian Anti-feminist Women Novelists* (Basingstoke: Macmillan, 1996).

16 See Brian Harrison, *Separate Spheres: The Opposition to Women's Suffrage in Britain* (London: Croom Helm, 1978), pp. 116–19 and Millicent Garrett Fawcett, 'The Appeal against Female Suffrage: a Reply', *The Nineteenth Century* 26 (1889), pp. 86–96.

17 Kathryn Gleadle, *The Early Feminists: Radical Unitarians and the Emergence of the Women's Rights Movements, 1831–1851* (London: Macmillan, 1995); Barbara Caine, *English Feminism* (Oxford University Press, 1996), pp. 57–65.

18 Barbara Taylor, *Eve and the New Jerusalem: Socialism and Feminism in the Nineteenth Century* (London: Virago, 1983).

19 Ibid., pp. 89–95.

20 Frances E. Mineka, *The Dissidence of Dissent: the Monthly Repository, 1806–1838* (New York: Octagon Books, 1972), pp. 195–200.

21 Mrs Leman Grimstone, 'Quaker Women', *Monthly Repository* n.s. 9 (1835), pp. 31–3.

22 Hoecker-Drysdale, *Harriet Martineau*, p. 31.

23 Bette Polkinghorn, 'Jane Marcet and Harriet Martineau: Motive, Market Experience and Reception of their Works popularizing Political Economy', in Mary Ann Dimand, Robert W. Dimand and Evelyn L. Forget, eds., *Women of Value: Feminist Essays on the History of Women in Economics* (Aldershot: Ashgate, 1995), p. 77.

24 Pichanick, *Martineau: the Woman and her Work*, pp. 46–71

25 Alfred Marshall, 'The Old Generation of Economists and the New', *Quarterly Journal of Economics* (January 1897), p. 117.

26 Polkinghorn, 'Jane Marcet and Harriet Martineau', see n. 23. Bette Polkinghorn and Dorothy Lampen Thompson, *Adam Smith's Daughters: Eight Prominent Women Economists from the Eighteenth Century to the Present* (Cheltenham: Edward Elgar, 1998).

27 David, *Intellectual Women*, p. 43.

28 Harriet Martineau, 'Political Non-Existence of Women', in *Society in America* 3 vols. (London, 1837), vol. 1, p. 3.

29 Martineau, *Society in America*, vol 1, p. 200.

30 Ibid., p. 202.

31 Ibid., p. 207.

32 Harriet Martineau, 'Female Industry', *Edinburgh Review* 109 (1859), pp. 293–336.

33 Ibid., p. 297.

34 Ibid., p. 300.

35 Ibid., p. 301.

36 Ibid., p. 329.

37 Harriet Martineau, letter to the *Daily News*, 28 December 1869, rptd in Yates, ed., *Harriet Martineau on Women*, pp. 252–6.

38 Frances Power Cobbe, *Theory of Intuitive Morals* (London, 1885).

39 Cobbe, *Life*, vol. 1, pp. 97–8.

40 Theodore Parker, *Discourse on Religion*, in *The Collected Works of Theodore Parker*, ed. Frances Power Cobbe (London, 1863), vol. 1, p. 306.

41 Frances Power Cobbe, *A Faithless World* (London, 1885), p. 6.

42 See the letter from James Martineau to Cobbe in the Frances Power Cobbe Papers, Huntington Library, Los Angeles.

43 France Power Cobbe, 'Progressive Judaism', in her *The Scientific Spirit of the Age and other Pleas and Discussions* (London, 1888), p. 88.

44 Frances Power Cobbe, *Studies New and Old on Ethical and Social Subjects* (London, 1865), p. 24.

45 F. P. Cobbe, 'The Medical Profession and its Morality', *Modern Review* 2 (1881), pp. 310–12.

46 Ibid., p. 297.

47 F. P. Cobbe, 'The Little Health of Ladies', *Contemporary Review* 31 (1878), p. 278.

48 Ibid., pp. 278–9.

49 Ibid., p. 294.

50 'Wife Torture in England', *Contemporary Review* 23 (1878), pp. 56–87.

51 Frances Anne Kemble, *Further Records 1848–1883* (London: R. Bentley, 1890), p. 80.

52 A. James Hammerton, *Cruelty and Companionship: Conflict in Nineteenth-Century Married Life* (London: Routledge, 1992) pp. 62–5.

CHAPTER SIX

Women's writing and the domestic sphere

Elizabeth Langland

In the nineteenth century, middle-class women were writing both within the domestic sphere and about it, shaping through their representations the context that was simultaneously enabling and disabling their own literary efforts. Although their working-class sisters still lacked the leisure and resources that could support sustained literary efforts, bourgeois women enjoyed increasing access to the conditions and means supporting writing and publication. Indeed, writing, along with teaching, presented itself as one of the very few ways to earn money for a respectable woman. Exigency, as well as talent, led many to pick up a pen, and, although they may have chafed at forces that continued to hamper their efforts, they challenged the odds and produced wonderful literature.

If we glance ahead to the early twentieth century to take a retrospective view of the preceding century, we recognize in Virginia Woolf's violent response to that avatar of the home, the 'Angel in the House', forces that threatened to cripple a creative writer's talents.[1] The woman writer suffered not only from a lack of privacy and insufficient time for concentration; at the same time her efforts were hampered by an expectation that the household Angel, the middle-class wife and mother, would sublimate all of her needs and desires in the well-being of her family. Woolf claims she had to kill her domestic predecessor to prevent her from stifling her creative energies: 'My excuse, if I were to be had up in a court of law, would be that I acted in self-defense. Had I not killed her she would have killed me. She would have plucked the heart out of my writing.'[2] For Woolf, the Angel flourished through her self-sacrifice for others: 'she never had a mind or a wish of her own' (p. 1385). But writing demands, pre-eminently, 'having a mind of your own'. For Woolf, that mind of her own could flourish only upon the foundation of 500 pounds a year and a private room.

Despite the fact that most middle-class women lacked the proverbial 'room of one's own' that enabled Woolf's fiction, many wrested an advantage from their situation through dint of sheer determination. The social nexus that structured their existence encouraged 'all the literary training that a woman had in the early nineteenth-century . . . training in the observation of character, in the analysis of emotion'.[3] And, despite the unquestioned difficulties, nineteenth-century women at home began writing prolifically. Jane Austen helped usher in the nineteenth century. She was, to Virginia Woolf, a kind of *lusus naturae*, whose literary gifts were perfectly matched to her constricted circumstances. The compatibility Jane Austen felt with her conditions, 'glad that a hinge creaked, so that she might hide her manuscript before any one came in' (p. 70), was not enjoyed by most of her successors, especially if they were wives with children and large households to manage.

Of course, it wasn't simply the burden of time that compromised aesthetic efforts but the weight of convention. On the brink of her career as a novelist, Charlotte Brontë solicited support from England's poet laureate, Robert Southey. His reply, which he referred to elsewhere as a 'cooling admonition', was characteristically disheartening, and, in answering his letter, Brontë reveals the conflicts it provoked:

You do not forbid me to write . . . You only warn me against the folly of neglecting real duties, for the sake of imaginative pleasure . . . I have endeavored not only attentively to observe all the duties a woman ought to fulfil, but to feel deeply interested in them. I don't always succeed, for sometimes when I'm teaching or sewing I would rather be reading or writing; but I try to deny myself.[4]

Elizabeth Gaskell and Margaret Oliphant, who both spoke eloquently about the multiple challenges facing them, were more typical of women writing within the domestic sphere while faced with myriad responsibilities for husbands, children and complex households. Gaskell professed to flourish as a housekeeper. In an early letter to Eliza Fox, she confesses her guilty delight in getting a house: compunction that so many people could not afford one, joy in the context it provided for her varied talents.[5] She represents her literary talents as stimulated by the household maelstrom, and her letters brim over with domestic details. Writing to her close friend Charles Eliot Norton, Gaskell depicts the close imbrication of household concerns with her literary aspirations. Ostensibly bemoaning her situation and its limitations, the buoyant, energetic tone belies her complaints:

I am sitting at the round writing table in the dining-room . . . If I had a library like yours, all undisturbed for hours, how I would write! Mrs Chapone's letters should be nothing to mine! I would outdo Rasselas in fiction. But you see every body comes to me perpetually. Now in this hour since breakfast I have had to decide on the following variety of important questions. Boiled beef – how long to boil? What perennials will do in Manchester smoke, & what colours our garden wants? Length of skirt for a gown? Salary of a nursery governess, & stipulations for a certain quantity of time to be left to herself. – Read letters on the state of Indian army – lent me by a very agreeable neighbour & and return them, with a proper note, & as many wise remarks as would come in a hurry. Settle 20 questions of dress for the girls . . . See a lady about an MS story of hers, & give her disheartening but very good advice. Arrange about selling two poor cows for one good one, – see purchasers, & show myself up to cattle questions, keep, & prices, – and it's not $\frac{1}{2}$ past yet! (*Letters* pp. 487–90)

Gaskell's role as household manager and her competence within that sphere lead seamlessly into comments about her literary efforts and success. Just how the two levels of activity can inform each other will become clearer when we turn later in this essay to the novels themselves.

Even writers who shared Gaskell's talent for organization often found themselves less happily situated within their households. Margaret Oliphant, for example, throughout much of her life was the primary breadwinner for her extended family: husband, children, mother, brothers, nieces and nephews. The pressures she faced struggling to produce an adequate income to support her establishment led her to adopt a more pragmatic tone. She claimed, 'I have written because it gave me pleasure, because it came natural to me, because it was like talking or breathing, besides the big fact that it was necessary for me to work for my children.'[6] In an oft-cited passage of her *Autobiography*, Oliphant imagines that George Eliot was kept 'in a mental greenhouse' (p. 5), a protected and nurturing context, in contrast to herself, who 'always had to think of other people, and to plan everything . . . To keep [her] household and make a number of people comfortable, at the cost of incessant work' (pp. 6–7). She, like Jane Austen, wrote in the family drawing room 'where all the (feminine) life of the house [went] on'; she doubted that she 'ever had two hours undisturbed (except at night, when everybody [was] in bed) during [her] whole literary life' (p. 24). Of course, as Virginia Woolf reminds us, even those writers in mental greenhouses could not easily banish the distractions of social expectations and convention. George Eliot was spared the exertions of running a large household, but her famous need to be sheltered from adverse reviews of her novels and her repeated protestations that writing functioned for her as a solemn moral duty reveal the 'mind-forged manacles' women writers strove daily to unlock.

The juxtaposition of George Eliot and Margaret Oliphant raises questions of their work's literary value, questions implicit in Oliphant's musings about Eliot's mental greenhouse. These queries also connect, I would argue, to the domestic sphere and its representation in their novels. Eliot's heroines chafe against the meaninglessness and restrictions of their lady's life; Oliphant's relish their command of local society and politics. In brief, the social and domestic conventions that structure the lives of middle-class and upper-middle-class women are represented differently in the novels of these two contemporaries. Eliot finds nothing but *ennui* and emptiness in the morning calls, afternoon teas, and dinner parties, in the highly structured routines of social introductions and cuts, in the elaborate conventions of dress. Oliphant locates in this complex semiotics of social life a route to political influence and control. It is this contrast between different representations and evaluations that is one of the most interesting features of our understanding of Victorian social life as we begin the twenty-first century. And it is here I locate the crux of this essay.

An analysis of this phenomenon asks that we look closely at three aspects of Victorian life: the social practices that controlled rhythms of the domestic sphere, the novels that represented domestic life, and the evaluations that have informed our appreciation of Victorian domestic fiction.

MIDDLE-CLASS DOMESTICITY IN NINETEENTH-CENTURY ENGLAND

Nineteenth-century middle-class women inhabited a world that became increasingly structured by the rhythms and routines of elaborate practices of etiquette. By the 1830s what had been a trickle of volumes addressing appropriate social decorum became a flood. In specifying the practices of middle-class life, these volumes, together with household management guides, architectural directories and philanthropic tracts, constituted what we may call a 'discourse' of domesticity. That is, they not only laid out its signifying practices but regulated who had authority, where, under what conditions, and within which social relationships. In short, we cannot regard these discursive practices as the negligible ephemera of Victorian culture as they have often been seen. They established power networks, enfranchising some, disenfranchising others. In England, they were a central mechanism for regulating class. Pierre Bourdieu's distinctions between economic and social capital help to reveal their significance. For Bourdieu, economic capital, the form of capital we recognize, manifest in money, property, possessions, constitutes only one way through which value is ascribed in an economy. Social prestige and prominence constitute another form of capital through which value accrues to its possessors.[7]

In Victorian England, through manipulating social signifying practices, middle-class women were capable of producing a corollary or complementary value to a man's income, a social capital. In fact, the house and its mistress served as a significant adjunct to a man's commercial endeavours. Whereas men earned the money, women had the important task of managing those funds towards the acquisition of social and political status.[8]

Although the nineteenth-century domestic novel often presented the household as a moral haven secure from economic and political storms, alongside this figuration one may discern another process at work: the active management of class power. The persistent myth of idle women in the home, isolated from industrial strife and class conflict and unriven by class contradiction, testifies to the power of domestic ideology and familial values that persist stubbornly today. Of course, by employing domestic servants, Victorians were introducing class issues directly into the home and setting up the home as a site for all the conflicts between labour and management that afflicted the nineteenth century generally. That they and others have refused to recognize this phenomenon testifies to effective management of conflicts within a regulatory system that reinterpreted domestic labour as 'help'.

The signifying practices of middle-class life through which domestic power was consolidated were spelled out in Victorian etiquette manuals, management guides and charitable treatises. Although these documents cannot be taken as straightforward accounts of middle-class life and cannot be read as reflecting a 'real' historical subject, their representations of middle-class life contributed to the public's understanding of what that life should be.[9]

THE PRACTICES OF MIDDLE-CLASS LIFE

Leonore Davidoff has commented that 'in the 1830s and 1840s there was a reinterpretation of the idea of Society and the expectation for individual behaviour to gain access to that society', an expectation whose historical origins stem, in part, from the presence in England of the untitled gentry. 'Tied to the nobility by marriage and similar life-styles' and to the farmers and middle-classes 'by family ties and farming interests', the untitled gentry played a crucial role in the English social hierarchy.[10] Lawrence and Jeanne Stone identify an 'aristocratic bourgeoisie' produced by this process of 'gentrification', a group who 'adopted genteel cultural patterns of behaviour' without following the economic and political practices of the upper class such as purchasing a country seat and agricultural estate. Although there were no 'legal barriers based on privilege', this genteel society 'was sliced and sliced again to extremely thin status layers, subtly separated from each other by the delicate but infinitely resistant lines of snobbery'.[11] Davidoff articulates the consequences more tellingly for our understanding of women's roles. Because 'formalised Society took the place of mobility controlled through legal classification', individuals sought stability in detailed decorums, which were in the hands of women.[12] Generally, with the rapid increase of wealth generated by the Industrial Revolution and the consequent social upheavals, status became a fluid thing, increasingly dependent upon the manipulation of social signs. This process, well under way in the eighteenth century, accelerated in the nineteenth.

Significantly, the etiquette books that detailed appropriate social behaviour were neither a continuing feature from eighteenth-century life nor a continuous aspect of the nineteenth century. In his study of this genre, Michael Curtin has discovered that no conduct manuals were published between 1804 and 1828. Suddenly in the 1830s, numerous new volumes found print. The rise in etiquette guides thus coincides with a period in British life inaugurated by the Reform Bill, a period marked by a drive to represent new forces in British politics and economics and a compensatory desire to stabilize the system along predictable lines. In 1837, the *Quarterly* reviewed eleven etiquette books, all published within the previous two years, some in several editions.[13] These guides, which highlighted the way 'social status could be indicated through a minute control of conventional behaviour', differed substantially from the earlier courtesy or conduct books.[14] The latter focussed on individual standards of moral and civil conduct and had as topics 'fortitude', 'honesty', 'fidelity', and so on – in sharp contrast to the etiquette manuals' chapters on 'balls', 'introductions and cuts', 'calls', and the like.[15] Whereas the conduct books were aimed at individual behaviour, the etiquette guides targeted the construction and consolidation of a social group.

Many of these etiquette guides were published anonymously, under such pseudonyms as 'A Lady' or 'Mentor', but the majority of writers, who were principally women, were only too glad to claim authorship.

These guides provided an avenue to publication for the obvious and established authorities on the subject: women within the domestic sphere. As the century advanced, the etiquette texts were joined in their tutelary functions by household management manuals and charitable treatises, also from the hands of women. One of the most famous, which went through several editions, is Isabella Beeton's *Book of Household Management* (1861), which sold 60,000 copies in its first year.[16]

It was not solely the opportunity to publish that made writing such a guide or manual attractive; publication was yoked with an affirmation of the social importance of one's domestic role. The manuals were precise and detailed, giving exact information, particularly on the most sensitive areas governed by etiquette: introductions, calls and cuts. The first two were mechanisms for defining and maintaining the group; the last was the mechanism for excluding undesirable individuals. Because of their central functions, all became highly elaborated.[17] A system so fully developed – specifying the way cards were to be left, the official timetable for visiting, the duration and content of calls – obviously plays a significant role in establishing and solidifying the Victorian hierarchy. *A Manual of Etiquette for Ladies* set an appropriately lofty tone in summarizing etiquette's function as establishing the 'rule of conduct which is recognized by polite society . . . that law to which obedience must be rendered; the sovereign to which authority and allegiance are due'.[18] Even if we are inclined to be sceptical about the possibility of persons observing such rules in daily life, the very popularity of the etiquette manuals reveals a pervasive awareness of and commitment to the class distinctions they create and reinforce.

The 'call', with its elaborated rituals, became the mechanism by which social groups were formed and consolidated. Because the custom of calling functioned to define and solidify a social group, women faced a heavy burden of maintaining acquaintance through visiting.[19] Such visits of ceremony, notes *Etiquette for Ladies*, are 'usually made in the morning – that is, before one o'clock'.[20] The student of etiquette would find elucidation in *How to Behave*: 'morning, in fashionable parlance, means any time before dinner'.[21] Ladies unable to receive visitors would have their servants announce that they were 'not at home', a message decoded in *Etiquette for Ladies and Gentlemen*: 'These last words are not, as they are sometimes thought, a falsehood, for everyone knows they merely mean you are engaged and cannot see visitors.'[22] The elaborate encodings of meanings speak eloquently of the privileged and privileging nature of this discourse.

The formulaic and ritualistic nature of the call enabled women constantly to police and maintain their social borders. In Oliphant's *Phoebe,*
Junior, a young lady gloats to her brother: 'Men may think themselves as
grand as they please . . . but their visits are of no consequence; it is ladies
of the family who must *call*.'[23] If calling conventions did not adequately
perform their policing function, the 'cut' was held in reserve. *Etiquette for
the Ladies* opines that it is 'almost unnecessary to hint that the introductions which are made at public balls and assemblies are for the night only.
It is strictly in Etiquette for a lady to cut even a nobleman on the
morrow.'[24] Like the call, the cut was almost entirely in the hands of
socially prominent women. It marked a refusal to recognize an individual as part of one's set and was carried out through various mechanisms:
not responding to a salutation, a bow, a card or a call; not answering a
letter or an invitation.

Our tendency in the past has been to read these often mind-numbing
rituals as empty and tedious, a sign of how bourgeois women wasted
their lives within the domestic sphere when they were not appropriately
engaged with their families. Florence Nightingale testifies passionately
in *Cassandra* to how women suffered from the rituals of etiquette, social
corsets as rigid as the physical corsets confining their bodies.[25] In
Charlotte Brontë's *Shirley,* Caroline Helstone memorably experiences
the social expectations laid upon her as a kind of 'brain lethargy.'[26] But
to take these attitudes as a measure of the whole cloth is to miss the
authority women were achieving in the home. Not only as managers of
their social capital but also as managers of their servants, they were professionalizing housekeeping and developing skills that would ultimately
lead their daughters and grand-daughters out of their homes and into
the workforce by the end of the century.

Middle-class women in the home were pursuing a 'career of sociabil-
ity',[27] the necessary complement to a man's career of monetarily remu-
nerated work. These were not separate, but integrated and integral
careers. Indeed, the celebrated domesticity of nineteenth-century
women tends to conceal the increasing domesticity of men, the expectation that a master would socialize at home in the evenings so that a
couple could develop and cultivate mutual acquaintances within their
social class.[28]

John Stuart Mill describes this phenomenon in *The Subjection of Women*:
'The improved tone of modern feeling as to the reciprocity of duty which
binds the husband towards his wife – has thrown the man very much more
upon home and its inmates, for his personal and social pleasures.'[29] What

I have described as a social career to match a monetary career is here represented by the phrase 'reciprocity of duty', which in its very generality disguises the pragmatic aspects of the relationship as affective bonds.

At the same time that the bourgeois woman was managing the family's social position within the middle classes through mastering the infinitely varied and precise signs of social status, so too was she helping to demarcate the distance between working and middle classes. A wife was, in Isabella Beeton's words, like 'the commander of an army' overseeing the smooth functioning of this demanding establishment; she was a specialist in 'Household Management' (always capitalized). Beeton speaks forcefully of 'proper management' and 'daily regulation', admitting that 'the performance of the duties of a mistress may, to some minds, perhaps seem to be incompatible with the enjoyment of life' (1–2). The mistress is cautioned to remember that she is 'the Alpha and the Omega in the government of her establishment, and that it is by her conduct that its whole internal policy is regulated' (18).

Beeton underscores only what is generally accepted in the etiquette guides and household manuals, but often mystified in novels, tracts and sermons: a mistress's key management role. *The Domestic Oracle*, a conduct book, anticipates the later etiquette manuals in sounding a cautionary note: 'Every mistress of a family ought to be convinced that every thing depends on her vigilance and studious care in the superintendence of her household.'[30] It is, of course, possible to read this description and argue that women have always been urged to define their work as 'superintendence of the household', the fine-sounding phrase masking the tedium of their menial, repetitive chores. But the Victorian age, historically distinctive in the numbers and availability of domestic servants, meant something quite different from our contemporary notions of 'homemaking'. The words they chose – management, governance, superintendence, generalship – emphasize that difference.

A bourgeois wife decided upon the household help required, drew up job descriptions, advertised, interviewed, hired, supervised, paid and fired. *Cassell's Book of the Household* underscores the importance of a mistress's superintendence:

Capable servants are produced by capable mistresses, who understand how work should be done, and insist upon it being properly done; who know when it is well done, what difficulties there are arising out of the special circumstances of the case, and how much time may reasonably be spent upon the due performance of the task; and who also make it evident that they are satisfied and pleased when the work is creditably accomplished.[31]

Such an analysis could be readily adapted to describe a successful master at a Victorian factory.[32] Mrs Henry Reeve's summation in 1893 could easily apply to both settings: 'In every household there must be the hands to do the work, the head to guide and to control the workers.'[33] The metonyms of 'hands' and 'heads' configure working class and bourgeoisie in harmony and mutual benefit within a healthy body politic.

The importance of a wife's management skills is glaringly evident in the monetary losses a family could sustain if she were inefficient and careless. Clever servants could cheat a family out of hundreds of pounds in the course of a year, especially if a housewife were lax enough to allow them to take payment in goods or covert commissions in lieu of or in addition to wages. Called 'perquisites', these extras ranged from taking a percentage from the tradesmen with whom the family did business to appropriating wax candle-ends, left-off garments, trimmings and trifles, and left-over food.[34] In the course of a year, these items 'amounted to a considerable value', and were 'the fruitful cause of extravagance and dishonesty'. The obvious consequence of system of perquisites was that 'the more wasteful the habits of the family, the more the servants gained; and it was to the interest of the servants that the master should suffer loss' (p. 158).

This understanding of the economy of a middle-class establishment – encompassing a man's salary and its application – enables us to appreciate the short step it became for women from management in the private sphere to management in the public realm. Florence Nightingale, for example, patterned the nursing profession on 'a wholly familiar model of female domestic management.'[35] However, mystifications of the household and household labour work against our recognizing the middle-class managerial woman.

QUEEN VICTORIA AND THE DOMESTIC SPHERE

It is illuminating to glance briefly at Queen Victoria's place in these emerging discourses of domesticity. The virginal young queen embodied a dramatic change from her predecessors, and she was readily seized upon as an icon of emergent bourgeois values. Writing in 1937 on the centenary of Victoria's accession to the throne, G. M. Young remarked of the period that the 'transference of the Crown from an elderly, undignified, and slightly crazy sailor to a girl endowed with remarkable self-possession and much force of character, could hardly be without its picturesque circumstances.' For him, it represented a 'waft of Arcadia'.[36]

On the one hand, as England's ruler, Victoria inhabited a sphere totally separate from that of the ordinary middle-class housewife. On the other hand, she and her public were busily representing and interpreting her as the embodiment of middle-class values. In her reliance on her husband Prince Albert and her professed inaptitude for public rule, Victoria presented herself through a screen of domestic virtues emphasizing home, hearth and heart. Associations of conventional propriety and familial devotion accumulated around Victoria despite the fact that, as Dorothy Thompson points out, 'if the stereotypical Victorian woman was well-mannered, self-effacing, demure and devoid of passion, Queen Victoria was so far from the stereotype as to be almost its opposite.'[37] Indeed, Victoria is memorable for her distress at repeatedly bearing children; she described herself as 'furious' when she learned of her first pregnancy, complained that an 'ugly baby is a very nasty object', and always expressed distaste for 'that terrible frog-like action' of newborns.[38] Albert, more maternal, was continually admonishing the Queen to be more of a mother and less of a monarch with her nine children. But the public conferred upon Victoria an image of itself that confirmed both the emergence and the importance of middle-class domesticity. That self-portrait was facilitated by the 'diffusion of cheap printed words and pictures [that brought] the image of the monarch and her family regularly into the consciousness of her subjects' (Thompson, *Queen Victoria*, p. 139). In 1867 Walter Bagehot summarized the effect of familiarizing the populace with a wifely and maternal Victoria: 'A *family* on the throne is an interesting idea. It brings down the pride of sovereignty to the level of petty life.'[39] Albert's death in 1861 further solidified Victoria's bourgeois image because she 'refused ever again to wear the robes of state, appearing in versions of widow's weeds' (*Queen Victoria*, p. 141).

That Victoria should, nonetheless, without disabling or disqualifying self-contradiction, take her place as head of the most powerful country in the world bespeaks her signal role in the construction of a new feminine ideal that endorsed active public management behind a façade of private retirement.

WOMEN WRITERS AND REPRESENTATIONS OF THE DOMESTIC SPHERE

The nonliterary domestic discourses we have just examined, such as etiquette guides and household manuals, tend to emphasize the bourgeois household manager more consistently than do literary representations, perhaps because the former carry the burden of explicitly addressing class issues, of at least acknowledging that middle-class life depends upon successful management of a servant class. Literary works – particularly domestic novels directed at middle-class audiences – have the luxury of ignoring or obscuring that fact, often burying it in the romance plot of boy meets girl, boy wins girl, boy marries girl.

It is to women writers and their representations of the domestic sphere that we will now turn both to highlight the tensions inhering in those depictions and to lay a groundwork for questions of value we will take up in conclusion.

Two writers, Elizabeth Gaskell and Margaret Oliphant, wrote novels that usefully amplify our understanding of women writers and the domestic sphere. Gaskell, as we saw earlier, conceived herself as a household manager whose managerial reach extended to the construction of narrative. Damned with faint praise by Henry James, who remarks the dependence of her art on 'modest domestic facts', Gaskell has represented precisely how realities are constructed out of quotidian 'feminine' details, a significance that has escaped many readers in addition to James. In this regard, Elizabeth Gaskell declares literary allegiance with Sarah Ellis, who was emboldened to write *The Women of England* by her conviction that the 'apparently insignificant detail of familiar and ordinary life' bears out the 'often-repeated truth – that "trifles make the sum of human things."'[40] True though it may be, the notion continues to meet stubborn resistance. In her book on the subject, Naomi Schor helps to explain the detail '*as negativity*' because it participates in a 'larger semantic network, bounded on the one side by the *ornamental*, with its traditional connotations of effeminacy and decadence, and on the other, by the everyday, whose "prosiness" is rooted in the domestic sphere of social life presided over by women.'[41] In short, 'the detail is gendered and doubly gendered as feminine' (p. 4). Gaskell is working to disrupt the ideological script that encodes the detail as trivial because of its association with the feminine. Her narrative procedures anticipate the conclusions of Michel Foucault, who recognizes behind 'minute material details' the presence of '"alien strategies" of power and knowledge'.[42]

Gaskell's *Cranford* and *Wives and Daughters* both highlight the tensions inhering in representations of women and the domestic sphere. The former depicts what are ostensibly 'old maids' and elderly ladies clinging to a dying way of life; the latter presents a particularly unpleasant household manager. *Cranford* the novel and Cranford the place are, quite simply, worlds structured by women's signifying systems: calling and visiting, teas and dinners, domestic economies, charitable activities and management of servants. Cranford, with its cultural capital, contrasts explicitly with the neighbouring city of Drumble, a world marked by expanding capital based on factories and production, money and investments. The former appears at first glance to be stagnant, even moribund. The ageing spinsters and childless widows who populate the town must eventually die. Given our conventional understanding that such lives are empty and trivial, the novel should tell a gloomy tale. Or, if it instead strikes a jocular note, it seems it must do so at the expense of the ladies. Yet those who know the novel can attest that its author finds its subjects neither risible nor morbid. They are, however, humorous, with a humour that arises from the fullness of meaning invested in the smallest details of daily life. *Cranford* brims over with engaged life; everything matters intensely because meanings are fluid, emerging moment by moment, producing valuable social capital for the ladies who are society's semioticians. The only cynic in the book, Mary Smith's father, represents the commercial world of Drumble, and the economic capital he stands for seems curiously unproductive and vulnerable. In short, the customary values have been reversed; his economic caution culminates in his exploitation, their social proliferations produce economic capital.

What the women term 'elegant' economy contrasts with the customary getting-and-spending one. 'Elegant' alludes to what we might now call renewable resources. Instead of the conspicuous consumption and waste of a 'vulgar' economy, the 'elegant' economy bases itself on recycling: old dresses, fragments of flowers, pieces of string, ends of candles, old notes and receipts. It privileges exchange over consumption: the newspaper circulating among the ladies early presages the way more substantial resources will circulate among them to protect their world, their ways, and their privilege. This Cranfordian 'elegant economy', though not productive of new material resources, is productive of substantial social capital and, therefore, calls into question the stability of currency in signifying rank. Indeed, *Cranford* points to the very instability of money as a sign of social standing; it is just one interpretable sign among many.

Gaskell's *Cranford* is written against the grain of traditional ideology that positions 'old maids' on the margins of productive activity. In its understanding of the ways in which women's discursive practices and their quotidian details constitute society and its meanings, it constructs another reality, another truth that counters that of domestic women's marginality, passivity and dependence. At the same time, *Cranford* points subtly to women's participation in the logic of class exploitation, which, in the frame of this earlier Gaskell novel, could be read positively as class synergy when, for example, Martha, the servant, ultimately bears the child that her mistress, Miss Matty, desires.

To explore class relationships that are more exploitative, I will turn to another Gaskell novel, *Wives and Daughters*, which represents a household manager, Mrs Gibson. When critics interpret Mrs. Gibson, they often dismiss her as a 'neat satire' of 'human deficiency'.[43] Laurence Lerner pinpoints in her 'little clevernesses of a mind that lacks the imagination really to understand that she has done wrong'.[44] But Gaskell's triumph of presentation, her demystification of domestic ideology, depends on simultaneously inscribing Mrs Gibson within two different scripts – the patriarchal and the bourgeois – and foregrounding their contradictions. In conventional gender terms, as wife and mother, Mrs Gibson appears insensitive and selfish. In class terms, as household and status manager, she demonstrates fine discrimination and familial loyalty. Her masterful negotiations of signifying practices – etiquette (including introductions, visiting, calls and cuts), dining rituals, household decor, and dress – make her a key player in the socially prestigious marriages of her daughter and step-daughter, marriages that install them permanently within the upper middle class and remove them from the ambiguous status of doctor's daughters and potential governesses.

At the same time that Mrs Gibson is putting her daughter and step-daughter into social circulation, she is attending to much-neglected household affairs, whipping up the entire establishment to a higher social standard, a process that begins with a renovation of household discipline. When the servants grumble about the work their new mistress demands of them, she summarily dismisses them – even Betty, Molly's nurse and surrogate mother, who has been with the family for sixteen years. We share Molly's point of view and distress over the dismissal, aggravated by the honeyed expression of Mrs Gibson's regret:

But, sweet one, you seem to forget that I cannot go against my principle [never to take an apology from a servant who has given notice], however much I may be sorry for Betty. She should not have given way to ill temper, as I said before; although I never liked her, and considered her a most inefficient servant, thoroughly spoilt by having had no mistress for so long, I should have borne with her (p. 212).

Mrs Gibson will not tolerate the kind of purposeful neglect practised by the servants when they want to 'mark their displeasure' (p. 210) with the family. Nor will she allow Molly to perform menial tasks when 'there are servants to do it' (p. 236). As a result, the organization of the house improves, the hierarchy is reasserted, and the insolence and carelessness disappear. The bourgeois manager reasserts middle-class ideals to the ultimate benefit of the middle-class family.

The premium Mrs Gibson places upon appearances may elicit a reader's laughter or censure, depending upon the particular context foregrounded, but the novel consistently depicts her efforts and emphases as socially productive rather than destructive. This is part of the text's substantial revision of cherished ideas, such as that substance counts for more than surface. In fact, as Gaskell demonstrates here, appearances are productive of substantial effects, and those who know how to manage the social signifiers are individuals to be reckoned with. The romance plot here is firmly focussed on the right boy meeting the right girl. Gaskell mixes this message of socially managed mobility into the romance plot, allowing certain illusions to be partially preserved in terms such as 'love'. Margaret Oliphant, one of her successors, was less interested in the illusions of romance. She represents the social managerial role of women as it extends from the home to the community, and the principal love affair for her heroines lies in their romance with a career.

Oliphant's depiction of her heroines' opportunistic negotiations of social discourses has produced dismay in critics both early and late, hearkening back to her publisher John Blackwood's initial critique of *Miss Marjoribanks* for its 'hardness of tone'.[45] Later critics follow Blackwood's lead. For example, of Phoebe Beecham, the eponymous heroine of *Phoebe, Junior*, Merryn Williams has said that she 'behaves in a way which most novel-readers would have found unpleasant'.[46] The heroines are too self-consciously manipulative and self-interested; they recognize and exploit the power conferred by mastery of the semiotics of social life. Marriage is represented as a means to an end, never as an end in itself. It must supply the proper 'field that was necessary for . . . ambition'.[47] Phoebe, too, insists that marriage provide her with political opportunities.

WOMEN WRITERS, THE DOMESTIC SPHERE AND LITERARY CANONS

Oliphant revises much more than the romance plot, and the negative comments are also responding to her demystification of the angelic ideal, her ironic staging of the feminine roles of dutiful daughter and *ingénue,* and her unrelenting focus on women's work that stresses the interpenetration of the political and the domestic, the way men's actions are informed by women's discursive practices. If we read canons as, in part, repositories of a culture's professed values and self-representations, we must ask if Oliphant's domestic novels have been consigned to obscurity, if not oblivion, for challenging so many Victorian sacred cows – romance, angels, feminine duty, innocence, passivity, and the separation of home and state. Oliphant's vision of reality, however faithful to quotidian affairs, pierced myths of the domestic sphere that were sedulously guarded in other depictions of Victorian life.

No one would accuse George Eliot of building a world out of etiquette and the related domestic discourses that Oliphant details in her novels. If someone did, there would be historical irony because Eliot fought shy of those discourses as a mark of 'silly novels'.[48] The fluidity of meanings and the constructed nature of identities that delight such artists as Gaskell and Oliphant are uninteresting, perhaps even troubling, to Eliot. Indeed, the hallmark of a character such as Dorothea Brooke in *Middlemarch* is that she desperately wishes to accomplish something outside the domestic sphere that seems so utterly inconsequential to her. Social life is represented only insofar as it confirms the triviality of women's lives.

It is in part because George Eliot is so consistently caustic about the emptiness of ladies' domestic lives that she has been hailed for her realism. Her vision coincides so perfectly with patriarchal orthodoxy about the inconsequence and inanity of society and woman's place within it that no one has felt compelled to place that truth within the context of other equally compelling truths. To do so is to recognize that, of course, Eliot's 'realism' is the product of a highly selective representation in which the signifying practices through which women organized society are severed from their larger meanings, and household management is erased as a topic. Eliot eloquently conjures up 'the stifling oppression of that gentlewoman's world', 'the gentlewoman's oppressive liberty' (p. 202).[49]

George Eliot's representational choices have significant consequences for our understanding of nineteenth-century women writers and the domestic sphere. To the extent that Eliot has been elevated above other women writers, her vision has claimed an authority that calls into question the seriousness and relevance of other representations. To be sure, Eliot's is a valuable view of crippling restrictions in the domestic sphere and the entire ideology of the Angel in the House, which underwrote it.

It also severs domestic order from 'good society' and masks the extent to which middle-class women were contributing to both.

As we pursue this question of canonical status, it is worthwhile thinking, not simply about what their novels represented, but also about how the woman writer immersed in the domestic sphere was herself regarded and represented. Because Oliphant compared herself to George Eliot and George Eliot herself resisted any comparison with Oliphant, it is illustrative to continue with these two contrasting contemporaries. If we return to Pierre Bourdieu's concepts of economic and social capital, we may now add another form of capital that affects an aspiring writer: cultural capital. For a woman to amass significant cultural capital was always difficult and helps explain the decision of many to adopt a male pseudonym. Bourdieu notes that cultural distinction is a generic refinement of manner that is coded as the outward manifestation of inner taste; we may add that it is also gendered masculine.

George Eliot was fashioning an aesthetic practice that generally underwrote a conventional logic of culture. For example, those who produce high culture should have a fund of educational capital on which to draw. A level of education might be generally conceded for a man of a certain class but could never be assumed in a woman. Thus, Eliot's *Middlemarch*, for example, demonstrates from chapter to chapter the extraordinary bank of educational capital on which its author could make generous drafts. Epigraphs are drawn not only from Cervantes, Milton, Spenser, Chaucer, Dante, Pascal and Shakespeare but also from Blake, Ben Jonson, Goldsmith, Beaumont and Fletcher, Burton, Donne, Alfred de Musset, Italian proverbs and so forth. A knowledge of Italian art, classical music, German higher criticism and philosophy in general, French, German and Italian languages, contemporary science, and the literatures of several nationalities constitutes only a part of the erudition that informs the narrator's commentary.

Social or class capital also has its subtle but pervasive presence. As Bourdieu points out, individuals of a superior class will always disdain the pleasures of the class or classes beneath them. And the 'Keepsake' album that Ned Plymdale proudly presents to Rosamond Vincy as the 'very best thing in art and literature' can be sneeringly dismissed by Lydgate as 'sugared invention' (pp. 198–9). It is the narrator whose complex assessment places each participant in this comic social drama of cultural distinction. That narrator also frames Lydgate within the scene as one who is 'so ambitious of social distinction' that the 'distinction of mind which belonged to his intellectual ardour' cannot save him from 'confusing acquiring substantial material possessions with the attainment of true culture' (p. 111).

Bourdieu's theories, then, offer some plausible explanations for George Eliot's achievement of the cultural distinction signified by canonicity. This is neither to fault nor to celebrate her works; rather, it simply foregrounds some factors that may have contributed to their elevation.

On Oliphant's claims to cultural distinction, I can be rather brief. She does not bank on any educational capital of the kind found in Eliot. In fact, early identified as Queen Victoria's favorite novelist, Margaret Oliphant has had her educational capital fixed at a low estimate: bourgeois woman's novelist.

Middlemarch, as we have seen, strategically lays out its claims to high culture, just as representations of the author's life lay claim to a social and economic distinction free from the worries of getting and spending. We know, in fact, that Eliot supported herself with income produced from her writing, but portrayals of her life often suggest a leisured withdrawal from such monetary concerns. She terms novel writing her 'true vocation', speaks of her books as 'deeply serious things to me', 'something worth living and suffering for', and celebrates her success in writing a novel that 'people say has stirred them very deeply'.[50]

Oliphant represents her own life in dramatically different terms.[51] And here I will touch only on the received truisms about that life because, as I wish to argue, it is precisely those truisms that have diminished her aesthetic capital as a writer. The key details are these: Oliphant wrote too fast and too much because she needed money. The mercenary motive, Oliphant's obsession with her income, and the fact that she claims that 'it was necessary for me to work for my children' (p. 4), seem to disqualify her as artist and turn her into a hack writer of sorts. That Oliphant also enjoyed certain social luxuries, like first-class travel and silk dresses, further jeopardized her stature as an artist, as if an austere lifestyle fostered great art and material prosperity were inversely related to cultural capital. Perhaps Virginia Woolf led the way, memorably encapsulating Margaret Oliphant's career in *Three Guineas*: 'Mrs Oliphant sold her brain, her very admirable brain, prostituted her culture and enslaved her intellectual liberty in order that she might earn her living and educate her children'.[52] Strains of incandescence return in this unabashed linking of economic, social, educational and cultural capital. Thereafter, the anecdotal Margaret Oliphant became a figure who 'wrote her way out of debt,'[53] was 'addicted to the trappings of a genteel style of life,'[54] 'never traveled other than first class . . . always wore silk,'[55] and continually hounded her forbearing publishers for advances. Not surprisingly, we arrive at this characteristic final estimate: 'all her books are flawed by speedy and careless writing' (Haythornthwaite, 'A Victorian Novelist', p. 38). The aesthetic judgment of the novels flows from an assessment of the novelist's economic and social dispositions.

The very paucity of jobs for women meant that writing, one of the few ways to produce income, figured very differently for women than for men in Victorian culture. That is, the economic imperative does not seem to operate so strongly as a disqualifier of artistic merit for men because of the subtle way that artistic labour is gendered in nineteenth-century England. Certainly, Charles Dickens supported his family through his writing. His endeavours were accorded the serious evaluation due to a man who, free to choose from an array of lucrative jobs, takes up art as the nobler and less prosperous enterprise. Far from being mercenary, he is celebrated for the sacrifices he makes for art. In contrast, women who wrote were faulted for their economic motives.[56]

Obviously, such questions of aesthetic assessment invite further thought. But, in conclusion, I would have us seriously consider how the educational, social and material capital that ground cultural distinction have gendered inflections and are, therefore, generally more problematic for a woman writer, particularly a woman writer in the domestic sphere, to achieve. She is forced to demonstrate an educational capital a man is presumed to have, and, if she speaks of money, she is denied the disinterestedness requisite to great art that he is granted. George Eliot brilliantly negotiated the Scylla and Charybdis of cultural distinction for women, and for that achievement, she has been praised for thinking like a man.

NOTES

1 The phrase 'Angel in the House' originated with Coventry Patmore, who created the prototype and gave that title to his poetic domestic epic in four volumes (1854–62).

2 'Professions for Women', in Sandra Gilbert and Susan Gubar, eds., *The Norton Anthology of Literature by Women: the Tradition in English* (New York: Norton, 1985), p. 1385. Subsequent references appear in the text.

3 Virginia Woolf, *A Room of One's Own* (New York and Burlingame: Harcourt, Brace and World, 1957), p. 70.

4 Ruth H. Blackburn, ed., *The Brontë Sisters: Selected Source Materials* (Boston: D. C. Heath and Company, 1968), p. 22.

5 *The Letters of Mrs Gaskell*, ed. J. A. V. Chapple and Arthur Pollard, (Manchester University Press, 1966), p. 208.

6 *Margaret Oliphant, The Autobiography*, arranged and edited by Mrs Henry Coghill (University of Chicago Press, 1988), p. 4.

7 See *Distinction: a Social Critique of the Judgement of Taste* (Cambridge, MA: Harvard University Press, 1984).

8 Significant work from both historians and literary theorists has challenged the historical portrait of Victorian women as the passive, dependent and idle creatures of prevailing ideology. See Leonore Davidoff's *Best Circles: Women and Society in Victorian England* (Totowa, NJ: Rowman, 1973), which examines the effect of the social conventions governing polite society as a 'linking factor between the family and political and economic institutions' (pp. 14–15), and Davidoff's collaboration with Catherine Hall, *Family Fortunes: Men and Women of the English Middle Class, 1780–1850* (University of Chicago Press, 1987), which argues for the 'centrality of the sexual division of labour within families for the development of the capitalism enterprise' (p. 13). Literary critics have also significantly revised our stereotypical notions of Victorian housewives. See, for example, Mary Poovey, *Uneven Developments: The Ideological Work of Gender in Mid-Victorian England* (University of Chicago Press, 1988); Nancy Armstrong, *Desire and Domestic Fiction: A Political History of the Novel* (New York: Oxford University Press, 1987); Catherine Gallagher, *The Industrial Reformation of English Fiction: Social Discourse and Narrative Form* (University of Chicago Press, 1985); Monica Cohen, *Professional Domesticity in the Victorian Novel: Women, Work, and Home* (Cambridge University Press, 1998); and Elizabeth Langland, *Nobody's Angels: Middle-Class Women and Domestic Ideology in Victorian Culture* (Ithaca: Cornell University Press, 1995).

9 Pierre Bourdieu usefully focusses on the fact that *all* language always exists within social relationships that it both reflects and creates. He speaks of the 'alchemy of *representation* . . . through which the representative creates the group which creates him' (*Language and Symbolic Power*, trans. Gino Raymond and Matthew Adamson, ed. John B. Thompson (Cambridge MA: Harvard University Press, 1991), p. 106).

10 Davidoff, *Best Circles*, p. 22.

11 Lawrence Stone and Jeanne Stone, *An Open Elite? England 1540–1880* (Oxford: Clarendon Press, 1984), p. 423.

12 Davidoff, *Best Circles*, p. 22. According to Michael McKeon, *The Origins of the English Novel, 1600–1740* (Baltimore: Johns Hopkins University Press, 1987), this breakdown in traditional forms originated in the eighteenth century; indeed, he claims that the emergence of the novel parallels conditions of 'status inconsistency' in early modern England.

13 Michael Curtin, *Propriety and Position: a Study of Victorian Manners* (New York: Garland, 1987). Leonore Davidoff, *Best Circles*, pp. 18, 41, and Duncan Crow, *The Victorian Woman* (New York: Stein, 1971), pp. 47–8, also comment on the phenomenon.

14 The etymology of 'etiquette' enforces this distinction. *Manners of Modern Society: Being a Book of Etiquette* (London: Cassell, Petter and Galpin) spelled it out in 1872: 'Centuries ago, the word "etiquette" conveyed to those who used it a far different signification than to us of the present day. The word – an Anglo-Norman one – originally specified the ticket tied to the necks of bags or affixed to the bundles to denote their contents. A bag or bundle thus ticketed passed unchallenged' (p. 35). The idea of passing unchallenged, of being certified, is certainly relevant to Victorian etiquette. The manual explains that codes of manners were written or printed on cards or tickets, and thus etiquette began to take on its current meaning (p. 35).

15 See Curtin, *Propriety and Position*, pp. 31–2, 130.

16 Isabella Beeton, *Book of Household Management* (1861, rptd London: Chancellor, 1982). An abridged edition, ed. Nicola Humble, is published in the World's Classics series (Oxford University Press, 2000).

17 Davidoff, *Best Circles* p. 41.

18 *A Manual of Etiquette for Ladies.* (London: T. Allman and Son, 1856), p. 3.

19 A practice of too frequent calls, however, could give one a bad reputation as a 'day goblin' or as 'one of those persons who, having plenty of leisure, and a great desire to hear themselves talk, make frequent inroads into their friends' houses' (*Etiquette, Social Ethics, and Dinner-Table Observances* (London: Houlston and Wright, 1860), p. 22). The implication is that one had to be privy to the requisite proportions of things.

20 *Etiquette for Ladies* (Halifax: Milner and Sowerby, 1852), p. 23.

21 *How to Behave* (London: Ward, Lock and Taylor, [1879]), pp. 68–9.

22 *Etiquette for Ladies and Gentlemen* (London: Frederick, 1876), p. 19.

23 Margaret Oliphant, *Phoebe, Junior* (Harmondsworth: Penguin, 1989), p. 173.

24 *Etiquette for the Ladies: Eighty Maxims on Dress, Manners, and Accomplishments* (London: Charles Tilt, 1837), p. 49.

25 Florence Nightingale (*Cassandra* 1852; Old Westbury, NY: Feminist Press, 1979).

26 (Harmondsworth: Penguin, 1974), p. 141.

27 Curtin, *Propriety and Position*, p. 302.

28 Michael Curtin, ibid., remarks that 'the wife's duties as family emissary in the matter of calls and cards seem to have expanded through the century. The fact that it became increasingly the normal pattern for husbands and wives to spend their evenings together . . . meant that the acquaintances of each of the spouses tended also to become family acquaintances' (p. 223).

29 Quoted in Asa Briggs, *Victorian Things* (University of Chicago Press, 1988), p. 220.

30 James Murray, *The Domestic Oracle* (London, [1826?]), p. 504.

31 *Cassell's Book of the Household*, vol. 1 (London: Cassell, [1890?]), p. 152.

32 *How to Woo; How to Win; and How to Get Married* (Glasgow: W. R. M'Phun, 1856) compares household management with captaining a vessel: 'While I am far from saying that a wife should be a species of drudge, or upper-servant, I would strongly urge upon all suitors, the importance of ascertaining whether

the objects of their choice be given to domestic duties, so far as the management or regulation of a house is concerned . . . It is a false and pitiful pride
which would feel hurt by being supposed to have knowledge of such matters.
The captain of a seventy-four loses nothing of his dignity, because he can tell
whether the buckets be properly cleaned, or the meanest rope sufficiently
tightened (pp. 24–5).

33 'Mistresses and Maids', *Longman's Magazine* 21 (March 1893).

34 See *Cassell's Book of the Household*, p. 157.

35 Anne Summers makes this argument in a *TLS* review of Mary Poovey's
    Uneven Developments (7–13 April 1989, pp. 357–8). Summers suggests that we
    should see Nightingale's evolution of the nursing profession as a fulfilment
    of bourgeois managerial ideals.

36 *Victorian Essays* (London: Oxford University Press, 1962), pp. 24–5.

37 *Queen Victoria: the Woman, the Monarchy, and the People* (New York: Pantheon,
    1990), p. 44.

38 *Dearest Child, Letters Between Queen Victoria and the Princess Royal, 1858–1861, a
    Selection from the Kronberg Archives*, ed. Roger Fulford (London: Evans Brothers,
    1964), p. 191.

39 Quoted in Thompson, *Queen Victoria*, p. 139.

40 Henry James, in a review of *Wives and Daughters* in the *Nation*, rptd in Angus
    Easson, ed., *Elizabeth Gaskell: the Critical Heritage* (London: Routledge, 1991),
    p. 465. Sarah Ellis, *The Women of England: their Social Duties, and Domestic Habits*
    (London: Fisher, 1839), p. 1.

41 Naomi Schor, *Reading in Detail: Aesthetics and the Feminine* (New York: Methuen,
    1987), p. 4.

42 *Discipline and Punish: the Birth of the Prison*, trans. Alan M. Sheridan (New York:
    Random House, 1979), p. 30.

43 Patsy Stoneman, *Elizabeth Gaskell*, (Bloomington: Indiana University Press,
    1987), p. 173.

44 Introduction, *Wives and Daughters*, ed. Frank Glover Smith (Harmondsworth:
    Penguin, 1969), p. 26.

45 Quoted in Leavis, *Collected Essays: the Novel of Religious Controversy*, vol. III of 3
    vols. (Cambridge University Press, 1989), p. 155.

46 *Margaret Oliphant: a Critical Biography* (New York: St Martin's Press, 1986), p.
    85. Williams's biography is, generally, a thorough and sympathetic account;
    nonetheless, it reproduces some of these critical truisms.

47 *Miss Marjoribanks* (Harmondsworth: Penguin, 1989), p. 114.

48 Alison Booth, *Greatness Engendered: George Eliot and Virginia Woolf* (Ithaca:
    Cornell University Press, 1992), citing Eliot's 'Silly Novels by Lady
    Novelists', points out: 'As though she has completely seen through the cult
    of woman's mission with its exaltation of minutiae . . . she heaps scorn on
    "mind and millinery" novels, with their combination of exquisite accessories
    and ignorant philosophies' (p. 71).

49 For a more extended analysis of this erasure, see Elizabeth Langland
    'Inventing Reality: George Eliot's *Middlemarch*', in *Nobody's Angels*, pp.
    181–208.

50 *Selections from George Eliot's Letters*, ed. Gordon Haight (New Haven and London: Yale University Press, 1985), p. 230.

51 Elisabeth Jay's biography of Margaret Oliphant notes that 'As the only woman admitted to the great tradition, until recent years, George Eliot then became the paradigm for discussing the woman's experience as writer. This exception really did begin to prove the rule by which other women writers were judged. This has proved damaging because, as it so happened, George Eliot's life and work could very neatly be fitted into another male-centred, nineteenth-century myth: the myth of progress' (*Mrs. Oliphant: 'a fiction to herself'* (Oxford: Clarendon Press, 1995), p. 246).

52 *Three Guineas* (New York: Harcourt, Brace and World, 1938), pp. 91–2.

53 Dale Trela, 'Jane Welsh Carlyle and Margaret Oliphant: an Unsung Friendship', *The Carlyle Annual* 11 (1990), p. 32.

54 Joseph H. O'Mealy, 'Mrs Oliphant, *Miss Marjoribanks*, and the Victorian Canon', *The Victorian Newsletter* (Fall 1992), p. 247.

55 J. Haythornthwaite, 'A Victorian Novelist and Her Publisher: Margaret Oliphant and the House of Blackwood', *The Bibliotheck: A Scottish Journal* 15 (1988), p. 38.

56 Bourdieu (*Distinction*) notes that literary works are often denied cultural distinction if they are believed to proceed from mercenary motives.

CHAPTER SEVEN

Women, fiction and the marketplace

Valerie Sanders

> I have now so large and eager a public, that if we were to publish
> the work without a preliminary appearance in the Magazine, the
> first sale would infallibly be large, and a considerable profit would
> be gained even though the work might not ultimately impress the
> public so strongly as 'Adam' has done.[1]

George Eliot, discussing with John Blackwood the best way to publish
The Mill on the Floss, sounds shrewd and confident. Her comments show
an awareness of the business issues involved in selecting the right
formula for a relative newcomer on the literary scene, and one whose
first appearance had set the public gossiping and speculating. Margaret
Oliphant's observation that the nineteenth century, 'which is the age of
so many things – of enlightenment, of science, of progress – is quite as
distinctly the age of female novelists', has now become a truism.[2] Yet the
ways in which professional women writers handled their careers
changed significantly from the early 1800s, when Jane Austen was being
ignored by publishers and reviewers, to the 1890s, when Mrs Humphry
Ward, riding high on the success of *Robert Elsmere* (1888), was insisting on
the early release of a cheap edition of *Marcella* (1894). According to John
Sutherland, 'the reprint of *Marcella* was the torpedo that sunk the three-
decker and by so doing stripped Mudie of his dictatorial powers'.[3]
Women novelists, who had begun the century in apologetic mode, ended
it, to a considerable extent, calling the shots. Yet the emergence of these
conditions was uneven and complex. Writers that we now regard as
'canonical' struggled for recognition, while those since relegated to
minor status seem to have exploited the marketplace on a scale that relatively few novelists achieve even today. Others, who started well, had to
rebuild their careers in mid-stream, and begin afresh, perhaps diversify-
ing into other genres. Many found ways of juggling their novel-writing
with contributions to the periodical press or literary reviewing.

Investigating how the conditions of the marketplace developed, what use women novelists made of them, and how they shaped their careers as they sought acceptance in the male-dominated world of publishing is the main purpose of this chapter.

The nineteenth century saw a major expansion of what might loosely be called the 'literature industry', and in particular a proliferation of new methods of novel publication. For much of the century, however, the expensive three-volume novel was the staple of the book-publishing industry. Selling at thirty-one shillings and sixpence for three volumes, the novel was clearly a luxury item, intended mainly for library stock. Mudie's Select Library, founded in 1843, was the chief bulk purchaser of novels, which meant that publishers had constantly to defer to library tastes. Margaret Oliphant later recalled that it seemed to her 'the patronage of Mudie was a sort of recognition from heaven'.[4] Without substantial orders from Mudie – 'the insatiable Mudie', 'the magnanimous Mudie', as John Blackwood called him (*George Eliot Letters*, vol. III, pp. 33, 289) – a novel was unlikely to make much money for either its author or its publishers, and, according to Gaye Tuchman, Charles Mudie's taste was 'that of a religious fundamentalist and patriarchal Victorian'.[5] While this may be a slight exaggeration, he certainly considered boycotting *The Mill on the Floss* when he discovered that its author was Marian Evans, living unmarried with George Henry Lewes (*George Eliot Letters*, vol. III, p. 209). Mudie also discouraged the issuing of cheap reprints (twelve- or six-shilling editions were the norm) before the three-volume library sets had had time to circulate widely: a year was his ideal time-lapse between first publication and first cheap reprint. John Blackwood refers in a letter of 1859 to a two-volume, twelve-shilling edition of *Adam Bede* as being 'intermediate to a people's edition' (*George Eliot Letters*, vol. III, p. 33). As with the difference now between hardback and paperback novels, the longer readers were prepared to wait, the cheaper a book would become, but the nineteenth century was very much an age when new novels caused a sensation and people were in a hurry to read them.

Publishers therefore looked to additional ways of selling their books to the public: hence the introduction of part serialization – both in separately bound and sold monthly parts (for which there were eighteenth-century precedents, taken up by Dickens for *Pickwick Papers*) and in magazines (which George Eliot accepted for *Scenes of Clerical Life*, but not for *The Mill on the Floss*). This method had the advantage of whetting the reader's appetite for more, thereby also increasing sales of the magazine, though it could reduce interest in the novel when serialization came to an end.[6] Occasionally, too, a novel serialization proved unpopular, and dragged down magazine sales with it – as happened with Gaskell's *North and South* in Dickens's *Household Words*. Part serialization, by both these methods, was particularly popular from the late 1830s until the 1860s, though magazine serialization quickly gained ascendancy over the monthly part.

Once a novelist had established a readership, there was an additional market for complete sets of novels, especially for cheap reprints at more affordable prices for the private purchaser. This was something that came into vogue in the 1830s, starting with Bentley's Standard Novels (1831), but was especially popular in the second half of the century when some of the greatest novelists had died and complete sets of their works could be issued. The Cabinet Edition of George Eliot's novels stretched to twenty-four volumes from 1878 to 1885, while the Cheap Edition came out in six volumes in 1881, with an additional twelve-volume 'fire-side edition' in New York in 1885. Collections of Elizabeth Gaskell's works (in fifteen volumes) were issued in Leipzig as early as 1849–57 when she was in mid career. Like many other Victorian novelists she was published in Tauchnitz's cheap English reprint series which began in 1837.[7] In 1879–80 Macmillan's brought out their famous sixteen-volume selection of Charlotte Yonge's works in the familiar blue-covered edition which copied the small-print format used by her original publishers, Parker.[8] Writers such as Margaret Oliphant and Eliza Lynn Linton, who were never reissued in a uniform edition, are now very much harder to recover except via odd second-hand copies. Yonge's works had a steady following among those who had grown up with her family sagas, whereas Oliphant and Linton were less consistently popular. Oliphant, moroever, was too prolific a novelist to be readily containable in a 'complete works'.

As John Sutherland has commented, 'high prices, multiple outlets, wide sales and abundant creative genius combined to make 1850–80 one of the richest periods that fiction has known'.[9] The women novelists discussed in this chapter were fortunate in living and working through a period of such productive activity in the fiction industry, but it was also a time when relations between novelists, publishers, libraries and readers were at their most personal and intense. Conditions favoured the arrival of fresh talent, and could turn high quality books into bestsellers, yet the balance of power between all the participants in a novel's launch was often precarious, with the novelist generally the most vulnerable party. As reviewers were only just coming to terms with the high-profile presence of women in the novel-writing market – moreover, women writing because they wanted to write, and not just because they needed the money – the stage was set for many a turbulent episode, as (mainly male) reviewers judged the work of (mainly female) new novelists, whose work had initially been accepted by male editors, many of them from publishing dynasties, like the Blackwoods.

Women novelists of the eighteenth century had already set an example of how to adapt to a system originally designed for and run by men. The most successful among them had attracted patronage and got up subscriptions when necessary, gradually winning the confidence of publishers and steadily raising their own earning power. Fanny Burney's career is a case in point. Having started small with £20 from Lowndes for *Evelina* (1778), she earned £2,000 for *Camilla* (1796) and built a cottage on the proceeds.[10] Though her earnings were less spectacular, Ann Radcliffe made an impressive £500 on *The Mysteries of Udolpho* (1794) and £800 on *The Italian* (1797). With Jane Austen, however, the story of women's publishing seems to restart more diffidently. She relied at first on male relatives to approach publishers, but her father failed in 1797 to sell *First Impressions* to Cadell, while her brother Henry's sale of *Susan* in 1803 for £10 to the publishers Crosby in London had produced no results six years later. Austen, calling herself 'Mrs Ashton Dennis' (the initials spelt 'MAD') was offered little choice but to buy back the manuscript at her own expense, or else wait indefinitely for its publication. When she did succeed in having a novel published, it was 'on commission', which meant that the author was herself responsible for the printing and advertising costs, while the publisher charged 10 per cent commission on each volume sold. As late as 1815, Austen took over her brother Henry's correspondence with John Murray over *Emma* apparently only because Henry was himself too ill to write, and then she stressed: 'I beg you to understand that I leave the terms on which the Trade should be supplied with the work, entirely to your Judgment'. Unlike her successors, especially Charlotte Brontë, Elizabeth Gaskell and George Eliot, she was never on intimate corresponding terms with her publishers. Her transactions with them remained formal and businesslike to the end. Nevertheless, Austen liked the idea of earning money and becoming a professional writer: 'I have now therefore written myself into £250 – which only makes me long for more', she told her brother Frank in 1813.[11] Overall, however, counting all her novels, she seems to have earned less than £700.[12] John Murray, who remaindered what he had left of her works in 1820, subsequently disposed of Austen's copyrights to Richard Bentley's firm.

Concern about earnings was something that affected most of her successors – not just because they needed the money to live on, but also because they wanted to be treated as professionals. Authorship, for men as well as women, had been gaining in dignity and credibility largely because successful novelists were being paid more realistic sums, yet also because they were entering the profession for more than purely economic reasons. Most nineteenth-century women novelists broached the marketplace as outsiders, excluded from the male 'clubland' of editors and publishers. A popular route was through journalism, which allowed the newcomer to establish some degree of confidence and authority in short articles and book reviews, often in magazines with a national, rather than a purely local, circulation, which might, in turn, lead to more extensive literary connections. Harriet Martineau's Unitarian family origins made W. J. Fox's *Monthly Repository* her natural point of entry; Fox's brother Charles ultimately published her hugely successful *Illustrations of Political Economy* (1832–4). Unlike George Eliot, who largely abandoned magazine journalism after the success of *Scenes of Clerical Life* in 1858, Martineau remained an active contributor to a wide range of quality newspapers and journals, most notably the *Edinburgh Review* and *Daily News*, for which she wrote on the progress of the American Civil War. George Eliot herself gained the courage and experience to write fiction partly through her apprenticeship as John Chapman's unofficial editor for the *Westminster Review*, while Elizabeth Gaskell came to writing through her contributions to *Howitt's Journal* in 1847 (though her first publication had been a poem, composed jointly with her husband, in the style of Crabbe, for *Blackwood's* in 1837): her contact with William Howitt, who read the manuscript of *Mary Barton* and passed it to John Forster, reader for Chapman and Hall, led to the publication of her first novel. Margaret Oliphant makes a great deal in her *Autobiography* of introducing Dinah Mulock to the publisher Henry Blackett: 'he, apparently with some business gift or instinct imperceptible to me, having made out that there were elements of special success in her' (p. 101). Hit-and-miss networking of this kind was often a woman's quickest route to finding the right publisher, though the direct approach with an unsolicited manuscript was always an alternative option.

Harriet Martineau's epic battle to find a publisher for her *Illustrations of Political Economy* in 1832 is recounted with considerable drama in the first volume of her *Autobiography*. Determined to publish her tales at whatever cost, Martineau was repeatedly told that the Reform Bill and the cholera epidemic would damage sales and make publication inadvisable.

After failing to interest any publishers by letter, Martineau set out for London and began seeing them personally. Even then, the terms she was offered by Charles Fox were so insulting that his brother was embarrassed to press them: the work was to be published by subscription, in the eighteenth-century style, 'and moreover, the subscription must be for five hundred copies before the work began'. She was also to sell 1,000 in the first fortnight, or the series would end after only two numbers. 'As Charles Fox had neither money nor connexion, I felt that the whole risk was thrown upon me', Martineau recalled.[13] As it happened, the series was a huge success, but Martineau remembered sending out circulars to all likely subscribers, including members of her own family who thought she was being rash and conceited. When the suspense was over, she felt permanently relieved from financial insecurity: 'The entire periodical press, daily, weekly, and, as soon as possible, monthly, came out in my favour, and I was overwhelmed with newspapers and letters, containing every sort of flattery' (1, 178). Martineau's narrative reminds us of how unstable and unpredictable the publishing industry was at that difficult time between the deaths of the great Romantic poets and the beginning of the Victorian period when the novel became the most popular genre.

Publishers had pointed ways of making it clear to their clients that they expected their works to fail. Discouraging terms and mean first payments were usually the best a new author could expect; moreover, many first novels by women were either published anonymously (*Frankenstein* and *Mary Barton* are good examples) or under pseudonyms, to protect them from prejudiced judgments by reviewers. For the Brontës, doing everything on their own, and without even the useful contacts that Martineau had made for herself by the time she was thirty, the battle to be noticed by publishers was often demoralizing. When Charlotte Brontë came to review her own and her sisters' fortunes with their novels, she felt they had had an arduous struggle for acceptance: 'The great puzzle lay in the difficulty of getting answers of any kind from the publishers to whom we applied', she recalled in the 'Biographical Notice of Ellis and Acton Bell'.[14] While Anne and Emily were prepared to accept disadvantageous terms from Newby, a notoriously roguish publisher, Charlotte found herself being offered nothing at all, as *The Professor* went its weary rounds – famously rewrapped in used paper, the next publisher's address added to the lengthening list each time the novel was rejected. That *Jane Eyre* was finally accepted and published with so much haste and enthusiasm was largely due to the enterprising outlook of one man, George Smith, who became her friend and adviser for the rest of her life.

What makes this period of literary history especially interesting is the peculiar conditions in which aspiring women novelists had to work professionally with equally ambitious young male editors in the best publishing houses. It is important to remember that there were no women editors at the top of Victorian publishing firms: the key publishers of the day were men – and young men at that – a new breed of keen, business-like operators, such as George Smith (1824–1901), John Chapman (1822–94) and John Blackwood (1818–79), who were eager to know their clients personally and, if necessary, help them with their personal problems. The blurring of lines between the professional and personal could be fruitful or it could be awkward. John Blackwood sent George Eliot a pug dog, and thought of the title for *The Mill on the Floss*; Charlotte Brontë asked George Smith for advice on investing the £500 she was paid for the copyright of *Shirley* (1849); he also sent her selections of new books to broaden her horizons, and, having finally persuaded her to visit his family, squired her around the sights of London. She even had a proposal of marriage from one of the firm, James Taylor (whom she rejected). Smith perhaps felt more comfortable with Elizabeth Gaskell, to whom he sent a valentine in 1864, urging her to write more of *Cousin Phillis* (which appeared monthly in the *Cornhill* from 1863 to 1864):

> More, more, he cried, e'er Phillis breathed her last,
> Three Volumes more, I want them quick and fast.
> Trollope's too long: Macdonald slow and tame
> There's only you can raise the Cornhill's fame.[15]

Gaskell, in turn, felt she could be humorous with Smith – so long as they were discussing anything except money. When he sent her an advance copy of *The Mill on the Floss*, she was ecstatic: 'Oh Mr Smith! your grandfather was a brick, and your grandmother an angel' (*Gaskell Letters*, p. 611).

As John Sutherland has observed, women novelists tended to stay longer than men with the same publishers:[16] hence the close working partnerships of John Blackwood with George Eliot and Margaret Oliphant; George Smith with Charlotte Brontë and Elizabeth Gaskell, later with Mrs Humphry Ward; Richard Bentley with Eliza Lynn Linton; and W. J. Fox with Harriet Martineau. In 1853, Gaskell declined to be lured away from Chapman and Hall by overtures from Richard Bentley via Dinah Mulock, partly because she had 'no complaint to make' against them, but also because they had taken 'the risk of *Mary Barton*, when Mr Moxon refused it as a *gift*' (*Gaskell Letters*, p. 250). Later, when she became disillusioned with them and was publishing with Smith, Elder, she confessed to being tempted by a better offer from Sampson Low, who had a lucrative American outlet: 'But I would much rather have 800£ from you than 1,000£ from them', she loyally told George Smith (p. 558). Not that these partnerships always proceeded smoothly. Martineau became disgusted with Fox's private life, while Eliot and Brontë struggled with editors who were kind-hearted and supportive, but not always entirely convinced by what their authors were trying to do. Significantly, Eliot continued addressing Blackwood as 'Dear Mr Blackwood', unlike the more relaxed Lewes, who was soon beginning letters, 'My dear Blackwood'. John Blackwood, initially stuck for how to address the author of *Scenes of Clerical Life*, tried 'My Dear Amos' (30 January 1857) after the hero of the first story. Although their relationship gradually warmed, its initial stages were complicated by the secrecy surrounding Eliot's identity, and Blackwood's sensitivity to her position. Like the Brontës, she was never entirely at ease in 'literary circles' (except perhaps in Germany), and at first avoided the full London literary life beyond the point where it had been useful to her during her *Westminster Review* years – though of course her position was greatly exacerbated by her unmarried relationship with Lewes. Towards the end of her life, when the public were more prepared to overlook her controversial history, she became more sociable, and held regular Sunday 'afternoons' at The Priory.

Jane Austen, Charlotte Brontë and Elizabeth Gaskell made little attempt to conceal their newcomer status when writing to their publishers. Austen had to back down over the dedication to the Prince of Wales in *Emma*, which she had instructed John Murray to put in the wrong place: 'it was arising from my ignorance only', she confessed, 'and from my having never noticed the proper place for a dedication' (*Austen Letters*, p. 305). Brontë, with no male intermediaries to act for her, had to ask even publishers who had turned her down for help in approaching others. 'For instance', she asked Aylott and Jones (who had published the 'Bell' brothers' poems) in 1846, 'in the present case, where a work of fiction is in question, in what form would a publisher be most likely to accept the M. S–? whether offered as a work of 3 vols or as tales which might be published in numbers or as contributions to a periodical'.[17] In fact Brontë always eschewed any form of publication other than the three-volume novel, but at this stage of her career, she was anxious to learn all the possibilities.

Elizabeth Gaskell sounds just as unsure of herself in her business correspondence with George Smith: 'Can you begin to print before you have the whole of the MS. That is a question I want much to have answered, & I'll tell you why', she explained when she was preparing the *Life of Charlotte Brontë* in 1856: 'I have 100 pages quite ready, – only with so many erasures, insertions at the *back* of the leaves &c (owing to the unchronological way in which I obtained information) that I should much like to correct all I can myself.' A week or two later she was confessing: 'I am no judge of type &c – and I find it difficult to say how far the MS will extend; I can scarcely tell what space it will occupy.'[18] It was not only the type that bothered Gaskell: money was another area that made her feel uncomfortable. 'I have a great dislike to bargaining, & I should not like to be (what the Lancashire people call) "having"; but if I must deal frankly with you, as I wish, the terms proposed for the Biography are below what I thought I might reasonably expect'. It is hard to tell with passages like this whether Gaskell was being entirely straight. After all, by 1856, she was an experienced novelist, with *Mary Barton* (1848), *Ruth* (1853) and *North and South* (1855) behind her. Indeed she uses her previous experience to substantiate her claims for more money: 'My way of reckoning was this – For "North and South" I received 600£ (from H[ousehold]. W[ords]. & Mr Chapman together,) retaining the copyright, having the Tauchnitz profit, – and only losing the American profit by my own carelessness in forgetting to answer the note, until some other American publisher had begun to reprint' (*Gaskell Letters*, p. 430). For good measure Gaskell added that the biography had been more arduous and expensive to write than a novel, and was also likely to interest a wider class of readers.

Smith was convinced and she succeeded in having her original offer of £600 for the copyright of the *Life* raised to £800, but her discussion of the issues at stake combines professional terminology and unprofessional disorder in a welter of facts, figures, opinions, and confessions of carelessness.

In her *Autobiography*, Margaret Oliphant insists that she was unable to bargain for the fabulous deals she felt had accrued to Trollope, Dinah Mulock Craik and Mrs Humphry Ward: 'I never could fight for a higher price or do anything but trust to the honour of those I had to deal with'.[19] In fact, as Elisabeth Jay's biography of Oliphant reveals, this was by no means the case. Oliphant did ask for better deals, and often reminded Blackwood of the going-rate for other novels which she felt were comparable with her own. Sometimes she got what she wanted, and sometimes not. Blackwood, who gave her £1,500 for *The Perpetual Curate* (1864), was less generous over *Miss Marjoribanks* (1866). Both had been serialized in *Blackwood's Magazine*, but, according to Elisabeth Jay, Blackwood, 'apparently put off by the harshness of tone of *Miss Marjoribanks*, which many subsequent readers have found her most accomplished work, refused to recognize her Carlingford series as the financial equal of Trollope's Barsetshire series'.[20] Though friendly with the whole Blackwood dynasty (she made John Blackwood her sons' official guardian, and held a big literary party at Runnymede in 1877 to celebrate her twenty-five years of authorship with the firm), Oliphant was sometimes hurt by his professional firmness. The complete version of her *Autobiography* opens with a painful memory of his rejecting 'paper after paper', whilst she choked back the tears, 'lest the hard men – who were very kind notwithstanding, and friendly and just – should see I was crying and think it an appeal to their sympathies' (p. 3). Blackwood was indeed 'kind' and 'friendly', doing his best to find Oliphant many and varied opportunities for increasing her salary as a professional author, while recognizing (as she did) that she would never be another George Eliot.

Relationships with editors could swing between cautious negotiation, mild flirtation, anger, disappointment and huffy withdrawal. There is every sign that such relationships were more complicated because the novelists were women negotiating with men: desperate to be taken seriously, but deeply conscious of their 'outsider' status, and unsure what tone to adopt in business negotiations; unsure, too, how to conduct the more personal side of the relationship. Achieving the correct balance between the two was a challenge, especially when the novelist needed to defend her own position. However inexperienced, many of them had firm ideas about what they could and could not manage. The Brontës and Jane Austen avoided serial publication in magazines, though Charlotte Brontë was invited to consider this for *Shirley*: 'I am not yet qualified for the task', she told W. S. Williams of Smith, Elder: 'I have neither gained a sufficiently firm footing with the public, nor do I possess sufficient confidence in myself, nor can I boast those unflagging animal spirits, that even command of the faculty of composition, which, as you say and I am persuaded, most justly, is an indispensable requisite to success in serial literature' (*Brontë Letters*, p. 574). Harriet Martineau went further in seeing serial publication of a novel as 'unprincipled', and 'a false principle of composition'. Her own *Illustrations of Political Economy*, serialized monthly over two years, were presumably exempt from disapproval because they came out as separate tales, complete in themselves; whereas John Murray's offer to publish a serialized novel on conspiratorial terms struck her as improper. 'He said that he could help me to a boundless fortune, and a mighty future fame, if I would adopt his advice', she recalls in the passage of her *Autobiography* (II, p. 116) describing the publication of *Deerbrook* (1839). In the end, Murray withdrew his offer as the humdrum domestic subject displeased him, and Martineau settled for a less spectacular, three-volume deal with Edward Moxon (who would later refuse *Mary Barton* as a gift).

While Martineau did her own negotiating, George Eliot continued using George Henry Lewes as her middle-man in discussions with Blackwood. The terms for each of her novels were laboriously debated as she weighed up what would be best for each book aesthetically and for herself economically. For Eliot, there were always conflicting considerations at stake, largely because, although she wanted to make money from her writing, she did not want to be seen *only* or *mainly* as writing for money. 'I don't want the world to give me anything for my books except money enough to save me from the temptation to write *only* for money', she told John Blackwood in 1859 (*George Eliot Letters*, III, p. 152). Nevertheless her instructions to Blackwood on the judicious timing of cheaper reprints are remarkably exact and anxious. 'I would on no account publish a 6/- edition of the books until the 12/- edition of the Mill has had a fair chance of disappearing from the shelves', she urged him in 1861; 'And pray print the smallest practicable number of Adam at 12/-., for I have a great dread of having my books printed to lie in warehouses' (*George Eliot Letters*, III, p. 392). She had learnt a great deal since the days of *Adam Bede*, when she declined to advise Blackwood on the timing of cheaper reprints, referring him instead to Lewes as 'a more experienced judge' (III, p. 33). From then on Eliot scrutinized every stage of the publication schedules for her novels. She also agonized about attaining the right kind of popularity. She wanted to be appreciated, but mainly by the more discerning kind of reader who would understand her moral earnestness; she wanted to push the more expensive editions of her books until the market was exhausted, but then she shrank from the shame of being remaindered. While Lewes continued proposing new publication arrangements (it was his idea that *Middlemarch* should appear in bi-monthly parts), Eliot tended to write more often about the niggling details of new editions. Her terror of bad reviews and habit of fleeing abroad immediately on publication of a new book testify to her continuing self-doubt in the world of mid-Victorian publishing, despite her own apparently unassailable position in it. Gaskell also timed her

1857 holiday so that she would be out of the country when her Brontë biography was published.

If it was difficult enough persuading publishers to believe in a new author, the problems of maintaining a literary career over a period of twenty or thirty years were no less daunting. Eliot herself made some decisions which now look strange, but at the time sounded convincing, as when she temporarily abandoned her best-selling line in Warwickshire rural tragedies, and turned to short tales, poems, and fifteenth-century Florence with *Romola* (1863), briefly also breaking with the Blackwood firm to publish with George Smith.[21] Smith offered Eliot an astounding £10,000 for *Romola*; though he reduced it to £7,000 for serialization in the *Cornhill*. When her next novel, *Felix Holt*, was up for negotiation, Eliot returned humbly to Blackwood, aware that the brief flirtation with Smith had been embarrassing all round.

The sums of money paid for copyright at this time varied, like other payments, according to the publisher's faith in his author; even with a promising first novel, some publishers were cautious until they had tested the market. George Smith, who was to be so generous with George Eliot, offered Charlotte Brontë only £100 for the copyright of *Jane Eyre*, which even she, with all her inexperience, thought rather mean: 'One hundred pounds is a small sum for a year's intellectual labour –', she told him despondently (*Brontë Letters*, p. 540) – though this was also what Gaskell was paid for *Mary Barton* the following year by Chapman and Hall. *Ruth* (1853), however, earned £500. Fees tended to rise encouragingly once publishers were confident that their authors were going to be successful. The question of keeping or selling copyrights was another problem new authors had to settle for themselves, without always being sure they were acting for the best. George Eliot clung carefully to hers, as one might expect. Harrison Ainsworth urged Mrs Henry Wood never to sell any of her copyrights, though she did dispose of *The Channings* to Bentley (Gettmann, *A Victorian Publisher*, p. 111). Gaskell, far less professional than Eliot, parted with the copyright of *Mary Barton*, without fully understanding what she was doing: 'but I was then so unknowing, and so little expected that it would ever come to a second edition, that I did not sufficiently make myself acquainted with the nature of the parchment document sent to me to sign' (*Gaskell Letters*, p. 132). While the selling of copyright brought in instant cash, it was a one-off payment, which might represent much less than a successful novel would eventually earn. Some authors, therefore, sold their copyrights for a fixed period of years, and then reclaimed them. Without literary agents to act for them (which was the case before the 1870s), all inexperienced Victorian novelists – men as well as women – were at risk of making the wrong decisions and losing considerable sums of money. According to Royal Gettmann, the royalty system, as we understand it today, came into play as late as 1885 with Eliza Lynn Linton's *Autobiography of Christopher Kirkland*. This ensured that novelists kept on being paid for successive sales of their work, once a certain number had been cleared.[22]

The market was also unpredictable in terms of taste. Whereas Eliza Lynn Linton was surprisingly successful with her first two historical novels, *Azeth the Egyptian* (1847) and *Amymone* (1848) – the first published at her own expense with Newby, the second by Bentley (who paid her £100) – her third novel, *Realities* (1851), so shocked the public that Linton abandoned novel-writing altogether for the next fourteen years. Faced with the need to redirect her career, she took up newspaper journalism, first with the *Morning Chronicle*, and later with the *Saturday Review*, which carried her notorious 'Girl of the Period' articles (1868). Though she returned to novel-writing with *Grasp Your Nettle* (1865), combining sensationalism with anti-feminism, her novels quickly came to seem old-fashioned and loosely constructed. She was still turning out three-deckers, such as *The One Too Many* (1894), when the new novelists of the next generation were writing shorter, tighter works in the novella style, and forcing Mudie to back down over the three-volume format.

Harriet Martineau, too, took several changes of direction within her long career – driven by her own political interests and declining taste for imaginative writing. Her novel *Deerbrook* (1839) was followed by only one other, *The Hour and the Man* (1841), an historical novel about Toussaint L'Ouverture. She then concentrated on writing up her own experiences of foreign travel, protracted illness, and visits to industrial sites in Birmingham (the last for Dickens's *Household Words*). Her lasting *métier* was as leader writer for the *Daily News* during the period of the American Civil War. Nevertheless, Martineau, in a curious experimental episode in 1851, nearly published a novel called *Oliver Weld*, using a pseudonym, but was persuaded not to go ahead with it by judicious criticism from Charlotte Brontë – a friend whose work Martineau herself criticized two years later when she was asked for her opinion of *Villette*. Brontë had actually offered to be her intermediary with George Smith, who hoped for another *Deerbrook*. What he was offered was a book full of religious and political controversy, which Martineau herself quickly suppressed as 'a foolish prank', admitting that her fiction-writing days were over.[23] The episode is perhaps more interesting for showing how quickly Brontë had moved from the role of humble petitioner to would-be patron of an older, more established writer, whose career had been more varied than Brontë's own.

By the middle of the century, women novelists were becoming distinctly more professional in their handling of their careers, and more directly involved in every stage of the publication process. During the 1860s, when many new magazines were started, several women took leading roles in running them. Mary Howitt had already edited, with her husband, *Howitt's Journal*, which had published Gaskell's early stories. Mary Elizabeth Braddon edited *Belgravia* from 1866 to 1876 and the *Belgravia Annual* from 1867 to 1876, quite apart from contributing to the other major literary journals of the day, including *Temple Bar* and *All the Year Round*. Mrs Henry Wood took over the running of Alexander Strahan's magazine, the *Argosy*, in 1867, and wrote much of the material herself, as did Charlotte Yonge for the *Monthly Packet*, which she edited from 1851 to 1890: as her entry in the *Oxford Guide to British Women Writers* (1994) confirms, 'one of the longest-serving editorships of any Victorian periodical'.[24] When Alexander Macmillan in 1865 offered Yonge the chance to edit the *Sunday Library for Household Reading*, she wanted to be sure that she would have total control over the contributions and editorial team as she had with the *Monthly Packet*, 'where I have been used to admit nothing that I do not quite go along with'.[25] Whereas Jane Austen and the Brontës took no part in the wider literary life of their times, it became increasingly common for women novelists to write for several journals simultaneously, review other novels, and work as publishers' readers – the best-known example being Geraldine Jewsbury, who not only reviewed regularly for the *Athenaeum*, but was also reader for Bentley's firm for twenty years, along with Maria Featherstonhalgh, Adeline Sergeant and Lady Dorchester. Not that women readers could be relied on to sympathize with up-and-coming women novelists. Jewsbury strongly opposed publishing Rhoda Broughton's *Not Wisely but Too Well* (1867), claiming: 'It will not do you any credit – indeed people will wonder at a House like yours bringing out a work so *ill* calculated for the reading of decent people' (Gettmann, *A Victorian Publisher*, p. 195). Having lost this round to Jewsbury, Bentley made sure that he published Broughton's next thirteen, besides publishing Mrs Henry Wood's *East Lynne* (1861), which Jewsbury had recommended, but with strong reservations about her ungrammatical writing. This was, however, a case of a woman reader preferring something that had been rejected by a man:

George Meredith, reader for Chapman and Hall. Bentley published it on a half-profit basis, but Wood received no payment for the various adaptations and dramatizations of the novel which were such a huge success.[26]

The connection between magazine serialization and book publication was particularly close in the 1860s, with many novels having their first public exposure in monthly instalments. Braddon's bestseller *Lady Audley's Secret* first appeared in the short-lived magazine *Robin Goodfellow* in 1861; when the magazine failed, the novel was rescued and continued in the *Sixpenny Magazine*. Rhoda Broughton's first novel, *Not Wisely but Too Well*, first appeared in the *Dublin University Magazine* in 1867, but established novelists such as Elizabeth Gaskell and George Eliot also continued publishing in magazines well into their careers. Gaskell's *Wives and Daughters* (1864–6), her final novel, was being serialized in the *Cornhill Magazine* when she died suddenly in 1865; Eliot also published *Romola* (1863) in the *Cornhill*. Margaret Oliphant, who mainly stayed loyal to *Blackwood's*, serialized stories in *Macmillan's Magazine*, *Cornhill*, and *Longman's*, among others.

Oliphant is an especially striking example of a woman who was determined on a literary career, and participated fully in all aspects of her profession. Besides reviewing regularly for *Blackwood's*, she wrote a history of their firm, *Annals of a Publishing House* (1897); two literary histories (*Literary History of England in the End of the Eighteenth and Beginning of the Nineteenth Century* (1882), and *The Victorian Age of English Literature*, (1892)); five biographies of her male contemporaries, including Edward Irving (1863) and her distant relative, Laurence Oliphant (1891); and several sets of 'historical sketches' – some from the reign of George II (1868–9), others from the reign of Queen Anne (1894). There was little she was unwilling to write about – whether it was John Stuart Mill's *Subjection of Women* or the latest 'sensation novel'. In 1884, she proposed writing a series of articles to be called 'The Old Saloon', which would allow her to comment on any aspect of current affairs and culture that caught her fancy: 'Short of politics', she suggested, 'I should be inclined to take in everything that was going on – theatre, pictures, books, even a taste of gossip when legitimate'.[27] Though some of her literary criticism now seems wrongheaded and limited in outlook, she recognized *Jane Eyre* as 'one of the most remarkable works of modern times' and Brontë herself as 'the most distinguished female writer' of the age.[28]

Not that Oliphant herself had a smooth career, and she certainly outlived her own reputation. It was a lasting disappointment to her that she was outperformed by George Eliot, Charlotte Brontë and Anthony Trollope – her own Carlingford series overshadowed by the latter's *Barchester Chronicles*. Oliphant regarded Carlingford as the crucial turning point that saved her career, when in the early 1860s John Blackwood kept rejecting her work: 'I dashed at the first story of the Chronicles of Carlingford and wrote it in two or three days feeling as if it was my last chance', she recalls in her *Autobiography* (p. 3). The series was 'pretty well forgotten now', she admits later, though 'it made a considerable stir at the time, and *almost* made me one of the popularities of literature. *Almost*, never quite, though "Salem Chapel" really went very near it, I believe' (*Autobiography*, p. 91). Reflecting on the difference between Trollope's career and her own, Oliphant decided her position as a 'friendless woman' had disadvantaged her. She always had the sense that other people (George Eliot in particular) did well because they were believed in and fussed over, whereas she had to do everything for herself.

Another writer whose success (to her inexplicable) she contrasted with her own was Mrs Humphry Ward, Matthew Arnold's niece and author of the surprising bestseller *Robert Elsmere* (1888). Entering her literary career, like so many nineteenth-century women, via journalism (articles on Spanish literature for *Macmillan's Magazine* in 1871–2), Ward's foray into novel-writing was at first unspectacular. Her novel *Miss Bretherton* (1884), published by Macmillan, made a loss of £22, as her editor, George L. Craik, explained to her in terse statistics: 'We printed 2500. We gave away 71. We have sold 1150. We have sent to America 750. We have on hand 521. The book sells at 6s. We gave you £50. We are out of pocket £22' (Sutherland, *Victorian Novelists*, p. 107). 'Quite dismayed at the results of *Miss Bretherton*' (in her own words), Ward neverthess declined Macmillan's offer of £100 for her next book, and took *Robert Elsmere* to Smith Elder – the publisher who, in nineteenth-century literary history, has the best reputation for 'discovering' women novelists disdained by other firms. Even so, the pre-publication history of Ward's novel was laborious and discouraging. At first the text was far too long and had to be rewritten. 'But how patient Mr Smith was over it', she recalls in her *Writer's Recollections* (1918), remembering his loyalty as friend and publisher for the next fourteen years. 'I am certain that he had no belief in the book's success and yet, on the ground of his interest in *Miss Bretherton* he had made liberal terms with me, and all through the long incubation he was always indulgent and sympathetic'.[29] The book's success – even this late in the century – hinged on library sales: according to Ward's own recollection of events, the 'circulating libraries were being fretted to death for copies' (p. 86). She was amused to find herself in a railway carriage with a woman she had just seen on the platform triumphantly waving the first volume of *Elsmere* which she had snatched against the odds from the library: '"Of course it was promised to somebody else; but as I was *there*, I laid hands on it, and here it is!"' the woman told Ward without realizing who she was (p. 87). Mudie had in fact taken only a cautious 200 copies of *Elsmere* initially, thus arousing Ward's distrust of the library's stranglehold on the publishing industry. Neither Mudie nor Smith could have predicted that *Elsmere* – the story of a country clergyman's religious doubts and his relationship with an intensely pious wife – would become a bestseller: the one-volume six-shilling version, for instance, ran through seventeen editions in 1888–9. She preferred the American system, which was based on the assumption that people wanted to *buy* books for their own homes, rather than borrow them from a library.

Though Ward remained popular for about a decade, and adapted her work successfully for the new single-volume market (as did Rhoda Broughton), she too lived to see tastes change, and her tales of spoilt beauties in country houses superseded by D. H. Lawrence's novels of working-class life in Eastwood and James Joyce's of Dublin's pubs and brothels. Gaye Tuchman, in *Edging Women Out: Victorian Novelists, Publishers and Social Change*, has argued that, by the end of the nineteenth century, women novelists were receiving less favourable contracts than men, and as the title of her book indicates, being 'edged out' of the literary marketplace. This may have been the case with Macmillan's, the publisher from whose archives Tuchman gained this impression, but a survey of nineteenth-century publishing history as a whole suggests a different picture. Although women writers rose to the heights of their profession in the late eighteenth century, it was not until the nineteenth that they fully established themselves as active participants in the rapidly evolving literature industry. Once there, their presence had to be accepted as a positive influence. Despite the centrality of Dickens, Thackeray and Trollope as popular novelists of the day, women novelists quickly established their right to be discussed on equal terms. It was repeatedly the advent of new *women* writers – Harriet Martineau, the Brontës, George Eliot, Elizabeth Gaskell, Mary Ward – that caused the greatest excitement, the most mystery, or the best Mudie sales, and many of these were lasting successes. Moreover, women novelists became fully involved in shaping their own profession, challenging the dominance of the three-volume novel, holding out for better terms, reviewing their peers, and rejecting modes of publication they found uncongenial. When H. G. Wells surveyed the state of the contemporary novel in 1911, deploring what he called the 'weary giant' attitude to novel reading and writing which he found in men, he exempted women from his criticism. 'Women are more serious, not only about life, but about books', he insisted, identifying in the literature of the 1890s, 'a rebel undertow of earnest and aggressive writing and reading, supported chiefly by women and supplied very largely by women, which gave the lie to the prevailing trivial estimate of fiction'.[30] By the end of the century the right of women novelists to be at the very heart of the marketplace was no longer questioned by any critic who wanted to be taken seriously.

NOTES

1 *The George Eliot Letters*, ed. Gordon S. Haight, 9 vols. (Yale University Press, 1954–79), vol. III, p. 151.

2 [Margaret Oliphant], 'Modern Novelists – Great and Small', *Blackwood's Magazine* 77 (May 1855), p. 555.

3 John Sutherland, *Mrs Humphry Ward: Eminent Victorian, Pre-eminent Edwardian* (Oxford: Clarendon Press, 1990), p. 148. It has to be said, however, that there was already mounting pressure against the 'three-decker', most notably from Arthur Mudie (Charles Mudie's son) and George Moore. See Royal A. Gettmann, *A Victorian Publisher: a Study of the Bentley Papers* (Cambridge University Press, 1960), p. 257; and John Feather, *A History of British Publishing* (London and New York: Routledge, 1988), pp. 154–5.

4 Mrs Oliphant, *Annals of a Publishing House: William Blackwood and His Sons, Their Magazine and Friends*, 2 vols. (Edinburgh and London: Blackwood, 1897), vol. II, p. 458.

5 Gaye Tuchman with Nina E. Fortin, *Edging Women Out: Victorian Novelists, Publishers and Social Change* (London: Routledge, 1989), p. 29.

6 Recognizing this, publishers usually produced the complete volumes simultaneously with the final part of the serial.

7 According to Gordon Haight, Tauchnitz 'had a stranglehold on English reprints on the Continent, many of which found their way into England'. George Eliot was so frustrated with Tauchnitz's terms (he paid her £30 for *Scenes of Clerical Life*, and £100 for *The Mill on the Floss*) that Lewes negotiated new terms for *Middlemarch* with Albert Cohn of Asher and Co., Berlin. 'The competition forced Tauchnitz to raise his offers for subsequent books', Haight notes in *George Eliot: a Biography* (Oxford: Clarendon Press, 1968), pp. 437–8.

8 Like Charles Kingsley, Yonge joined Macmillan when John Parker went out of business in 1863: Charles Morgan, *The House of Macmillan (1843–1943)* (London: Macmillan, 1944), p. 65.

9 John Sutherland, *Victorian Novelists and Publishers* (London: Athlone Press, 1976), p. 39.

10 Cheryl Turner, *Living By the Pen: Women Writers in the Eighteenth Century* (London and New York: Routledge, 1992), p. 114.

11 *Jane Austen's Letters*, ed. Deirdre Le Faye (3rd edn, Oxford University Press, 1995), pp. 304, 217.

12 Jan Fergus, 'The Professional Woman Writer', in Edward Copeland and Juliet McMaster, eds., *The Cambridge Companion to Jane Austen* (Cambridge University Press, 1997): she actually earned 'something over £631' (p. 28).

13 *Harriet Martineau's Autobiography* (1877; rptd ed. Gaby Weiner, 2 vols. London: Virago, 1983), vol. 1, p. 167.

14 The 'Biographical Notice of Ellis and Acton Bell' (1850) is frequently reprinted in editions of *Wuthering Heights*: for example in the Penguin English Library edition, ed. David Daiches (Harmondsworth: Penguin, 1965) or in *Case Studies in Contemporary Criticism: Wuthering Heights*, ed. Linda Peterson (New York: St Martin's Press, 1992).

15 Jenny Uglow, *Elizabeth Gaskell: a Habit of Stories* (London and Boston: Faber and Faber, 1993), pp. 338–9.

16 Sutherland, *Victorian Novelists and Publishers*, p. 84.

17 *The Letters of Charlotte Brontë*, ed. Margaret Smith, vol. 1 *1829–1847* (Oxford: Clarendon Press, 1995), p. 462.

18 *The Letters of Mrs Gaskell*, ed. J. A. V. Chapple and Arthur Pollard (Manchester University Press, 1966), pp. 426–7. Gaskell found it difficult to judge space, as shown in her troubled relations with Dickens over the serialization of *North and South* in *Household Words*. Peter Ackroyd comments that Gaskell was 'somewhat difficult' as a contributor, 'particularly in her inability or slowness to cut her text as Dickens desired' (Peter Ackroyd, *Dickens* (London: Minerva, 1991), p. 745).

19 *The Autobiography of Margaret Oliphant: the Complete Text*, ed. Elisabeth Jay (Oxford University Press, 1990), p. 91.

20 Elisabeth Jay, *Mrs Oliphant: a Fiction to Herself: a Literary Life* (Oxford: Clarendon Press, 1995), p. 280.

21 Margaret Harris and Judith Johnston see Eliot's Italian tour of 1860 as a turning point in her career: 'in the shift from the working out of childhood memories to more studied work on the past in relation to the present, both reading the past in relation to the present and writing it . . . There is a consciousness in the journal of history being constantly remade' (*The Journals of George Eliot*, ed. Margaret Harris and Judith Johnston (Cambridge University Press, 1998), pp. 333–4).

22 Gettmann, *A Victorian Publisher*, p. 116.

23 *The Brontës: Their Lives, Friendships and Correspondence*, ed. T. J. Wise and J. A. Symington, 4 vols. (Oxford: Shakespeare Head, 1932), vol. III, pp. 320–2.

24 Joanne Shattock, *The Oxford Guide to British Women Writers* (Oxford University Press, 1994), p. 481.

25 *Letters to Macmillan*, ed. Simon Nowell-Smith (London: Macmillan / New York: St Martin's, 1967), p. 88.

26 Shattock, *The Oxford Guide to British Women Writers*, p. 473.
27 Vineta and Robert A. Colby, *The Equivocal Virtue: Mrs Oliphant and the Victorian Literary Market Place* (New York: Archon Books, 1966), p. 164.
28 'Modern Novelists – Great and Small', *Blackwood's Magazine* 77 (May 1855), pp. 558, 568.
29 Mrs Humphry Ward, *A Writer's Recollections*, 2 vols. (London: Collins, 1918), vol. II, pp. 65–6.
30 H. G. Wells, 'The Contemporary Novel', *Fortnightly Review* 96 (1 November 1911), p. 861.

CHAPTER EIGHT

Women poets and the challenge of genre

Virginia Blain

What form is best for poems? Let me think
Of forms less, and the external. Trust the spirit,
As sovran nature does, to make the form;
For otherwise we only imprison spirit
And not embody. Inward evermore
To outward – so in life, and so in art
Which still is life.

(Aurora Leigh, fifth book, lines 223–7)

Romanticism's rejection of classical generic convention in the language and form of poetry was a great boon for women writers. While Thomas de Quincey, lamenting his brilliant mother's lost talents, extols the hidden genius of women letter-writers, he still unthinkingly boasts of his own prowess in Greek and Latin, learned while a public school-boy, and a mark of privilege rarely available to women and girls in the nineteenth century.[1] While De Quincey may have followed the Wordsworths to Dove Cottage, he apparently did not share Samuel Coleridge and William Wordsworth's egalitarian notions of language, whereby poetry was redefined, in the famous Preface to *Lyrical Ballads* (2nd edn, 1800) as the words of 'a Man speaking to Men'. This new definition brought poetic language back into the common sphere, linking it once more with its roots in oral culture, where, in spite of such an apparently masculist formulation, it was soon taken up by a broadening band of women poets. Among these, of course, were some who, like Elizabeth Barrett herself, were privileged enough to have gained access to an education in the classics, however unsystematic that might have been, and who had been able to draw on that knowledge in producing their poetry.[2] For example, Mary Tighe (1772–1810), famous for her extended Spenserian allegory *Psyche; or, the Legend of Love* (1805), which became immensely popular after her death and inspired the young John Keats, came from a wealthy family with a highly educated mother who encouraged her daughter's classical reading. More commonly, however, women poets relished the chance to be able to speak their own language. Caroline Bowles Southey (1786–1854), although not particularly an admirer of Wordsworth's (she thought him too egotistical) was moved by something of the same spirit to produce her own verse autobiography (*The Birthday*), published in 3,000 lines of splendidly conversational blank verse in 1836, fourteen years before *The Prelude* appeared.[3]

Among Caroline Bowles's other works, her meditation on mortality, 'That's What we Are', stands out in its stripping away of the protective wraps in which we shield ourselves from our own corporeality and its inevitable end in death and decay. It is instructive to compare this ironic and meditative lyric, set in a churchyard in which the sexton is opening an ancient tomb to inter the last member of an old family (it is cheaper to bury him here than in the pauper's grave he might otherwise have been allotted), with the far more formal address to 'The Grave' by Bowles's younger contemporary, Caroline Clive (1801–73). Clive writes containedly, in quatrains, and her style is of the eighteenth century:

> Unspoken tongues, perchance in praise or woe,
> Were character'd on tablets Time had swept;
> And deep were half their letters hid below
> The thick small dust of those they once had wept.

Here she uses the figure of an (ungendered: therefore, by convention, male) poet–observer wandering through an ancient tomb to draw the classic contrast between human aspirations after immortality and the obliterating effects of time. The tone is dignified and impersonal, and although her poem is as clear-eyed about mortality as Bowles's, and makes much the same point about the mortality of letters as well as bodies, it lacks the dramatic impact of Bowles's more direct and personal approach, where the lady-like female poet-narrator asks the sexton to explain where the old coffins are, for all she can see among the 'mortuary emblems half-effaced' with their illegible lettering, are 'a few fragments of dark rotten wood, / And a small heap of fine, rich, reddish earth'. Having patronizingly described the old sexton 'with his hard gray face' as himself 'a living tombstone', the narrator then has to take the lesson ('plain-spoken homily') dealt by 'that unlettered man', when he answers her with the sardonic statement: 'That's what we are!'

Both poems combine anxieties about the survival of writing with their more overt anxiety about the decay of the body, and, in their distinctive ways, they each deal with the topic of death with an almost pagan relish that vivifies their pessimism. Bowles draws a Christian moral at the end of her poem, but it is by no means its point, as Christina Rossetti's Christian belief was to be the point of her poems about death written later in the century. The concern shared by Clive and Bowles for the survival of the written word (even letters carved in stone will disappear in time) is one that was by no means unique to female poets: yet it was itself obliterated in women's poetry during the early years of the nineteenth-century by the more immediate anxiety about whether or not women had any business with seeking poetic immortality at all. Fame, as Felicia Hemans and others were fond of pointing out, posed a difficult problem for a woman: it could not provide her with moral support in the way that a husband's love could be expected to; instead, it would lead her into the morally ambiguous territory of the public domain, away from the 'private sphere' of home and hearth.[4] Hemans (1793–1835) was one of the major poetic voices in the nineteenth century, her popularity ensuring that a copy of her poems made its way into almost every literate household. We shall probably never know if it was the unpleasant prospect of being married to a famous woman that drove her husband away while she was pregnant with their fifth child, but, despite her disavowal of Fame's allure for a woman, she would have been hard-pressed to support her family without it.[5]

At the other end of the spectrum from the populist Hemans were poets like Emily Brontë (1818–48) and Dorothy Wordsworth (1771–1855). Like the male Romantics, they each sought their own kind of salvation in Nature. Brontë's poetry does not trouble with the dilemma of woman and fame; nor does the immortality of her work appear to be an issue. Instead, it is the survival of the human soul against 'the steadfast rock of immortality' that she stakes her words upon ('No coward soul is mine'). Brontë's poetry has received a lot more attention in recent times,[6] where previously it was her one novel (*Wuthering Heights*, 1847) that commanded the bulk of the critical notice. Dorothy Wordsworth, equally unconventional in her personalized form of religious faith, never presumed to call herself a poet, suppressing her own gift, as she wrote herself, precisely because she so greatly '*reverenced* the Poet's skill' ('Irregular Verses', 1827). Those who knew her well, including her brother of course, believed, like Thomas de Quincey, that 'some subtle fire of impassioned intellect apparently burned within her', which, whenever it became 'conspicuous', was 'immediately checked in obedience to the decorum of her sex and age, and her maidenly condition'.[7] Her nature descriptions in her journals provided material for her brother's poems as well as her own,[8] and her poetic voice is characteristically attuned more to speech rhythms than to the artificial dictates of metre. Eliza Hamilton (1807–51),[9] another sister of a more famous brother (Sir William Rowan Hamilton, poet and astronomer: see *DNB*), also lived an intense spiritual life, though in her case it was bounded within a more conventional frame, her puritanical Moravian faith.

In her approach to poetic form, Hamilton seems to fall somewhere between Tighe and Dorothy Wordsworth. Like Tighe, she is drawn to formal poetic language and to the Spenserian stanza, but, like Wordsworth, she opens her verse in the direction of speech rhythms. Where Tighe end-stops her lines, Hamilton's derive their emotional force from the seemingly inexorable tidal pull from one line to the next:

> And woman's lips in silence have a power
> Changed when their tones go forth upon the winds;
> Their safety is in secrecy, their hour
> The lone & still one when the heart unbinds
> Its hidden feelings to the few beloved -
> Or to the living one whose trueness has been proved.[10]

Hamilton was Anglo-Irish, born and raised in a Dublin family of genius, somewhat reminiscent of the Brontës (there were five gifted children, all but one being girls; the mother died early; the children relied largely on each other's company; William, like Branwell, as the male child, was provided with every opportunity to develop his gifts, while the girls 'made do'). Eliza's ambition was always to be a poet (although her brother tried to train her as an astronomer) and in 1830 she and William spent a summer with the Wordsworths during which she received a good deal of practical criticism of her poems, as well as considerable respect from the great man for her gift. Her first publication was in the *Dublin University Magazine*, which proved a fair supporter of a number of women poets, including Mary Ann Browne, later Gray (1812–44). Interestingly, this very masculist journal provided a forum – rather like *Blackwood's Edinburgh Magazine* for Felicia Hemans and Caroline Bowles – in which women could encounter each other's work and through which they could become known to each other in person, or at least begin a conversation among themselves. For example, Browne made contact with Hamilton as a result of reading her work in the magazine, and Hamilton made reply in a poem which begins by referring to the ghostly presence of the recently dead Letitia Landon (1802–38):

Dear Lady! of the soft-voiced lyre
Another music gone
Steeped in her heart's extinguished fire
Whose dirge is ocean's moan
By Afric's coast – song, Lady! song
Hath made thee ours in vision long
A vivid dream by poets prized
As all by song etherialized!-
(from: 'To an Unknown Poetess (Miss M. A. Browne
A reply to a message of hers in 1841')

This poem not only marks the impact of Landon's untimely death in Africa so soon after her impetuous marriage, but also honours the importance of women's poetry to other women poets. It is as though the poetry, through its release from materiality, its etherialization, is paradoxically the only tangible 'remains' of the poet whose life is cut tragically short, just as Browne's was to be, at the age of thirty-two, from the effects of childbirth, and Hamilton's also, at forty-four, apparently from cancer.

Letitia Elizabeth Landon (always known as 'L. E. L'.) had been a publishing phenomenon during the 1820s and 1830s. The mystery of her true identity, coupled with her special line in romantic love poetry – abandoned women who lament their condition to the strains of a harp or lyre, and who are vaguely based on a Sapphic model, popularly misread as exalting suicide for the sake of unrequited love[11] – brought her almost a cult following. Various attempts have been made to recuperate her verse project for modern feminism, but to my mind they remain unconvincing.[12] Nevertheless, Landon was a shrewd manipulator of the literary marketplace, and her tragic and mysterious death in Africa in 1838 cut short a career that showed promise of new directions. Her influence on subsequent female poets was profound, whether or not they chose to learn from her methods. Christina Rossetti (1830–94) and Elizabeth Barrett Browning (1806–61) both, like Hamilton, wrote poems memorializing L. E. L. while at the same time gently taking her to task for what they (especially Browning) saw as an over-indulgence in self-pity:

Downstairs I laugh, I sport and jest with all;
But in my solitary room above
I turn my face in silence to the wall;
My heart is breaking for a little love.
(Rossetti: 'L. E. L'.)

'Do ye think of me, as I think of you?' –
O friends, – O kindred, – O dear brotherhood
Of all the world! what are we, that we should
For covenants of long affection sue?
(Barrett Browning: 'L. E. L's Last Question')

Of course, Landon's removal to Africa with her new husband, George Maclean, the stern Governor of Cape Coast Castle, took her at one magical stroke away from the London world of literary hackwork and often scandalous innuendo, which, as a single woman, she had had to endure in her struggle to support herself and her family by her writing, and transported her into the realm of the exotic, a place no other woman poet of her standing had visited, let alone inhabited. We might wonder if Landon had any notion before she got there that the Castle was one of a number of coastal strongholds in which Africans were imprisoned prior to their forced enshipment to the slave plantations of the Americas. Contemporary accounts of her marriage and departure certainly make no mention of this unsavoury fact. After her mysterious death from an overdose of prussic acid, her poetry naturally received a boost in popularity which enabled her to rival Hemans in sales for the next twenty years or so.

Despite Landon's silence on political issues like slavery in favour of a more insular focus on the sorrows of romantic love, many other women poets did choose to embrace political causes in their verse. Landon's friend and one-time housemate, Emma Roberts (*c.* 1794–1840), for example, who spent some time in India, wrote poems in condemnation of the practice of suttee; while, more notably, poets like Anna Laetitia Barbauld (1743–1825), Hannah More (1745–1833), Helen Maria Williams (1762–1827) and Amelia Opie (1769–1853) all protested forcefully against slavery and the slave trade, while Barbauld's niece Lucy Aikin (1781–1861) took a strong stand in her *Epistles on Women*[13] on the side of feminism and anti-imperialism generally. Anne K. Mellor has argued[14] that this group of female poets can be seen as forming a separate tradition from that of the more conventional 'poetess', who, like Landon, may not have thought so deeply about the implications of buying into the imperialist project.

However, to pursue a line tracing a rigid divide between politically engaged 'female poets' and more conventionally feminized 'poetesses' may be inadvertently to encourage a kind of post-feminist sexism. Any simple divide between the 'poet' who deals with 'real' issues, and the 'poetess' who deals mainly with romantic love and sentimentalized nature description (subjects deemed fit for women), is likely to break down under critical examination. For the serious 'poet' may also deal with the issue of romantic love (Barrett Browning, for example, published extensively on political subjects as well as producing her famous series of love sonnets to her husband), and who is to say it is not a 'real' issue, even a political issue: one of the tenets of modern feminism, after all, has been that 'the personal is political'. Romantic love can be treated in ways that bring this out: Barrett Browning's extraordinary verse-novel *Aurora Leigh*, a narrative poem in nine books published in 1857 [1856], is one work dedicated to bringing this point home through its extensive exploration of the workings of sexual politics.

Sentimentality, too, can have its own expressive purpose.[15] This is the case with poets as widely spaced as Felicia Hemans (d. 1835) and Jean Ingelow (1820–97). Hemans's most anthologized poem, 'Casabianca' ('The boy stood on the burning deck'), often taken in the past as the epitome of a sentimentalized exaltation of patriotic heroism, can now be read quite differently, as offering a 'between-the-lines' critique of the sacrifice of children in the name of a (dead or absent) father.[16] Jean Ingelow, enormously popular mid-century for her colourful romantic ballads – 'The High Tide on the Coast of Lincolnshire' and 'Divided' were two of the best-known – also repays a more deconstructive reading, as Isobel Armstrong and others have shown.[17] Yet neither Hemans nor Ingelow focussed exclusively, or even largely, on the theme of love between men and women. They held out instead for a high-minded ideal of loyalty as a kind of social and domestic adhesive. The peculiar dilemma faced by any female artist in a patriarchal culture who longs both to develop her difference from other women, but also to keep her commonality with them, can be traced in one form or other through the work of many women poets of the century. Some poets ('Michael Field' is a prime example) struggled as much against female identity as for it.

It is noticeable that, among the number who come to terms more readily with the problem of gender, are those whose work, like that of Hemans and Ingelow, appears to be less reliant on the romantic myth of heterosexual bliss: these include Augusta Webster, Constance Naden, Mary Coleridge, May Kendall and Michael Field. 'Michael Field' was the pen-name adopted by two women poets who actually lived together as lovers, and who jointly produced a large number of volumes. These were Katharine Bradley (1846–1914) and Edith Cooper (1862–1913), an aunt and niece, who vowed early to dedicate themselves to poetry and to each other (see their poem entitled 'Prologue': 'My love and I took hands and swore / Against the world, to be / Poets and lovers evermore') and who were enabled to do so for the rest of their lives thanks to their possession of inherited wealth. Such a privileged social position enabled them to hold themselves aloof from marketplace pressures. Although their main aspiration centred on the writing of (very unfashionable) verse tragedies in the Shakespearean tradition, as time went on they also produced eight volumes of lyric poetry, the best of which is often the love poetry (where the 'voice' adopted is generally that of a male lover, an imitation of the conventional romance myth subverted by the joint female authorship). Michael Field's initial reception by reviewers was excellent – 'he' was hailed by critics (including Robert Browning) as a major new voice: 'a poet of distinguished powers', 'something almost of Shakespearean penetration', 'a fresh gift of song'.[18] Once their secret was out, however, and people knew that 'Michael Field' was a woman – worse, *two* women – their work was no longer taken seriously, except by a few who saw in it something noble and who admired the writers' dedication to their love of beauty and each other. So their work, too, sank without much trace somewhere between the two world wars, once those who championed them had died.[19]

Not only was Michael Field relatively untrammeled by the more usual constraints imposed upon women under patriarchy, this pair also managed, until late in their lives at any rate, to avoid the penitential meshes of conventional Christianity that so troubled many women poets. Bradley and Cooper, indeed, took great pride in their avowed paganism, declaring themselves to be 'maenads' in their rebellion against the cultural stereotypes of femininity.[20] Again, unlike less privileged women, they had both studied Greek, and knew that the Meinades, or Bacchantes – priestesses of Bacchus – renowned for their seeming madness or frenzy in their worship, could keep *hoi polloi* at bay and find new freedom by embracing such an outrageous identity. This did not prevent them admiring the work of some devoutly Christian poets – for example, Christina Rossetti (to whom they composed a sonnet) and also the Roman Catholic poet Alice Meynell; although Bradley, with characteristic impatience, once declared that Dorothy Wordsworth was the only woman she regarded as a true poet.[21]

Their own lasting strength as poets, though, owes much to their unswerving sense of vocation, a sense shared by some, if not all, of the poets included in this discussion. Again, such a sense is largely underwritten by privilege: access to education and contact with a supportive literary milieu. Certainly Barrett Browning had it, and so did Rossetti, though she never had the private income which in Barrett Browning's case enabled her to support her husband and fellow-poet Robert Browning as well as herself. Neither woman had to work for a living, though if Rossetti had been stronger, she might well have been obliged to go out teaching as a governess, like her sister Maria.[22] Although Rossetti and Barrett Browning each published some prose works, they certainly regarded themselves first and foremost as poets, and received enough acclaim for their work during their lifetime to maintain such a belief in themselves.

In the Introduction to his recent anthology of Victorian verse, Daniel Karlin has argued that for a poet to take his (or her) work seriously, as Barrett Browning claimed to do, was actually a mistake. She wrote: 'Poetry has been as serious a thing to me as life itself . . . I never mistook pleasure for the final cause of poetry; nor leisure, for the hour of the poet.'[23] To take one's art seriously in this manner was to bypass the pleasure principle so forcefully extolled by Wordsworth in his Preface to the *Lyrical Ballads*. For Wordsworth, poetry is written out of 'the necessity of giving immediate pleasure to a Human Being', an argument he elaborates eloquently, and of which Karlin highly approves.[24] Yet, despite Wordsworth's admirable determination to remove poetry from its exclusive domain in an ivory tower, there is a sense in which the exaltation of a pleasure principle is in itself a very patrician move.[25] To assume the kind of intellectual freedom that can insist upon its centrality in writing and reading is to assume a position of immense privilege. Karlin's argument about Wordsworth is a very important one in my view, because it points, by implication, to one of the chief difficulties under which women poets, as a 'muted' group, so much less sure of their right to be heard, had to labour in the nineteenth century, at least until the 1870s or 1880s. It is reminiscent of early (male) reactions to women as undergraduates in the universities,[26] where they were constantly ridiculed for taking their studies too seriously, taking too many notes, being altogether too earnest. Many women poets in the earlier part of the century felt keenly their position of exposure in the public eye, at the same time as they desperately wanted to be taken seriously as poets and have their poetry given the dignity of a worthy life's work rather than having to be disguised, in a way, under some such title as is alluded to in Barrett Browning's remark, for example the very common (and commonly self-deprecating) 'Lays of Leisure Hours'.[27] To write purely from a motive of pleasure would have been an idea quite literally out of reach. Only when we get to poets like Michael Field, writing in the 1870s and 1880s, a very privileged and patrician pair, does the pleasure principle surface in women's production of poetry. Whether it then acts as the kind of spiritual–sexual leaven recommended by Wordsworth is perhaps open to debate.

However, compared with women novelists, who usually wrote for money (and often with great success), poets were placed in a very different position. During the 1830s, particularly with the popularity of the annuals and gift books, verse was a highly prized commodity, but from the late 1840s prose fiction began to dominate the market. This had consequences both good and bad for the production of poetry. While Felicia Hemans and Letitia Landon were each able to support an extended family by their writings during the 1830s (and Landon also published novels), the pressure of this financial expectation could often compromise their poetry as art. Later poets like Augusta Webster (1837–94) who wrote most of her poetry in the 1860s, and Mathilde Blind (1841–96), publishing mainly in the 1880s and 1890s, on the other hand, developed quite a different professional attitude, producing journalism for money, and poetry as a non-profit-making exercise. Neither of them was reliant on their writing for their economic survival, however. Yet the seriousness with which they took their poetry was likely to be different in kind, if not in degree, from that of the earlier writers. They experienced, it would be fair to say, a more even-handed reception than Hemans and Landon had experienced: the 'let us now pay homage to the fair poetess' kind of patronage had long gone out of fashion. In part, this changing attitude was the product of women's own input into literary criticism. As the century drew on, there emerged other women poets like Webster herself, who reviewed for the *Athenaeum*, or Alice Meynell (1847–1922), who published a number of volumes of influential literary essays (the first was *The Rhythm of Life*, 1893) after making her presence felt early as a poet with the publication of her first volume, *Preludes*, in 1875 (followed by many more in later years).

Poetic tastes and styles changed immensely throughout the nineteenth century. The romantic glorification of abandonment in love, for example, dropped quickly out of fashion in favour of a burgeoning Victorian interest in the psychology of couples.[28] The motif of abandonment did not disappear entirely, but was given a different slant, most notably in Christina Rossetti's verse, both secular and devotional. A significant portion of her secular verse addresses the theme of lost love: often almost lovingly dwelt upon (Wordsworth's 'pleasure principle'

(p. 172 above) peeping through, perhaps), as in poems like 'An Apple-Gathering', for example. Although her manner, as Virginia Woolf once noted, can be 'exquisitely playful',[29] and although recent criticism has paid more attention to her whimsical sense of humour,[30] her poem 'A Birthday' (composed in 1862) which begins, famously, 'My heart is like a singing bird', is possibly the only one that expresses a sense of joy in love. Her devotional verse is seldom joyous either – her relationship with her God is not an easy one. Woolf also wrote of Rossetti, memorably, that when God was finally called to account, Rossetti would be one of the chief witnesses for the prosecution.[31] By this she meant that, in her view, Rossetti's poetic gift had been grossly compromised by her religious belief. But Woolf was part of the generation that was determined to throw off the shackles of the Victorians who were their immediate ancestors, and we can now recognize other ways of looking at this issue. For example, it can be argued that, for the truly devout, the realm of religion was a space marked out separately from the everyday, and that, since souls are unsexed, gender hierarchies could be kept at bay in this private space. Rossetti herself was comforted by this belief: 'one final consolation remains to careful and troubled hearts: in Christ there is neither male nor female, for we are all one (Gal. iii. 28)'.[32] Such a sense of sanctuary might help to account for at least part of the strong attraction towards religion shown by many women poets of the period. Barrett Browning, for example, always retained her firm belief in a Christian God, which runs like a silk thread through the fabric of her writing: not always visible, but always firmly there. Alice Meynell converted to Roman Catholicism in 1872 and remained a devout Catholic for the rest of her life. She was a strong admirer of Rossetti and developed something of her subtle meditative style in her poetry. Dora Greenwell (1821–82), another friend and admirer of Rossetti's and author of a number of theological essays as well as devotional and other poems, once wrote that mixing Christianity with poetry was like eating honey off the tip of a spear[33] – a telling image of the powerful sway still occupied by Christian thinking at the time.

Others, however, especially those of more radical tendencies, like Mathilde Blind, step-daughter of Karl Blind, a German revolutionary, were influenced by scientific and evolutionary thinkers to abandon Christianity altogether. Constance Naden and May Kendall were followers of the new sciences rather than the old belief systems; Naden (1858–89) wrote philosophical treatises as well as poetry, and Kendall – whose real name was Emma Goldworth (1861–1943) – also produced satirical novels. Amy Levy (1861–89) was another highly intelligent and well-educated woman, who grew up in and later rebelled against the orthodox Anglo-Jewish community of north London. It is now widely believed that she too was what we would today call 'lesbian',[34] though, unlike the two women behind Michael Field, she was not destined to find the happiness of a reciprocated love. While her work never confronts the theme of same-sex desire directly, certainly it can lend itself to this interpretation by modern readers accustomed to looking for coded hints of even heterosexual desire in nineteenth-century writing. Another social outsider, Adah Isaacs Menken (1839?–1868), took a Jew as one of her numerous husbands (it is not known whether there were four or five) and, to some extent at least, also took upon herself the role of Jewish champion. Like Levy though, and with as much cause (for Menken was an actress – still a marker of social undesirability – as well as an alien, being American born and bred), she felt isolated and deeply unhappy in the London society of her time, and she died in Paris a week before publication of her single volume of poems. Also dying tragically early, Levy committed suicide at the age of twenty-eight, despite her burgeoning career as published novelist and poet. Clearly, to be an outsider because of one's extreme Christian devotion, one's Jewishness or, even, one's atheism was one thing in Victorian society, but to be an outsider because of one's sexuality was quite another, and even more irredeemable. Paradoxically, Levy produced some of the most profoundly erotic love poetry written by a woman at this time: for example, her 1884 poem 'Sinfonia Eroica', about listening to Beethoven at a concert, is a *tour de force* in the way it combines the sensual ecstasy of musical experience with the orgasmic experience of bodily release:

> I, with the rest,
> Sat there athirst, atremble for the sound;
> And as my aimless glances wandered round,
> Far off, across the hush'd, expectant throng,
> I saw your face that fac'd mine.
> Clear and strong
> Rush'd forth the sound, a mighty mountain stream;
> Across the clust'ring heads mine eyes did seem
> By subtle forces drawn, your eyes to meet.
> Then you, the melody, the summer heat,
> Mingled in all my blood and made it wine.
> Straight I forgot the world's great woe and mine;
> My spirit's murky lead grew molten fire;
> Despair itself was rapture.

> Ever higher,
> Stronger and clearer rose the mighty strain;
> Then sudden fell; then all was still again,
> And I sank back, quivering as one in pain.
> Brief was the pause; then, 'mid a hush profound,
> Slow on the waiting air swell'd forth a sound
> So wondrous sweet that each man held his breath;
> A measur'd, mystic melody of death.
> Then back you lean'd your head, and I could note
> The upward outline of your perfect throat . . .
> . . . And I knew
> Not which was sound, and which, O Love, was you.

Levy was also one of the poets more gifted at using the most potent formal quality of verse, its power of rhythm. Tragically, like Beethoven, she too became aware of an advancing deafness, which was to cut her off from hearing her beloved music, though not from the inner cadences of her own verse – 'Wordsworth located the pleasure of poetry where you might think it was most apparent, but where it has often been least regarded: in rhythm, in the constitutive and elemental principle of poetic form' (Karlin, *Penguin Book of Victorian Verse*, p. lviii). Viewed in this light, Levy would earn approval for poems like this: but they are not the only type she produces. Elsewhere (as in 'Magdalen', a poem about a 'fallen woman'), she raises concerns about the ethics of pleasure that are common to a lot of women poets of the mid to late nineteenth century. In a sense, lyric poetry is the only form which can escape an ethical environment and remain purely ontological. Once poetry narrates action, it joins fiction in becoming ethical; that is, it implies consequences to human behaviours, including the behaviour of pleasure-seeking.

In *Aurora Leigh*, Barrett Browning invented a unique and – as it turned out – profoundly influential way of giving voice to the ideals as well as the tribulations of the woman poet. The poem went through thirteen editions by 1873. The form chosen, that of 'verse-novel', consciously brought poetry as close as possible to the realm of prose fiction without actually going over the edge. But the whole purpose of the work is the debate it raises about various ethical issues, by which I mean issues which have to do with human behaviour (rather than any absolute sense of good and evil, or even right and wrong, though these may have some relevance). The overarching question raised in the work is the eternal one: how best to live one's life? In this case, how best to live one's life as a female artist in a constrictive society? The heroine Aurora enacts the struggle of the serious female artist figure to achieve an autonomous status in an unusually hostile environment, encountering opposition not just from her insufferably priggish cousin, Romney, but also from her often fraught negotiations with other female characters, who might represent alternative female roles; the 'man's woman' Lady Waldemar, the fallen woman (Marian Erle), even the embittered stepmother from the beginning of the poem. Despite what some have regarded as the compromised ending, in which Aurora does marry Romney after all, this remarkable poem made its mark in depicting the possibility of a full rich life for a single woman who was dedicated to a poet's existence. No subsequent female poet could afford to ignore it – many quoted it, consciously or unconsciously, in their own work: 'But most of all I think Aurora Leigh', wrote Adelaide Procter (1825–64), in 'A Woman's Answer', which is a poem paired with her 'Woman's Question' – both being explorations of the paradoxical nature of romantic love for another human being, and the difficulty of balancing one's own needs with those of another. These poems also raise common anxieties not just about one's way of being in the world, but, linked with these, anxieties about genre, or one's way of being in poetry. Barrett Browning's poem was a deeply strengthening model, which almost seemed to lend legitimacy to women's desire to have both love and creativity in their lives, and not to have to choose between them. It seemed at one stroke to do away with a kind of wavering self-apology which had marred too many female-authored poems in the first half of the century.

It also opened up the way for women poets wanting to expand into longer narrative works, whether or not they were based on Barrett Browning's autobiographic model. Some that were not, but were rather closer to dramatic productions, were Emily Pfeiffer's experimental mixed-genre *Rhyme of the Lady of the Rock, and How it Grew* (1884) – which embeds a folk-ballad on a historical subject into a contemporary prose commentary – and Mathilde Blind's politically engaged verse narratives on the entrenched misogyny of the Christian church (*The Prophecy of Saint Oran*, 1881) and the scandal of the Highland clearances in Scotland (*The Heather on Fire*, 1886). These three narrative poems all engage strongly with ethical issues. Pfeiffer's poem explores a number of contemporary issues: marital rape is one of them. She manages to deal with such a sensitive topic by distancing it through a technique of framing. She sets her poem within a double frame: firstly, it tells (in prose) an amusing but matter-of-fact story of a woman poet travelling in the Western Isles of Scotland, where she finds herself at a place (Duart Castle, on the Isle of Mull) which harbours a particular legend that appeals to her so much she decides to make a poem of it. This poem is then given to the reader piecemeal, as it is composed; and each portion (or Fitte) is again framed by the remarks and byplay of assorted characters who assemble each evening to listen and to criticise as the poem is read aloud. The legend narrated in the poem is of a woman sold into marriage from one clan to another, and eventually set to perish on an ocean rock for refusing to sleep with her new chieftain, and defending herself against rape with her dagger:

> She set herself as a hind at bay,
>   She straightened her back to the wall;
> 'I that am come as a hostage here,
>   Would you use me as a thrall?'
> 'Not so', quoth he, 'but by limb and life,
>   I'll use you as my wedded wife.'
>
> (Fitte the second, st. 22, p. 122)

One of the auditors in the poem's prose frame, a passing pedlar, comments (tellingly, to the poet's husband, who has read the Fitte aloud, and not to the poet):

'"Your lady has set her pen to work on a perilous subject as addressed to your 'Philister' English public", said he.

'My visions were scattered in a moment; like a jewelled window through which a bullet has passed, the hues of fancy grew dark and dull with the inlet of common day.' (pp. 127–8).

Mathilde Blind's poems also deal with the political subject of coercion of the weaker by the stronger – not, this time, of a wife by a husband, but (in *Heather on Fire*) of a whole village of innocent people forcibly evicted from their homes by a powerful English landlord during the Highland clearances, and (in *Saint Oran*) of a young monk persecuted and eventually killed by his own church for the sin of falling in love. The monk returns from the dead like Lazarus, but with a very different message:

> Slowly he raised his voice – once rich in tone
> Like sweetest music, now a mournful knell
> With full sepulchral sounds, as of a stone
> Cast down into a black unfathomed well –
> And murmured, 'Lo, I come back from the grave –
> Behold, there is no God to smite or save.
>
> 'Poor fools! wild dreamers! No, there is no God;
> Yon heaven is deaf and dumb to prayer and praise;
> Lo, no almighty tyrant wields the rod

> For evermore above our hapless race;
> Nor fashioned us, frail creatures that we be,
> To bear the burden of eternity'.
>   (Part Four, sts. xi and xii, pp. 60–1)

Of course his brother monks are enraged at this prophecy, and rush to take revenge:

> 'The fool says in his heart, There is no God,'
> Cried St Columba, white with Christian ire
> 'Seize Oran, re-inter him in the sod
> And may his soul awake in endless fire:
> Earth on his mouth – the earth he would adore,
> That his blaspheming tongue may blab no more'.
>   (st. xx, p. 64)

Other poets became even more engaged with the dramatic end of the narrative spectrum, exploring the possibilities not only of dramatic monologue but of full-scale verse drama, a form which attracted a surprising number of women poets. The influence of Robert Browning was a potent one in this regard: his willingness to explore, through dramatization, viewpoints other than that of the conventional bourgeois male, endeared him to women writers. Augusta Webster, for example, a strong admirer, produced many dramatic monologues as well as some fine dramas, which tackle a number of contentious contemporary issues under cover of a historical setting; verse drama was also written copiously by Michael Field and by Emily Pfeiffer. It is important to realize that this genre was so popular with many women poets. Drama thrives on conflict, and direct expression of conflict was something convention denied to young women. Dramatic forms offered the opportunity to imitate or inhabit less socially acceptable positions without taking direct responsibility for them; with the lyric forms, by contrast, poets were too often assumed to BE the speaking 'I' of their poem, and in the case of women poets, this readerly assumption was a powerful agent for writerly self-censorship.

In the nineteenth century, the more 'classical' forms like verse tragedy and epic were supposedly unavailable to women, owing to their exclusion from the universities, and, in many cases, from any form of serious schooling. However, a surprisingly large number of future poets did manage to scrounge an education for themselves; vicars' daughters like Frances Havergal listened in on their father's tutoring sessions; younger sisters like Emily Brontë and Eliza Hamilton persuaded their more fortunate brothers to teach them; wives of enlightened husbands, like Mary

Howitt,[35] went on educating themselves after marriage; clever daughters of rich men, like Elizabeth Barrett and Constance Naden, were allowed tutors of their own; women who lived with female partners, notably Katharine Bradley and Edith Cooper, supported each other's efforts to overcome deficiencies in formal education. Amy Levy was the only one to attend university (Newnham College at Cambridge). The thirst for knowledge remained intense. Knowledge of the classics was particularly prized for its association with the idea of true learning at Oxbridge, and for its relative inaccessibility to females. In fact, classical translations as well as – to a lesser extent – translations from the modern romance languages became something of a status symbol among nineteenth-century women poets. Elizabeth Barrett and Augusta Webster each produced scholarly translations from the Greek; both had benefited from a classical education, at least in the sense that they had been enabled to study Greek in a serious manner and reach a level of proficiency high enough for them to produce original translations (see Webster's 1866 verse translation of Aeschylus' *Prometheus Bound*, and her 1868 *Medea*; Barrett Browning also translated *Prometheus Bound* (first attempted 1833, revised in 1845 for publication in 1850)).

In a sense, of course, this kind of work was always undertaken by women in order to prove a point: to illustrate their own ability in what too often went unchallenged as male intellectual territory. But, though creative (much more so than is often credited), it was not original work, and we need to move on to ask the hard question about the scope and nature of women's creative contribution to poetry. To a large extent, post-Romantic women poets were obliged to find a way to utilize or to abandon an inherited stockpile of expressive machinery that increasingly appeared to be stiff, creaky and cumbersome, and in which the allotted role of 'woman' did not at all chime with their own desire. Different poets rose to this challenge in different ways. Some, most notably the American poet Menken who came to live in London and published her poetry there (cheekily dedicating her volume to Charles Dickens – whom she must have met backstage), responded to the challenge by ditching 'feminine' expressive forms altogether. Instead, by adapting Walt Whitman's chanting speech-rhythms, throwing in a dash of Swinburne's highly coloured rhetoric and imbuing the whole with a fair dose of feminist rage, she created a new and quite shocking voice: as Judith, for example, in her poem of that name, she warns the (Victorian male) populace:

Stand back, ye Philistines!
Practice what ye preach to me . . .
I am no Magdalene waiting to kiss the hem of your garment.
It is mid-day.
I am Judith!
I wait for the head of my Holofernes!

It should be noted that Menken's defiant refusal to identify with the female victim-figure of Magdalene, the fallen woman, was not universally shared. A number of women poets do deal sympathetically with one of the most notorious social evils of the time, that of prostitution – and they deal with it in a manner which recognizes their own unique and yet implicated position as middle-class women. It is instructive to compare the poems on this subject by Augusta Webster ('The Castaway'), Amy Levy ('Magdalen') and – less well-known – 'The Message', by Mathilde Blind. In Webster's poem, the speaker is an intelligent prostitute (a contentious concept to begin with, for many contemporary readers). She has no illusions about herself or her ostracized position in a hypocritical society:

> And, for me,
> I say let no one be above her trade;
> I own my kindredship with any drab
> who sells herself as I, although she crouch
> in fetid garrets and I have a home
> all velvet and marqueterie and pastilles,
> although she hide her skeleton in rags
> and I set fashions and wear cobweb lace:
> the difference lies but in my choicer ware,
> that I sell beauty and she ugliness;
> our traffic's one – I'm no sweet slaver-tongue
> to gloze upon it and explain myself
> a sort of fractious angel misconceived –
> our traffic's one: I own it. And what then?
> I know of worse that are called honourable.

(lines 65–79)

If we turn from these words to a poem like Dante Gabriel Rossetti's 'Jenny' (published in the same year: 1870),[36] often acclaimed for its anti-moralistic sympathy with the prostitute of its title, it is interesting what uneasy gaps and cover-ups suddenly appear, and how much more patronizing its (male) narrator becomes in this context. To treat the same subject from the opposite gender position makes a surprising difference.

Certainly, women wrote about traditional lyric subject-matter – love poetry, devotional poetry, poems of elegy and meditation, poems about nature (and about the city) – but very often these are poems which adopt quite a different perspective from the one most readers of Victorian poetry will expect. To take one example: Augusta Webster's fine, though sadly unfinished, sequence of sonnets written to her daughter, 'Mother and Daughter', published posthumously in an 1895 edition by W. M. Rossetti, attests to this power of a different viewpoint in a manner more striking even than 'Sonnets from the Portuguese' or 'Monna Innominata'. It is unique in its celebration of maternal same-sex love within the classical format of traditional heterosexual romantic love:

> II
> That she is beautiful is not delight,
>   As some think mothers joy, by pride of her,
>   To witness questing eyes caught prisoner
> And hear her praised the livelong dancing night;
> But the glad impulse that makes painters sight
>   Bids me note her and grow the happier;
>   And love that finds me as her worshipper
> Reveals me each best loveliness aright.
>
>   Oh goddess head! Oh innocent brave eyes!
> Oh curved and parted lips where smiles are rare
> And sweetness ever! Oh smooth shadowy hair
> Gathered around the silence of her brow!
>   Child, I'd needs love thy beauty stranger-wise:
> And oh the beauty of it, being thou!

This claims affinity with Felicia Hemans's poetry, which laid such an emphasis on what she called 'the domestic affections', particularly maternal love, yet it goes a step further in its appropriation of the category of traditional love poetry. That Webster knew she was mortally ill when she was writing the sequence no doubt accounts for some of the intensity with which her speaker's voice is imbued as she dwells on the beloved with such evident longing to somehow 'fix' her love, to give her daughter some tangible evidence of value (hers for her mother; her mother's for her) that would last beyond the grave.

This is naturally one of the works which is most vividly illustrative of the difference in women's poetry. Angela Leighton has made the claim that 'to be a woman poet in the nineteenth-century, much more than to be a woman novelist, was to belong to an electively separate female tradition'.[37] Yet I am not convinced that all of the poets themselves wished to be thought of as 'different' from male poets, and none was in any way trying to be what we now call 'separatist', that is, writing consciously in an exclusively female tradition. It seems fair to say that while almost all of them held strong views on issues such as the education of girls and women, most would have seen their own writing as contributing, in whatever way, to a poetic mainstream rather than a realm of women poets. This is an attitude that showed marked changes over the period we are dealing with. While Felicia Hemans, for example, had no objection to being labelled a 'poetess', the feminized title with its connotations of 'prettiness' and 'lightness' became less popular as the century went on.[38] Elizabeth Barrett Browning may have lamented the absence of literary grandmothers,[39] but this has since been shown to be evidence only of the general suppression and 'forgetting' of earlier work by women, not of their non-existence. Perhaps also, like Michael Field and Mathilde Blind and possibly Mary Coleridge, Barrett Browning cared more to find acceptance with male readers than with female. Mary Coleridge (1861–1907), a wonderfully subtle and intelligent poet, was especially alert to the difficulties of her position as bearing the name of a famous male poet (who happened to be her great-great-uncle). In her decision to publish anonymously, she appears to have been torn between not wishing to hang on the coat-tails of a famous name, and a fear of being dismissed by readers and critics as a mere 'she', a 'poetess': 'Indeed I don't want to be thought a her – how could I? – I only don't want to be thought me – which is bad grammar, & as feminine as all the rest of it, I'm afraid!'[40]

It might be premature to assume that the work of these women can be read as part of an isolated female tradition: on the contrary, it contains numerous traces of influence by male poets, including many examples of what can best be described as a dialogue, either with a particular male poet or poem, or with certain assumptions underlying male-authored poetry. This dialogue is most noticeable in the love poetry written by women. Here, many of them are concerned to point the difference of their own gendered subjectivity, in terms of a poetic tradition predicated on a male viewpoint and speaking position. This kind of challenge to male authority had of course been initiated in similar ways by women poets in earlier periods. But Victorian women poets seem to have their own characteristic ways of continuing the discussion. Robert Browning's well-known poem, 'Any Wife to Any Husband', is one which clearly struck a chord with women poets, as so many of them wrote ripostes, from Rossetti ('Wife to Husband') to Pfeiffer ('Any Husband to many a Wife').

Rosamund Marriott Watson (1860–1911), who initally published under the pseudonym 'Graham Tomson', joined the growing debate about sexual politics late in the century. In the 1880s and '90s she wrote a number of chilling ballads about marital betrayal, disguised as folk legends (for example, 'Ballad of the Bird-Bride', 'A Ballad of the Were-Wolf') and often tinged with a profound sense of alienation and loss. Herself married three times, she knew the pain of losing her children through divorce; such losses are a recurring theme in her poetry. Here, for example, is a shorter poem of hers, 'Old Pauline' (1884):

> So your boys are going to Paris? That's how I lost my own.
> Lonely? Ah yes, but I know it, the old are always alone.
> You remember my boys, Euphrasie? No? Was it before your day?
> Each, when his turn came, kissed me, and cried; but they went away.
> How I longed for them, always, vainly! and thought of them, early and late;
> I would start and look round in the pasture if any one clicked the gate.
> But a greater sorrow fell on me: my Marie, with eyes so blue,
> Grew restless, poor bird! in the home-nest – she must seek her fortune too.
> And, once the desire is on them, 'tis a fever, they cannot stay;
> And Marie, my poor little Marie! well, I missed her one bright spring day.
> 'Twas *then* that my heart broke, 'Phrasie, for my children gay and tall,
> For fair, vile, glittering Paris had taken them all.
> Yet the good God is merciful always; I live, and I have no pain,
> Only the old dumb longing for the children home again.
> Still I watch the road to the city, up the glistening sun-set track,
> But they never come back, Euphrasie – never come back!

Moving beyond the domestic environment, how did women poets in the second half of the century react to the controversies between the new science and established religion? Mathilde Blind published in 1889 an entire volume of poems devoted to evolutionary themes, called *The Ascent of Man*. Unlike Tennyson's more gloomy view (in *In Memoriam*, 1850), her poetry appears unequivocally to welcome and celebrate progressivist theories foretelling the continued improvement of the human race. Not for her any hankering after established religion: she sets her face against such worn-out creeds and places her faith in the innate capacity of human beings to change and adapt. Louisa S. Bevington (1845–95) was another poet who spurned traditional religion, becoming a Darwinist and anarchist in later life and earning for herself the sobriquet 'the poetess of evolutionary science' from Alfred H. Miles in 1891 – though he does rather dash her down with his final comment: 'Her chief defects are the over-facility common to so many poetesses, and a deficient perception of the humorous'.[41] In other words, she wrote passionately about social injustice to women.

Other women poets who were particularly concerned with the new scientific discoveries and the changing world view these brought into focus, were Constance Naden and May Kendall. Neither, thankfully, could be accused of lacking a sense of humour. These two poets were very different from the morally earnest Bevington and Blind, being much more intellectually astringent, and inclined to tackle esoteric subjects with a disruptive wit rather than a cloudy idealism. Naden, extremely intelligent and exceptionally well-educated, is more inclined to metaphysical speculation than Kendall, and less class-conscious; that is, she is not self-reflexive about her own social position of privilege in the way Kendall can be. Her sense of humour comes out particularly in the series entitled 'Evolutionary Erotics', in poems like 'Scientific Wooing' and 'Natural Selection'. Kendall goes further however, deftly driving her sly critique of science and scientists to the edge of farce, with wickedly comic, almost absurdist, poems like 'The Philanthropist and the Jellyfish' and 'Lay of the Trilobite':

> How wonderful it seemed and right,
>   The providential plan,
> That he should be a Trilobite,
>   And I should be a Man!
>
> And then, quite natural and free
>   Out of his rocky bed,
> That Trilobite he spoke to me,
>   And this is what he said.

What the Trilobite says to the Man and how it punctures Man's complacency forms the substance of the poem. A more serious Kendall poem, 'Church Echoes', which contrasts the viewpoints of the vicar's daughters with that of the poor charity children and also of the tramp, setting them quizzically against an orthodox Christian frame, is soberingly pessimistic in its conclusions; certainly very far from the meliorism offered by Blind's *Ascent of Man*.

It may be objected that I have concentrated in this discussion on the work of middle-class poets. Privilege is always relative, and although there were periods when women poets in general found it harder to achieve public recognition than their male counterparts, it is also true that educated middle-class women, especially those who had connections in the literary world, and who wrote with an eye to their popular appeal, did not always find it so very difficult to find a publisher as the century progressed, especially in the wake of trail-blazers like Hemans, Landon and Barrett Browning. For working-class women who wished to publish poetry, it was generally a different story. Many found only a relatively ephemeral place in cheap newspapers of the day. Some were taken up by the wealthy: Mary Colling (b.1805), for example, a servant who taught herself to read, was encouraged by her mistress, Anna Bray (a writer herself), who published in 1831 Colling's *Fables and other Pieces in Verse* by subscription. Given these circumstances, it is not surprising to find that these poems are muted in their critique of social mores, despite Colling's deft turn for wit and satire. Janet Hamilton (1795–1873), daughter of a Scottish shoemaker, was taught to read by her mother, but never learned to write, later dictating to her husband and son. Her verse includes many lively pieces in Scots dialect, commenting outspokenly on issues such as women's work and the evils of drink. She became very well known in her local community and beyond, attaining celebrity status by the end of her life. Ellen Johnston (1835–73), also Scottish, was known as 'the Factory Girl'. She too was self-taught. It is perhaps no accident that these strong women's voices both hail from Scotland, since Scottish law was kinder to women than English in a number of ways; for example, *de facto* marriages carried the same legal rights and responsibilities as regular marriage. However, Johnston had a tough life, working in a factory from the age of eight, and later having an illegitimate daughter for whose support she began to publish her poems and also her autobiography. A number of other lesser-known working-class poets are gradually coming to light as researchers turn their attention to the newspaper archives.[42] It needs to be remembered, though, that these women were firmly embedded in an oral culture, not a literary one, and their work utilizes other discourses than those developed by their middle-class sisters. Nor would their work have reached the same kind of audience. Caroline Bowles and Caroline Clive, from early in the century, may have wondered with some anxiety about the possible survival of their work; for working-class women, even its initial production was something of a miracle.

It has not been possible in such a brief account to cover more than a fraction of the rich material still waiting in the wings of the nineteenth century, as it were. So much has now been unearthed by assiduous researchers, and is being slowly but surely disseminated to a wider audience by way of reprints in anthologies and single volumes. It is exciting to realize that this 'new' women's poetry of the nineteenth century has been one of the most remarkable growth areas in literary scholarship over the last ten years, generating an increasing number of anthologies, journal articles, essay collections, dissertations and books.[43] There are literally dozens of wonderful poets to be reckoned with now, whose work was previously only available in research libraries. Their poetry so often has the power to move us strongly, to make us laugh, make us cry, make us wonder, and make us celebrate our inheritance with the utmost pleasure: it has indeed survived.

NOTES

1 See the first chapter of his autobiography, in *Confessions of an English Opium-Eater together with Selections from the Autobiography of Thomas De Quincey*, ed. E. Sackville-West (London: Cresset Press, 1950), p. 9.

2 For Barrett Browning's own account of her education, see her essay 'Glimpses into My Own Life and Literary Character' (1820), *Browning Institute Studies* 2 (1974), pp. 119–34.

3 See Virginia Blain, *Caroline Bowles Southey, 1786–1854: the Making of a Woman Writer* (Aldershot: Ashgate, 1998).

4 For a sound discussion of the issues involved in this dilemma of 'going public', see Dorothy Mermin, *Godiva's Ride: Women of Letters in England, 1830–1880* (Bloomington: Indiana University Press, 1993), especially chs. 1 and 2.

5 See Paula Feldman's account of Hemans's earning power, in her essay 'The Poet and the Profits: Felicia Hemans and the Literary Marketplace', in Isobel Armstrong and Virginia Blain, eds., *Women's Poetry, Late Romantic to Late Victorian: Gender and Genre, 1830–1900* (Basingstoke: Macmillan Press, 1999), pp. 71–101.

6 Margaret Homans's fine study, *Women Writers and Poetic Identity: Dorothy Wordsworth, Emily Brontë, and Emily Dickinson* (Princeton University Press, 1980), initiated a reconsideration of her poetic achievement.

7 Thomas de Quincey, *Recollections of the Lakes and Lake Poets*, ed. David Wright, from journals written between 1834 and 1848 (Harmondsworth: Penguin, 1970), p. 131.

8 Mary Moorman's 1971 edition of *Journals of Dorothy Wordsworth* (Oxford University Press) made strong claims about William Wordsworth's use of his sister's journals in his poetry, by printing poems linked with journal extracts. More recently, these claims have been disputed: Anne K. Mellor, *Romanticism and Gender* (London: Routledge, 1993), refers to this area of controversy in Wordsworth studies in some detail, p. 168.

9 See Virginia Blain, 'Letitia Elizabeth Landon, Eliza Mary Hamilton, and the Genealogy of the Victorian poetess', *Victorian Poetry* 33 (Spring 1995), pp. 31–52.

10 From an unpublished ms poem held in Trinity College, Dublin. Sir William Rowan Hamilton papers, MS 2502, f. 23. The poem, entitled 'An Unfinished Preface', has no punctuation.

11 See Yopie Prins, *Victorian Sappho* (Princeton University Press, 1999), for an important discussion of the reception of Sappho in Victorian England.

12 Perhaps the most persuasive is Isobel Armstrong's account in her chapter on women's poetry in *Victorian Poetry: Poetry, Poetics and Politics* (London: Routledge, 1993).

13 *Epistles on the Character and Condition of Women, in various ages and nations* (1810).

14 Mellor, *Romanticism and Gender*, pp. 82ff., sees women's didactic religious Evangelical poetry as precursor of feminist poetry.

15 Eve Kosofsky Sedgwick gives a fascinating thumbnail sketch of the history of the notion of sentimentality, tracing it from its origins as a term of praise in the eighteenth century to opprobrium in the twentieth, via a Nietzschian path involving the concept of vicariousness. Her argument destabilizes it as any kind of critical category. See *Epistemology of the Closet* (Berkeley: University of California Press, 1990), especially pp. 147–54.

16 See Tricia Lootens, 'Hemans and Home: Victorianism, Feminine "Internal Enemies", and the Domestication of National Identity', *PMLA* 109 (1994), pp. 238–53. Lootens was the first to make this point, and her article paved the way for later revaluations of Hemans.

17 See Isobel Armstrong, 'Misrepresentation: Codes of Affect and Politics in Nineteenth-Century Women's Poetry', in Armstrong and Blain, eds., *Women's Poetry, Late Romantic to Late Victorian*, p. 23. See also Jennifer A. Wagner, 'In her "Proper Place": Ingelow's Fable of the Female Poet and her Community in *Gladys and Her Island*', *Victorian Poetry* 31 (1993), pp. 227–39; Heidi Johnson, '"Matters That a Woman Rules": Marginalized Maternity in Jean Ingelow's A Story of Doom', *Victorian Poetry* 33 (1995), pp. 75–88.

18 See reviews cited by Mary Sturgeon, *Michael Field* (London: G. G. Harrap, 1922; rptd New York: Arno Press, 1975), pp. 27–8.

19 These were Michael Field's literary executor, Thomas Sturge Moore, who published an anthology of the verse as *A Selection from the Poems of Michael Field* (London: The Poetry Bookshop, 1923) and edited selections from their journals as *Works and Days* (London: John Murray, 1933); their biographer, Mary Sturgeon, who published *Michael Field* (London: G. G. Harrap, 1922); and Emily Fortey, who edited some of the posthumous work for publication, as *The Wattlefold: Unpublished Poems of Michael Field* (Oxford: Basil Blackwell, 1930).

20 This is made explicit in a letter they wrote to Richard Garnett around 1898, the year *World at Auction: a Drama in Verse* was published. About its title page, which was possibly designed, like the book's cover, by their artist friend Charles Ricketts, they write that the intimate appreciation of Bacchic worship that it evinces is 'most gratifying to us Maenads!' (A. L. S. n.d. no. 59, quoted by permission of the Harry Ransom Humanities Research Center, University of Texas at Austin). In 1907, however, they both converted to Roman Catholicism.

21 See Bradley's letter to Cooper held in the Bodleian Library, Oxford, quoted by permission: 'Dorothy Wordsworth . . . is the only English woman I rank as a poet – a divine creature for whom William could not have altogether sufficed. What other woman has ever had her heart right toward nature, has

ever felt of one blood with the forests, the little hills, & the mountain breezes'
(Ms Eng. poet d.56 ff. 135–6, n.d.).

22 'I am rejoiced' she once wrote, 'to feel that my health does really unfit me
for miscellaneous governessing'. See *The Family Letters of Christina Rossetti*, ed.
W. M. Rossetti (London: Brown, Langham, 1908), p. 24. Rossetti did,
however, make some attempt to help her mother run a day school, and she
also undertook charitable work at a penitentiary for fallen women in
Highgate, London, from the late 1850s.

23 Daniel Karlin, ed., *The Penguin Book of Victorian Verse* (Harmondsworth:
Penguin, 1998), pp. lv–lix. He quotes from Barrett Browning's Preface to her
1844 *Poems* on p. lv.

24 Ibid., p. lviii.

25 It is tempting to bring in Roland Barthes and his now classic *Pleasure of the
Text* (trans. Richard Miller (New York: Noonday Press, 1975)) at this point,
but, although the topic invites further elaboration, there is no room for it
here, beyond the remark – I hope not too contentious – that Barthes's work,
splendidly original as it is, in no way negates my point about a patrician
standpoint.

26 Women were not admitted to degrees at London University until 1878, and
at Oxford until 1920. Women were allowed to take degrees at Cambridge
in 1921 but were not admitted as full members of the university until 1948.

27 Maria Jane Jewsbury (1800–33: sister of the more well-known Geraldine) is
a good example of an extremely talented poet who nevertheless, in the
name of religion, placed her duty to others well above any poetic production of her own. Her 1829 volume, *Lays of Leisure Hours*, indicates this in its
title. She married, travelled to India with her missionary husband, and died
the next year.

28 See P. M. Ball, *The Heart's Events: the Victorian Poetry of Relationships* (London:
Athlone Press, 1976), for a development of this notion.

29 *The Essays of Virginia Woolf*, vol. 1, ed. Andrew McNeillie (London: Hogarth
Press, 1986), p. 226.

30 See, for example, the generous selection of her nonsense poems for children
reprinted in Angela Leighton and Margaret Reynolds, eds., *Victorian Women
Poets: an Anthology* (Oxford: Blackwell, 1995), pp. 397–9.

31 See *The Diary of Virginia Woolf*, vol. 1, ed. Anne Olivier Bell (London:
Hogarth Press, 1986), pp. 178–9 (Monday, 4 August 1918).

32 Christina Rossetti in *Seek and Find: a Double Series of Short Studies of the Benedicite*
(London: SPCK (Society for the Promotion of Christian Knowledge), n.d.
[1879]), p. 32.

33 See her essay 'An Inquiry as to How Far the Spirit of Poetry is Alien,and
How Far Friendly, to Christianity' in her *Liber Humanitatis* (1875). The essay
ends: '[though the Christian] may sometimes taste of song's sweet, intoxi-
cating wild honey, it will be as did the mighty men in the scriptural story, but
"sparingly, and on the tip of his spear"'.

34 The process whereby women's friendships were publicly labelled deviant is

complex and uneven, as Martha Vicinus demonstrates in her important essay 'Distance and Desire: English Boarding-school Friendships, 1870–1920', in *Hidden from History: Reclaiming the Gay and Lesbian Past*, eds. M. Duberman, M. Vicinus and G. Chauncey Jr (New York: NAL Books, 1989), pp. 212–29.

35 Frances Havergal (1836–79) was a poet and hymnist, devoting herself to study of languages and to the spiritual life. Mary Howitt (1799–1888), wife of William Howitt, was a lively-minded Quaker who wrote for a living: novels and translations as well as poems. For the Howitts, see Carl Woodring's *Victorian Samplers: William and Mary Howitt* (Lawrence: University of Kansas Press, [1952]), and Joy Dunicliff, *Mary Howitt: Another Lost Victorian Writer* (London: Excalibur Press, 1992).

36 See Angela Leighton's important essay '"Because men made the laws": the Fallen Woman and the Woman Poet', *Victorian Poetry* 27 (1989), pp. 109–27. Susan Brown has also written a useful essay on this topic, 'Economical Representations: Dante Gabriel Rossetti's "Jenny", Augusta Webster's "A Castaway", and the Campaign against the Contagious Diseases Acts', *Victorian Review* 17 (1991), pp. 78–95.

37 Angela Leighton, *Victorian Women Poets: Writing against the Heart* (London: Harvester Wheatsheaf, 1992), p. 123.

38 For a further discussion of the usage of the term 'poetess', see Marlon Ross, *The Contours of Masculine Desire: Romanticism and the Rise of Women's Poetry* (Oxford University Press, 1989); Leighton, *Victorian Women Poets*; Mellor, *Romanticism and Gender*; and Blain, *Caroline Bowles Southey*.

39 'England has many learned women . . . and yet where are the poetesses? . . . I look everywhere for grandmothers and see none' (*The Letters of Elizabeth Barrett Browning*, ed. F. Kenyon, 2 vols. (London, 1898), vol. I, p. 231).

40 From an unpublished letter to Robert Bridges held in the Bodleian Library, Oxford, and quoted by permission (Dep. Bridges 108 fols. 5–6).

41 Alfred H. Miles, ed., *The Poets and Poetry of the Nineteenth Century*, vol. IX (Rossetti to Tynan); 1st edn, 1891; (London: George Routledge, 1907), p. 229: 'It is not surprising that Mrs Guggenberger [her married name] should have broken the spell which for fifteen years had confined Darwin to the world of prose, for her part is emphatically that of the poetess of evolutionary science'. The entry finishes (p. 230) with the quote given in the text above.

42 See the pioneering work by Florence Boos: for example, '"Cauld Engle-Cheek": working-class Women Poets in Victorian Scotland', *Victorian Poetry* 33 (1995), pp. 53–71.

43 See Guide to Further Reading for anthologies and critical works.

CHAPTER NINE

Women and the theatre

Katherine Newey

The theatre of the nineteenth century offered women irresistible opportunities for independence, action, agency, fame and money. Yet participation in the theatre also threatened loss of position and reputation,
exhaustion, frustration, exploitation and poverty. The theatre as a profession (for middle-class women particularly) challenged the ideals of
self-effacement and control of women's 'natural' voracious desires which
Mary Poovey argues are at the heart of the idea of the 'proper lady'.
However, as Kerry Powell argues in the case of actresses, the theatre also
offered women the opportunity to 'speak compellingly'.[1] In spite of the
difficulties of negotiating this tricky territory, women moved into the
theatre in large numbers throughout the nineteenth century, and their
participation in the theatre industry constitutes one of the more visible
instances of women's increasing autonomy and self-definition through
work in the period. Women's participation in the theatre was all the
more important as the theatre was, in effect, a mass medium of the
nineteenth century.[2] But the theatre in the nineteenth century was not
simply an entertainment industry: it was an important part of the discursive construction of English (and I use this term deliberately) national
culture. If we adopt Benedict Anderson's concept of the nation as an
'imagined community', then the theatre was a vital part of that imagin-
ing, and women in the theatre were defining and participating in one of
the more significant constructions of 'cultural nationhood' in the period.
In these terms, women's work in the theatre was an exercise of cultural
citizenship, and all the more significant because of their exclusion from
political citizenship.

The nineteenth century was both fascinated and repelled by the
actress on the stage. It was principally through the body of the actress
that ambivalent attitudes towards women in the theatre were played out.
Entrance onto the stage put middle-class women's respectability on
public trial, much as her physical body was on display. Valerie Sanders

notes the suspicions attached to the actress: that she 'lives fast: . . . and
one *season* gives her more experience, more of the nerve and hard features of the world – than a whole life of domestic duties could do'.[3] Yet
star actresses, such as Fanny Kemble, Helen Faucit, Ellen Terry, Madge
Kendal and Mrs Patrick (Stella) Campbell, were celebrated throughout
the century, while the visual spectacle of the theatre was increasingly
organized around the suffering or passionate female character. The
nineteenth century was also the period of the international actress,
beginning with Rachel Félix in the 1840s, and continuing with Sarah
Bernhardt and Eleanora Duse who were international stars until their
deaths in the 1920s. This cult of female celebrity is one of the many con-
tinuities between the theatre and film industries, to the extent that the
idea of the star has become a constitutive element of the mainstream
film industry in the twentieth century.

   In the first half of the nineteenth century the threat of social exclusion for actresses was in part mitigated by the growth of stardom, and
the reformulation of the narratives of actresses' lives to stress their con-
formation to 'middle-class standards for domestic femininity'.[4] Fanny
Kemble's account of her debut as Juliet at Covent Garden in 1829 is narrated as an example of filial obedience over which she had little control,
and she regarded her profession with ambivalence,[5] while Helen Faucit's
career and subsequent marriage to Sir Theodore Martin can be plotted
as a melodrama of upward mobility, from struggling young actress to
leading lady for William Macready, the principal tragedian of the day,
to wife of Sir Theodore Martin, memoirist of Queen Victoria. Both
Kemble and Faucit made their reputations in the 'legitimate' theatre –
that loosely defined but culturally important identification of the West
End theatres licensed to present the spoken drama. Frances Kemble first
played with her father, Charles Kemble, at the Theatre Royal, Covent
Garden, and Helen Faucit played opposite Macready at Covent Garden
and Drury Lane in the 1830s and 1840s. Faucit was particularly
renowned for her 'womanliness' and 'sympathetic' acting style. Her
Rosalind 'charmed us by the simplicity, the delicacy, the purity of the
delineation'.[6] Gail Marshall argues that it was precisely Faucit's 'forget-
fulness of self' – her literal and metaphoric artlessness – which drew
praise.[7] Such commentary is typical, demonstrating a paradoxical combination of anxiety about women's deliberate self-assertion with a clear
enjoyment of its results.

   While Fanny Kemble's debut was the most successful of that season,
and she became a celebrity after just one performance, her case was

unusual and her career overdetermined by her family network (as daughter of Charles Kemble and niece of Sarah Siddons), reflecting the importance of family networks in the profession. As Tracy Davis points out, the star performer was an anomaly in the nineteenth century, as the majority of performers throughout the century worked as chorus girls, character and bit-part or walk-on actors.[8] Although Michael Baker and Michael Sanderson posit a gradual increase in respectability and status for performers throughout the century,[9] more recent economic and demographic evidence suggests that this is a 'myth',[10] of a piece with the general historiographic convention of the progressive 'improvement' of the theatre towards bourgeois values. Yet it was a functional myth which governed the profession's own sense of itself, and particularly discussions of the social position of the actress in the second half of the century. The 'surplus woman problem' of the 1850s, which led to the theatre becoming a possibility for middle-class women who needed to support themselves, and changes instituted in the fashionable theatres of the West End (see below on Marie Wilton), meant that these theatres tended to replicate Victorian ideals of domestic femininity. Public views of star actresses focussed on their feminine and domestic characters, or excused their waywardness as part of their aesthetic charisma. This public indulgence of celebrity actresses was a double-edged sword, allowing actresses to mask often irregular private lives behind the demands of art, but requiring that they disguise artistic endeavour as art*less* femininity. While these actresses may be unrepresentative of the majority of the profession (*pace* Davis), the rhetorical effect of such personal power should not be underestimated. The passionate performances of Ellen Terry, or Stella Campbell, or even the more intellectual and political work of Elizabeth Robins – whose performance as Hedda Gabler was reviewed by Clement Scott as touching 'the keynote of genius'[11] – may have been construed as the unselfconscious work of women rather than artists, but their presence as powerful artists on the stage persisted, nonetheless. Together with the increasing number of women writing for the theatre in the last third of the century, and the plethora of women's texts dramatized for the stage, the feminization of popular culture must constitute one of the more significant cultural changes of the late nineteenth century.

Although the actress was the most visible example of female transgression of the persona of the 'proper lady' in the nineteenth-century theatre, it was in the work of manager or actress–manager where women's physical, intellectual and aesthetic independence was most

clearly marked. Yet such autonomy could not be insisted on too vehe-
mently. In her study of actress–manager Jane Scott and actress–writer
Elizabeth Macauley, J. S. Bratton shows how women's attempts to construct and control their careers attracted overt contempt and covert
erasure from history, particularly because these two women 'achieved
what they did without benefit of sexuality . . . they were not worthwhile
objects of the male gaze'.[12] Madame Vestris and Marie Wilton are presented here as examples of the ways in which individual women negotiated the tensions between respectability and sexuality which faced
women wishing to make a career in the theatre. Of course, Vestris and
Wilton were not the only women managers of the century, but their
styles represent the kinds of constraints within which women managers
worked, and the strategies by which they constructed careers.

Madame Vestris took on management in her own right in 1831. She
leased the Olympic Theatre, which was licensed only for the performance of 'burletta', a generic term used to describe a range of musical
entertainments, extravaganzas, and comedies with music. The theatre
attracted a fashionable audience, who took pleasure in seeing a theatrical version of their own world presented on stage. The company consisted mainly of comic actors (including John Liston, Frank Raymond,
Mrs Glover and Charles Mathews), and also included the playwright
James Robinson Planché, whose extravaganzas such as *The Olympic
Revels* came to define the theatre's house-style. The productions were
carefully rehearsed (not always a given in this period) and presented with
lavish settings and costumes, which were deliberately designed to give a
picturesque overall effect. Vestris is credited with 'inventing' the box set,
an arrangement of stage flats which approximated the walls and ceiling
of the middle-class drawing-room. While such coherence in production
is the industry standard today, and invested with aesthetic significance
and seriousness, it was novel in the theatre of the early nineteenth
century. According to Clifford Williams, Vestris's chief managerial inno-
vation was to introduce 'considerate management', with a modicum of
security and comfort for actors and audience.[13] In most contemporary
opinions, Vestris's principal capital was still held in her person. Known
as the 'fair lessee', Vestris's physical presence and appearance on the
Olympic stage was still the guarantee of success, as Planché's opening
address written for her emphasizes:

> Noble and Gentle-Matrons-Patrons-Friends!
> Before you here a venturous woman bends!
> A warrior woman – that in strife embarks,

> The first of all dramatic Joan of Arcs!
> Cheer on the enterprise, thus dared by me!
> The first that ever led a company![14]

As with all the examples I discuss in this chapter, there is a choice of interpretations here, which each raise important issues. Is Vestris's address here an example of her subservience to male ventriloquism and a masculinist conception of the public woman? Or is Vestris appropriating Planché's words to make her own self-definition and claim for historical significance?

Vestris worked in the London theatre during its period of greatest perceived decline, when, during the 1820s and 1830s, demographic changes brought new audiences into the Theatres Royal, and also fed the growth of theatres beyond the West End which did not hold Royal Patents. Whatever commentators then and theatre historians now might argue about the 'decline of the National Drama', the fact that such a decline was perceived inevitably affected the reputations of those who worked in the theatre. Whenever reputations were at issue, it was women's reputations that were most vulnerable. Vestris pursued a theatre career at the time of high anxiety about the position of women and a backlash against women working in the theatre. As a performer, Vestris specialized in singing and dancing roles, and was a scandalous success in a series of 'breeches roles' in musical comedy, roles designed primarily to display the actress's legs. Throughout her career she was plagued by the appropriation of her image and reputation in a series of pornographic pseudo-biographies and images, over which she had no control, and her private life, particularly her partnership with Charles Mathews, was open to scrutiny and criticism.[15] In the atmosphere of anti-theatrical feeling and surveillance within which she was working, Vestris's assumption of the management of the Olympic Theatre was more complex than simply a part of the inevitable progress of the English theatre to its achievement of middle-class mimetic realism.

After this perception of a decline in the standards of the drama from the early nineteenth century, the beginning of Marie Wilton's managerial career in 1865 is hailed as the moment of revival.[16] Like Vestris's management at the Olympic, Wilton's managerial policies – particularly her attention to realistic stage detail – and Tom Robertson's plays, such as *Caste*, *MP*, *Ours* and *Play* (the so-called 'cup-and-saucer' comedies), reflected the middle-class audience back to itself. The story of Wilton's rescue of the Queen's Theatre, a 'dust-hole' just off Tottenham Court Road, and her transformation of it into the fashionable and comfortable

Prince of Wales's Theatre, with pale blue stalls seats with white lace anti-macassars, high admission prices and shortened playbills, is repeated almost without question in the standard histories of the nineteenth-century theatre. In the conventional historiography of the nineteenth-century theatre, Vestris's and Wilton's managements fostered key developments in the inexorable progress of the representation of respectable middle-class life on stage, in ways that established domestic realism and psychological naturalism as the natural goals of English drama. What is also clear, but unstated in this narrative, is the way in which Vestris and Wilton have been cast as midwives or mothers of male playwrights or schools of theatre. But such an interpretation is not inevitably a model of subservience to patriarchal structures: each woman appears to have traded on this nurturing 'feminine' role to gain autonomy and agency over her career. Vestris's irregular private life was subsumed in her exquisite productions, and Marie Wilton converted her infantilized theatrical 'line' of *gamine* roles into a managerial persona of authority and respectability. Jane Moody suggests that such control of theatre programmes and promotion of playwrights and production styles is akin to authorship, and, indeed, to see the work of manageresses in this light usefully blurs otherwise hegemonic notions of authorship as ownership.[17]

What this narrative does not give room to is the multiplicity of theatrical voices which crowd the nineteenth-century stage (more of which were women's than we generally recognize), and a long view of how we construct our own cultural histories. As significant as Vestris and Wilton were – not least as two prominent female managers succeeding in the masculinist club of the theatre profession – to suggest that the nature of English theatre turned solely on these (or any other) specific moments is to erase the major portion of English theatrical history. Wilton's 'discovery' of Tom Robertson has been used as part of an orthodox history of the theatre which has valued (and still does value) the élite over the popular, art over entertainment, the literary over the non-literary drama, and Englishness over foreignness; and Vestris's management was seen to pave the way for Wilton's work. What is excluded here is the popular and the ephemeral, and in the discussion of women playwrights which follows, I want to offer a corrective to the hegemonic teleology of English theatre, in which the drama evolves necessarily towards the ultimate goal of psychological and representational realism. The work of women is crucial in challenging this model, and here I propose Mary Braddon and Ellen Wood as counter-canonical voices against the realist canon of Robertson, Arthur Wing Pinero and George Bernard Shaw.

Braddon's work in particular makes claims for popular culture as a determinant of modernity, and places the middle-class woman at its centre as a consumer and producer of its fantasies.

In spite of the barriers of class, respectability and access to the profession, patterns of female dramatic authorship in the nineteenth century demonstrate both the lure of the theatre and its maddening conditions of work for women. Over the century, some 500 women wrote some 1,200 theatrical or para-theatrical titles. This output constituted approximately 12% of the total dramatic literature of the nineteenth century.[18] This was not on the same scale as women's fiction writing, as studies show that women made up between 35% and 50% of novelists in the same period.[19] However, the sheer volume of titles and range of generic work within the broad category of 'drama' that this 12% represents constitutes a major area of women's writing which has only recently been recognized as being of significance. Theatrical writing – whether it be for commercial production (as in the case of Catherine Gore) or for the closet (as in the case of George Eliot's dramatic poems *Armgart* and *The Spanish Gypsy*) – attracted most women writers in the nineteenth century at some time or other during their careers; indeed, of women writers familiar to the student of nineteenth-century fiction and poetry, only the Brontë sisters and Elizabeth Gaskell did not attempt dramatic writing of some kind. On surveying the range of women playwrights over the nineteenth century, it is as if a whole school of new work by women has been 'discovered', and there are now some 500 *new* authors who must be incorporated into our understanding of women's writing in the nineteenth century. Such quantitative analyses (albeit crude and approximate) begin to counter the long-standing assumption that, as Dorothy Mermin recently put it, by 1830, 'Drama had entered a long decline, so that the paucity of female playwrights did not materially affect the literary landscape'.[20]

At one level, the attraction of the stage as a scene of writing is easily understood. In the eighteenth century, playwriting could be a lucrative source of income, and in the early nineteenth century the idea of the large financial returns from writing for the stage persisted. Furthermore, the performance of a play promised an immediate response from an audience, and the possibility of long-lasting popularity. At the end of the nineteenth century, writing for the theatre promised political visibility as well as income and fame, as the theatre was harnessed by Elizabeth Robins, Cicely Hamilton, Githa Sowerby and Florence Bell – to name the most prominent women – for feminist causes, including explorations of female poverty (*Alan's Wife*, by Robins and Bell), women's work (*Diana of Dobson's* by Hamilton, and *Rutherford and Son* by Sowerby) and women's suffrage (*Votes for Women!* by Robins). But, however tempting were the promises of fame and money in the theatre, the professional and physical organization of the London theatre industry posed barriers to participation for women playwrights. John Russell Stephens describes the London playwriting world as a 'strange mixture of tawdriness and grandeur, raffishness and respectability',[21] with a network of clubs (the Athenæum and the Garrick particularly) through which playwrights met and mixed with other professional men. Of course, these clubs were not open to women members (at the time of writing this chapter, both still do not admit women members) and therefore part of the networking so important to getting plays read and accepted by managers, engaging the right casts, getting them favourably reviewed, and being offered further work, was not available to women. In the practicalities of getting a play successfully produced, Ellen Donkin has shown how essential matters of successful production such as the customary first reading of a play by its playwright to the theatre management and company, the playwright's presence at rehearsals, and involvement in the details of the production could not be taken for granted: '[B]ackstage space was still gendered: . . . women who worked there ran very real risks of no longer being treated as "ladies"'.[22]

Mary Russell Mitford was representative of a number of Romantic women playwrights who were attracted to the theatre for the opportunities it offered for participation in an important cultural institution, as well as the promise of income. Her playwriting career follows that of Joanna Baillie, Elizabeth Inchbald, Hannah More and Anne Yearsley, and is contemporary with Sarah Flower Adams, Felicia Hemans and Isabel Hill. Like these writers, Mitford's desire to write plays in the high cultural tradition of verse tragedy – the 'national' drama represented by the Elizabethans, and pre-eminently Shakespeare – was an effective strategy by which to establish her seriousness and her respectability. Like these writers, she experienced problems with managers and actors in getting satisfactory productions of her plays mounted. But despite these difficulties Mitford's self-image as a playwright overrode the other more lucrative fiction writing she did, and demonstrates the enduring power of the theatre as a cultural field in the early nineteenth century.

Mitford wrote eight full-length plays: from *Julian*, first performed at Covent Garden in 1823, to her opera libretto, *Sadak and Kalasrade* performed at the English Opera House in 1835, to *Otto of Wittlesbach*, begun in 1829, published in 1854, but never performed, in spite of Mitford's attempts to have it produced in the early 1830s. Mitford's plays were historical tragedies, which impressed her literary friends such as Thomas Noon Talfourd, persuaded star actors and managers such as William Macready and Charles Kemble to perform in them, entertained middle-class audiences at the London Theatres Royal, Drury Lane and Covent Garden, and impressed theatre critics. Her play *Foscari* (first performed at Covent Garden, 1826) caused her to be hailed as a dramatist who had 'in some measure rescued the stage from these moving nuisances, those puning [*sic*] pirates who infest the purlieus of the theatres, under the assumed name of authors'.[23] By any standards of judgment, this is the record of a successful playwright. Her plays – together with her sketches collected as *Our Village*, and subsequent series *Belford Regis* and *Country Stories*, and her general 'woman of letters' work such as editing *Finden's Tableaux* and annuals for Colburn – supported her spendthrift father and invalid mother, all the while maintaining the family's sense of itself as genteel middle-class. Yet Mitford's abiding sense of herself was of her failure as a playwright. Her letters to her friends are full of accounts of the frustration, desperation and outright illness she suffered as a result of the trials of dramatic authorship, and her application for a state pension in 1837 outlined the combination of circumstances which led her to apply to Lord Melbourne: 'I had been compelled during the last winter . . . by the state of the theatres to withdraw a tragedy for which I had seemed certain to be paid in ready money – that this disappointment had been followed by a failure of health & spirits which had nearly taken away the power of execution which that very disappointment had rendered doubly necessary'.[24] Mitford's increasing bodily frailty was of a piece with what Norma Clarke finds to be the general 'propensity to mental and physical collapse of so many women writers in the nineteenth century'.[25] However, this should not be seen as an indication of women's weakness, and it is important that we do not write off Mitford's career as a failure. What Mitford felt to be the extremity of her sufferings can be seen as an indication of how great were the obstacles she faced, and how determined she was to control her life and circumstances.

Mary Russell Mitford was unusual as a playwright in the nineteenth century in that she was not connected to the theatre through familial or conjugal networks. As with other areas of the profession, the 'largest identifiable group [of women playwrights] is the 15 per cent who were actresses or members of theatrical families'.[26] In the field of popular theatre – entertainment which flourished while tragedy and high comedy were apparently in decline – a number of women playwrights was active in the middle third of the century. Mary Ebsworth, Marie-Therese Kemble, Catherine Gore, Eliza Planché, Mrs Denvil, Elizabeth Polack, Eliza Cooke, Mrs Alfred Phillips, Caroline Boaden, Mrs Herman Merivale and Anna Maria Hall all worked in and for the popular theatre. Paradoxically, although these women were closely linked to the theatre through family networks, and suffered fewer of the frustrations felt by Mitford, Isabel Hill or Felicia Hemans in having their work accepted in the theatre, their individual careers were obscured by those very family connections. Apart from their published plays, they leave few traces, and, as playwrights, they are 'invisible', their existences inferred from the remnants of documentation which surround their identities, but rarely comment directly upon them. While the plays written by these women do not constitute an aesthetic school, they do have common features, particularly in their use of generic conventions. Most of the plays written for the minor theatres by women were comedies or melodramas. In the case of the comedies particularly, plays were written to provide roles for their authors, thus sidestepping the assumption of the times that plays were chosen for 'the size and dramatic possibilities of the central male character'.[27]

The work of Mrs Alfred Phillips is a good example of a woman writing quite specialized roles for herself, although she does not write herself as the heroine. In her one-act farce, *An Organic Affection*, Mrs Alfred Phillips (she is given no other name in cast lists, title pages, or any of the standard indexes) plays a caricature of a French actress, Mademoiselle Joliejambe, who is, unsurprisingly, famous for her beautiful legs (the resonances of Vestris or Celeste here are inescapable). The part requires Phillips to use an extreme stage French accent, misuse words in a comic way, and make and become the butt of gags about her body which sail very close to the wind of mid nineteenth-century propriety. The plot, such as it is, revolves around the difficulties of Penelope, a poor but honest seamstress, who was attacked by a group of men in the street, resulting in a black eye which obscures her actual beauty. She is judged by these damaged looks by the male characters who neither value her character nor see her beauty, until the destitute Doublequill Bun learns he has inherited a large sum of money and, seeing Penelope without her bandages, realizes she is beautiful and schemes to marry her. After a series of delaying plots, which involve the discomfiture of various dissolute male characters who are hangers-on of Mlle Joliejambe, the play ends predictably with Doublequill and Penelope's marriage. There are choices about how we might read this play: on the one hand, it can be read as participating in the misogynist practice of ridiculing actresses such as Madame Vestris and Celeste who made their careers from their foreignness, and, in Vestris's case, from her legs. On the other hand, the play is ultimately so extravagant in its triviality – and almost all its characters, not just Mlle Joliejambe, are shown to be vain and silly – that it could be read as a satire on that very masculinist knowledge which sexualizes the stage and the women on it. In this reading, the melodramatic triumph of the poor but honest hero and heroine establishes firmly where the moral lines of the stage *should* be drawn.

Working in the latter part of the nineteenth century, Florence Marryat (1838–99) was typical of another type of woman playwright who included playwriting as part of her broader career as a 'woman of letters' – a middle-class professional woman who supported her family by her writing. Marryat was known principally as a novelist (she wrote over ninety novels), and these were frequently dramatized; at one time nine adaptations of her novels were running simultaneously in provincial theatres.[28] She collaborated with Sir Charles Young in dramatizing two of her novels, *Miss Chester* and *Charmyon. Miss Chester*[29] is a full-blooded domestic melodrama of the upper classes (and in this respect different from the melodramas of working-class life prevalent in the 1820s and 1830s), in the mould of the sensation dramas adapted from the novels of Ellen Wood and Mary Braddon. Although Marryat's work lacks the explicit political dimension of her near contemporary 'New Woman' writers, her dramatization of the feeling woman as a passionate and powerful speaking subject is ideologically challenging, and all the more interesting in its location in the popular theatre, rather than the 'fringe' of private theatres, clubs and experimental venues emerging in the late nineteenth century.

The plot of *Miss Chester* brings the past history of the complicated relationships of an aristocratic family to work on the present situation of the characters, ending, in the convention of melodrama, with a series of public confessions of wrongdoing and contrition, and the public vindication of the virtuous and the victimized. It is concerned with revealing the true identities of Miss Chester, her husband Sir Arthur Ashton, who first appears as the Bohemian drinker and gambler Michael Fortescue, and their son Rupert, who first appears as the second son of the Earl of Montressor. The ending of the play demonstrates a concern with the complicated nature of family relationships, and a dramatization of the ways in which legal, economic and emotional elements are entangled in the construction of personal identity and relationships. The play is of interest for the way that it shifts the focus from the plot of the love triangle between the juvenile lead characters – Rupert, Michael (the Earl of Montressor's eldest son) and his cousin Isabel – to a searing dramatization of the pain of an older woman, the abandoned Miss Chester. It is her voice which is dominant in the play, whether it be her feigned stance of anti-romanticism, in which she tells her charge, Isabel, that 'if you wish to fight successfully the battle of the world, you must ignore the very existence of a heart' (p. 7), or her private voice of pain, revealed only to the audience. The sense of a female authorial voice is strong here, and counters Kerry Powell's argument that the numbers of adaptations of women's novels (principally by male playwrights) 'represent a massive assault against women writers that is both textual and sexual in nature'.[30]

As Powell makes clear, the issue of the adaptation of women's texts for the theatre is an important one, and, again, demonstrates the complicated nature of the relationship between women and the theatre. While women playwrights struggled to participate on something like equal terms with their male colleagues, the theatre was voracious in its devouring of women's fictional texts. Adaptations of novels by men and women were constant presences in the theatre throughout the century (the works of Walter Scott and Charles Dickens the most prominent), but in the latter part of the nineteenth century it was the fiction of women which dominated the stage. Amongst canonical novels by women, there were numerous adaptations for the London stage. For example, Elizabeth Gaskell's *Mary Barton* was dramatized in three versions, including Dion Boucicault's adaptation, *The Long Strike* (1866). There were four versions of *Jane Eyre* between 1848 and 1882, and three adaptations of early novels by George Eliot – *Adam Bede* (1862) and *Silas Marner* (1871 and 1876).

While Marie Wilton was working with Tom Robertson to produce his comedies of middle-class society at the Prince of Wales's, theatre-goers all over the English-speaking world were delighted by adaptations of three sensation novels by women, Ellen Wood's *East Lynne*, and Mary Elizabeth Braddon's *Lady Audley's Secret* and *Aurora Floyd*. *East Lynne* was published as a novel in 1861, but its adaptations remained part of the standard repertoire of commercial theatres until the beginning of the Second World War. Dramatizations of the novel first appeared in New York in 1863, and then in Britain in 1864 as *The Marriage Bells*. This adaptation was followed by a number of English versions playing in all the

London theatre districts, from the Surrey Theatre on the south bank in 1866, to the Lyceum Theatre in 1867. *Lady Audley's Secret* was first published in book form in October 1862, and by March 1863 the story of the blonde bigamist had appeared on five stages in London, filling both the usually class-differentiated West End and East End theatres. The play's notoriety and popularity is confirmed by the appearance at the St James's Theatre of a burlesque version opening on Boxing Day, 1863 (always the opening day for the new Christmas pantomime): Henry Byron's 'Comical Conglomerative Absurdity', *Eighteen Hundred and Sixty Three; or, The Sensations of the Past Season, with a Shameful Revelation of "Lady Someone's Secret"*. Adaptations of *Aurora Floyd* followed closely on the heels of *Lady Audley's Secret*, mirroring the appearance of two novels, which were published in the same year, and which Braddon herself referred to as 'my pair of Bigamy novels'.[31] Both Benjamin Webster Jnr's version, and Charles Smith Cheltnam's adaptation, *Aurora Floyd; or, The Deed in the Wood*, opened on 11 March 1863, at the Adelphi and at the Princess's Theatres respectively. These were followed by another four adaptations, including a production at the Théâtre du Chatelet, Paris, in July 1863. Versions of all three plays toured the United States and Australia and New Zealand for at least the next thirty years.[32]

In their concentration on the passions of contemporary domestic life, the roles of Lady Isabel, Lady Audley, or Aurora provided opportunities for women to speak. When Lady Audley or Aurora took centre stage, a space was created for an independent, articulate and passionate female voice in a time and society in which women were idealized into passivity and silence. As melodramas, these plays emphasize the physicality of sensation and crime, through showing action and conflict expressed bodily as well as linguistically. Nowhere is this more powerful than in the staging of femininity in these plays. The 'irruption into the narration of that feeling . . . which is repressed in the narrative'[33] which Lyn Pykett finds in fictional melodrama is made manifest on stage as emotion codified and formularized into a set of gestures, vocal usages and physical poses, which became visual icons of femaleness under great stress. Through their impassioned speeches, these female characters indicate realms of experience and emotion beyond the quotidian and limited notion of the domestic sphere, and, in this gesture towards broad experience, they provide a partial model for liberation of female experience. However partial and problematic, in that Lady Isabel and Lady Audley must die for their transgressions, and Aurora must be subdued and humbled, the power and energy of expression in such performances is ultimately liberating. Furthermore, the continued popularity of these plays undercuts the historiographical model of a smooth evolutionary development of the theatre towards psychological realism and representational naturalism at the end of the nineteenth century. The feminized text in popular culture endured, in spite of high cultural critics such as Henry Morley deeming sensation plays such as *Aurora Floyd* as 'garbage' fitted only for the 'literary taste in the uneducated'.[34] The staying power of such texts is undoubtedly connected with their involvement with varieties of femininity – those socially sanctioned and those not – a feature of mass entertainment which was readily apparent when women's texts were transferred to the new medium of popular entertainment. According to Lilian Gish, early Hollywood director D. W. Griffith felt that if women did not like a movie it would be a failure; if they liked it, it would become a success.[35]

For all the information we have about performances of the past, the presence of the audience is perhaps the most elusive element of the theatrical exchange. The experience of the audience – without whom a performance can hardly be said to have taken place – has remained largely unrecovered. Where they exist, discussions of nineteenth-century spectatorship have tended to be driven by class concerns, and derived from class-based assumptions about the behaviours and tastes of various theatre audiences. But what is the effect of looking at audiences and spectatorship through the lens of gender, rather than class? Do traces of Jill Dolan's ideal 'resistant spectator' exist, and are they recoverable?[36] Unlike women's reading of fiction, which Kate Flint argues was 'a means . . . of becoming part of a broader community . . . [which] may stretch far beyond the reader's immediate social world to incorporate other readers whom she may never meet . . . but with whom she shares horizons of expectations,'[37] theatre-going encouraged little sense of community for women. In spite of – or perhaps because of – the necessary physical community of a theatre audience, discussions of women's theatre-going emphasize differences between women. Macready's management of Drury Lane, for example, ordered that 'after this evening, the money of women of the town should be refused altogether at the doors'.[38] On Macready's retirement as manager, he was praised by the *Illustrated London News* as highly for his attempts to elevate 'the moral character of his temple' as for his artistic policies in promoting the 'legitimate' or 'National Drama'. The *ILN* makes clear the divisions between groups of women, remarking that at Drury Lane 'fathers, husbands, and brothers did not dread for their fair charges a rude, insulting contact with the flaunting insolence of vulgar and shameless morality'.[39] This connection between theatre and prostitution, made almost universally throughout the nineteenth century, although, as Tracy Davis argues, not founded in professional practice,[40] had inevitable consequences for women spectators. The social geography of London popular entertainment meant that the prostitution and theatre districts were virtually identical. The morally loaded nature of these spaces meant that the behaviour of any woman in these areas was automatically under suspicion, and so respectable female attendance at the theatres required male escort. Ironically, the identity between theatre and prostitution was most pronounced in London's West End, where the high cultural respectabilities of the 'National' or legitimate drama clashed directly with the notoriety of the prostitutes of Drury Lane and Covent Garden.

For women who aspired to work as theatre critics, this collision of London's social geography with notions of female propriety resulted in serious professional limitations, which extended beyond the overdetermined spaces of London's theatre districts. Like playwrights, theatre critics formed interlinked masculinist social and professional networks, centred on time spent together in Parliament, the courts and the clubs, 'formulating a sense of collectivity through their interactions'.[41] Theatre criticism was surely one of the most challenging forms of female spectatorship transgressing those codes of behaviour which constituted the 'proper lady', and, moreover, directly threatening such male collectivity. Female theatre criticism tended to come from arenas of professional writing already positioned in an oppositional relationship to the mainstream, such as the circles of suffrage and socialist intellectuals late in the nineteenth century. Eleanor Marx Aveling is a prominent example of the latter, closely connected (initially through her father Karl Marx) with late nineteenth-century socialist intellectuals, and interested in using theatre as part of her general critique of contemporary social relations. Marx Aveling was a translator of Henrik Ibsen, appeared as Nora in a private performance of *A Doll's House*, and used her social and intellectual capital to promote causes of a radical and libertarian nature; her involvement in theatre translation, performance and criticism was part of this larger project.

Notwithstanding important female (and feminist) challenges to patriarchal assumptions about spectatorship and taste to be found in women's theatre criticism, perhaps the most powerful evidence of female spectatorship is to be found in the fictional and diary accounts of individual spectators. Such records also provide further information about the social location of the female spectator within the territory of the 'proper lady'. Admittedly, these records are scant, and focussed on female star performers, but the intensity of recorded experiences suggests the very dangers of theatricality and strong feeling of which nineteenth-century moral pundits were so fearful. Fears of female loss of control could be expressed in extreme ways; standard psychological theory of the nineteenth century held that if women's moral or religious principles were weakened or removed, the female mind became tempestuous as 'subterranean fires become active, and the crater gives forth smoke and flame'.[42] Women's own contradictory fears of loss of control, yet elation at powerful feeling, are implicit in their responses to some of the great actresses of the period. For example, Lady Monkswell's diary response to seeing Sarah Bernhardt as Adrienne Lecouvreur makes explicit the divided feelings of a spectator at once powerfully affected and appalled: 'I make a vow I will not go to be harrowed up again in this most wanton manner . . . Whatever people say Sarah B. has genius'.[43] Queen Victoria recorded similarly mixed feelings of pleasure and alarm in seeing the ghost scene in *The Corsican Brothers*, and was castigated for her public display of these responses.[44]

But it is in fiction where the most intense accounts of female spectatorship are to be found. The use of theatrical scenes and metaphors in women's fiction is widespread: prominent examples in women's writing across the century include Jane Austen's use of Kotzebue's comedy, *Lovers' Vows*, to intensify her plot of mis-matched lovers in *Mansfield Park*; Lady Audley's life-as-performance in Mary Braddon's *Lady Audley's Secret*; and the stage and drawing-room performances of the Alcharisi, Gwendolen, and Herr Klesmer in George Eliot's *Daniel Deronda*. Charlotte Brontë's description of the actress playing Vashti in *Villette*, drawn from her experience of seeing Rachel Félix perform, is surely one of the most vivifying scenes of theatricality in Victorian fiction. About the real Rachel as Camilla, Brontë wrote that the actress was: 'terrible as if the earth had cracked deep at your feet and revealed a glimpse of hell . . . she made me shudder to the marrow of my bones: in her some fiend has certainly taken up an incarnate home. She is not a woman – she is a snake.'[45] Brontë's description of the fictional actress Vashti is not only one of the most powerful descriptions of performance in Victorian fiction but is also central to the characterization of her protagonist, Lucy Snowe. Lucy describes the last moments of the play as the actress's triumph of will – but a triumph achieved at the cost of her life. Vashti had an inordinate will, convulsing a perishing mortal frame, bent it to battle with doom and death, fought every inch of ground, sold dear every drop of blood, resisted to the latest the rape of every faculty, *would* see, *would* hear, *would* breathe, *would* live, up to, within, well nigh *beyond* the moment when death says to all sense and being -

'Thus far and no farther!'[46]

Lucy's description can be read as an identification with the actress of her own frustrated and pent-up emotional power. Her description constantly slips between a response to the role and the actress playing it, typical of the blurring of the boundaries between the private and public characters of performing women in this period. For Lucy such slippage is necessary and even therapeutic, as it allows identification without open rebellion, so Vashti allows Lucy to dramatize her ambivalence over her own will to power. The consequences of such public display of a woman's emotions find their objective correlative in the fire which breaks out at this moment in the theatre, making physical the psychological metaphors cited above. As John Stokes argues, Vashti is Brontë's answer to G. H. Lewes's troubled ambivalence about female power; in Brontë's version, Vashti embodies 'the truth that the representation of female desire, however diabolic it might appear, could be vehement proof of the reality of female identity'.[47] Writ large, we can read Vashti as a paradigm for articulate women's attitudes towards personal power and agency in the nineteenth century: through the theatre, these desired but dangerous powers could be experienced and experimented with.

NOTES

Research for this chapter was supported by the Australian Research Council and the Society for Theatre Research. My thanks to Margaret Leask, Sylvia Martin, Gillian Sykes and Tiffany Urwin for their research assistance.

1 Kerry Powell, *Women and Victorian Theatre* (Cambridge University Press, 1997), p. 3.
2 Tracy C. Davis, 'The Sociable Playwright and Representative Citizen', in Tracy C. Davis and Ellen Donkin, eds., *Women and Playwriting in Nineteenth-Century Britain* (Cambridge University Press, 1999), p. 19.
3 From the *Quarterly Review* (1835), cited in Valerie Sanders, *The Private Lives of Victorian Women: Autobiography in Nineteenth-Century England* (Hemel Hempstead: Harvester Wheatsheaf, 1989), p. 109.
4 Mary Jean Corbett, *Representing Femininity: Middle-Class Subjectivity in Victorian and Edwardian Women's Autobiographies* (Oxford University Press, 1992), p. 108.
5 Sanders, *The Private Lives of Victorian Women*, pp. 112–13.
6 Donald Mullin, comp. and ed., *Victorian Actors and Actresses in Review. A*

Dictionary of Contemporary Views of Representative British and American Actors and Actresses, 1837–1901 (Westport, CT: Greenwood Press, 1983), pp. 182 and 185.

7   Gail Marshall, *Actresses on the Victorian Stage: Feminine Performance and the Galatea Myth* (Cambridge University Press, 1998), pp. 50–1.

8   Tracy C. Davis, *Actresses as Working Women* (London: Routledge, 1991), p. 163.

9   Michael Baker, *The Rise of the Victorian Actor* (London: Croom Helm, 1978), and Michael Sanderson, *From Irving to Olivier: A Social History of the Acting Profession in England, 1880–1983* (London: Athlone Press, 1984).

10 Davis, *Actresses as Working Women*, p. xiii.

11 Angela V. John, *Elizabeth Robins: Staging a Life, 1862–1952* (London: Routledge, 1995), p. 55.

12 J. S. Bratton, 'Miss Scott and Miss Macauley: "Genius Comes in All Disguises"', *Theatre Survey* 37:1 (May 1996), p. 72.

13 Clifford John Williams, *Madame Vestris: A Theatrical Biography* (London: Sidgwick and Jackson, 1973), p. 95.

14 Cited in Williams, *Madame Vestris*, p. 101.

15 Davis, *Actresses as Working Women*, p. 108.

16 Clement Scott, *The Drama of Yesterday and Today*, 2 vols. (London: Macmillan, 1899), vol. I, pp. 471 and 484–7, and William Archer, *The Old Drama and the New* (London: William Heinemann, 1923), p. 338.

17 Jane Moody, 'Illusions of Authorship', in Davis and Donkin, eds., *Women and Playwriting*, pp. 102–3.

18 These figures are based on my tabulations of the following sources: James Ellis and Joseph Donohue, eds., *English Drama of the Nineteenth Century, An Index and Finding Guide* (New Canaan: Readex Books, 1985); Allardyce Nicoll, *A History of English Drama 1660–1900*, vols. IV–VI (Cambridge University Press, 1959–70); Donald Mullin, *Victorian Plays. A Record of Significant Productions on the London Stage, 1837–1901* (Westport, CT: Greenwood Press, 1987); and indexes to the Pettingell Collection, University of Kent at Canterbury.

19 John Sutherland, *Victorian Fiction: Writers, Publishers, Readers* (London: Macmillan, 1995), p. 160, and Gaye Tuchman with Nina E. Fortin, *Edging Women Out: Victorian Novelists, Publishers, and Social Change* (London: Routledge, 1989), p. 7.

20 Dorothy Mermin, *Godiva's Ride: Women of Letters in England, 1830–1880* (Bloomington: Indiana University Press, 1993), p. 43.

21 John Russell Stephens, *The Profession of the Playwright: British Theatre 1800–1900* (Cambridge University Press, 1992), p. 10.

22 Ellen Donkin, *Getting into the Act: Women Playwrights in London, 1776–1829* (London: Routledge, 1995), p. 136.

23 *The Theatrical Examiner; or, Critical Remarks On the Daily Performances, with Bills of the Play*, 5:39 (7 November 1826), n.p.

24 Mary Russell Mitford, 13 May 1837 (Letters from Mary Russell Mitford to Sir Thomas Noon Talfourd, Eng Mss, 665, John Rylands Library, University of Manchester).

25 Norma Clarke, *Ambitious Heights. Writing, Friendship, Love – The Jewsbury Sisters, Felicia Hemans, and Jane Welsh Carlyle* (London: Routledge, 1990), p. 51.

26 Gwenn Davis and Beverly A. Joyce, comps, *Drama by Women to 1900: a Bibliography of American and British Writers* (London: Mansell, 1992), p. xi.

27 Julie Holledge, *Innocent Flowers: Women in the Edwardian Theatre* (London: Virago Press, 1981), p. 22.

28 Helen Black, *Notable Women Authors of the Day* (Glasgow: David Bryce and Son, 1893), p. 90.

29 Florence Marryat and Sir Charles Young, *Miss Chester* (London: Samuel French, n.d.), first performed at the Holborn Theatre, 6 October 1872.

30 Powell, *Women and Victorian Theatre*, p. 101.

31 Robert Lee Wolff, 'Devoted Disciple: the Letters of Mary Elizabeth Braddon to Sir Edward Bulwer-Lytton, 1862–1873', *Harvard Library Bulletin*, 22:1 (January 1974), p. 12.

32 Sources for this performance history are: Brian J. Burton, 'Introduction', *East Lynne; or, Lady Isabel's Shame* (Birmingham: C. Combridge, 1965); Weldon B. Durham, ed., *American Theatre Companies, 1888–1930* (Westport, CT: Greenwood Press, 1987); Sally Mitchell, 'Introduction', *East Lynne* (New Brunswick: Rutgers University Press, 1984); Donald Mullin, *Victorian Plays: a Record of Significant Productions on the London Stage, 1837–1901* (Westport, CT: Greenwood Press, 1987); Allardyce Nicoll, *A History of English Drama, 1660–1900*, vol. v, *Late Nineteenth Century Drama, 1850–1900* (Cambridge University Press, 1946; 1975); George C. Odell, *Annals of the New York Stage* (New York: Columbia University Press, 1945–); *Playbills and Programmes from London Theatres 1801–1900 in the Theatre Museum, London* (Cambridge: Chadwyck-Healey, 1983); Ruth Vasey and Elizabeth Wright, comps. and eds., *Calendar of Sydney Theatrical Performances, 1870–1879* (Sydney: Australian Theatre Studies Centre, 1986); Richard Waterhouse, *From Minstrel Show to Vaudeville: the Australian Popular Stage, 1788–1914* (Kensington: University of New South Wales Press, 1990); J. P. Wearing, ed., *The London Stage, 1890–1899. A Calendar of Plays and Players* (Metuchen: Scarecrow Press, 1976).

33 Lyn Pykett, *The 'Improper' Feminine: The Women's Sensation Novel and the New Woman Writing* (London: Routledge, 1992), p. 97.

34 Henry Morley, *The Journal of a London Playgoer*, ed., with an Introduction by Michael R. Booth (Leicester University Press, 1974), p. 243.

35 Lizzie Francke, *Script Girls: Women Screenwriters in Hollywood* (London: British Film Institute, 1994), p. 5.

36 Jill Dolan, *The Feminist Spectator as Critic* (Ann Arbor, MI: UMI Research Press, 1988).

37 Kate Flint, *The Woman Reader, 1837–1914* (Oxford: Clarendon Press, 1993), p. 42.

38 J. C. Trewin, ed., *The Journal of William Macready* (London: Longmans, 1967), entry for 19 January 1842, p. 178.

39 *The Illustrated London News* (17 June, 1843), p. 421.

40 Davis, *Actresses as Working Women*, p. 78.

41 Gay Gibson Cima, '"To Be Public as a Genius and Private as a Woman": the Critical Framing of Nineteenth-Century British Women Playwrights' in Davis and Donkin, eds., *Women and Playwriting*, p. 35.

42 John Bucknill, cited in Sally Shuttleworth, '"The Surveillance of a Sleepless Eye": the Constitution of Neurosis in *Villette*', in George Levine and Alan Rauch, eds., *One Culture: Essays in Science and Literature* (Madison: University of Wisconsin Press, 1987), p. 321.

43 E. C. F. Collier, ed., *A Victorian Diarist. Extracts from the Journals of Mary, Lady Monkswell, 1873–1895*, 2 vols. (London: John Murray, 1944), vol. I, p. 43.

44 Cited in Richard W. Schoch, *Shakespeare's Victorian Stage* (Cambridge University Press, 1998), pp. 133–4.

45 Cited in Juliet Barker, *The Brontës* (London: Weidenfeld and Nicolson, 1994), p. 677.

46 Charlotte Brontë, *Villette* (Harmondsworth: Penguin English Library, 1979), p. 342.

47 John Stokes, 'Rachel's "Terrible Beauty": an Actress Among the Novelists', *ELH* 5:4, (Winter 1984), p. 783.

CHAPTER TEN

Women writers and self-writing

Linda Peterson

In 1826 the publishers John Hunt and Cowden Clarke advertised a series on life writing provocatively entitled *Autobiography: a Collection of the Most Instructive and Amusing Lives Ever Published, Written by the Parties Themselves*. In their initial 'Advertisement' they featured no women's self-writing; their list of forthcoming volumes included only men's accounts, classified not by genre or mode but by the writers' public roles: statesmen (Sully, Bubb Doddington), men of genius and literature (Gibbon, Hume, Marmontel), religious enthusiasts (John Wesley, George Whitfield), artists (Benvenuto Cellini), dramatists and players (Colly Cibber, Carlo Goldini), mystics and impostors (William Lilly, James Hardy Vaux).[1] Within a year, however, for reasons unknown, Hunt and Clarke had decided to include two examples of women's autobiography: the scandalous memoirs of Mary Robinson, an actress known in the late eighteenth century as the mistress of the Prince of Wales, later as a Romantic poetess, and the *Life* of Charlotte Charke, a picaresque narrative by the daughter of Colley Cibber, famous in her day for her cross-dressing onstage and off.[2]

From our vantage point almost two centuries later, we might wonder why these early nineteenth-century publishers took so narrow a view of women's self-writing – narrow both in the sense that they published so little of it and in that they chose only one subgenre, the *chroniques scandaleuses*. By contrast, in 1881, when Margaret Oliphant embarked on a series of critical essays on autobiography for *Blackwood's Edinburgh Magazine*, she featured women's self-writing in three of her seven instalments: the *Autobiography* of Margaret, Duchess of Newcastle, in the third; the Interregnum memoirs of Lucy Hutchinson and Alice Thornton in the sixth; and the historical account of Madame Roland, heroine (and victim) of the French Revolution, in the last. Admittedly, in the 1870s and 1880s Oliphant had become fascinated with the genre of autobiography, having begun her own at about the same time. Yet the difference was not simply one of personal interest or prejudice. In the fifty-five years between Hunt and Clarke's series – to my knowledge, the first of its kind, the first to capitalize on the newly named genre of *autobiography* – and Oliphant's essays in *Blackwood's*, the literary status of, and public knowledge about, women's self-writing had dramatically changed. What had seemed a minor genre at the beginning of the century, written primarily by religious enthusiasts (spiritual confessions) or socially dubious women (scandalous memoirs), had become a common, even privileged genre by the late Victorian period, with not only famous women producing memoirs of their professional careers but also ordinary wives and daughters composing accounts of family and domestic life.

This change was due, in part, to the democratization of self-writing in the post-Romantic period. When Robinson wrote her *Memoirs* (1801), it was with the sense that she was an imaginatively gifted, rather unusual and talented individual; at the end of the century, when Camilla Crosland wrote *Landmarks of a Literary Life* (1893), it was with the conviction that 'the recollections of *any* truth-loving, truth-telling individual who has passed the allotted three-score years and ten of life, mixing in the society of the great metropolis, ought to be worth recording'.[3] The burgeoning interest in and production of women's self-writing was also due, perhaps more importantly, to the archival work of nineteenth-century editors and scholars who resurrected and published women's manuscripts from earlier periods and to literary critics like Oliphant in *Blackwood's* or Edith Simcox in the *North British Review* who paid increasing attention to life writing, including specimens by women.[4] Beginning in the second decade of the nineteenth century and steadily increasing throughout, Victorian antiquarians, scholars and critics searched for, discovered and edited the texts we cite today when we write about the 'emergence' of British women's self-writing: Margaret Cavendish's *True Relation of the Birth, Breeding, and Life* (1814); the *Memoirs of Ann Lady Fanshawe* (1829); *A Legacy, or Widow's Mite, Left by Alice Hayes* (1836); the *Autobiography of Mary Countess of Warwick* (1848); *The Autobiography of Mrs Alice Thornton* (1875); *The Autobiography of Anne Lady Halkett* (1875); and numerous spiritual accounts written by Nonconformist women of the working and middle classes.[5]

The Victorians resuscitated and wrote about these women's autobiographies for reasons with which we can readily sympathize: for their historical interest, for the social and cultural information they contained, for their contribution to discussions of a 'new' literary genre, for their relevance to present-day lives, for their influence on contemporary approaches to life writing. The publication of earlier texts and the reconstruction of literary history help to explain the growing popularity of self-writing among nineteenth-century women, professional and amateur alike. Their editorial work anticipates our own efforts at understanding the genres of women's self-writing, including those women inherited and those they created.

When Hunt and Clarke selected women's self-writing for their *Autobiography* series, they published examples of the *chroniques scandaleuses*. When Oliphant wrote her series for *Blackwood's*, she emphasized the family or domestic memoir. Both genres were important for nineteenth-century women's life writing – the first suggesting the dubious light in which women who publicized their experiences were initially viewed, yet also anticipating the professional artist's lives that their successors would write; the second representing a more respectable form of autobiography, indeed the most common form of women's self-writing in the nineteenth century. Also important, though unrepresented in these two series, were the spiritual autobiographies and missionary memoirs that women of various religious persuasions composed and that were increasingly published by their descendants or their churches.

FROM CHRONIQUES SCANDALEUSES TO PROFESSIONAL ARTIST'S LIFE

The *chroniques scandaleuses*, as Felicity A. Nussbaum has taught us, is predominantly an eighteenth-century genre, 'the first significant public form of self-writing that women take up, other than spiritual autobiography'. Scandalous memoirs present the female self ambivalently: on the one hand conforming to conventional dichotomies of class and gender that associate female sexuality with lower-class, fallen women and thus encouraging middle-class women readers 'to regulate themselves', on the other hand disrupting conventional paradigms of female character in that such memoirs offer an apologia for the woman autobiographer's (mis)deeds and 'demand public published space' in which patriarchal relations might be challenged.[6] As a genre, such memoirs were associated with women of dubious character (or, in Pope's phrase, 'no character at all') – that is, with actresses, prostitutes and women authors.

The two *chroniques scandaleuses* that Hunt and Clarke published – Charke's an eighteenth-century account, published originally in 1755,

Robinson's a Romantic account, published in 1801 – exemplify this paradigm. Robinson's *Memoir* is introduced, for example, as an autobiography that 'show[s] the exposed situation of an unprotected beauty' and,
unlike other 'autobiography of this class', is not 'dangerous'.[7] That the
editors judge the *Memoirs* to be without danger suggests, perhaps, their
need to rationalize its risqué moments. Yet it also suggests a shrewd sense
that Robinson's self-writing is safe because it stays within the known
boundaries of the feminine. Its two main plotlines juxtapose the autobiographer's progress in one set of roles (daughter, mother) against her
regress in another (wife, mistress). The first plot traces the fall of a beautiful young woman from chastity to infidelity; as Robinson looks back on
her life, she sees a sensitive, talented girl left unprotected by her father,
too quickly married off to a duplicitous London rake, too readily
exposed to the temptations of the stage, and too naively charmed by the
amorous supplications of a prince (who loses interest after she becomes
his lover). The second plot, amplified and completed by Maria
Robinson, her daughter, tells of Robinson as a loving mother, dutiful
daughter and faithful wife. Robinson superimposes this second plot on
the less commendable course of her actions, explaining her marriage to
Thomas Robinson as an act of filial obedience and her fidelity to him,
even during the worst of his profligacies, as a commitment to her children and family. She insists that she consented to his marriage proposal
only because 'of being still permitted to reside with my mother'; she
hints, too, of latent maternal impulses: 'only three months before I
became a wife, I had dressed a doll'. Shortly after her marriage, when
she discovers his infidelities and indifference to her sexual honour, she
describes her sole joy as prospective motherhood: 'I divided my time
betwixt reading, writing, and making a little wardrobe for my expected
darling. I little regretted the busy scenes of life; I sighed not for public
attention'.[8]

Perhaps needless to say, very few Victorian women embraced the *chroniques scandaleuses* as a form of life writing, and much of the nineteenth-
century life writing of professional women can be seen as a reaction
against this genre and a (re)turn to or experimentation with other possibilities. Nonetheless, Robinson's autobiography represents a seminal
text for women's self-writing in its account of authorship and in the editorial role that her daughter played in the composition and publication
of the text.

As a professional actress and author, Robinson was uncertain about
the relationship of maternal and artistic roles. She claims that she turned

to poetry, then the theatre to support herself and her daughter, but she never fully persuades us that maternal concerns motivate her professional career or that her life as an actress was compatible with her responsibilities as a mother; indeed, she acknowledges that she may have instigated the death of her second child, Sophia, by working too hard and dancing too much while still nursing and thus sending the child into 'strong convulsions'.[9] This tension between motherhood and artistry, between biological and literary (re)production, continues to vex women's self-writing, as in Mary Howitt's *Autobiography* (1889), with its agonized account of her son's death as she struggled over an unfinished piece of hackwork ('How often did he beg and pray to me to put aside my translation just for that one day, that I might sit by him and talk or read to him!'), or in Margaret Oliphant's *Autobiography* (1899), with its probing self-inquiry about the possible negative influence of her writerly life on her sons' failures in their careers ('it was one of my foolish ways to take my own work very lightly, and not to let them know how hard pressed I was sometimes, so that he [her son Cyril] never, I am sure, was convinced how serious it was in that way, and certainly never was convinced that he could not, when the moment came, right himself and recover lost way').[10] Only accounts by single women without children manage to escape this tension, though even these frequently record obstacles or restrictions imposed by family life, as in Harriet Martineau's tale of her mother's refusal to allow her to accept an editorial position in London, or in Florence Nightingale's semi-autobiographical *Cassandra* (1852), where the speaker bitterly complains that women are prohibited from following Christ, especially his teaching that his disciples must foresake father and mother, brothers and sisters: 'But if *we* were to say that, we should be accused of "destroying the family tie", of diminishing the obligations of the home duties'.[11]

Mary Robinson's daughter Maria, who edited the *Memoirs* and added a narrative of her mother's last years, suffers from no such ambivalence about women's roles. A Victorian before her time, Maria firmly links the plot of authorship to that of maternity. As she completes the *Memoirs*, she dates the 'commencement of her [mother's] literary career' from 1788. In that year Mrs Robinson began not only to write, but to nurse her daughter back to health: 'Maternal solicitude for a beloved and only child now wholly engaged her attention: her assiduities were incessant and exemplary for the restoration of a being to whom she had given life, and to whom she was fondly devoted'. In the daughter's revision, maternal devotion pays off in literary production (or, alternatively, literary production reactivates maternal conscience). As Maria puts it, 'the silence of the sick-chamber prov[ed] favourable to the muse'.[12] Thus, in editing her mother's life, Maria Robinson effects what her mother's narrative only hints: that a safe, culturally viable myth of female artistry could be created by shifting the narrative focus from romantic to domestic love. We might say that Maria anticipated the virtues of linking the artist's autobiography generically with the domestic memoir.

This link between domesticity and authorship or artistry was explicitly made in many women's auto/biographies of the nineteenth-century; with a few notable exceptions, most memoirs by women authors and artists turn away from the *chroniques scandaleuses*, with its association of women's self-writing and indecorous self-display, even prostitution, and embrace instead the genre of domestic memoir. Fanny Kemble, for instance, explains her acting career in *Record of a Girlhood* (1879) as purely an act of self-sacrifice and family necessity; to save her father and his theatre from bankruptcy, she volunteers to go out as a governess but instead, on the advice and appeal of her parents, makes her *début* in the role of Juliet, becoming 'a great success' and saving the Kemble family from 'domestic catastrophe'.[13] In her 'Reminiscences of My Life', later amplified and published as her *Autobiography* (1889), Mary Howitt incorporates a letter to her sister Anna Harrison, written in 1836, in which she explains her writing of children's verses and tales as an extension of her maternal role:

Just lately things were sadly against us. Dear William could not sleep at night. The days were dark and gloomy. Altogether I was quite at my wits' end. I turned over in my mind what I could do next, . . . [t]hen I bethought myself of all those little verses and prose tales that for years I had written for the juvenile annuals. It seemed probable to me I might turn them to account.[14]

Howitt did in fact 'turn them to account', producing not only a steady stream of juvenile literature, including translations of Hans Christian Andersen, but also the highly successful *Peter Parley's Tales*, which includes the still-famous children's verse, 'Come into my parlor, / Said the spider to the fly'. Howitt's *Autobiography* is fully a domestic production, composed with her younger daughter Margaret, who sifted through the family letters to provide the basic materials, and illustrated by her elder daughter Anna Mary, who sketched her parents' final home in Switzerland just as she had, years before, sketched the family homes in London.

Oliphant's *Autobiography*, too, domesticizes authorship and includes several familial scenes of writing. In an account of her writerly origins, she explains that she took up fiction while nursing her mother through 'a bad illness'; instead of doing needlework, she 'wrote a little book in which the chief character was an angelic sister, unmarried, who had the charge of a family of motherless brothers and sisters, and who had a shrine of sorrow in her life in the shape of the portrait and memory of her lover who had died young'.[15] This myth of the good daughter, which appeared first in the novel *Christian Melville* (1845), again in *Kirsteen* (1890), finally in the *Autobiography* (1899), redeems authorship from the transgressive mode it held in much early nineteenth-century ideology. In Oliphant's account, writing strengthens rather than disrupts domestic life: the 'little book' pleased her ailing mother and older brother Frank; her fiction-writing provided work for her alcoholic brother Willie, who became her amanuensis and later published the 'little book' under his own name; and her writerly career gave an alternative direction to a family history of crisis and failure.

In its most dramatic form, Charlotte Elizabeth Tonna's *Personal Recollections* (1842) enacts the turn from transgressive self-writing to redemptive authorship by rendering her account in the genres of both domestic memoir and spiritual autobiography. Her *Personal Recollections* begin with chapters on home and family life that might have come from virtually any ordinary, pious life writing; with simple titles like 'Childhood', 'Youth' and 'Early Days', character sketches of father, grandmother and brother, and details of life in provincial Norwich, they resemble many other memoirs by Victorian women. And, in fact, that is the point. Quite overtly, Tonna's celebrate the virtues of the 'rural English HOME' in which she grew up and on which she considers English prosperity and political freedom to be founded (p. 37). Resisting any presentation of herself as 'the heroine of some strange romance', Tonna emphasizes her religious conversion and dedication to Christian work; she insists that her writing is but one example of the labour 'every good Christian' must undertake. The connection between conversion and authorship is crucial to Tonna's account. Just as male spiritual autobiographers had traditionally followed their narratives of conversion with calls to the ministry,[16] so Tonna records her call to didactic literature. She describes writing her first religious tale in an all-night fit of inspiration, the next morning receiving a letter requesting a contribution to the Dublin Tract Society. 'I saw in it a gracious acceptance of my free-will offering at His hands to whom it had been prayerfully dedicated' (p. 136), she adds, implicitly interpreting the experience as a sanction of female authorship. The conventional pattern of spiritual autobiography, modified to fit her circumstances, provides the divine and literary authority she seeks.

The authority that Tonna, like many other nineteenth-century women, gained by such rhetorical manoeuvres has been well analysed by scholars like Mary Jean Corbett and Valerie Sanders, who emphasize the woman writer newly invested with power for 'producing and reproducing the ideologies that structure Victorian culture'.[17] This new authority instigates (or perhaps develops simultaneously with) a significant phase in the history of women's self-writing. Women gained credibility for their personal narratives and, more generally, for their literary productions by aligning them with women's cultural work. When, in Elizabeth Barrett Browning's semi-autobiographical poem, Aurora Leigh imagines the future of poetic production, 'the burning lava of a song', as emerging from 'the full-veined, heaving, double-breasted Age', she, too, is drawing on maternal metaphors to justify and celebrate the achievement of women's writing.[18] However, when autobiographers like Tonna speak of their writing as a 'literary avocation' or, in biblical terms, as a 'free-will offering', they are also limiting its range. The amateurism implied by *avocation* represents a refusal of professional status consonant with Tonna's belief that her writing should be of a 'homely simplicity', fully intelligible to a five-year-old.[19] The use of *free-will offering* reinforces a conception of women's writing not as professional labour, but as one of many possible forms of Christian service, all extensions of ordinary, womanly roles and responsibilities.[20] The implications of the domestic mode, in other words, differ from one woman's text to another's.

Of course, not all women authors and artists justified their work in religious terms or produced autobiography in the domestic mode. In her *Autobiography* (1877) Harriet Martineau pointedly insists on the distinction between amateurism and professionalism, feminine work and masculine labour, the 'needle' and the 'pen'. When her first articles for the *Monthly Repository* appeared in print, her eldest brother Henry praised her literary efforts and sanctioned a career as a *professional* author. In her *Autobiography* she describes the incident as a priestly laying on of hands: 'He then laid his hand on my shoulder, and said gravely (calling me "dear" for the first time) "Now, dear, leave it to other women to make shirts and darn stockings; and do you devote yourself to this". . . . That evening made me an authoress'.[21] Henry articulates a distinction that Martineau observes throughout her self-writing, whether in the *Autobiography* or her many personal letters: that professional work is different from, not an extension of, domestic responsibility; that the female author must leave her needle and the domestic circle behind in order to take up the pen. This is masculine wisdom, initially resisted by female family members. That Martineau rejected this feminine sentiment and viewed her literary career as an entry into a masculine profession we can gauge from a letter to her mother written in July 1832, when she left Norwich for London permanently: 'I fully expect that both you and I shall occasionally feel as if I did not discharge a daughter's duty, but we shall both remind ourselves that I am now as much a citizen of the world as any professional *son* of yours could be'.[22]

More generally, Martineau introduces an ungendered paradigm to present her intellectual and moral development, thus suggesting that there should be no *fundamental* difference between men's and women's self-writing. As she explained in her translation of Auguste Comte's *Positive Philosophy* (1853), individual development is a specific version of general, human progress:

The progress of the individual mind is not only an illustration, but an indirect evidence of that of the general mind. The point of departure of the individual and of the race being the same, the phases of the mind of a man correspond to the epochs of the mind of the race. Now, each of us is aware, if he looks back upon his own history, that he was a theologian in his childhood, a metaphysician in his youth, and a natural philosopher in his manhood.[23]

Within a Comtean framework, she interprets her life as moving from an early religious or 'fictitious' stage (1802–19) through what she calls a 'metaphysical fog' (1819–39) to a final stage of scientific or 'positivistic' understanding (1839–55). These Comtean phases become Martineau's hermeneutic substitute for the biblical typology of orthodox spiritual autobiographers and her alternative to the domestic model of other women autobiographers. In rejecting (or avoiding) the domestic model, she is followed by later women autobiographers, including Annie Besant (*An Autobiography*, 1893), Frances Power Cobbe (*Life*, 1895), and Mrs. Humphry Ward (*A Writer's Recollections*, 1918), whose self-writing charts their intellectual and moral growth within the intellectual currents of their time.

THE RISE OF THE DOMESTIC MEMOIR

The adoption of a domestic mode in professional women's life histories was part of a larger revival of a form that had emerged in the seventeenth century but had remained private, often in manuscripts, until nineteenth-century scholars made them public. As Oliphant explained in her series for *Blackwood's*, autobiographies divide themselves between records of public life and more private, domestic accounts, the latter usually given lower status. Yet in her opening article on Benvenuto Cellini, as she distinguishes between *res gestae*, the autobiographies of important public figures who 'leave behind a record of many things worth knowing, clear up, perhaps, some historical mysteries of the period, and keep the incidents of [their] own life alive among men', and 'domestic records', the autobiographies of persons over whose head 'these events have passed', Oliphant praises the latter as self-writing that 'widens our experience of human nature' and is thus as 'interesting and instructive as any other part of the perennial drama'.[24] In so judging, she echoes (or perhaps anticipates) a growing interest in the private lives of public figures and in domestic life itself.

Oliphant's distinction between public, *res gestae* and private, domestic memoirs was both conventional and original. As Felicity Nussbaum suggests in her account of biography and autobiography in the eighteenth-century volume of *The Cambridge History of Literary Criticism*, 'England unquestionably led Europe in its intense interest in the personal, the private, and the ordinary, turning for its biographical subjects from the lives of the eminent and learned to the middle ranks and below',[25] and Oliphant's preference for the private and domestic reflects this national trend. In terms of women's self-writing, Oliphant was perhaps the first critic to see the link between this trend and domestic memoirs by women. In her sixth article, on the seventeenth-century memoirs of Lucy Hutchinson and Alice Thornton, Oliphant virtually defines the genre of domestic memoir and genders it feminine:

> Mrs Hutchinson's memoirs were not intended for the public. The compilation of family histories was a fancy of the time. In the leisure of widowhood and age, when her children were out in the world and her noonday over, a woman who had been full of fancy and vivacity all her life – without leisure, in the vicissitudes of an active career, for more than a copy of verses now and then, or a religious meditation jotted down among the simples in her recipes-book – would amuse herself in the ease of her later days by writing down all that happened, if not to herself, 'to your father', in all the principal chapters of his existence.[26]

Here are the key elements clearly identified: life writing by an older woman, a mother, for the purpose of conveying family memories, attitudes and achievements, her own as well as the family's.[27] Such auto/biographies are what we would today term 'relational', emphasizing not an autonomous self or individual achievement, but presenting the writer within a network of family and friends and as the recorder of a communal history.

It has taken modern autobiography studies several decades to reach a similar understanding of the importance of such self-writing in the nineteenth century. As scholars such as Estelle Jelinek, Sidonie Smith and Susan Stanford Friedman have pointed out, autobiography studies prior to 1980 relied on men's self-writing to theorize about the genre, the result being a conception of autobiography as representing an autonomous self, public achievement and individual progress. The re-inclusion of women's texts in major critical studies has required new approaches to and theories about women's life writing, as well as a re-consideration of nineteenth-century women's discussions of the genre, as in Joanne Shattock's study, in 'Victorian Women as Writers and Readers of (Auto)biography', of how Margaret Oliphant and Eliza Lynn Linton read the lives of Brontë and Eliot in thinking about their own.[28]

Despite Oliphant's relegation of domestic memoirs to a historically remote 'fancy of the time', the form continued to be written – indeed, it flourished – in the Victorian era. Seventeenth-century domestic memoirs, like Lucy Hutchinson's *Memoirs of the Life of Colonel Hutchinson . . . to which is prefixed the Life of Mrs Hutchinson, Written by Herself* (1810), *The Autobiography of Mary Countess of Warwick* (1848) and Ann Lady Halkett's *Autobiography* (1875), placed great emphasis on social continuity and family service in national causes, thus revealing their essentially aristocratic origins and modes of self-definition. Similarly, the upper- and middle-class wives of Victorian diplomats, politicians, civil servants, clergymen and others carried on the tradition, incorporating their personal lives into the predominantly public accounts of their husband's achievements; they conceptualized their experiences under such titles as *Foreign Courts and Foreign Homes, Our Home in Cyprus, At Home in India* or *Garden of Fidelity*.[29] Moreover, in a uniquely Victorian version of the form, ordinary wives and daughters wrote reminiscences of domestic life in middle-class homes for their children and grandchildren, implicitly asserting the value of the domestic as equal to that of the public. These memoirs are what William Matthews, the great bibliographer of British autobiography, classifies simply as autobiographies of 'domestic and family life', self-writing in which autobiographers, mostly women, recorded their memories of home life and social mores in a fast-changing Britain.[30]

Domestic memoirs flourished as well among the families of professional artists and authors, particularly in a subgenre we might call 'family memoirs' or 'dynastic histories': the *Memoir and Letters of Sara*

Coleridge (1873); the *Memoirs of the Life of Anna Jameson, by her Niece, Gerardine Macpherson* (1878); Fanny Kemble's *Record of a Girlhood* (1879); *Mary Howitt: an Autobiography, edited by her Daughter Margaret Howitt* (1889); Anne Thackeray Ritchie's *Chapters from Some Unwritten Memoirs* (1895); *Autobiography and Letters of Mrs Margaret Oliphant* (1899); and Mrs Humphry Ward's *A Writer's Recollections* (1918). Like their seventeenth-century counterparts, these memoirs emphasized a family tradition of public achievement, in literature and the arts rather than in political or military service. Unlike their predecessors, however, the nineteenth-century women who wrote these memoirs were not merely recording the actions and achievements of their fathers, husbands and brothers but were, quite consciously, writing themselves into that family history, often as the culmination of it, sometimes as a principal actor or originator of a family dynasty.

Sara Coleridge and Fanny Kemble present themselves as inheritors of a family tradition in literature and the theatre respectively. As Coleridge begins her memoirs, she dwells much on her father, the poet, and despite plans to narrate her full life story, never writes much beyond her childhood under his influence. Kemble also contextualizes her career within a family tradition, in this case of acting, beginning her autobiography with reference to her 'aunt Siddons', the great eighteenth-century tragic actress, and discussing 'the dramatic talent of the Kembles', of which she modestly disclaims any 'specific gift'.[31] Kemble's *début* is fully a family affair, with Fanny playing Juliet, her mother Lady Capulet, and her father Mercutio; 'my father not acting Romeo', she adds, 'deprived me of the most poetical and graceful stage lover of his day'.[32]

If these women wrote of their lives and careers within family contexts, others presented themselves as originators or founders of a professional tradition. Margaret Oliphant seems to express this intention when she records, in her *Autobiography*, the marriage proposal of her cousin Francis Oliphant: that they should 'build up the old Drumthwacket together'.[33] Although Frank Oliphant, a painter, died of tuberculosis early in his career, leaving Margaret with three young children to support, the *Autobiography* nonetheless records his primary works of art and faithfully includes the literary attempts (they can scarcely be called achievements) of their two sons, Cyril and Cecco. Oliphant's *Autobiography* might be read, then, as a modernized version of the domestic memoirs she reviewed for *Blackwood's*, but with much more prominence given to the woman's professional life.

Mary Howitt, too, seems to have had a family history in mind when she composed the 'Reminiscences' that her daughter Margaret later expanded into the *Autobiography*. A collaborative model of writing was especially important to Mary Howitt, who had come to love literature through joint study with her sister Anna, with whom she had jointly published juvenile poetry.[34] With marriage, her husband William replaced Anna as primary companion and collaborator, but it was Anna Mary, the oldest child, who eventually came to replace both sister and husband, becoming the daily companion of – and a collaborator with – her mother. As early as 1833, when Anna Mary was ten years old, Howitt wrote about her daughter's help with drawings for a poetic manuscript: 'I wish I could send you some specimens of Anna Mary's drawings. She is now illustrating my "Seven Temptations." She designs heads to illustrate the different characters. William has them with him in London, and has astonished several artists with them'.[35] Years later, when Mary began her autobiography, Anna Mary, who had subsequently trained to work as a professional painter, illustrated her mother's account. As Howitt's *Autobiography* attests, we need to think of some, perhaps even most, nineteenth-century women's self-writing as *collaborative* writing. Not only did women construct life stories from many different kinds of materials (letters, diaries, documents provided by others in the family), but they often wrote with the help of, or were edited by, other family members, usually other women.

Even an individually composed account like Mary Ward's *A Writer's Recollections* shows the traces of (indeed, the skilful use of) this kind of family memoir. Ward's *Recollections* fits within a common, sometimes termed 'masculine', tradition of intellectual and professional life writing: in the first half, Ward traces the primary currents of intellectual and literary influence that led her to become a writer; in the second half, she records the circumstances of her major novelistic achievements from *Robert Elsmere* to *Eleanor*. Yet Ward's autobiography is also a family history, beginning with her memories of her grandfather Thomas Arnold, the famous headmaster of Rugby, and continuing with her uncle Matthew Arnold, the Victorian poet, critic and Inspector of Schools, as well as many other friends and family who participated in a tradition of educational reform and professional criticism. Because of this strain of family memoirs, Ward's autobiography has sometimes been denigrated as lacking 'inner drama' and offering instead 'public information'.[36] Yet in her writing about family members with notable public accomplishments, she is also writing herself into a distinguished family history, as perhaps the first woman to deserve a place therein.

CONTINUITY AND CONFLICT WITHIN WOMEN'S SPIRITUAL AUTOBIOGRAPHY

As Felicity Nussbaum suggests in her comment (cited above) about early forms of women's self-writing, spiritual autobiography had a strong influence on women's self-conception and presentation in earlier centuries. Like their male counterparts, women from various Protestant groups and of all classes used self-writing to trace their salvation from sin, their spiritual progress or regress, and their contributions to the work of the church. Early modern women writers readily adopted the traditional form of spiritual autobiography. They treated their lives as a struggle between opposing forces of good and evil. They delineated a pattern of spiritual progress from bondage in sin and spiritual darkness to enlightenment and victory over the world, flesh and devil. Moreover, they composed their lives without a sense that they were appropriating a masculine tradition or that their experiences were radically different from men's. Indeed, Quaker and other Nonconformist women participated early and directly in the writing of English spiritual autobiography and, by composing powerful personal accounts, helped shape its conventions.

Many of these early accounts were reprinted (often reedited) in the nineteenth century, thus offering religious women an unbroken tradition of self-writing. For example, Elizabeth Stirredge's *Strength in Weakness Manifest*, originally published in 1711, was included in *The Friends' Library* in 1838 as *The Life and Testimony of that Faithful Servant of the Lord, Elizabeth Stirredge*. Stirredge's account follows the general formula for spiritual autobiography, beginning with her earliest recollections of religious seriousness and her 'dread and terror' in contemplating death; she recalls at great length her temptations to sin (the most serious being a hankering after 'fine clothes'), her wanderings without spiritual guidance (like the children of Israel in the wilderness), her conviction of sin and conversion under Quaker preaching, and finally her persecution for religious conscience.[37] Similarly, Alice Hayes's *A Legacy, or Widow's Mite* appeared initially in 1749, later in an American edition of 1807, and again in a British edition of 1836. Such documents of personal spiritual history continued to be written in the nineteenth century, sometimes only for the writer's private edification, often for circulation within the religious community, occasionally for publication as an exemplary life.

Two important variations on the spiritual autobiography emerge in nineteenth-century women's life writing: the 'heroic' missionary memoir, and the chronicle of doubt and faith, loss and gain.

Until the 1830s only male clergymen were officially sent to foreign lands, thus making men the subjects of the earliest missionary memoirs. By 1835, however, single women were being approved for service by the Society for Promoting Female Education in China, India and the East, a branch of the Church Missionary Society, and various sectarian groups began to appoint both single and married women to serve with missionary families and husbands – largely, it seems, because of the extraordinary successes of a small core of women, including Ann Hasseltine Judson, Sarah Hall Boardman and Margaret Wilson, who had gone out to India unofficially in the 1820s and whose lives were widely publicized in memoirs of the 1830s and 1840s.

Margaret Wilson was a Scotswoman famous for establishing the Bombay School for Destitute Girls in the 1830s; her namesake, another Mrs Wilson, did similar educational work in Calcutta.[38] Ann Judson, an American-born missionary, was noted for pioneering work in Burma and for her eloquent pleas on behalf of female education in the East.[39] Sarah Boardman (later Judson) founded schools in Burma where, under British rule, the government made appropriations throughout the provinces for a network of schools 'to be conducted on the plan of Mrs Boardman's schools at Tavoy'.[40] What the journals and auto/biographies of these female missionaries helped to create was a form of self-writing in which the woman subject emerged as heroic, capable of undertaking difficult work and surviving (even thriving) in harsh climates and circumstances.

In reviewing the *Memoir of Mrs Judson*, Margaret Wilson, then a missionary in Bombay, observed: '[This account] introduces us to individuals, formed by nature for a subordinate sphere of action, and deprived, in a great measure, of those powerful motives to exertion which the eager pursuit of knowledge, a love of honourable distinction, and the expectation of reward, impart to their possessors'.[41] Despite the rhetoric of separate spheres, what Wilson implies – that her fellow missionary found opportunity for heroic action and honourable distinction in India and Burma – becomes an explicit argument in subsequent auto/biographies of Judson and her associates. In the 1851 preface to new memoirs of Ann and Sarah Judson, the author Arabella W. Stuart begins with the claim: 'Among the many benefits which modern missions have conferred on the world, not the least, perhaps, is the field they have afforded for the development of the highest excellence of female character . . . The missionary enterprise opens to women a sphere of activity, usefulness and distinction, not, under the present constitution of society, to be found elsewhere'.[42] In the poetics of female missionary biography, the cause of converting the non-Christian or educating Indian women becomes complementary to the feminist cause of expanding western women's work.

The self-writing of these early women missionaries, usually in the form of narratives extracted from journals or letters written to female friends, may seem conservative in terms of religious beliefs or social practices. What is remarkable, however, is that women missionaries and their editors developed a new form of Victorian life writing, one that represented women taking heroic action, women engaged in serious work outside the home. As a biographer, Arabella Stuart was quick to note the absence of such literature and thus the innovativeness of her book: 'How few of the memoirs and biographical sketches which load the shelves of our libraries, record the lives of women!' Margaret Wilson noted, too, the possibilities for a new 'species of biography' that recorded the 'lives of distinguished females' who would otherwise have been 'deprived' of 'honorable distinction'.[43] These auto/biographers depict themselves and other women in heroic modes – braving long ocean voyages, enduring the physical hardships of life on mission posts, living without the companionship of English-speaking women, facing customs and practices that would have shocked their European counterparts. Moreover, they show women taking action in political crises, even intervening in military campaigns. Their editors emphasize the heroism of women's characters and actions: 'Females, who in this country of order and security, tremble at the idea of being left for one night alone in their strong and guarded dwellings, may perhaps conceive the feelings of Mrs Boardman on being thus left'.[44] In her memoirs there is no evidence that Sarah Boardman trembled.

If women missionaries adapted the form of spiritual autobiography to new ends, Victorian women of quite different religious convictions (or none at all) engaged in another new kind of life writing: the autobiography of de-conversion, of loss or alteration of faith. Harriet Martineau's adoption of Comtean philosophy, discussed above, reflected her loss of Unitarian beliefs and her intellectual conversion to a 'scientific' system of self-understanding. This conversion entailed an eventual separation from her Unitarian family and some friends, although her *Autobiography* (1877) rationalizes, even naturalizes this separation by presenting it as a version of all human development. Martineau's other life writing, however, suggests a more disruptive personal history. When she wrote *Letters on Mesmerism* (1845) and then co-published the agnostic *Letters on the Laws of Man's Nature and Development* (1851) with H. G. Atkinson, several family members broke ties, including her much-beloved brother James, who wrote a scathing review of the latter book. These two books, largely based on personal experience, suggest the potentially disruptive effects of women's self-writing when it rejected traditional forms and engaged in contemporary religious or political debates.

Annie Besant's *Autobiography* (1893) embraces this disruptive force as it traces her deconversion from Anglicanism to her discovery of atheism, socialism and then theosophy. In her testimony, her unhappy marriage to a conventional clergyman led her to recognize the link between patriarchal religion and patriarchal family structures, both of which had 'enshrouded' her 'own bright life' in 'pain' and 'rendered [her] degraded by an intolerable sense of bondage': 'My religious past became the worst enemy of the suffering present. All my personal belief in Christ, all my intense faith in His constant direction of affairs, all my habit of continual prayer and of realisation of His Presence – all were against me now.'[45] Her autobiography dissevers her 'self' from the forms that, in life and life writing, caused such pain, first breaking with her husband and his patriarchal ideologies and later writing of her life within paradigms learned from Madame Blavatsky's theosophy.

Frances Power Cobbe, too, broke from the Anglicanism of her father, but her *Life* (1895) chooses not to associate this break with a rejection of family or domestic life. Indeed, Cobbe safely contains her account of her sojourn to Theism within a chapter on 'Religion', treating her change of religious views as a matter of intellectual inquiry, not as a matter of feminist politics. Cobbe's later work in reformatories and ragged schools can be seen, moreover, as a traditional extension of woman's work in the home to a larger world in need of domestic aid. In her chapter on 'Workhouse Girls', for instance, she assumes a decidedly womanly point of view:

It was never realized by the *men* (who, in those days, alone managed our pauper system) that girls cannot be trained *en masse* to be general servants, nurses, cooks, or anything else. The strict routine, the vast half-furnished wards, the huge utensils and furnaces of a large workhouse, have too little in common with the ways of family life and the furniture of a common kitchen to furnish any sort of practising ground for household service.[46]

Cobbe's *Life* records the improvements that she and women colleagues made to the social system.

That Besant and Cobbe could, in their accounts of religious deconversion, employ such different modes of self-representation suggests both the diversity of nineteenth-century life writing and the hybridity of its major examples. If Charlotte Elizabeth Tonna could link religious autobiography and domestic memoir in her *Personal Recollections*, Annie Besant could argue the incompatibility of the two in *An Autobiography*. If Margaret Oliphant could frame the story of her authorship within a family memoir, Harriet Martineau could choose to write a more individuated, 'masculine' version of her professional career. By the end of the nineteenth century the field of self-writing was rich indeed. Spiritual autobiography had consolidated itself as a form and had developed interesting variations in the heroic memoirs of missionary women and in the probing intellectual analyses of Nonconformists, agnostics and other religious thinkers. The *chroniques scandaleuses* of the eighteenth century had quietly disappeared or been transformed into the respectable artist's life (what William H. Epstein has called 'life-course') of the professional woman.[47] The domestic memoir, a Victorian variation on the family histories of the seventeenth and early eighteenth centuries, flourished in a culture that celebrated the joys of home, family and private life. Perhaps most important, women writers were experimenting with these forms in various combinations and permutations.

NOTES

1 These categories and names come from the 'Advertisement' that prefaces *Autobiography: a Collection of the Most Instructive and Amusing Lives Ever Published, Written by the Parties Themselves* (London: Hunt and Clarke, 1826), n.p. In 1829 the series was taken over by the publishers Whittaker, Treacher and Arnot, who seem to have been more interested in translating and publishing contemporary accounts (as vols. 27–34 attest). The series ceased publication in 1833.

2 *Memoirs of the Late Mrs Robinson, Written by Herself* (London: Hunt and Clarke, 1826) and *A Narrative of the Life of Mrs Charlotte Charke, Youngest Daughter of Colley Cibber, Esq., Written by Herself* (London: Hunt and Clarke, 1827). The two autobiographies are bound together as vol. VII in all editions I have seen.

3 *Memoirs of the Late Mrs. Robinson Written by Herself, with Some Posthumous Pieces* (London: Wilks and Taylor, 1801); Mrs Newton Crosland, *Landmarks of a Literary Life, 1820–1892* (London: Sampson Low, Marston and Company, 1893), p. 1.

4 Margaret Oliphant published six of the 'Autobiography' series anonymously in *Blackwood's Edinburgh Magazine* between January 1881 and July 1882, with the seventh appearing in April 1883. Edith Jemina Simcox's 'Autobiographies', published in January 1870 in the *North British Review*, is reprinted in *Prose by Victorian Women: an Anthology*, ed. Andrea Broomfield and Sally Mitchell (New York: Garland, 1996), pp. 528–61. As Broomfield and Mitchell remark, Simcox's study appeared 'before most of the major Victorian autobiographies (including those by Mill, Martineau, Carlyle, and Oliphant) were published', and it gives little (virtually no) attention to issues of gender and self-writing.

5 *True Relation of the Birth, Breeding, and Life of Margaret Cavendish, Duchess of New Castle, Written by Herself*, ed. Sir Egerton Brydges (Kent: Johnson and Warwick, 1814); *Memoirs of Lady Fanshawe*, ed. E. Harris Nicolas (London: Henry Colburn, 1829); Alice Hayes, *A Legacy, or Widow's Mite, Left by Alice Hayes* (London: Darton and Harvey, 1836); *Autobiography of Mary Countess of Warwick*, ed. T. Crofton Croker (London: Percy Society, 1848); *The Autobiography of Mrs Alice Thornton*, ed. Charles Jackson (London: Surtees Society, 1875); *The Autobiography of Anne Lady Halkett*, ed. John Gough Nichols (Westminster: Camden Society, 1875). Except for Cavendish's *True Relation*, first published in the seventeenth century, and Hayes's *Legacy*, published in the eighteenth, these texts are all 'Victorian', and would be lost to literary history but for the efforts of Victorian editors. There is a modern edition of *The Memoirs of Anne, Lady Halkett and Ann, Lady Fanshawe*, ed. John Loftis (Oxford: Clarendon Press, 1979). Excerpts from Alice Thornton's autobiography and Margaret Cavendish's *True Relation* are included in Elspeth Graham, ed., *Her Own Life* (London: Routledge, 1989).

6 Felicity A. Nussbaum, *The Autobiographical Subject: Gender and Ideology in Eighteenth-century England* (Baltimore and London: Johns Hopkins University Press, 1989), pp. 179–80.

7 Robinson, *Memoirs*, p. v. Citations are to the 1826 Hunt and Clarke edition.

8 Ibid., pp. 34, 59–60.

9 Ibid., p. 69.

10 Mary Howitt, *An Autobiography* (Boston: Houghton, Mifflin, 1889), vol. II, pp. 17–18; Margaret Oliphant, *Autobiography*, ed. Mrs Harry Coghill (Edinburgh and London: Blackwoods, 1899), p. 148.

11 Florence Nightingale, *Cassandra*, ed. Myra Stark (London: Feminist Press, n.d.), p. 54. The text was written in 1852 and first published in 1928 in Ray Strachey's *The Cause*.

12 Robinson, *Memoirs*, pp. 130–1. Maria gives the date as 1787, but the chronological sequence makes it clear that they arrived back in England at the beginning of 1788.

13 Frances Ann Kemble, *Record of a Girlhood* (New York: Henry Holt, 1879), pp. 186–9.

14 Howitt, *Autobiography*, vol. I, pp. 249–50.

15 Oliphant, *Autobiography*, pp. 16–17.

16 Roger Sharrock discusses this feature of spiritual autobiography in the introduction of his edition of Bunyan's *Grace Abounding to the Chief of Sinners*.

17 Mary Jean Corbett, *Representing Femininity: Middle-Class Subjectivity in Victorian and Edwardian Women's Autobiographies* (New York: Oxford University Press, 1992), p. 15; this version of the argument follows closely Nancy Armstrong's approach in *Desire and Domestic Fiction: a Political History of the Novel* (New York: Oxford University Press, 1987). In *The Private Lives of Victorian Women: Autobiography in Nineteenth-Century England* (London: Harvester Wheatsheaf, 1989), Sanders emphasizes the adoption of a religious perspective and rhetoric as a means of overcoming personal frustration, emotional turmoil and intellectual boredom; see also her article, '"Absolutely an act of duty": Choice of Profession by Victorian Women', *Prose Studies* 9 (1986), pp. 54–70.

18 Elizabeth Barrett Browning, *Aurora Leigh and Other Poems*, ed. John Robert Glorney Bolton and Julia Bolton Holloway (London: Penguin, 1995), bk v, lines 214–15.

19 Charlotte Elizabeth [Tonna], *Personal Recollections*, 4th edn (London: Seeleys, 1854), pp. 221, 136, 179. Tonna explains her style in these terms: 'My little books and tracts became popular; because, after some struggle against a plan so humbling to literary pride, I was able to adopt the suggestion of a wise Christian brother, and form a style of such homely simplicity, that if, on reading a manuscript to a child of five years old, I found there was a single sentence or word above his comprehension, it was instantly corrected to suit that lowly standard' (p. 179).

20 The Old Testament explains the free-will offering as a 'tribute' given 'as the Lord thy God hath blessed thee' (Deut. 16:10, King James Version) in contrast to the required tithe or burnt offering.

21 Harriet Martineau, *Autobiography* (London: Smith, Elder, 1877), vol. I, p. 120.

22 Ibid., vol. III, p. 91.

23 Harriet Martineau, trans., *Positive Philosophy of Auguste Comte* (London: John Chapman, 1853), vol. I, p. 3.

24 [Margaret Oliphant], 'Autobiographies, No. I. – Benvenuto Cellini', *Blackwood's Edinburgh Magazine* 129 (January 1881), pp. 1–3. Laura Marcus's important survey of nineteenth-century criticism in *Auto/biographical Discourses: Theory, Criticism, Practice* (Manchester University Press, 1994), pp. 11–55, reveals that nineteenth-century critics tended to treat autobiographical genres in terms of historical progress or evolution – as in Edith Simcox's use of Comtean terminology (Monumental, Positive, Metaphysical) in the *North British Review* (Jan. 1870). Oliphant is the only critic I have found who begins with the generic distinction between public *res gestae* and private domestic memoirs.

25 Felicity A. Nussbaum, 'Biography and Autobiography', in H. B. Nisbet and Claude Rawson, eds., *The Cambridge History of Literary Criticism* (Cambridge University Press, 1997), p. 306.

26 [Margaret Oliphant], 'Autobiographies: No. VI, – In the Time of the Commonwealth: Lucy Hutchinson–Alice Thornton', *Blackwood's Edinburgh Magazine* 132 (July 1882), p. 80.

27 In the article on Margaret Cavendish, Duchess of Newcastle, moreover, Oliphant articulated the autobiographical function of such memoirs, recognizing Cavendish both as an autobiographer and a 'family historian' and terming her biography of the Duke 'a second autobiography'. See [Margaret Oliphant], 'Autobiographies: No. III', *Blackwood's Edinburgh Magazine* 129 (May 1881), p. 638.

28 The exclusion of women's autobiographies from major theoretical studies is well documented by Jelinek in *The Tradition of Women's Autobiography* (Boston: Twayne, 1986), pp. 1–8; Smith in *A Poetics of Women's Autobiography* (Bloomington: Indiana University Press, 1987), pp. 3–19; and Friedman in 'Women's Autobiographical Selves: Theory and Practice', in Shari Benstock, ed., *The Private Self* (Chapel Hill: University of North Carolina Press, 1988), pp. 34–62. About this exclusion, Smith asserts: 'The poetics of autobiography, as the history of autobiography, remains by and large an androcentric enterprise. Despite the critical ferment brought about by feminist critiques of the academy, of disciplinary methodologies, of the canon, the majority of autobiography critics still persist in either erasing women's story, relegating it to the margins of critical discourse, or, when they treat women's autobiographies seriously, uncritically conflating the dynamics of male and female selfhood and textuality' (p. 15). Shattock's study, 'Victorian Women as Writers and Readers of (Auto)biography', in V. Newey and P. Shaw, eds., *Mortal Pages, Literary Lives: Studies in Nineteenth-Century Autobiography* (Aldershot: Scolar Press, 1996), pp. 140–52, theorizes the ways in which women wrote about themselves by analysing other women's life writing.

29 See William Matthews, *British Autobiographies: an Annotated Bibliography of British Autobiography Published or Written before 1951* (1955; Hamden, CT: Archon Books, 1968), s.v. 'diplomats' and consuls' wives' and 'politicians' wives'.

30 See Matthews, *British Autobiographies*, s.v. 'domestic and family life' and 'housewives'. Women wrote two-thirds of the memoirs listed under these headings.

31 Sara Coleridge, *Memoirs and Letters of Sara Coleridge*, ed. her daughter (London: Henry S. King, 1873); Frances Ann Kemble, *Record of a Girlhood* (New York: Henry Holt, 1879), pp. 1–2.

32 Kemble, *Record*, p. 193.

33 Oliphant, *Autobiography*, p. 28.

34 See ch. III, 'Girlhood', in Howitt's *Autobiography*, vol. I, pp. 74–113.

35 Howitt, *Autobiography*, vol. I, p. 237. There are no illustrations in the first edition of Mary Howitt's *The Seven Temptations* (London: Richard Bentley, 1834), though Anna Mary later published the illustrations to other children's books written by her mother.

36 These complaints were made by Alan W. Bellringer, 'Mrs Humphry Ward's Autobiographical Tactics: a Writer's Recollections', *Prose Studies* 8 (1985), p. 41, who also recognizes that Ward 'establishes a continuity in the network of intellectual families who sustain the "history of ideas"'.

37 See *The Life and Testimony of that Faithful Servant of the Lord, Elizabeth Stirredge,*

in William and Thomas Evans, *The Friends' Library* (Philadelphia: Joseph Rakestraw, 1838), vol. II, pp. 187–212, and *A Legacy, or Widow's Mite, Left by Alice Hayes* (London: Darton and Harvey, 1836).

38 John Wilson, ed., *Memoir of Mrs Margaret Wilson* (Edinburgh: John Johnstone, 1838), includes several chapters about the Bombay school for girls. The minutes of the Society for Promoting Female Education in China, India and the East (later called the Female Education Society) include numerous notes of women approved for service in Calcutta and other Indian schools; see 'Missions to Women', in the *Church Missionary Society Archive*, sec. II, part I.

39 Ann Judson, 'Address to the Females of America' and her 'Address to Females in America, relative to the situation of Females in the East', rptd in *Memoir of Mrs Ann Judson*, ed. James D. Knowles, 3rd edn (Boston: Lincoln and Edmands, 1829), pp. 313–24.

40 See Arabella W. Stuart, *Lives of Mrs. Ann H. Judson and Mrs Sarah B[oardman] Judson* (Auburn: Derby and Miller, 1852), p. 300. The primary difference between Mrs Boardman's school and others in Burma was that, while Mrs Boardman was allowed to continue religious instruction, British schools were officially prohibited from teaching the Christian religion on the grounds that it disrupted relations with – and created rebellions of – the native inhabitants.

41 *Memoir of Margaret Wilson*, p. 611.

42 Stuart, 'Preface' to *Lives of Mrs Ann H. Judson and Mrs Sarah B. Judson*, p. iii. The other Mrs Judsons were subsequent wives of Adorinam Judson, the first male missionary to Burma.

43 Stuart, *Lives of Mrs Ann H. Judson and Mrs Sarah B. Judson*, p. iii; John Wilson, *Memoir of Margaret Wilson*, p. 611.

44 Stuart, *Lives of Mrs. Ann H. Judson and Mrs. Sarah B. Judson*, p. 242.

45 Annie Besant, *An Autobiography* (London: T. Fisher Unwin, 1893), pp. 90–1.

46 *Life of Frances Power Cobbe by Herself* (Boston: Houghton, Mifflin, 1895), vol. I, p. 298.

47 William H. Epstein, 'Recognizing the Life-Course', in *Recognizing Biography* (Philadelphia: University of Pennsylvania Press, 1987), pp. 138–71.

CHAPTER ELEVEN

The professionalization of women's writing: extending the canon

Judith Johnston and Hilary Fraser

In 1856 George Eliot wrote an article entitled 'Silly Novels by Lady Novelists' for the radical *Westminster Review*. Sometimes offered as evidence of Eliot's lack of empathy with other women writers and her failure as a feminist, the article comes at the very moment when women's writing is beginning to be considered seriously as professional writing, perhaps for the first time, at least by women. Eliot's essay is in fact a call to arms, a plea to women not to prostitute their gifts because, as she points out, 'the most mischievous form of feminine silliness is the literary form, because it tends to confirm the popular prejudice against the more solid education of women'.[1] At the end of the article she writes in admiration of women writers of genius and points out that women must have 'patient diligence, a sense of the responsibility involved in publication, and an appreciation of the sacredness of the writer's art' (p. 460). These qualities are finally distilled into one pertinent phrase, 'precious speciality' (p. 461), which specifically separates women's writing from that of men. Eliot cannot envisage rising altogether above conventional gender distinctions, but she can envisage a time when women's writing will be accepted as a serious contribution to the profession.

Eliot's article also expresses consciousness of a sea-change, consciousness that women at least need no longer consider themselves dainty amateurs (mere dilettantes), but should and must consider themselves as professional writers, who must approach their craft, the sacred 'writer's art', with the proper professional attitudes. Of course what Eliot does not signal here is that women had actually been writing professionally throughout the century, often merely posing as amateurs, in an attempt to negotiate gendered discursive boundaries, and often disclaiming professional credentials, qualifications and sometimes even competence[2] in order to construct themselves as writing within a domestic discourse and conforming to a domestic ideology. Mary Jean Corbett describes such discursive practices as the 'discourse of femininity', adding that it was 'something many public women consciously appropriated as a means of legitimating their public identities, of achieving professional success, of making political change'.[3] Moreover, Corbett also points out that the term 'professional' itself shifts and changes. She writes, '[u]sed loosely to characterize all literary workers who earned money from their writing, the word "professional" has in different historical contexts, specific connotations' (p. 19), and quotes Feltes on the subject, who sees the word as specifying a 'field of ideological tension' (quoted, p. 188). Professionalism is a category, then, that is neither meaningful outside history nor empty of ideological signification; indeed, the professionalization of women's writing in the period may be seen to have been constitutive of ideology, a critical site for the negotiation and contestation of gender ideology.

In the nineteenth century generally, and especially in the periodical press, part of the ideological tension is the need to acknowledge the role of women within the profession but to try and make as little of the fact as possible. Thus William Brighty Rands in his 1858 article 'Literature as a Profession' determinedly genders his professional writers for the most part as male ('there are thousands of writing men'[4]), but nevertheless concedes 'there are other men and women of letters, who live by their pens' (p. 164), the only occasion in the article when women are included. Sometimes this tension emerges in quite strange ways. Richard Simpson's review of George Eliot's novels in the *Home and Foreign Review* of 1863 suggests that George Henry Lewes has a viable share in the writing: 'there is an organic unity in the career of these two authors, which allows us to consider them as a double mouth-piece of a single brain'.[5]

To return to 'Silly Novels'. It is no longer sufficient, George Eliot argues, for 'us' to imagine that women write only out of necessity, 'struggling for a maintenance' (p. 443) and she designates such women as 'fair writers' (p. 444) using the specifically male term which simultaneously genders and denigrates. What is more, Eliot's 'us' here, while making the reader complicit with her approach to the topic, may be read as a direct address to fellow writers and critics of both sexes; that is, it represents professional writers generally. Any professional critic, Eliot argues, who forms 'a high estimate of the share women may ultimately take in literature, will, in principle, abstain from any exceptional indulgence towards the productions of literary women' (p. 460). Eliot thus demands a balanced equity and rigour regardless of sex in professional critical practice.[6]

Astute though Eliot's article is, it is a rhetorical piece of writing, and contains views that demand to be complicated. Perhaps the first thing to point out is that of course many women writers did write out of necessity, even if that was not their only motivation, for authorship was one of the few professions open to middle-class educated women. An article in *Tait's Edinburgh Magazine* two years later in 1858 invokes 'the unfortunate authoress who steeps her fingers in ink up to the second joint, and then hawks her manuscripts from publisher to publisher', and who 'works far harder than the wretched drab at eight pounds per annum, who cleans the parlour for "the lady as writes"'.[7] Many examples there were of successful and talented female authors – Harriet Martineau, Anna Jameson, Margaret Oliphant – whose writing was their livelihood. Indeed, Margaret Oliphant specifically compares her own professional career, which she sees as having been determined by the fact that she was always obliged to write potboilers in order to make money to support her extended and impecunious family, with George Eliot's less financially and domestically circumscribed, and consequently more illustrious, one.[8]

Kept, as she was, according to the envious Oliphant, 'in a mental greenhouse and taken care of' (p. 15), Eliot did indeed enjoy many of the privileges of the male professional writer that most women conspicuously lacked. A room of her own, for example, of the kind that guaranteed literary men their intellectual space, such as is described in an article of 1831 in *Fraser's Magazine*: 'It was evident that the room was appropriated to one individual, and to one purpose. Retirement was here the obvious accompaniment of literature . . . The room was evidently for *himself*.'[9] Contrast Anna Jameson's writing situation, upon first moving to her cottage in Ealing:

the arrangement is like an American Wigwam – we have each our own corner – our own chair – our own drawer – our own peg – our own half of a toilet table . . . Yesterday we had not room to move . . . there was not space to stir my elbow – I stood and worked from 10 to 3 – and then from five to 9 – today we revel in space and repose and I write to you from my own domain – a corner about 3 feet square.[10]

Oliphant's own working space was no more dedicated or sequestered than Jameson's:

I had no table even to myself, much less a room to work in, but sat at the corner of the family table with my writing-book, with everything going on as if I had been making a shirt instead of writing a book . . . My mother sat always at needlework of some kind, and talked to whoever might be present, and I took my share in the conversation, going on all the same with my story . . . up to this date, 1888, I have never been shut up in a separate room, or hedged off with any observances. My study, all the study I have ever attained to, is the little second drawing-room of my house, with a wide opening into the other drawing-room where all the (feminine) life of the house goes on; and I don't think I have ever had two hours undisturbed (except at night, when everybody is in bed) during my whole literary life.[11]

Florence Nightingale makes a similar point in 'Cassandra' when she observes, 'Women never have half an hour in all their lives (excepting before or after anybody is up in the house) that they can call their own', and they 'have no means given them, whereby they *can* resist the "claims of social life"', having been 'taught from their infancy upwards that it is wrong, ill-tempered, and a misunderstanding of "woman's mission" (with a great M) if they do not allow themselves *willingly* to be interrupted at all hours'.[12] Some women such as Martineau, and Nightingale herself, could protect their professional lives from such unwelcome social incursions by withdrawing to the invalid's couch, but for the most part women either worked on regardless or, like Frances Trollope, wrote through the night.

To be a professional writer meant different things for men and women. Even the most fundamental definition of the term – that it refers to writers who earn money from their work – cannot always be applied to women. Eliot herself fulfilled her duties as assistant editor of the *Westminster Review* in an unpaid capacity, while, before the passing of the Married Women's Property Acts of 1870 and 1882, women who had the misfortune to be married had no legal right to their earnings, as writers such as Caroline Norton and Annie Besant complained. For the latter, it was a cruel discovery that her imagined new-found economic independence as a published writer was mistaken: 'I had not realised then the beauty of the English law, and the dignified position in which it placed the married woman; I did not understand that all a married woman earned by law belonged to her owner, and that she could have nothing that belonged to her of right.'[13] Less tangibly, the woman who would be a professional writer had to challenge and to manage discursively all the ideological prescriptions that constructed women as passive, self-sacrificing, domestic goddesses who inhabited the private sphere rather than the noisy world of public debate. Virginia Woolf was later to write of the need to 'do battle' with 'The Angel in the House' before she could enter the profession of writing; and of the need to decorate and furnish the 'room of one's own' that had been so hard won.[14]

At the same time, of course, as Woolf points out, writing was the one profession which could be carried out within the domestic sphere; although when it came time to manage such issues as copyright and payment and authorial identity, women packed their bags and went to Town. Famously the Brontë sisters, Charlotte and Anne, presented themselves to the publisher George Smith as the only means of proving the separate identities of Currer and Acton Bell, and Anna Jameson, in the confidence of her professional literary status, took the publisher John Murray to task in the public columns of the *Athenaeum* for taking liberties with her copyright.[15] These few citations of many examples show to what extent ideology was in conflict with actual practice. Women defended their professional status vigorously and, like George Eliot herself, reveal a degree of business acumen that shows that, while they remained victims of the system, they nevertheless refused for themselves the role of victim. Gaye Tuchman suggests that nineteenth-century women writers should not be considered professional because they did not control significant elements of their work,[16] but we would argue that the constant efforts to maintain that control, even if they were unsuccessful, show to what extent women regarded themselves as professional and behaved professionally.[17]

Women were more readily acknowledged as professional writers in some fields than in others. From the late eighteenth century, fiction, or the novel, to be more specific, was considered an appropriate writing genre for women, and by the mid-Victorian period the feminization of the genre had become a commonplace. In allowing this there was simultaneously an implied denigration of the form. In 1835, the anonymous reviewer of a misogynistic book with the title *Woman as She is and as She should be* caustically summarizes its author's views on female authorship: 'They are most successful in *novels*; but, then, what a contemptible branch of literature is the novel! . . . Female authors may know something of "society and manners", we are told; "but they are grossly ignorant of human life"'.[18] It was believed that writing a novel required no extensive education and, more importantly, it was work which could be done at home. It was also perceived as a kind of activity that came relatively naturally to women. As an 1865 article on 'Women Writers' in 'The Ladies' Pages' of the magazine *Bow Bells* contends, the feminine mind is characterized by the prominence of the emotions rather than the intellect, and is therefore more suited to literature than philosophy; and 'Of all departments of literature, fiction is the one to which, by nature and by circumstance, women are best adapted.'[19]

In 1863 Julia Kavanagh published *English Women of Letters*, a survey that begins with Aphra Behn and ends with Lady Morgan, and which is designed to trace the development of the profession of fiction writing. Kavanagh's timing is significant, we suggest, for the general re-appraisal of women's role in the profession of letters that seems to have been taking place at mid-century along with renewed activity and interest in women's issues generally. Kavanagh concludes:

Fiction is going on its wonderful career like Saturn devouring its own children. The time when novels were few has gone by; we shall never see its return. It is the only branch of literature in which women have acquired genuine distinction and exercised undoubted influence . . . We cannot open a novel of to-day on which these past and faded novelists have not left their trace.[20]

Kavanagh believes this 'trace' is 'worthy of attention and record' (p. 330). For all her equivocation, as suggested by the unpleasant Saturnine metaphor, and her criticism of the literary grandmothers she cites, her publication celebrates the role of women in the development of fiction as a form, and, albeit indirectly, claims fiction as a profession for women.

While Kavanagh's assertion that fiction is the only branch of literature in which women can claim distinction is incorrect, as we will show, nevertheless it is with fiction that women were first able to earn a respectable living. Ann Radcliffe's famous Gothic novels established this pattern (she earned £800 for *The Italian* in 1797). Kavanagh's *English Women of Letters* appeared in the same year the serialization of George Eliot's *Romola* was drawing to a close, a work for which Eliot was initially offered the 'magnificent' sum of £10,000 by the publisher George Smith.[21] By 1876 the *Contemporary Review* in a brief article entitled 'Recent Novels' is confidently claiming that the 'course of fictitious literature in our day is upward and not downward' and adds that work of a high class is especially produced by ladies. The reviewer cites George Eliot specifically as producing novels which carry 'the whole weight of modern culture, or at least a good part of it'.[22]

Eliot herself, in 'Silly Novels', nominated fiction as the one area of intellectual endeavour in which women can compete on equal terms: 'No educational restrictions can shut women out from the materials of fiction, and there is no species of art which is so free from rigid requirements. Like crystalline masses, it may take any form, and yet be beautiful' (p. 461). The genres from which women could be, and often were, shut out included science, history, philosophy and politics. Yet interestingly enough fiction itself often gave them an opportunity to explore these forbidden fields, and it is not uncommon to find the language of science, history, religion and so on discursively appropriated in the novels and critical writings of literary women, including, of course, Eliot herself. When she writes 'Like crystalline masses' in the above quotation, for example, she invokes a scientific discourse with which she is obviously familiar. The simile is appropriate, it is informed, it is scientifically correct. Moreover, as critics such as Gillian Beer and Sally Shuttleworth have amply demonstrated,[23] in her later novels Eliot consistently incorporates science into her metaphoric language in a similar way. As her partner George Henry Lewes developed his study of more scientific subjects so she too studied those same topics by his side. She is written into his 'Sea-Side Studies', published by *Blackwood's Edinburgh Magazine* in August 1856, as a lady carrying a landing-net who 'has taken the precaution of putting on things which "won't spoil"',[24] and her obvious pleasure in the studies comes through in her journal: 'the tide being then low, we went out on our first zoophyte hunt. The littoral zone at Ilfracombe is nothing but huge boulders and jutting rocks of granwacke or clay slate, which when not made slippery by sea-weed are not very difficult to scramble over.'[25]

As T. W. Heyck has shown, scientists split away from the general 'men of letters' category into 'professionalized academic disciplines' attacking the 'men of letters' as 'shallow, dilettantish, amateurish, and out of date'.[26] Eliot's term 'rigid requirements', cited from 'Silly Novels' above, shows how acutely she comprehended the changes taking place. George Henry Lewes, writing on philosophy and later turning to science, had to endure specific attacks prompted by his perceived amateur status.[27] These circumstances militated naturally enough against women writers to an even greater degree. Barbara Gates and Ann B. Shteir explain that the focus of women's education shifted in the late 1860s from natural science to the classics, ironically equalizing one aspect of women's education with that of men, while at the same time discouraging women from engaging in scientific studies. This they attribute directly to the 'masculinization of science',[28] but it is also clear that, like 'amateur' male writers, women's exclusion can also be attributed to the professionalization of scientific discourse as a whole.[29]

Yet women were professionally engaged in the writing of books on science throughout the nineteenth century, from Jane Marcet's *Conversations on Chemistry* (1806), to Anne Pratt's *Things on the Sea Coast* (1850) and Margaret Gatty's *British Seaweeds* (1862), to Alice Bodington's *Studies in Evolution and Biology* (1890). It was even argued that women were particularly well adapted to engage in certain branches of science. Writing towards the close of the eighteenth century (and before Humphrey Davy was to transform the science), Maria Edgeworth suggests that:

Chemistry is a science well suited to the talents and situation of women; it is not a science of parade; it affords occupation and infinite variety; it demands no bodily strength; it can be pursued in retirement; it applies immediately to useful and domestic purposes: and whilst the ingenuity of the most inventive mind may in this science be exercised, there is no danger of inflaming the imagination, because the mind is intent upon realities, the knowledge that is acquired is exact, and the pleasure of the pursuit is a sufficient reward for the labour.[30]

Botanical writing too was similarly deemed to be 'a safe subject [for women], just sufficiently aesthetic without any danger of being intellectual, and properly sexless'.[31] Its science was not quite scientific and its practice based on minute observation of particulars, something women were supposedly more able to do than men. As Elizabeth Rigby asked, comparing men's writing to that of women:

Who . . . has not turned from the slap-dash scrawl of your male correspondent – with excuses at the beginning and haste at the end, and too often nothing between but sweeping generalities – to the well-filled sheet of your female friend, . . . overflowing with those close and lively details which show not only that observing eyes have been at work, but one pair of bright eyes in particular?[32]

Gates and Shteir argue that scientific narratives shaped by women writers typically 'merged gender with genre, and became pioneering contributions by women to the cultural transmission of science' (p. 8). The women writing early in the century domesticated their topics by presenting scientific discourse in the form of 'conversations' or 'talks' in a 'female mentorial tradition' (p. 9) in which they mediated scientific information to children, to women and to working-class people alike, functioning 'not as groundbreakers but as educators' (p. 10).

The periodicals of the day were well aware of, and perhaps even contributed to, this particular role for women. William Empson, reviewing works on political economy by Marcet and Martineau for the *Edinburgh Review*, manages to devote almost the entire article to Martineau but in the end hands the prize to Marcet. He lays the groundwork by declaring political economy to be a fit subject for women because it comes within the province of home, both their own and that of their poorer neighbours. These are interests, says Empson, which will satisfy 'any reasonable personal ambition'.[33] It is clear from this statement that not just women found it necessary to negotiate discursive boundaries. When it came to dealing seriously with the work of professional women writers, it seems that male reviewers also had to acknowledge the ideology of the day. Empson subsequently explains Martineau's methodology by stating that scientific tales are not to be confused with moral ones, and adds in metaphoric language that suggests both the scientific experiment and a cooking recipe: 'By the help of a well-contrived fiction, she puts society, as it were, into a sieve, and takes out of the commingled mass of human affairs, one by one, the particular amount and description of persons and circumstances which an actual experiment would require' (pp. 6–7). However, it is in his declaration that 'Discoverers are seldom the best teachers' (8) that we find Empson cheerfully handing the lesser role of disciple (that is, popularizer or mediator) to these women who will prove 'more successful missionaries' than the discoverers themselves. Empson has earlier made it clear that the 'discoverers' are male with his reference to Martineau's 'rescue of her beloved science – the science of Adam Smith' (p. 2). Despite his preoccupation with Martineau and her work, Empson ultimately takes her to task for her excellences and her genius and declares in favour of Mrs Marcet who, although lacking imagination and poetry, is 'a more judicious reasoner, and a surer guide' (p. 39). As George Eliot so rightly suggests in 'Silly Novels':

No sooner does a woman show that she has genius or effective talent, than she receives the tribute of being moderately praised and severely criticized. By a peculiar thermometric adjustment, when a woman's talent is at zero, journalistic approbation is at the boiling pitch; . . . Harriet Martineau, Currer Bell, and Mrs Gaskell have been treated as cavalierly as if they had been men (p. 400)

The increasing professionalization of science saw many women pushed aside but women can also be said to have created a counter-discourse, continuing to relay scientific information in other forms. This counter-discourse manifested itself not just in periodical articles and texts like those named above, but also took shape in the work of women novelists and poets, travel-writers and essayists. These women, like the English writer Louisa Anne Meredith, describing plant and insect life in colonial Australia in a publication categorized as travel-writing, were careful to disclaim any scientific knowledge whatsoever. As Meredith puts it: 'I cannot for a moment flatter myself with the idea of conveying information to those skilled in scientific detail; . . . I have sketched every-day things with a faithful and homely pencil.'[34] Yet their work within any number of disguising genres, with disclaimers suggesting a mere amateur and domestic status, consistently demonstrates a broad, but detailed scientific knowledge predicated upon the Linnaean system and other forms of recognized scientific discourse.

Later in the century, women of science like Arabella Buckley no longer felt the need to disguise their work in this way. Buckley's 'Darwinism and Religion', written for *Macmillan's Magazine,* is authoritative, knowledgeable and forthright. She presents a description of Darwin's position and then proceeds to argue from this to her own: 'I believe that this fear, if it be founded upon the theory of the moral sense, as set forth in the "Descent of Man", is a groundless one; and the object of the present essay is to attempt to show . . . [t]hat Mr Darwin, if his theory be approximately true, has given a new impulse to the Utilitarian philosophy.'[35] Far from proffering disclaimers, at one point Buckley writes 'I cannot discover from writers on physiology and psychology that I am mistaken' (p. 49) although when her argument becomes speculative she offers it 'with much hesitation' (p. 50). On the whole, however, she argues confidently that evolutionary theories offer no threat to established religion and she argues progressively, always shifting beyond a particular position but keeping, as she herself says, 'strictly and logically to facts' (p. 51). Buckley's language is driven in part by her subject, but also in part by a new confidence that she can be a professional writer, rewriting 'Darwin for the future'.[36]

The domestication of science as a genre might be compared with history as another genre interdicted to women but appropriated by them nevertheless. When Eliot looks with a scientific eye to the history of common life, her methodology, as Alison Booth explains: 'can serve, then, both to subordinate the individual . . . and to exalt any individual as contributor to grand historical developments, which in turn must be seen as the cumulative effects of multitudes of common lives.'[37] Eliot's novel *Middlemarch* is not simply a 'history of man' as she posits in the 'Prelude', it is also a very precise history of a very particular moment in English political life, the passage of the 1832 Reform Bill into law. *Middlemarch* demonstrates how an historical, social and political agenda can shape a domestic narrative, inform it and yet remain closely tied to a particular fictional space that denies any historical subtext. This said, Christina Crosby has argued convincingly that Eliot 'is on the wrong side, as it were, of an asymmetrical difference crucial to the identity of man as a properly historical subject. She writes as a male manqué.'[38] In novels such as *Felix Holt, the Radical* (1866), *Middlemarch* (1871–2) and *Daniel Deronda* (1876) it could be said that she achieves her historical ends by radically excluding women.

Crosby contends more generally that in the nineteenth century history is 'produced as man's truth' which requires that women be 'above, below or beyond properly historical and political life' (p. 1). This proved to be a particular challenge to professional women historians. Early in the century histories by women are often about women. Lucy Aikin published *Memoirs of the Court of Queen Elizabeth* in 2 volumes in 1818; Anna Jameson published *Memoirs of the Celebrated Female Sovereigns* in 1831; Hannah Lawrance began *Historical Memoirs of the Queens of England* (1838 and 1840); and Agnes Strickland published her *Lives of the Queens of England* in twelve volumes between 1840 and 1848, to provide just a small sampling.

It is clear that women could achieve two major aims when confining themselves to histories about women. Firstly, they could legitimately locate a space for themselves in the writing of women's history as a profession. As one reviewer remarked of Hannah Lawrance, her ambitious style and elaborate ornament 'do not ill become a female historian, especially when her themes are persons of the same sex'.[39] These women did, however, pay due regard, even homage, to the recognized male historians such as the Scottish philosopher David Hume, in much the same way as women contented themselves with the teaching of science in preference to cutting-edge practice. Secondly, they could reclaim a place for the women of history within the genre by rectifying omission and correcting the record. As a *Monthly Review* article 'Woman in England' points out in discussing Lawrance's work, she is of necessity 'an expounder of slender and scattered facts' but the writer praises her ability to 'show how much she has learnt and can indicate by means of few and feeble lights'.[40]

History, as Heyck has shown, belonged principally to the 'letters' category and was written for 'commercial publication . . . [and] offered for sale to the general reading public through a market system',[41] along with philosophy, novels, poetry and journalism, particularly reviews. Considered therefore a professional genre, for this reason the competition was keen, and women, even when they confined themselves to the writing of women's histories, were open to attack on the grounds that history was a masculine subject. C. S. M. Phillips attacks Agnes Strickland in the pages of the *Edinburgh Review* as a woman who 'assumes masculine functions' without assuming 'masculine gravity and impartiality'.[42] Earlier the *Gentleman's Magazine* had complained of a heaviness in her writing as inevitable when politics and petticoats are mixed together.[43] Macaulay, Whig historian and Strickland's chief male rival in this period, wrote of her in his diary as a 'vulgar, mendacious, malignant

scribbler',[44] revealing the extent to which he felt professionally threatened by her. These comments show clearly that history was very much
contested ground, even when the historical subjects were women themselves.

Women did not after all confine themselves to producing accounts of
historical women. Harriet Martineau, for instance, produced among
other histories *The History of England during the Thirty Years' Peace,
1816–1849* (1849–50); *Introduction to the History of the Peace from 1800–1815*
(1851); and *British Rule in India: a Historical Sketch* (1857). Valerie Pichanick,
comparing Martineau's practice to that of Macaulay, shows that
Macaulay's satisfaction that 'by the mid-nineteenth century the ends of
progress had been achieved' is in sharp contrast to Martineau's recognition 'that her England was not yet Utopia', revealing only 'partial
advance towards the grand slow general change'.[45] D. T. Coulton's
'Contemporary History – Mr Roebuck and Miss Martineau' for the
Quarterly Review considers Martineau's *History of England* and Roebuck's
History of the Whig Ministry of 1830. He accuses both of partisanship and
animosity and, while favouring Martineau, nevertheless attacks her
qualifications as a professional historian, citing 'feeble and feminine
mimicries', but not as a professional writer: 'we think her book likely to
survive the fleeting publications of the day'.[46] Reception of much of
Martineau's work was in this style. The *Athenaeum*, reviewing her
Introduction to the History of the Peace, sententiously decides that while her
writing shines: 'we cannot exactly point to the writer as furnishing an
exception to the case of no woman having been a first-rate historian.
None of the fair sex have ever taken that rank in history . . . the truth is
that history is acted by men, – and the historian has to narrate manly
transactions in a manly spirit.'[47]

In an article on 'popular authorship' in the *London Quarterly Review* of
1855–6 the anonymous journalist effectively disposes of both science
and history with a complaint uncannily similar to that of George Eliot
in 'Silly Novels': 'As a body, our authors are no longer prompted by
unusual gifts or guided by the loftiest principles; but vanity supplies the
place of inspiration, and sordid motives are in the stead of high ambition. Hence the endless compilations of history and science in which
(with many admirable exceptions) truth is let down and diluted more
and more.'[48] Interestingly enough, such comments echo those frequently made more specifically about the periodical press. John Henry
Newman in *The Idea of a University* (1852) condones the role of 'periodical literature and occasional lectures and scientific institutions [in]

diffus[ing] through the community' a 'superficial acquaintance with chemistry, and geology, and astronomy, and political economy, and modern history, and biography, and other branches of knowledge' and thereby enabling the acquisition of 'a graceful accomplishment, and a suitable, nay, in this day a necessary accomplishment, in the case of educated men'.[49] Those who wrote for periodicals were widely perceived to be 'stimulated by the prospect of gain rather than by the workings of genius', to write 'in a small and smattering way' on subjects of which they only have 'superficial' knowledge.[50] The geologist Hugh Miller, in an article of 1870 on 'Periodicalism' sees periodical writing as issuing forth 'from the closets of over-toiled *littérateurs*', and being responsible for 'an excited superficiality [that] creeps out upon the age'.[51] As the language of the above quotations suggests, by the mid-Victorian period, writing for the periodical press had become feminized for some critics; an intellectual activity of which women might be capable.[52] According to William Hazlitt, in his 1823 article on 'The Periodical Press', periodicals exemplify modern literature, which he describes as 'the directress of fashion', as 'a gay Coquette, fluttering fickle vain . . . [which] trifles with all sorts of arts and sciences . . . glitters, flutters, buzzes, spawns, dies, – and is forgotten'. 'Instead of solemn testimonies from the learned', he avers, 'we require the smiles of the fair and the polite . . . let Reviews flourish – let Magazines increase and multiply'.[53]

Increase and multiply they did, and by mid-century many of the anonymous multitude of contributors to the periodical press were from the ranks of 'the fair' sex. And for many, including George Eliot, Harriet Martineau and Margaret Oliphant, periodicals were the platform from which extremely successful and high-profile professional writing careers were launched. The practice of anonymous journalism enabled women to enter the field in greater numbers than was generally suspected, in their own time and later, and allowed them to address topics not generally thought of as suitable to a woman's pen, because theoretically no-one except the editor knew who the author of a particular piece was. By the 1840s women and their writing were becoming a force to be reckoned with in Victorian Britain. It is clear from articles such as that of G. H. Lewes writing for *Fraser's Magazine* in 1847 that their considerable presence in the writing scene generally was making an impact, judging from the language Lewes uses which, while humorous, nevertheless expresses considerable anxiety that writing as a profession is being invaded by 'speculators' and that the once well-trained 'army' of writers is being 'swelled and encumbered by women, children, and ill-trained troops'.[54] He thinks of the profession of writing as an exclusive club of which men are the chief members. But women by this date had already begun to claim particular areas of writing for themselves. Travel writing, for example, was an area in which women were beginning to dominate, highlighted by the influential *Quarterly*'s 'Lady Travellers' review, written by Elizabeth Rigby, who celebrates the particular qualities women brought to travel writing, and firmly believes the Englishwoman is superior by far to any foreign lady as a 'traveller or writer of travels', because she is 'well-read, solid thinking . . . educated with the refinement of the highest classes, and with the usefulness of the lowest'.[55]

Women writers themselves, while appearing to perpetuate the commonly held stereotypes regarding women so prevalent in the nineteenth century, would often also explain, as Rigby does, that their lack of education hampered their ability to achieve the same level of expertise as men. Thus while women rarely attempted, in the early years of the century anyway, to operate outside the system, they nevertheless did attempt to change that system from within, employing varying styles of discourse, an issue recognized in R. H. Horne's *A New Spirit of the Age* which he published in 1844 and which was written in collaboration with Elizabeth Barrett Browning.[56] In the section entitled 'Harriet Martineau and Mrs Jameson' the following statement is made:

Both these fine writers have, as we have seen, advocated a remodelling of our institutions with regard to their own sex. The one represents the intellect of the question, the other the feeling; one brings to it an acute abstract comprehension, the other all the sympathies of a woman; one reasons from observation, the other from experience; one has been roused to the cause by general benevolence, the other, probably, by personal suffering.[57]

Most existing studies of letters as a profession, both nineteenth-century and modern, make gendered assumptions. The very term 'men of letters', so definitively stated by Carlyle in the 1840s, implies that women can only be pretenders in the profession:

There are genuine Men of Letters, and not genuine; as in every kind there is a genuine and a spurious. If *Hero* be taken to mean genuine, then I say the Hero as Man of Letters will be found discharging a function for us which is ever honourable, ever the highest; and was once well known to be the highest. He is uttering-forth, in such way as he has, the inspired soul of him; all that a man, in any case, can do.[58]

Yet many women who were Carlyle's contemporaries defined themselves, like Elizabeth Barrett Browning's fictional poet Aurora Leigh, fundamentally as professional writers: 'I write', the eponymous heroine states baldly,[59] and this is the keynote of so many women writers' auto-biographical self-representations. In the genre of autobiography (and autobiography can take various forms, such as journals and diaries, commonplace books, even fiction), women were concerned to record not their private lives so much as their professional lives. George Eliot turned her journal upside down and recorded in the back 'How I came to Write Fiction' and 'History of Adam Bede', conscious that fiction would be to her the real profession for which journalism was merely an apprenticeship. Autobiographical forms of self-representation justify the choice of vocation, suggest women's qualifications, explain or negotiate their resistance to the separate spheres ideology, and often claim, as carefully as possible, either a place for themselves within the canon, or at least equal status with male writers. Why else would George Eliot take the trouble at the outset of her career to write down how it all came about unless she had an eye to posterity and a sense that professionally she had arrived?

Similarly, biographies, like those of professional male writers, focus on the life only as it served the career, rather than how the profession may have framed the life. The biography of Anna Jameson started by her niece Gerardine Macpherson and on her death completed by Margaret Oliphant, even in its title, *Memoirs of the Life of Anna Jameson* (1879), which plays on the titles of various of Jameson's publications, signals at the outset that this will be a writing life. Charlotte Dempster, in her review of this book for the *Edinburgh Review*, wrote that 'the life of Anna Jameson was truly dedicated to art. It became her work and her profession; she loved it truly, and it rewarded her largely', not financially she hastens to point out, but in friendships and study 'the artist-woman was soothed, dignified, and consoled'.[60] There is clearly a recognition, even a validation, here, of a professional career from one of the more conservative of the major journals. Margaret Oliphant, for the similarly conservative *Blackwood's Magazine*, in 'Two Ladies', reviews Jameson's biography (despite her part in its publication) and Fanny Kemble's autobiographical *Record of a Girlhood*. Oliphant acknowledges that, whenever necessary, 'women *have* toiled, have earned money, have got their living . . . in total indifference to all theory', but concludes with a sigh that nowadays 'literature is becoming, or has become, a profession like any other'.[61]

In another year George Eliot too would be dead, perhaps the most successful professional of them all. For her the obituaries did not hint at limitations of mind and talent as they universally had twenty years earlier in recording the death of Anna Jameson in 1860. George Eliot, in the intervening twenty years, had benefited from the recognition that literature is a profession and was celebrated for her contribution to it. Julia Wedgwood, writing for the *Contemporary Review* in 1881, entitled her piece 'The Moral Influence of George Eliot' and placed Eliot in illustrious company, with Walter Scott, Shakespeare and Elizabeth Barrett Browning. 'In literature', she writes, 'many are called and few chosen',[62] and the word 'genius' is offered without qualification. Later the same year Wedgwood produced a similar essay on Carlyle and in her opening paragraph wrote:

The inclement season has ended two lives . . . Thomas Carlyle and George Eliot, though separated by the interval of a bare generation, represented two intellectual eras – the great Englishwoman who has made fiction the vehicle of an impressive moral doctrine belongs wholly to the present; the great Scotchman who has done the like by history belongs to a phase of development that we have already left far behind us.[63]

In claiming Eliot for the present, Wedgwood locates the particular stage of arrival in the professionalization of women's writing. Virginia Woolf was born a year after Eliot's death, and was later to acknowledge the ways in which her own professional writing career was facilitated by such literary mothers: 'for the road was cut many years ago – by Fanny Burney, by Aphra Behn, by Harriet Martineau, by Jane Austen, by George Eliot – many famous women, and many more unknown and forgotten, have been before me, making the path smooth, and regulating my steps. Thus, when I came to write, there were very few material obstacles in my way.'[64] Moreover, by the time of writing *A Room of One's Own* (1929), it was possible for Woolf to assert unequivocally:

it is certainly true that women no longer write novels solely. There are Jane Harrison's books on Greek archaeology; Vernon Lee's books on aesthetics; Gertrude Bell's books on Persia. There are books on all sorts of subjects which a generation ago no woman would have touched. There are poems and plays and criticism; there are histories and biographies, books of travel and books of scholarship and research; there are even a few philosophies and books about science and economics. And though novels predominate, novels themselves may very well have changed from association with books of a different feather.[65]

Woolf is in error when she comments that women of a previous generation limited their literary activities to the writing of fiction, which only serves to confirm her more general view in *A Room of One's Own* of the invisibility of women in conventional literary history. As this chapter has attempted to argue, the very diversity of their literary output was a crucial factor in women's struggle to be recognized as professional writers.

NOTES

1 George Eliot, 'Silly Novels by Lady Novelists', *Westminster Review* 66 (1856), pp. 442–61, 454.
2 These are the qualifiers used to describe the term 'professional' in Linda K. Robertson, 'Who is a Professional Scholar? George Eliot and George Henry Lewes Considered', in Martin Hewitt, ed., *Scholarship in Victorian Britain* (Leeds: Trinity and All Saints / Leeds Centre for Victorian Studies, 1998), pp. 102–13, 111.
3 Mary Jean Corbett, *Representing Femininity: Middle-Class Subjectivity in Victorian and Edwardian Women's Autobiographies* (Oxford University Press, 1992), p. 15. For further discussion of the question of professionalism, see Deirdre David, *Intellectual Women and Victorian Patriarchy: Harriet Martineau, Elizabeth Barrett Browning, George Eliot* (London: Macmillan, 1987); Dorothy Mermin, *Godiva's Ride: Women of Letters in England, 1830–1880* (Bloomington: Indiana University Press, 1993); Thaïs E. Morgan, ed., *Victorian Sages and Cultural Discourse: Renegotiating Gender and Power* (New Brunswick: Rutgers University Press, 1990); H. Perkin, *The Rise of Professional Society: England since 1880* (London: Routledge, 1990); Julia Swindells, *Victorian Writing and Working Women: the Other Side of Silence* (Cambridge: Polity, 1985).
4 William Brighty Rands, 'Tangled Talk. Literature as a Profession', *Tait's Edinburgh Magazine* n.s. 25 (1858), pp. 162–6, 164.
5 Richard Simpson, 'George Eliot's Novels', *Home and Foreign Review* 3 (1863), pp. 522–49, 524.
6 Though at the end of the century Arnold Bennett is still complaining of the 'exceptional indulgence' meted out to women journalists: 'they are not expected to suffer the same discipline, nor are they judged by the same standards. In Fleet Street femininity is an absolution, not an accident', Arnold Bennett, *Journalism for Women. A Practical Guide* (London: John Lane, 1898), p. 10.
7 Anon., 'Woman and Womankind VI', *Tait's Edinburgh Magazine* 25 (1858), pp. 348–58, 348.
8 *The Autobiography of Margaret Oliphant*, ed. Elisabeth Jay (Oxford University Press, 1990), pp. 14–17.
9 Anon., 'On the Libraries of Celebrated Literary Men', *Fraser's Magazine* 3 (1831), pp. 408–9, 408.
10 A. L. S. from Anna Jameson to Lady Byron, 16 November 1842, British Library MS Box 75, Letters 252, 254.
11 Oliphant, *Autobiography*, p. 30.
12 Florence Nightingale, *Cassandra and Other Selections from* Suggestions for Thought, ed. Mary Poovey (New York University Press, 1993), pp. 213–14.
13 Annie Besant, *Autobiographical Sketches* (London: Freethought Publishing Company, 1885), p. 46.
14 Virginia Woolf, 'Professions for Women', in *Virginia Woolf: On Women and Writing*, ed. Michèle Barrett (London: Women's Press, 1979), pp. 58, 63.

15 Anna Jameson, 'Rights of Authors', *Athenaeum* 1595 (22 May 1858), p. 659; and John Murray, 'Rights of Authors', *Athenaeum* 1596 (29 May 1858), p. 688.

16 Gaye Tuchman with Nina E. Fortin, *Edging Women Out: Victorian Novelists, Publishers, and Social Change* (New Haven: Yale University Press, 1989), p. 36.

17 See also Ellen Miller Casey's article challenging Tuchman's *Edging Women Out*: 'Edging Women Out?: Reviews of Women Novelists in the *Athenaeum*, 1860–1900', *Victorian Studies* 39 (1996), 151–71; and Corbett, *Representing Femininity*, pp. 57–9, on the problematics of negotiating the private and public spheres for the nineteenth-century woman writer.

18 Anon., 'A Blast against the Monsterous Regimente of Womene', *Tait's Edinburgh Magazine* 2 (1835), pp. 707–14, 711.

19 Anon., 'Women Writers', *Bow Bells* n. s. 3 (1865), p. 139.

20 Julia Kavanagh, *English Women of Letters* (1863; n.p.: n.pub., n.d.), p. 330.

21 Eliot could not agree to a May 1862 starting date, and eventually they agreed on £7,000 for twelve monthly instalments.

22 Anon., 'Recent Novels', *Contemporary Review* 29 (1876–7), pp. 527–8, p. 528.

23 See Gillian Beer, *Darwin's Plots: Evolutionary Narrative in Darwin, George Eliot, and Nineteenth-Century Fiction* (London: Routledge and Kegan Paul, 1983); Sally Shuttleworth, *George Eliot and Nineteenth-Century Science: the Make-believe of a Beginning* (Cambridge University Press, 1984).

24 George Henry Lewes, 'Sea-Side Studies', *Blackwood's Edinburgh Magazine* 80 (1856), pp. 184–97, 190.

25 *The Journals of George Eliot*, ed. Margaret Harris and Judith Johnston (Cambridge University Press, 1998), p. 265.

26 T. W. Heyck, 'From Men of Letters to Intellectuals: the Transformation of Intellectual Life in Nineteenth-Century England', *Journal of British Studies* 20 (1980), pp. 158–83, 179. See also Heyck's subsequent study, *The Transformation of Intellectual Life in Victorian England* (London: Croom Helm, 1982).

27 Rosemary Ashton, *George Henry Lewes: a Life* (Oxford University Press, 1991), p. 146.

28 Barbara T. Gates and Ann B. Shteir, *Natural Eloquence: Women Reinscribe Science* (Madison: University of Wisconsin Press, 1997), p. 17.

29 Though note that Lydia Becker, in a signed article 'On the Study of Science by Women', *Contemporary Review* 10 (1869), pp. 386–404, mounts a strong argument against the refusal of professional recognition to women scientists.

30 Maria Edgeworth, *Letters for Literary Ladies* (London: J. M. Dent, 1993), p. 21.

31 Joanna Trollope, *Britannia's Daughters: Women of the British Empire* (London: Hutchinson, 1983), p. 156.

32 Elizabeth Rigby, 'Women Travellers', *Quarterly Review* 76 (1845), pp. 98–137, 98–9.

33 William Empson, 'Illustrations of Political Economy. Mrs Marcet – Miss Martineau', *Edinburgh Review* 57 (1833), pp. 1–39, 1.

34 Louisa Anne Meredith, *Notes and Sketches of New South Wales during a Residence in that Colony from 1839 to 1844* (London: John Murray, 1846), pp. vii–viii.

35 Arabella Buckley, 'Darwinism and Religion', *Macmillan's Magazine* 24 (1871), pp. 45–51, 46.
36 Barbara Gates, *Kindred Nature: Victorian and Edwardian Women Embrace the Living World* (University of Chicago Press, 1998), p. 61.
37 Alison Booth, *Greatness Engendered: George Eliot and Virginia Woolf* (Ithaca: Cornell University Press, 1992), p. 93.
38 Christina Crosby, *The Ends of History: Victorians and 'The Woman Question'* (New York: Routledge, 1991), p. 43.
39 Anon., 'Notices. Historical Memoirs of the Queens of England', *Monthly Review* 151 (1840), p. 124.
40 Anon., 'Woman in England', *Monthly Review* 160 (1843), pp. 495–502, 498, 500.
41 Heyck, 'From Men of Letters to Intellectuals', p. 159.
42 C. S. M. Phillips, 'Miss Strickland's Queens of England', *Edinburgh Review* 89 (1849), pp. 435–62, 436.
43 Quoted in Judith Johnston, *Anna Jameson: Victorian, Feminist, Woman of Letters* (Aldershot: Ashgate, 1997), p. 67.
44 Thomas Pinney, *The Letters of Thomas Babington Macaulay*, vol. v (Cambridge University Press, 1981), p. 233.
45 Valerie Kossew Pichanick, *Harriet Martineau. The Woman and her Work, 1802–76* (Ann Arbor: University of Michigan Press, 1980), p. 143.
46 D. T. Coulton, 'Contemporary History – Mr Roebuck and Miss Martineau', *Quarterly Review* 91 (1852), pp. 160–95, 169.
47 Anon., 'Martineau's Introduction to the History of the Peace', *Athenaeum* 1230 (1851), pp. 543–5, 544–5.
48 Anon., 'Popular Authorship – Samuel Warren', *London Quarterly Review* 5 (1855–6), pp. 464–80, 465.
49 John Henry Newman, *The Idea of a University, Defined and Illustrated*, ed. I. T. Ker (Oxford: Clarendon Press, 1976), p. 128.
50 Anon., 'Modern Periodical Literature', *Dublin Review* 51 (1862), pp. 275–308, 276–7.
51 Quoted in Hilary Fraser with Daniel Brown, *English Prose of the Nineteenth Century* (London: Longman, 1997), p. 12.
52 Another perspective arises from mid-century reviews, by Walter Bagehot and Leslie Stephen among others, of the early contributors to the *Edinburgh Review*, which suggest that the status and weight of journalism had in fact increased with the new professionalization. Stephen, for example, writes that the standard of periodical writing then was 'so low that writing which would now be impossible passed muster without an objection' ('The First Edinburgh Reviewers', *Cornhill Magazine* 38 (1878), p. 222). And for Bagehot, writing in the modern periodical press, far from being feminized, is likened approvingly to 'the talk of the man of the world' ('The First Edinburgh Reviewers', *National Review* 2 (1855), p. 256).
53 Quoted in Fraser with Brown, *English Prose of the Nineteenth Century*, pp. 7–8.
54 George Henry Lewes, 'The Condition of Authors in England, Germany, and France', *Fraser's Magazine* 35 (1847), pp. 285–95.

55 Rigby, 'Women Travellers', p. 102.
56 See Elizabeth Barrett Browning and Robert Browning, *The Brownings' Correspondence*, ed. Philip Kelley and Ronald Hudson, 8 vols. (Winfield, KS: Wedgestone, 1984–92), vol. VIII, p. 341. The editors note that Elizabeth Barrett Browning expended 'much effort on her collaboration with R. H. Horne for the two volumes of critical essays published in *A New Spirit of the Age*'.
57 R. H. Horne, *A New Spirit of the Age* (1844; London: Oxford University Press, 1907), p. 299.
58 Thomas Carlyle, 'The Hero as Man of Letters', in *On Heroes, Hero-Worship and the Heroic in History* (1841; London: Harrap, 1929), p. 192.
59 Elizabeth Barrett Browning, *Aurora Leigh*, ed. Kerry McSweeney (Oxford University Press, 1993), p. 5, Book I, l. 29.
60 Charlotte Dempster, 'Memoirs of Mrs Jameson', *Edinburgh Review* 149 (1879), pp. 84–104, 103–4.
61 Margaret Oliphant, 'Two Ladies', *Blackwood's Edinburgh Magazine* 125 (1879), pp. 206–24, 206, 209.
62 Julia Wedgewood, 'The Moral Influence of George Eliot', *Contemporary Review* 39 (1881), pp. 173–85, 176.
63 Julia Wedgewood, 'A Study of Carlyle', *Contemporary Review* 39 (1881), pp. 584–609, 584.
64 Woolf, 'Professions for Women', p. 57.
65 Virginia Woolf, *A Room of One's Own* (London: Hogarth, 1931), p. 119.

CHAPTER TWELVE

Women writers and religion
'A self worth saving, a duty worth doing and a voice worth raising'

Elisabeth Jay

> But after that faith is come, we are no longer under a schoolmaster
> . . . There is neither Jew nor Greek, there is neither bond nor free,
> there is neither male nor female: for ye are all one in Christ Jesus.
>
> Galatians 3.28[1]

St Paul's teaching promised an end to slavery and gender inequity, but the first half of the nineteenth century witnessed heated religious debate over the ushering in of Christ's kingdom on earth, some seeing the abolition of slavery and the growth of missionary and philanthropic societies as signs that the millennial period of Christ's second coming had already begun, but others, wanting evidence of more catastrophic intervention, postponed the realization of Paul's vision to heaven, or an earth that could only be transformed by Christ's arrival in person. Meanwhile the religious dispensation of a beneficent Providence, represented on earth by an educative paternal authority, was subject to successive attacks from Deists, geologists and those who found it hard to see the purposive love of God in the industrial and domestic slavery they saw around them.

Elizabeth Gaskell's novel, *North and South* (1855), depicts a world where 'Masters and Men' between them have signally failed to bring about the lineaments of a Christian state. Gaskell juxtaposes two nineteen-year-old girls, Bessy and Margaret, to suggest a spectrum of the latest generation of women's responses to this failure. Bessy, the dying factory girl, passively accepts 'pain and sorrow' as women's prophetic lot. Confined 'to suffer and be still'[2] upon a sick-bed, she laments the disputes 'between masters and men' that have prevented even the minimal factory reforms that might have saved her life, but refuses to apportion blame. Instead, her appropriation of suffering results in a death-centred theology that postpones any hope of resurrection to the afterlife. The self-sacrificial identification with Christ that was so often preached to women has no visible redemptive effect upon her father's drinking and so the impulse is internalized as self-reproach and guilt. 'Hale', the heroine's surname, by contrast serves as a clue to the author's approval of Margaret's robust championship of a more positive female stance. In a chapter emphatically entitled 'Masters and Men' (ch. 15), it is Margaret who is forced into voicing the Christian challenge to a Dissenting industrialist when he declares that 'in the Platonic year, it may fall out that we are all – men, women and children – fit for a republic', but, meanwhile, as a capitalist he is entitled to behave as an 'autocrat'. This lengthy debate takes place in the presence of her father, a former Church of England clergyman, who in renouncing his ministry has abdicated the authority of Apostolical Descent to which John Henry Newman's first *Tract for the Times* famously claimed the Anglican ministry entitled him.[3] This absence of paternal authority prompts Margaret to occupy the ministerial role of appealing to 'passages in the Bible'. Gaskell repeatedly describes Margaret's remarks as self-deprecatory and voiced in a low tone, but her conviction of the importance of the message she carries tempts her beyond bearing witness in her own and others' homes, into the public arena when she seeks to disperse an angry crowd of workmen (ch. 22). Gaskell's treatment of Margaret's behaviour at this point is equivocal. Margaret's voice fails her, her gender affords none of the protection she had presumed upon and her behaviour is the cause of deep social embarrassment. Yet, as the pebble thrown by one of the workmen hits her, she echoes Christ's words from the Cross: 'You do not know what you are doing', and the visual iconography of her limp body encircled in a man's arms offers a daring reversal of the Madonna Pietà pose.

This may seem an unlikely reading of an image 'safely' encoded within the embrace sanctioned by a romantic plot, until we remember that Gaskell wrote part of *North and South* while staying at the Derbyshire home of the Nightingales, where she encountered Florence, a more outspoken theological revisionist:

The great reformers of the world turn into great misanthropists, if circumstances or organisation do not permit them to act. Christ, if He had been a woman, might have been nothing but a great complainer. . . ..

The next Christ will perhaps be a female Christ.[4]

Gaskell's letters record that she and Nightingale had crossed swords over the text 'Who is my mother? and who are my brethren?', quoted immediately after this passage in Nightingale's text. Nightingale's view that nothing, let alone domestic ties, should stand in the way of great teachers and preachers, for Gaskell involved an over-radical dismissal of the notion of a woman's sphere:

There is just that jar in F. N. to me. She has no friend – and she wants none. She stands perfectly alone, half-way between God and his creatures . . .

She and I had a grand quarrel one day. She is, I think, too much for institutions, sisterhoods and associations, and she said if she had influence enough not a mother should bring up her child herself.

Margaret Hale, like her creator, is a girl to whom the love and respect of family and friends mean much, and it is here that, again like Gaskell, she will pay the price for her impulsive decision to practise the imitation of Christ in a public sphere. Margaret may have the final speech in the novel, but her very last words acknowledge that her active pursuit of the path of conscience invites women of the previous generation to stigmatize her as 'That woman!' When Gaskell had chosen, in her previous novel *Ruth* (1853), to 'speak my mind out' about the undiscriminating blame cast upon seduced women, even within Christian communities who theoretically believed in a redemption open to all, she received similar treatment from her Unitarian husband's flock:

I think I must be an improper woman without knowing it, I do so manage to shock people. Now *should* you have burnt the 1st vol. of Ruth as so *very* bad? even if you had been a very anxious father of a family? Yet *two* men have; and a third has forbidden his wife to read it; they sit next to us in Chapel and you can't think how 'improper' I feel under their eyes.[5]

Religion, congregations were told, was a matter of individual conviction, but it was not a thing apart from daily life: it was imbibed and practised in the context of social relationship and institutional framework. This tension between the inner life of the spirit and cultural expectation was felt particularly acutely by women whose very being was frequently described in relational terms (a view neatly summarized by George Eliot's Lawyer Wakem as 'We don't ask what a woman does – we ask whom she belongs to.')[6] 'Cultural expectation' itself, of course, was not a unified entity but differed according to class, creed, chronology and even geographical location, and that makes generalization about women's religious lives a particularly hazardous enterprise.

This chapter inevitably focusses mainly upon the views expressed by literate, middle-class women who sometimes, in their very desire to acquaint their readers with a broader social discourse, found themselves unwittingly playing the patriarchal game of appropriating the voice of and 'speaking for' the excluded. Sensitive though they were to

the practical challenges faced by their working-class sisters, they often
assumed a middle-class ideal of religious behaviour as universalizable
while implicitly denying that a belief in spiritual equality might reasonably awaken aspirations for a higher social position from which to exercise religious influence more effectively. *Adam Bede* (1859) was written by
George Eliot, the grand-daughter of a carpenter, but the entire tenor
of that novel is designed to discourage any reader from making the
mistake of believing that the gentleman traveller, through whose eyes
we first see the surprising 'feminine delicacy' of Dinah Morris, the
working-class, Methodist female preacher, could ever see such a woman
as someone he might consider marrying.[7] Manuals of advice and moral
tales addressed to working-class women tempered the advantages to be
derived from the protestant work ethic with frequent reminders of
women's especial capacity for self-sacrifice and longsuffering in adver-
sity.[8] The Bible, which remained throughout the century a central
feature on reading lists composed for the female servant classes, theoretically provided a shared discourse between mistress and servant, but
the uses of the literacy for which it provided an incentive were carefully monitored and emphasis was placed upon following the example
of Christ the 'suffering servant' when middle-class women writers
mediated its teaching to the working classes.

    Looking after the moral and religious instruction of the servant classes
was a recognized part of an English gentlewoman's duty, along with educating other women, children of both sexes, and 'inferior races'.
Distributing Bibles and improving tracts, composing manuals delineat-
ing women's special religious mission, retelling Bible stories, writing
religious verse and hymns, and producing broadly based Christian meditation upon religious subjects, also lay within a woman's remit.
Teaching was the easiest of the Christian 'gifts' to justify in a woman
since it involved either the simple transmission of experience, or relay-
ing 'received' wisdom. Prophecy was permissible if it allowed women to
position themselves as 'vessels', inspired by a revelation beyond their own
powers; and 'spirituality' could be associated with the private and experiential, and defined, in binary mode, against the notions of meddling
with questions of ecclesiastical polity, or intruding upon the rational,
specialized discourse, which the nineteenth century was increasingly
bent on 'professionalizing'.[9] In an era noted for its doctrinal warfare, the
non-sectarian flavour of so much women's religious writing is striking.
There were gender-determined reasons for this. Marriage sometimes
involved women in a change of denomination: in such cases it was more

than likely that the woman, unwilling to brand her own or her husband's family as heretical would broaden her tolerance of liturgical difference and develop a broader view of what constituted the fundamentals of Christian behaviour. Sarah Stickney Ellis, noted for her conduct books, *The Mothers of England* (1843), *The Wives of England* (1843), *The Daughters of England* (1845) and *The Women of England* (1850), for example, was raised as a Quaker before marrying a Congregational clergyman. The exigencies of daily domestic life as a governess or a poor relation exposed such women as Caroline Wilson (née Fry), author of *Assistant of Education, Religious and Literary* (10 vols., 1823–8), or Charlotte and Anne Brontë to a variety of theological nuance and practice. Those like Ellis, or Caroline Woodroffe, author of *Shades of Character; or, Mental and Moral Delineations; designed to promote the formation of the female character on the basis of Christian principle* (2 vols., 1824; 7th edn., 1855), who chose to supplement their husband's income by running boarding schools for girls from the higher classes, would also have needed to ensure that religious shibboleths did not discourage the families of potential pupils.[10]

There were, of course, women who felt that the temper of the times, or the extremity of their personal experience, legitimated their writing about the world of ecclesiastical politics, but the fictional polemic of such women as Elizabeth Harris, whose novels, *From Oxford to Rome* (1847) and *Rest in the Church* (1848), offered thinly veiled, portentous accounts of her secession to Rome from Anglo-Catholicism, was commonly dismissed as 'viewy'.[11] George Eliot's article, 'Silly Novels by Lady Novelists', provides an acerbic contemporary synopsis of such 'oracular' offerings, 'which are generally inspired by some form of High Church, or transcendental Christianity . . . and the *white neck-cloth* species, which represent the tone of thought and feeling in the Evangelical party'.[12]

In one of the nineteenth-century's most famous guides to ideal womanly behaviour, Ruskin gave hysterical expression to this feeling that the fair sex should not meddle with Theology: 'Strange in creatures born to be Love visible, that where they can know least, they will condemn first, and think to recommend themselves to their Master, by crawling up the steps of His judgement-throne to divide it with Him'.[13]

The extreme vehemence with which Ruskin expressed himself has been in danger of masking the typicality of his view, which has little to do with guarding the purity of orthodox faith and everything to do with attitudes to gender; for Ruskin had abandoned orthodox Christianity seven years before writing this lecture. Henry James, who did not share Ruskin's nostalgic tenderness for elements of an orthodox upbringing,

vented similar views about George Eliot's religious thought. It is not that
the male character in James's dramatized discussion of Eliot's novel,
Daniel Deronda, has any particular quarrel with her theology, only with
the 'unnaturalness' of her embarking upon such activity.

She does not strike me as naturally a critic, less still as naturally a sceptic; her
spontaneous part is to observe life and to feel it, to feel it with admirable depth.
Contemplation, sympathy and faith – something like that, I should say, would
have been her natural scale. If she had fallen upon an age of enthusiastic assent
to old articles of faith, it seems to me possible that she would have had a more
perfect, a more consistent and graceful development, than she has actually had.
If she had cast herself into such a current – her genius being equal – it might
have carried her to splendid distances. But she has chosen to go into criticism,
and to the critics she addresses her work; I mean the critics of the universe.
Instead of feeling life itself, it is 'views' upon life that she tries to feel.[14]

The manuscripts of notable women writers of this period leave us in no
doubt that they indulged in theological speculation, but finding a public
voice was harder. A late nineteenth-century survey book, *Religious
Thought in the Nineteenth Century*, devoted only 8 of its 396 pages to
women's contributions.[15] Macmillan was happy to publish Christina
Rossetti's poetry but not so willing to put out her books of devotional,
moral and exegetical reflection on biblical texts and Church offices.[16]
Florence Nightingale compiled a three-volume theological work:
Suggestions for Thought to the Searchers after Truth among the Artizans of England,
and had six copies privately and anonymously printed.[17] Opinion is
divided as to whether Benjamin Jowett and J. S. Mill, to whom she presented copies, encouraged or discouraged its publication:[18] what is
certain is that it remained unpublished until the twentieth century. This
literary episode is interesting in ways that go beyond the work's passionate prophetic discourse. Her family circle brought her into contact with
liberal and unorthodox thinkers of the day: in her early twenties, for
instance, she met Sara Hennell, an advocate of 'theistical pantheism',
then governess at the house of Nightingale's cousin, Sir John Bonham
Carter. Sara was shortly to become a member of the freethinking
Coventry set of Brays, Brabants and Hennells who were the catalyst for
George Eliot's break with orthodoxy.[19] Cocooned within her suppor-
tively unorthodox circle, Sara went on to publish a series of 'palpably
serious and earnest'[20] tomes on contemporary theology and philosophy,
but Florence Nightingale's rare excursions into public theological discourse[21] omitted the radical feminine Christology of her unpublished

work, which she presumably thought would damage her practical attempts to introduce women to the front-line of public engagement.

A further interesting aspect of Nightingale's theological 'non-event' was that *Suggestions* had begun life in two manuscript books, denominated 'Religion' and 'Novel'.[22] Writing fiction, in as far as it was a permissible form of preaching, was so because it was grounded in 'experience' rather than in any claim to 'knowledge' of the rules of classical literature. Despite the challenge to feminine modesty that publication inherently posed, it was possible to interpret the production of a morally wholesome domestic novel as a performative instance of female religious witness in that it reinscribed the women's sphere of witness within the home. Such an explanation may help to account for the popularity, even in highly orthodox Christian circles, of George Eliot's fiction.[23] Her heroines repeatedly explore how a woman can live a life of religious vocation without the structures lent by orthodox doctrinal conviction. The bookish Romola, though living in fifteenth-century Florence, tries out the thoroughly nineteenth-century roles of lay sister and missionary-nurse, before discovering that the only route, for the single woman, to Madonna-like fulfilment lies in the self-sacrificial role of proxy mothering.[24] By the Finale of *Middlemarch*, Dorothea Brooke, purged of the scholarly and reforming ambitions that had initially deprived her of the normal happiness of 'a Christian young lady of fortune [who] should find her ideal of life in village charities' and seek for models 'in the perusal of *Female Scripture Characters*' (ch. 3), has apparently only opted for a more turbulent way to arrive at living 'faithfully a hidden life', restricted to being 'known in a certain circle as a wife and mother'.

There were, however, a variety of secondary routes into public theological discourse that a woman writer could employ. Margaret Oliphant, most prolific of Victorian women writers, ventured upon a theological critique of Frederick Denison Maurice's writings in one of her earliest essays for *Blackwood's Edinburgh Magazine*. The commissioning editor's apparent daring was counterbalanced by two safety nets: the trivialization of the piece implied in the title 'Modern Light Literature – Theology' and the masculine persona Oliphant employed.[25] The liberal theologian, Principal Tulloch of St Andrews, suggested in the dedicatory preface to his lecture series, *Movements of Religious Thought in Britain during the Nineteenth Century*, that this book formed only part of a far larger project 'which used to engage our discussion many years ago, and in the treatment of which you were to bear what would have proved by far the most interesting part'. As it continued, however, his tribute to her subtly shifted the terms into qualities less at odds with the conventional understanding of female religious piety, transforming her from his theological equal into a good woman: 'I know of no writer to whose larger powers, spiritual insight, and purity of thought, and subtle discrimination of many of the best aspects of our social life and character, our generation owes so much as it does to you.'[26]

It was not only men who drew such distinctions: women writers often policed the boundaries just as efficiently. Oliphant's female literary executors excised their relative's fiercest theological speculation from her published autobiographical writing,[27] and it was Dinah (née Mulock) Craik, a fellow novelist, not afraid to express socially progressive views about women's roles, who rapped her sister novelist's knuckles when Oliphant dared to abuse domestic fiction by using it, in the wake of her ten-year-old daughter's sudden death, to explore her unorthodox understanding of the doctrine of Atonement: 'I think you will yet be sorry for having written "Agnes": – because it does not "justify the ways of God to men" – and its doubts may trouble weaker souls long after you have conquered them and lived to see that His ways are right – and His mercy endureth for *ever*.'[28]

It took Oliphant another twenty years to develop, in her 'Stories of the Seen and the Unseen', a genre in which, through fantasy, the supernatural, allegory, Utopian and dystopian visions, she could voice a radical feminist theology. The comparative absence of authoritative biblical texts on questions of immortality and the afterlife provided a theologically uncolonized space into which a woman's interpretative voice could be interpolated. Although Oliphant had been dismissive of the wave of spiritualist enthusiasm that had swept America and England in the 1860s, gathering such eminent women writers as Elizabeth Barrett Browning, the novelist Anna Hall, and the noted essayist, Mary Howitt and her daughter, Margaret, in its embrace,[29] she nevertheless saw how the 'otherness' of another world might be appropriated by the 'other sex' to offer a critique of terrestrial society, especially if legitimated by claims that such tales, unlike her domestic and social fiction or melodramatic romances, 'presented' themselves to her without her volition.[30]

In the course of her long career Oliphant tried her hand at three other genres through which women could engage with religious discourse: translation, religious verse and biography.[31] Women's alleged capacity to absorb and imitate made the acquisition of foreign languages a suitable accomplishment that could then be put to good religious use in the 'secondary' art of translation. St. John Rivers' persuading Jane Eyre to 'sacrifice' her German studies to acquire Hindustani, for the sole purpose of furthering his missionary ambitions, nicely illustrates the 'handmaiden' status of this skill. Oliphant, who developed distinctly matriarchal habits, passed on the task of translating Montalembert's *Les Moins d'Occident* to a younger relative when the first volumes had served the financial turn she needed. The task of translating David Friedrich Strauss's *Das Leben Jesu*, was passed around the womenfolk of the Coventry circle of freethinkers: Sara Hennell agreed to revise the initial work of her sister-in-law 'Rufa' (née Brabant) and then of Mary Ann Evans ('George Eliot') to whom the task was given in 1844.

Nineteenth-century religious verse by women enjoys a dispiriting reputation,[32] for two reasons: first its sheer volume, which makes it a laborious exercise to winnow the wheat from the chaff; and secondly it too frequently displayed a tendency to narrow the Romantic sensibility into piously sentimental versifying or the expressions of a limited range of acceptable postures and attitudes, where 'Mothers meek' and 'maidens mild' were celebrated and heavenly bliss promised to those who learned to 'Wait patiently upon the Lord'. The volume and the conventionality were not unrelated: sacred poetry enjoyed a legitimacy, not shared by fiction, within even the strictest sects, and the vanity of publication was more easily justified if God's name rather than the poet's was central to the enterprise. Nowadays readers find it easier to appreciate Christina Rossetti's manipulation of the quiescent acceptance of a woman's lot, traditionally endorsed by such poetry, so as to give vent to the 'selfish, souring discontent' and 'silent envy nursed within' that bred her creative resentment. Her domestic ballad, 'The Lowest Room' (1856), perfectly encapsulates the ostensible praise of dutiful resignation to the Victorian understanding of female Christian heroics, within an evocation of a pagan Homeric world whose energy lingers to animate the 'trumpet-burst' of the last verse and plant the suggestion that among the 'deep secrets' to be disclosed at Judgment Day will be a female discontent finally revealed as divine rather than as sinful in origin.

The domestic hagiography involved in producing religious biographies and memoirs was, like hymn-writing, fit work for women's pens because both could draw their exemplary images from the experiential world, and provide material aimed as much at family worship as at a more public function.[33] Family-edited memoirs encouraged the 'angel in the house' to adopt the stance of 'recording angel', whose duty it was to preserve a loving and compassionate account of an exemplary Christian life. 'Saving a life' was female redemptive work, although in practice a woman's input might vary from the chore of 'laying out' the correspondence and anecdotes for a more famous male author to use, to the shaping task implicitly involved in a genre which Victorians saw as properly teleological. This underlying conviction, that, in George Eliot's words, 'a real "Life"' should set forth 'briefly and vividly the man's inward and outward struggles, aims, and achievements, so as to make clear the meaning which his experience has for his fellows'[34] was one of Christianity's most enduring gifts to those who abandoned its overarching metanarrative. The permeability of the biographical genre ensured that as a philosophy it continued to inspire the fictional output of many a religiously unorthodox woman novelist. Eliot's criterion could have served as the bedrock upon which Mrs Humphry Ward was to build her bestselling novel, *Robert Elsmere* (1888). For a host of minor women writers, religious biographies and moral tales offered the transition between the domestic and the public sphere necessary to launch them into professional writing, while for more established writers such commissions provided their 'bread and butter'.[35]

Religion offered alternative networks to women who were excluded from the clubland where male authors and editors made their contacts. Emily Gosse, whose most popular tract sold half a million copies, must have actively sought access to a religious network well beyond the 'few extreme Calvinists' to whom her son, in his anxiety to be seen to have arrived at the cultural 'centre', limited her acquaintance.[36] The Quaker connection, in which they had been raised, was to provide useful contacts for both Mary Howitt and her protégée, Sarah Stickney Ellis.[37] Charlotte Elizabeth Phelan Tonna and Emma Jane Worboise received editorships of Christian journals and magazines for women, courtesy of the Evangelical press, and Felicia Skene edited the Anglican High Church *Churchman's Companion*. Although Charlotte Yonge, the Tractarian novelist, was always painfully anxious to acknowledge her father and her spiritual mentor, the Revd John Keble, as her formative influences, women's networks played an important part in her subsequent career. Much of her early educational writing was commissioned by an older woman friend who ran a near-by school for village girls, or by Ann Mozley, who edited *Magazine for the Young*, launched in 1842. In her turn Yonge became editor of the *Monthly Packet* (1851–99), aimed at wealthier private schoolrooms. Over the years younger relatives and friends, such as the young Mary Arnold (later to become bestselling novelist, Mrs Humphry Ward), were encouraged by 'Aunt Charlotte' to write for privately circulated magazines and then to become fully fledged contributors.[38] Elizabeth Charles (1828–96), author of a popular series of novels offering religious exemplars in the guise of historical drama (*The Chronicles of the Schonberg-Cotta Family* (1863) inaugurated the series), had derived great benefit from her youthful membership of a women's essay-writing group.[39]

These female writing communities and networks had their institutional counterpart in religious sisterhoods. Under the auspices of Oxford Movement teaching, 1845 saw the first Church of England sisterhood formed by the Sisters of Mercy at Park Village West, Regents Park. The numbers of sisters within the Church of England grew steadily: by 1861 there were 86, by 1878, 700 and, by the end of the century, between 2,000 and 3,000.[40] During the century Roman Catholic nunneries in England and Scotland also mushroomed from 21 in 1800 to 90 distinct congregations and over 600 individual communities in 1900, containing over 6,000 nuns.[41] Since this institutional religious commitment took place against the background of a national culture that might variously be interpreted as either increasingly non-sectarian or downright secular,[42] the phenomenon deserves comment. The accompanying shift in emphasis from the contemplative to an active life of service in the surrounding community suggests that sisterhoods succeeded by offering single women meaningful work and a valid alternative to a life regarded as barren or 'without issue'. Like their nursing 'sisters', these women donned a uniform that permitted them to move freely in areas formerly held inappropriate for middle-class women, whose religiously inspired philanthropic work required delicate negotiation to enable the extension of their expressions of Christian love from the domestic to the wider community in which they lived.[43] The social class of the preponderance of recruits is nicely indicated by an observation made in 1881, by Pusey, the Oxford Movement leader who had lent much support to this development: 'I am so glad of a Novice who can't quite spell correctly. I think it is a greater love of God to call them.'[44] In what proportions these developments mirrored, were encouraged by, or themselves fostered women's growing sense of their separate identity and usefulness, it is not always easy to tell. However, the way in which women writers, such as Anna Jameson (*Sisters of Charity: Catholic and Protestant* (1855)) and Dinah Craik ('About Sisterhoods' (1883)), who were not themselves attracted by the conventual life or Anglo-Catholicism, wrote approvingly of this development is in itself interesting.[45] Even more striking is the support some High Church women writers derived from involvement with religious sisterhoods.

Charlotte Yonge and Christina Rossetti became lay associates of sister-hoods and Felicia Skene was a signatory on the foundation documents of an Oxford sisterhood though she did not progress to formal membership. This lay participation in formally validated women's work for God seems to have provided support for their own vocational dedication. In 1850, at the age of nineteen, Rossetti wrote *Maude*, a novelette, in which three middle-class girls are shown embarking on adult life: Magdalen joins a convent, Mary marries and Maude, an anorexic, consumed by a complex mixture of self-loathing and pride in her vocation as a poet, dies in an accident on the way to Mary's marriage, though the best of her work survives. The tale's analysis of the hothouse spiritual atmosphere in which Maude overanalyses her daily life for evidence of 'sin' at times reads like a parody of Charlotte Yonge's portraits of finely strung girlish consciences. During the next decade, however, Rossetti discovered that work with the 'magdalenes' of Highgate Penitentiary provided the framework for more positive sororal plots of the kind found in her poem, *Goblin Market* (1859), in which a woman becomes the agent of her sister's redemption.[46] There were also women writers as varied in their religious positions as the agnostic Eliza Lynn Linton and the Protestant Charlotte Brontë who expressed their revulsion for the unnaturalness of a life 'among a community of women unchecked by masculine influence'.[47]

The great doctrinal and ecclesiastical controversies of the nineteenth century were not for the most part overtly gender-specific, but as they were interpreted in the web of daily life, gender inevitably became an issue. Behind the famous examples of female literary engagement with particular systems of belief that are mentioned here it is possible to infer a vast hinterland of individual protest and accommodation by women working with and against the grain of the belief groups they encountered. It is customary to think of women as inherently more conservative, as guardians of the household gods, and in some mid nineteenth-century households where the view of the way in which God was to be worshipped changed with alarming frequency the tension between personal belief and marital duty was stretched to breaking point. Mrs Humphry Ward rehearsed, in *Robert Elsmere*, the pattern, if not the credal details, that had inflected her own troubled upbringing as daughter of Thomas Arnold, who first turned his back upon his father's inclusive concept of a national church for the anti-erastian notions of the Oxford Movement, before subsequent secessions to Roman Catholicism in 1854, back to Anglicanism in 1865, and then once more to Catholicism in 1876. The consequent job losses took his family from Tasmania, where he had emigrated, to Dublin and Oxford, before the last change deprived him of his Oxford post and the remnants of his wife's support. The daughter's fictional attempt to resolve the problem that had proved insoluble for her parents in effect admits the task too great. The eponymous hero, whose intellectual pilgrimage leads to his giving up his Anglican ministry and founding 'the New Brotherhood of Christ' in the East End of London, dies before he and his wife, who has remained an Anglican, have to face the questions of their small daughter's religious upbringing. The perfect wife and mother is freed, by killing off 'the thinker in the house', to remain true to contradictory family pieties: 'Every Sunday morning, with her child beside her, she worshipped in the old ways; every Sunday afternoon saw her black-veiled figure sitting motionless in a corner of the Elgood Street Hall [the centre of the Brotherhood's gatherings]'(ch. 51).

With depressing frequency women authors, like Mrs Humphry Ward and George Eliot, who had succeeded in emancipating themselves from orthodoxy, painted portraits of fictional heroines who do not. Whether distressed by the price their own freedom had exacted, convinced of their own exceptionality or anxious to prove the morality of their intellectual scepticism by the orthodoxy of their views on women's role, Ward and Eliot repeatedly consign girls who attempt to think things through for themselves to premature death or the subjugation of their intellectual independence to the requirements of nurturing a harmonious family.[48] The silencing of these heroines speaks to the power of the model by which women were enjoined, like Mary, 'to ponder these things in their heart' rather than put them into words.

The centrality of the Word, the duty to spread the Word, and the supremacy of individual judgment over the tradition of the Church's teaching might all, by contrast, seem to encourage the assumption that the Evangelical faith, the age's dominant orthodoxy, would have worked as an unequivocally liberating force for women in both social and literary spheres.[49] Yet, as Christine Kreuger has suggested, the inheritance of the female preaching imperative was so hedged about with qualificatory clauses that it provided a curiously problematized access to the roles of teacher, critic and prophet.[50]

Hannah More (1745–1833), for instance, friend of Dr Johnson, acclaimed poet and dramatist, and doyenne of Evangelical women writers, knew that if she wished her message to penetrate the hearts and minds of the highest in the land, she would need to rely upon male voices to sanction her preaching. It was her success in gaining the Bishop of London's praise for her essays directed to the 'Great' and to the 'Fashionable world',[51] that resulted in his commissioning her to produce a riposte to Tom Paine's *Rights of Man*, in a manner intelligible to the 'vulgar reader'. The act of writing 'Village Politics' (1793) involved its own act of submission: 'I heartily hope I shall not be discovered', she wrote to a female friend, 'as it is the sort of writing repugnant to my nature.'[52] And yet the time she had spent in 'mastering' a colloquial rhetoric for the purpose of projecting Establishment anti-propaganda to the lower classes paid dividends in the *Cheap Repository Tracts* begun in 1795. Backed again by the male support offered by that Evangelical constellation of the upper-class governing élite known as the Clapham Sect, she wrote over fifty moral tales and ballads, aping the production values of the chap-books they were designed to usurp. Whereas it had been possible for the Establishment to dismiss the earlier eighteenth-century Methodist tracts as tainted by sectarian fanaticism and political and social disruption, More's experience of writing across the class gap ensured that her work sold to both traditional hawkers and those from higher classes who approved her message sufficiently to wish to buy and disseminate it more widely. The sale within the first year of 2 million copies in this series has led to Hannah More being posthumously acclaimed as a major force in the democratization of literature,[53] yet posterity's verdict should not blind us to the fact that for More and her Victorian successors their route from their religious tradition to a public voice for women was by no means unambiguously clear.

Relying upon male voices for legitimation often meant more than appealing to men as patrons: it also frequently involved an act of ventriloquism, adopting a male persona and pseudonym, or, if publishing anonymously, being assumed to be male. The first famous Evangelical novel by a woman, Hannah More's *Coelebs in Search of a Wife* (1808), gives something of the flavour of the complicated accommodations that women writers had to engage in before preaching their message. At first glance this might seem a radical revision of the male epic quest story; here the hazardous adventures the male hero undergoes are resituated in a domestic world and the ultimate test will be marriage, the event traditionally assumed in fiction of the period to be the defining moment of a *woman's* life,[54] but the radicalism of this revision is qualified. The novel introduces us to a spectrum of female misbehaviour viewed from the supposedly male subject-position of the narrator. Moreover, the fact that the author had probably achieved a prolific literary output precisely because she remained single (as had those other Bluestocking 'fore-mothers' she smuggled into her work as objects for veneration)[55] did not prevent her from, and may even have pushed her towards, wrapping her religious message in the patriarchal plot that charts a woman's progress by the approval of a discerning male and is foreclosed by marriage and motherhood. 'Remember that the fairest creature is a fallen creature', Coeleb's mother implores him before setting out her religiously oriented socialization programme for women:

The education of the present race is not very favourable to domestic happiness. For my own part I call education, not that which smothers a woman with accomplishments . . .but that which inculcates principles, polishes taste, regulates temper, cultivates the reason, subdues the passions, directs the feelings, habituates to reflection, trains to self-denial, and more especially, that which refers all actions, feelings, sentiments, tastes, and passions, to the love and fear of God. (vol. 1, ch. 2).

This Evangelical educational agenda for women had been formulated in the context of late eighteenth-century society and continued into the new century almost untouched by Romanticism's analysis of the significance of childhood experience, its emphasis upon the place of feeling, and the importance it placed upon the uniquely individual response. In those Evangelical families and schools where Wordsworth's poetry and Scott's novels formed permissible reading matter alongside works of Evangelical practical piety, the cultural cross-currents set in train could be profoundly transformative. One such family, brought up far from the urbane circles envisaged in More's novel, in early childhood experienced this clash of cultures, almost unmediated by the interaction with their social peers that might both have softened their perception of the process and have deprived them of their creative subject matter. Their father, Patrick Brontë, endeavoured to provide his daughter Charlotte's biographer with an account of the way in which his religious opinions had facilitated and complicated his own social odyssey from the poverty of his Irish origins through a university education at Cambridge to the gentlemanly connotations of the Anglican ministry, by way of an explanation of the upbringing his children had experienced in Haworth parsonage:

The truth of the matter is – that I am, in some respects, a kindred likeness to the father of Margaret, in 'North and South' peacable [*sic*], feeling, sometimes thoughtful – and generally well-meaning. Yet unlike him, in one thing – by occasionally getting into a satirical vein – when I am disposed to dissect, and analyze human character, and human nature, studying closely its simples and compounds, like a curious surgeon – And being in early life thrown on my own resources – and consequently obliged, under Providence, to depend on my own judgement, and exertions, I may not be so ready as some are, to be a follower of any man, or a worshipper of conventionalities or forms, which may possibly to superficial observers, acquire me the character, of a little exccentricity.[56]

Despite his attempt to locate the experience within the grasp of Elizabeth Gaskell's imaginative comprehension, the mind-set he described was almost unintelligible to a woman whose milieu was the sociable, intellectually eclectic world of mid nineteenth-century Unitarianism. His son Branwell, educated at home, never managed to resolve the discrepant forces inherent in his upbringing into the ballast of an independent adult life. Patrick's young daughters, however, were exposed to an abrupt contrast between their father's interpretation of Evangelical piety – where individual judgment and accountability were held at a premium, and no mother's voice was heard, offering socializing advice – and the world of institutional and socialized Evangelicalism encountered at school and in the families where they gained employment. In this wider world, the Brontë sisters discovered, the teaching and example of social conformity, rather than the preaching of religious integrity, formed the minimum qualification for the post of governess for which they were intended. In a 'literary conversation' that was to prove the fictional equivalent of the Wordsworth–Coleridge dialogue, they explored the challenge of living the life of the spirit in the body of a woman constrained by society's construction of genteel femininity. Four novels appeared in swift succession: *Agnes Grey* (1847), *Wuthering Heights* (1847), *Jane Eyre* (1848) and *The Tenant of Wildfell Hall* (1848).

In *Agnes Grey*, Anne charted the progress of a young girl who begins her governessing career with naive idealism, believing that her task was 'to make Virtue practicable, Instruction desirable, and Religion lovely and comprehensible' (ch. 1). By the end of the novel her conscience remains uncompromized, but she has recognized the almost insurmountable difficulties of effecting moral and spiritual reform in a social milieu where she is little more than a servant. Her aspiration is now limited to diligent pursuit of the duty appointed by God without hope of visible results: 'If happiness in this world is not for me, I will endeavour to promote the welfare of those around me and my reward shall be hereafter' (ch. 21). Emily Brontë's last known composition began,

> No coward soul is mine
> No trembler in the world's storm troubled sphere
> I see Heaven's glories shine
> And Faith shines equal arming me from Fear

Wuthering Heights's anarchic power partly derives from the way in which the novel shows the spirit's flux and desire for unity operating at a similar cosmic level which fails to translate into acceptable social practice. Catherine Earnshaw's clinging to the essence of selfhood leads her to transgress in turn the roles of exemplary daughter, sister, wife and mother. It is not difficult to see why, in Gaskell's picture of the three sisters, Anne's patience was praised and the inviolable independence of spirit that led to Emily's intractable refusal to accommodate socially was demonized as obstinate selfishness.[57]

In *Jane Eyre* Charlotte accumulated a comprehensive list of indictments against the cultural assumptions, enshrined in the familial, educational, economic and religious structures of the first half of the nineteenth century, that served to curb and suppress 'that still small voice which interprets the dictates of conscience' (ch. 19). Jane's 'inward power' and 'sense of influence' battles with physical coercion, conventional morality, the male 'ownership' of learning and the clergy's right to interpretative authority (ch. 27). Although she shares with Agnes Grey the very Protestant conviction that 'We were born to strive and to endure' (also ch. 27), she is not prepared for the total submission of her own will for the benefit of others, nor to defer all visible reward to 'the hereafter'. She knows that her cousin St John Rivers's dictate, 'A missionary's wife you must – shall be', is based upon a preferred theological construction of her gender as 'docile' and inclined to 'mistrust yourself' (ch. 34). Protestant spirituality's gender-liberating power has rarely been as fully realized as it is in Jane's adieu to Rivers:

I told him to forbear question or remark; I desired him to leave me: I must and would be alone. He obeyed at once. Where there is energy to command well enough, obedience never fails. I mounted to my chamber; locked myself in; fell on my knees; and prayed in my way – a different way to St. John's, but effective in its own fashion. I seemed to penetrate very near a Mighty Spirit; and my soul rushed out in gratitude at His feet. (ch. 35)

Anne's *The Tenant of Wildfell Hall* meditates upon the recipes for spiritual resistance encoded in her sisters' novels, attempting to discriminate between tussles of will and the path of conscience by respecting the social norms wherever possible and stressing the sad alternatives offered in a fallen world, where a wife's conviction of her lack of moral influence over her husband may force her to concentrate her exercise of it in the only relationship where women could enjoy temporary power: motherhood.[58]

Read against the passionate, and occasionally bitter protests of the

Brontë sisters, compelled to wrestle with any external authority that seemed to challenge the inner workings of conscience, it is easier to understand the appeal of Charlotte Yonge's preaching of the Tractarian virtues of submission, obedience and humility before the authority of the Church and her earthly representatives. Yet Yonge's own carefully restricted life, constructed according to the pattern of quiet service and sacrifice for others that her writing endorsed, could be interpreted as an apology for the sheer excess of more than 200 works of fiction and non-fiction. The paradox involved in the empowering conviction of a duty to express 'silent self-sacrifice' as the Christian woman's goal is stunningly illustrated in a passage from Yonge's *A Book of Golden Deeds* (1864) – a favourite with her exacting clerical mentor, John Keble. Canonized for her 'golden' selflessness is

Le*ae*na, the Athenian woman at whose house the overthrow of the tyranny of the Psistratids was concerted, and who, when seized and put to the torture that she might disclose the secrets of the conspirators, fearing that the weakness of her frame might overpower her resolution, actually bit off her tongue, that she might be unable to betray the trust placed in her. The Athenians commemorated her truly golden silence by raising in her honour the statue of a lioness without a tongue, in allusion to her name, which signifies lioness. (Ch.1. 'What is a Golden Deed').

This small example of Yonge's re-reading of Greek history also serves as a reminder of the multiple ways in which nineteenth-century women writers strove to reclaim the patriarchal texts. Alongside this one might place Christina Rossetti's refiguring of biblical typologies, Hannah More's and Elizabeth Barrett Browning's attempts to reposition Eve at the centre of Milton's cosmic drama, *Paradise Lost*,[59] and countless female reinterpretations of that other Protestant classic, Bunyan's *Pilgrim's Progress*. Like all appropriation, however, the work of women writers anxious to realize the Pauline vision of a world where all distinctions between Jew and Greek, male and female, would be obliterated in a Christocentric economy, ran the risk of neglecting alternative spiritual heritages. Only George Eliot amongst the major novelists, benefiting from her exposure to German Higher Criticism's comparative readings of religious texts, sought to explore how being raised a Jew, Dissenter, Catholic, or semi-educated attender at church or chapel might impact differently upon a woman's interpretation of her religious duty. Nineteenth-century religious history is only slowly being liberated from the danger, not entirely resisted by this summary chapter, of picturing this period as a Christian hegemony, and thus defining the faithful against any voice of protest along a binary divide. The rediscovery of Jewish writers such as Grace Aguilar (1816–47) and Amy Levy (1861–89), both poets and novelists, is beginning to reveal the subtle variations in the problems encountered by women as they strove to access the literature of their own religious tradition and negotiate the gap between private and public utterance.[60] A brief discussion is also inclined to re-marginalize voices from the colonies, the women involved in harem or zenana missionary work, or wives striving to utilize a husband's posting to plant the ideal of a Christian household in an alien culture,[61] or Olive Schreiner's *Dreams* (1891) offering a South African reworking of Paul's vision of equality. Striving for the balanced account also neutralizes the scandalously exceptional such as Annie Besant's spiritual ricochets (1847–1933) from Evangelicalism to atheism to theosophy, or Adeline Sergeant's troubled trajectory (1851–1904) from a Wesleyan childhood to periods spent as an Anglican and an agnostic before reception into the Roman Catholic Church.[62]

Restrictive as the construction of the 'devout woman' could be in the nineteenth century, the wealth and diversity of female activity fostered or provoked in the name of religion, remains testimony to the way in which religion could also provide women with a sense of a self worth saving, a duty worth doing and a voice worth raising.

NOTES

1 Christina Rossetti offered this text as a consolation to hearts that remained troubled 'by the limit of God's ordinance concerning our sex (*Seek and Find: a Double Series of Short Studies of the Benedicite* (London: SPCK [Society for the Promotion of Christian Knowledge],1879), pp. 31–2).

2 Martha Vicinus adopted this phrase from Sarah Ellis's comment that a woman's 'highest duty is so often to suffer and be still' (*The Daughters of England* (London, 1845), p. 73) as the title for an influential anthology of feminist essays, *Suffer and Be Still: Women in the Victorian Age* (Bloomington: Indiana University Press, 1972), p. xv).

3 Newman's privately circulated tract, 'Thoughts on the Ministerial Commission, respectfully Addressed to the Clergy' (September 1830), formed the opening salvo of a plea for a reappraisal of the Anglican tradition undertaken in a Catholic rather than a Protestant spirit, that was to become variously known as the Oxford Movement and Tractarianism.

4 *Florence Nightingale: Cassandra and Other Selections from Suggestions for Thought*, ed. Mary Poovey (New York University Press, 1993), p. 230.

5 *The Letters of Mrs Gaskell*, ed. J. A. V. Chapple and Arthur Pollard (Manchester University Press, 1966), pp. 319–20, 220–3.

6   George Eliot, *Mill on the Floss* (1859), Book VI, ch. 8.

7   The Epilogue to *Adam Bede* leaves the question open as to whether the
    Methodist Conference of 1803 was right to ban women from preaching: the
    issue had been reawakened in the year of the novel's publication by the suc-
    cessful British tour of Phoebe Palmer, an American evangelist who attracted
    'intense crowds and criticism for daring to preach publicly to "promiscu-
    ous" (mixed) audiences' (Elizabeth K. Helsinger, Robin L. Sheets and
    William Veeder, *The Woman Question: Society and Literature in Britain and America,
    1837–83*, 2 vols. (Chicago and London: University of Chicago Press, 1983,
    1989), vol. II, p. 180). The oblique reference to religious debates contempo-
    raneous with the novel's publication, rather than its setting, is characteristic
    of the use to which Eliot puts her Preludes and Epilogues. Her assertion in
    the Prelude to *Middlemarch* that 'later-born Theresas were helped by no
    coherent social faith and order . . . Their ardour alternated between a vague
    ideal and the common yearning of womanhood' may have carried little res-
    onance in the 1832 of the novel's setting, but, as Florence Nightingale com-
    plained, flew in the face of the evidence in 1872, as numbers of religious
    sisterhoods grew and women's active participation in philanthropy prolife-
    rated ('A "Note" of Interrogation', *Fraser's Magazine* 8 (1873), pp. 567–77).

8   See June Purvis, *Hard Lessons: The Lives and Education of Working-Class Women
    in Nineteenth-Century England* (Cambridge: Polity Press, 1989), pp. 59–70; and
    Kate Flint, *The Woman Reader, 1837–1914* (Oxford: Clarendon Press, 1993),
    pp. 13–14, 112–15.

9   The nineteenth century saw the rise of training colleges and more detailed
    specification of ordination requirements, together with the introduction, in
    the 1870s, of Theology as a separate degree subject at Oxford and
    Cambridge. See Alan Haig, *The Victorian Clergy* (London and Sydney:
    Croom Helm, 1984), and, Anthony Russell, *The Clerical Profession* (London:
    SPCK, 1980).

10 Religious writing directed at children belongs more properly to the next
    chapter. Margaret Nancy Cutt, *Ministering Angels: a Study of Nineteenth-Century
    Evangelical Writing* (Wormley, Herts.: Five Owls Press, 1979), provides a useful
    introduction to a particular section of the market; whereas Judith
    Rowbotham's chapter on 'Religion as a Control on Reality', in *Good Girls
    Make Good Wives: Guidance for Girls in Victorian Fiction* (Oxford: Basil Blackwell,
    1989), pp. 53–98, employs a wider range in pursuit of her argument.

11 See the Guide to Further Reading for numerous discussions of polemical
    religious fiction of the nineteenth century.

12 *Westminster Review* 66 (1856), pp. 455–61.

13 J. Ruskin, 'Of Queen's Gardens' (1865) in *The Works of John Ruskin*, ed. E. T.
    Cook and A. Wedderburn, 39 vols. (London: George Allen, 1903–12), vol.
    XVIII, p. 128.

14 Henry James, 'Daniel Deronda: a Conversation', in *Partial Portraits* (London
    and New York: Macmillan and Co., 1888), pp. 83–4.

15 J. Hunt, *Religious Thought in the Nineteenth Century* (London: Gibbings, 1896).

He included Hannah More, Sara Hennell, Francis Power Cobbe and Harriet Martineau.

16 See Jan Marsh, *Christina Rossetti: a Literary Biography* (London: Pimlico, 1994), pp. 267–9, 450–4. Despite Rossetti's disguising the genre by the inclusion of poetry, and being at pains to emphasize 'the second-hand' nature of her scholarship and rebut the slur of 'a reputation for prevalent originality' ('The Key to My Book', *Called to Be Saints: the Minor Festivals Devotionally Studied* (London: SPCK, 1895), p. xiii), these works were, nonetheless, theological.

17 *Suggestions* (London: Eyre and Spottiswoode, 1860) was written and revised between 1852 and 1859. Extracts have been reprinted in *Florence Nightingale: Cassandra and Other Selections from Suggestions for Thought*, ed. Mary Poovey (New York University Press, 1993).

18 A letter from Benjamin Jowett to Florence Nightingale, dated 9 February 1865, leaves it unclear whether he would have applied this general encouragement to *Suggestions*: 'I sometimes wish that you would write more . . . Your writings appear to me to be very effective. Don't you think that if one has any true ideas – whether about the Army, the position of women, or about subjects of theology – it is a duty not to let them be lost?' (*Dear Miss Nightingale: a Selection of Benjamin Jowett's letters to Florence Nightingale, 1860–1893*, ed. Vincent Quinn and John Prest (Oxford: Clarendon, 1987) p. 42).

19 Sara Sophia Hennell (1812–99) and her close-knit family were thought to have provided the 'original' upon which the Meyrick family of George Eliot's *Daniel Deronda* were modelled. Sara met George Eliot in 1842 at the home of her younger sister, 'Cara', and her husband, the philanthropical freethinker and Coventry manufacturer, Charles Bray. It was at the same house, a few weeks later, that Eliot met Elizabeth ('Rufa') Brabant, daughter of a medical doctor who had studied German in order to acquaint himself with Higher Criticism: 'Rufa' married the Hennell girls' brother, Charles, a natural theist, the following year. The appeal of this cultivated, well-travelled, mercantile circle, prepared to discuss the latest German thought, to the clever young Eliot, already anxious to transcend the orthodoxies of her staid 'yeoman' family, is not hard to fathom.

20 The phrase employed by William Ewart Gladstone, *Nineteenth Century* 38 (1895), pp. 715–39, when refuting the argument of her *Essay on the Sceptical Tendency of Butler's Analogy* (1859).

21 See n.7 and the follow-up article, 'A Sub-"Note of Interrogation": What will be our Religion in 1999?', *Fraser's Magazine* 88 (1873), pp. 25–36.

22 *Florence Nightingale*, ed. Poovey, pp. vii–viii.

23 Charlotte Yonge's *The Clever Woman of the Family* (1865), ch. 24, cites *Silas Marner* as approved reading in a Tractarian clergyman's household.

24 George Eliot was by no means immune to the growth of Marian worship beyond the confines of Roman Catholicism during the nineteenth century. The complex permutations of this phenomenon are usefully summarized in Helsinger, *et. al.*, eds., *The Woman Question*, vol. II, pp. 94–201.

25 *Blackwood's Edinburgh Magazine* 78 (1855), pp. 72–86.

26 *Movements of Religious Thought in Britain during the Nineteenth Century* (London: Longmans, Green, and Co.), pp. iii–iv.

27 *The Autobiography of Margaret Oliphant: the Complete Text*, ed. Elisabeth Jay (Oxford and New York: Oxford University Press, 1990), restores the order and content of the manuscript text.

28 DMC to MOWO, 2 November 1865, National Library of Scotland, MS 23194.

29 For the next generation of Victorian women's involvement in this movement, see Alex Owen, *The Darkened Room: Women, Power, and Spiritualism in late nineteenth-century England* (London: Virago Press, 1989).

30 *Autobiography and Letters of Mrs Margaret Oliphant*, ed. Mrs Harry Coghill (Edinburgh and London: 1899; reprinted with an introduction by Q. D. Leavis, Leicester University Press, 1974), pp. 321–2.

31 Oliphant wrote biographies of five men involved in religious life: Edward Irving, Laurence Oliphant, John Tulloch, Thomas Chalmers and the Count de Montalembert. Her religious verse was unremarkable other than in demonstrating that the genre was a popular page-filler in literary magazines. For a fuller discussion of her religious output see Elisabeth Jay, *Mrs Oliphant: 'A Fiction to Herself': A Literary Life* (Oxford: Clarendon Press, 1995), ch. 5.

32 See the Guide to Further Reading for accounts of nineteenth-century religious verse.

33 See the tradition described in Christopher Tolley, *Domestic Biography: the Legacy of Evangelicalism in Four Nineteenth-Century Families* (Oxford: Clarendon Press, 1997). Given her inheritance it was no accident that Virginia Woolf should have cut her publishing teeth upon the 'Note on Father' that she contributed to F. W. Maitland's life of that Evangelical renegade and biographer supreme, Leslie Stephen.

34 G. Eliot, 'Thomas Carlyle's Life of John Sterling' *Westminster Review* 57 (1852), pp. 247–51.

35 Christina Rossetti expressed herself willing to contribute the lives of Elizabeth Fry, Mary Lamb and Adelaide Procter to an Eminent Women series, but rejected George Sand, George Eliot and Harriet Martineau as subjects because their views were antipathetic to her own religious position (Jan Marsh, *Christina Rossetti: a Literary Biography* (London: Pimlico, 1994), p. 495).

36 Cf. E. Gosse, *Father and Son* (1907), ch. 1, and Ann Thwaite, *Edmund Gosse: a Literary Landscape 1849–1928* (Oxford and New York: Oxford University Press, 1985), p. 29.

37 See Henrietta Twycross-Martin, 'The Drunkard, the Brute and the Paterfamilias: the Temperance Fiction of the Early Victorian Writer Sarah Stickney Ellis', in Anne Hogan and Andrew Bradstock, eds., *Women of Faith in Victorian Culture: Reassessing the Angel in the House* (London: Macmillan, 1998), pp. 6–30.

38 Christabel Coleridge, *Charlotte Mary Yonge: Her Life and Letters* (London: Macmillan and Co., 1903), pp. 148–9, 201.

39 *Our Seven Homes: Autobiographical Reminiscences of Mrs Rundle Charles*, ed. Mary Davidson (London: John Murray, 1896).

40 Arthur M. Allchin, *The Silent Rebellion: Anglican Religious Communities 1845–1900* (London: SCM Press, 1958), pp. 119–200. For further discussion of the place of religious sisterhoods in nineteenth-century culture, see the Guide to Further Reading.

41 Herbert Thurston, 'Preface', in Francesca M. Steele, *The Convents of Great Britain* (London and Dublin: Sands; M. H. Gill, 1902), pp. x–xi.

42 The debate is usefully rehearsed in the introductory chapter to Sarah Williams, *Religious Belief and Popular Culture in Southwark, c. 1880–1939* (Oxford University Press, 1999).

43 In an effort to reach the poorest classes, working-class 'Bible-women' were employed in the 1850s as 'native agents', dispensing Bibles and domestic advice in London's poorest areas; by 1862 almost every town in England had its Bible-woman. See Frank K. Prochaska, *Women and Philanthropy in Nineteenth-Century England* (Oxford: Clarendon Press, 1980), pp. 126–30. See also D. M. Lewis, '"Lights in Dark Places": Women Evangelists in Early Victorian England', in William J. Sheils and Diana Woods, eds., *Studies in Church History: Women in the Church*, 27 (Oxford: Blackwell, 1990), pp. 415–27.

44 Quoted in Allchin, *The Silent Rebellion*, p. 135.

45 'About Sisterhoods', *Longman's Magazine* 1, (1883), pp. 303–13. Mysteriously retitled, when reprinted in *Christina Rossetti, 'Maude'; Dinah Mulock Craik, 'On Sisterhoods'; 'A Woman's Thoughts about Women'*, ed. E. Showalter (London: William Pickering, 1993), pp. 47–58.

46 For further discussion of the significance of Rossetti's involvement with religious sisterhoods, see Diane D'Amico, '"Choose the stairs that mount above": Christina Rossetti and the Anglican Sisterhoods', *Essays in Literature*, 17 (1990), p. 204. See, also, Frederick Roden, 'Sisterhood is Powerful: Christina Rossetti's *Maude*', in Hogan and Bradstock, eds., *Women of Faith in Victorian Culture*, pp. 63–77.

47 Eliza Lynn Linton, 'Tact and Temper', *Ourselves: a Series of Essays on Women* (London and New York: G. Routledge, 1870), pp. 108–30. Charlotte Brontë's *Villette* (1853) depicts a fascinated revulsion for the conventual life.

48 For further discussion see Elisabeth Jay, 'Doubt and the Victorian Woman', in David Jasper and Terence R. Wright, eds., *The Critical Spirit and the Will to Believe* (London: Macmillan, 1989), pp. 88–103.

49 As Sean Gill notes in *Women and the Church of England: from the Eighteenth Century to the Present* (London: SPCK, 1994), pp. 79–80, scholarly assessment of nineteenth-century Evangelicalism's impact on women varies widely – for differing estimates of its alleged empowering effect, see: Frank K. Prochaska, *Women and Philanthropy in Nineteenth-Century England* (Oxford: Clarendon Press, 1980), pp. 1–17; Barbara Taylor, *Eve and the New Jerusalem: Socialism and Feminism in the Nineteenth Century* (London: Virago Press, 1983); and David Bebbington, *Evangelicalism in Modern Britain: a History from the 1730s to the 1980s* (London: Unwin Hyman, 1989), p. 129.

50 Christine L. Kreuger, *The Reader's Repentance: Women Preachers, Women Writers,*

and Nineteenth-Century Social Discourse (Chicago and London: University of Chicago Press, 1992).

51 Hannah More, *Thoughts on the Importance of the Manners of the Great to General Society* (1788) and *Estimate of the Religion of the Fashionable World* (1790).

52 Hannah More to Mrs Boscawen, 1793, quoted in Mary Gwladys Jones, *Hannah More* (Cambridge University Press, 1952).

53 For instance by R. D. Altick, *The English Common Reader: a Social History of the Mass Reading Public 1800–1900* (University of Chicago Press, 1957; rptd 1963), pp. 73–7.

54 A speech delivered by Coeleb's father underlines the feminization of his son's position: "I know your domestic propensities; and I know, therefore, that the whole colour of your future life will be, in a particular manner, determined by the turn of mind of the woman you may marry. Were you to live in the busy haunts of men; were you of any profession, or likely to be engaged in public life, though I would still counsel you to be equally careful in your choice, yet your happiness would not so immediately, so exclusively depend upon the individual society of a woman, as that of a retired country gentleman must do." (Hannah More, *Coelebs in Search of a Wife,* 2 vols. (1808; 3rd edn, London: T. Cadell and W. Davies, 1809), vol. I, pp. 18–19).

55 Elizabeth Carter and Elizabeth Smith are honoured in *Coelebs,* vol. II, p. 250.

56 Patrick Brontë to Elizabeth Cleghorn Gaskell, 3 November 1856. Quoted in Juliet Barker, *The Brontës* (London: Weidenfeld and Nicolson, 1994), p. 792.

57 For a fuller discussion, see Elizabeth Cleghorn Gaskell, *The Life of Charlotte Brontë,* ed. Elisabeth Jay (London: Penguin, 1997), pp. xix–xxi.

58 For an essay that develops this division of the 'angelic role', see: Siv Jansson, '*The Tenant of Wildfell Hall*: Rejecting the Angel's Influence', in Hogan and Bradstock, eds., *Women of Faith in Victorian Culture,* pp. 31–47.

59 More, *Coelebs,* vol. I, ch. 1. The theme obsessed Elizabeth Barrett Browning, from *A Drama of Exile* (1844), which offers a fairly conventional view of woman's place in the drama of redemption, though giving a woman's theological anxieties pride of place, to the conclusion of the epic *Aurora Leigh* (1857) where the modern Eve, 'Aurora', attains her status as the lead partner in humanity's pilgrimage to the New Jerusalem by feminizing blind Romney's role: he is now reduced to finding contentment working 'among Christ's little ones'.

60 See the Guide to Further Reading for recent work on nineteenth-century Jewish writers.

61 See the Guide to Further Reading for research into women's participation in missionary work, a comparatively recent focus of research interest.

62 See Carolyn C. Nelson, 'Novels of Religious Doubt and Faith: Adeline Sergeant and John Oliver Hobbes', *British Women Fiction Writers of the 1890s* (New York and London: Twayne; Prentice Hall International, 1996), pp. 59–69.

CHAPTER 13

Women writing for children

Lynne Vallone

Along a cool sequestered way,
    Her quiet walk she winds;
Sheds milder sunshine on his day,
    His brow with flowers binds.

Of art intuitive possest,
    Her infant train she rears;
To virtue by her smiles carest,
    Or chastened by her tears:

Beside the flitting midnight lamp,
    With fond and wakeful eye,
Wipes gently off the dying damp,
    Or sooths the parting sigh: –

'Tis here that Woman brightest shines
    (Though bright in other spheres):
Her name is drawn in fairest lines,
    When written by her tears.

Yet not the weak, the puny thing,
    Subdued to silly woe;
The firmest dignity may spring,
    Where softest feelings grow.
      From 'Remonstrance' by Ann Taylor Gilbert (1807)[1]

INTRODUCTION

In a century that defined the role of the 'proper' woman as the care of her home and the monitoring of the spiritual and physical welfare of the family, (literate) women often wrote for children, whether privately (through homemade primers, stories, poems and instructive correspondence) or through publication.[2] As nursery monitors, moral arbiters and domestic managers – whether mothers, spinster aunts or maiden daughters, and even as they perhaps worked beside their husband or brothers in trade, or headed households – women were responsible for bringing up the next generation. Middle-class girls were trained in this ideology of 'woman's mission' from a very young age, and numerous instructive books on 'professional motherhood' existed to guide them. One typical text of this type is *Practical Hints to Young Females on the Duties of a Wife, a Mother and a Mistress of a Family* (1815), by Ann Martin Taylor, mother of poets Ann and Jane Taylor.[3] As her daughter suggests above in her poem 'Remonstrance' – countering the misogynistic view that women are inferior to men – Ann Martin Taylor argues that the domestic female performs an essential and valuable service to the family and to the nation: 'To promote domestic virtue, and preserve the domestic happiness of the fireside is an effectual, as well as simple means of increasing national prosperity.'[4]

The gender politics surrounding the novel as a threatening genre for girls to read and for women to write, and the ever-burgeoning market for appropriate literature for young (again, middle-class) readers, made the children's tale an increasingly viable option for women writers of the nineteenth century. These women writers, Julia Briggs argues, 'felt they must prove themselves to be serious and persuade others to take them seriously, and this mood of seriousness was reflected in what they wrote'.[5] Mitzi Myers casts this seriousness in a somewhat different light: in their didactic fiction, the focus of women writers at the turn of the eighteenth century on wise mother–teachers 'signal[ed] a shifting female cultural ideal, a bourgeois invention of womanhood in the stylish new mode of enlightened domesticity'.[6] Women's writing for children served a dual purpose, then: as an extension of their home duties, writing didactic or instructive works for children was sanctioned as a proper pursuit; and as paid work, women authors were rewarded for their creative efforts within the market economy generally closed to them through the pervasiveness of the conventionally narrow framework of accepted women's roles. The history of children's literature in the nineteenth-century, then, is also the history of women's writing.

This survey of nineteenth-century children's literature is too brief to discuss adequately women's writing for working-class children. However, it would be a mistake to conclude from my overview that women were not writing for working-class children as well as those from the middle class. For instance, tract fiction, such as that produced by the Religious Tract Society (RTS), was designed for the poor child: made cheaply, priced accordingly, and often given as prizes in Sunday Schools. The

Child's Companion (1824–1932) was a successful RTS penny monthly of primarily religious stories directed towards working-class children. As Charlotte Yonge, the children's novelist and editor of the *Monthly Packet* (founded by Yonge in 1851 'For Younger Members of the English Church'), reminds us in her review of children's literature for *Macmillan's Magazine* (1869), 'skim milk, innocent fluid as it may seem, is apt to turn sour, and . . . nobody ought to attempt to write for the poor (any more than for the rich) who cannot do so with sense and spirit, as well as with a good moral'.[7] Although much tract fiction for the underprivileged child was imbued with preaching and prohibition, the child audience was taken seriously, and the best writers sought to encourage and entertain working-class children as well as to guide them.

Of course, the nineteenth century could not be an era of writers for children if it were not also an era of child readers. The nineteenth century was remarkable for its production of literary material of all kinds. Literacy rates for adults and children grew steadily throughout the nineteenth century, and there was great need for books and periodicals to satisfy an energetic reading public. For example, serialized numbers of Dickens's novels would sell about 40,000 copies each. A legislative commitment to reading was made by the Elementary Education Act of 1870 which held that the government was responsible for providing educational opportunities for all children in the areas where schools were not already available.[8]

The focus on education and on childhood in general begun in the Romantic era helped to develop a specialized literature for children. Although it may be tempting to define children's literature in sweeping, general terms, such as the struggle between 'fantasy and reason'[9] or the need to 'express an absence, a loss, a distance between parents and children,'[10] nineteenth-century children's literature belies such easy or provocative assessments. As Myers coyly opines, 'hasty analysis [of the Moral Tale] climaxes in premature evaluation'.[11] Perhaps one way to understand the century in terms of children's books is through the concept of 'hybridity'. The 'hybridity' found in nineteenth-century children's literature – in realistic family dramas that blend into Evangelical tracts, fantasies that are also moral tales, geography lessons that double as Bible study, etc. – can be said to reflect a nineteenth-century understanding of 'the child' (here middle-class, mostly) as a weak yet beloved 'class' that, with its incongruous combination of both innocence and potential for corruption, required moral and practical instruction through its literature.

This emphasis on instruction and moral behaviour incited the ire of some critics. Charles Lamb's infamous dismissal of much of women's writing for children casts blame upon the authors of moral tales and Evangelical tracts, such as Anna Laetitia Barbauld and Sarah Trimmer, for withering childhood imagination. These insults were hurled in 1802 within a letter written to Samuel Taylor Coleridge, whose genius, Lamb implies, was fed by stories of fancy heard as a youth: 'Think what you would have been now, if instead of being fed with Tales and old wives fables in childhood, you had been crammed with Geography and Natural History? *Damn them*. I mean the cursed Barbauld Crew, those *Blights and Blasts* of all that is *Human* in man and child'.[12] Following Lamb, some twentieth-century observers likewise privilege imaginative writing over any other form of children's literature. Yet, we can dispute that the 'Golden Age of children's literature' relies primarily upon the work of male fantasists of the later Victorian and Edwardian eras. Indeed, we can identify another 'golden age' in the realist/moralist tradition of nineteenth-century women writers for children.[13]

MORAL TALES AND EVANGELICAL TRACTS

The Evangelical revival responsible for the conversion to 'vital religion' of large numbers of people, begun in the mid eighteenth century, spilled over into the nineteenth century and influenced the politics, culture and social conscience of an entire age. William Wilberforce, Hannah More (herself an author of religious tracts for children used in her literacy programmes and as Sunday School rewards for poor children), and Anthony Ashley Cooper, seventh Earl of Shaftesbury, energized followers within the Church of England to return to the Gospel and 'the doctrine of salvation by faith in the atoning death of Christ'.[14] As the very fabric of society was being rewoven by the earnest application of Evangelical doctrine in every aspect of life, Evangelicalism not surprisingly had a significant impact on the development of nineteenth-century children's literature as well. Mrs Sherwood, author of the wildly successful didactic religious novel of domestic life, *The History of the Fairchild Family* (vol. 1, 1818), and her sister Mrs Cameron, adaptor of one of the earliest works of children's literature written in English – the Puritan James Janeway's *A Token for Children* (originally published in 1672 and revised by Cameron in 1828) – and Mary Louisa Charlesworth, whose *Ministering Children* (1854), celebrated pious and helpful youngsters, all participated in blanketing the children's literature market with religious works for children.[15] Mrs. Trimmer's evangelically minded *The Guardian of Education* (1802–06) – the first periodical to review children's book – was specifically geared to aid mothers in their choice of Christian books for their children.

By the mid-Victorian years, as Charlesworth's rather overwrought novel demonstrates, Evangelicalism had joined with sentimentality. A striking example of this kind of hybridization can be found in the work of Hesba Stretton (pseudonym of Sarah Smith), author of numerous Evangelical tracts for children, of which the 'waif romance' *Jessica's First Prayer* (1867) is probably the most famous.[16] In this tale, young Jessica, a hungry and abused child whose mother is an actress and an alcoholic, befriends a greedy old man, Daniel. Neither Jessica nor Daniel is exactly as appearance would seem to dictate: though a 'street arab', Jessica proves to be an honest girl, and the respectable chapel-keeper Daniel also keeps a clandestine coffee-stall to feed his avarice. Jessica is unsatisfied by her ignorant state, and once her physical hunger is lessened by Daniel's donations of coffee and buns, her spiritual hunger awakens and she becomes a devoted member of Daniel's church. Her simple faith leads both the worldly Daniel and the earnest minister back to Christ's teachings about compassion, love and gratitude, as she makes her first earnest prayer, 'O God I want to know about You. And please pay Mr Dan'el for all the warm coffee he's give me'.[17] Finally, Jessica's inevitable grave illness brings Daniel to contrition for his miserliness, and, repentant, he informally adopts the girl, who ultimately recovers her health. Thus, the child who is destitute in all but faith can lead privileged adult sinners to true happiness and charity through knowledge of God.

The Evangelical tract (many such tracts were published by the RTS[18]) operates within an economy of tears in its message of repentance and salvation. The tale progresses within a cycle of 'liquid' value through the tears of sorrow, joy, gratitude or penitence, liberally expressed. The innocent child – particularly the cast-off child – serves as the perfect catalyst for the conversion of corrupt adult characters within the text and, more importantly, as an example for the child reader – who may also shed pleasurable tears of remorse for his/her own sinfulness. Along the way, the Evangelical writer exposes some of the upper-class neglect or mistreatment of the poor. In these ways, Evangelical fiction is a powerful literary genre advocating social change, and the women (and men) who wrote it were active reformers working towards reformation of society as well as the reclamation of souls.

Although concomitant with the beginnings of the Evangelical revival,

and firmly entrenched in the didactic tradition, Maria Edgeworth's
moral tales for children, written late in the eighteenth century and into
the nineteenth, have been called 'refreshingly secular'.[19] With her father,
Richard Lovell Edgeworth, Maria Edgeworth was an inheritor of
Enlightenment ideals such as reason and knowledge by experience.
Edgeworth was never a mother, but she was a loyal daughter – deferring
to her rather eccentric father in most matters – and a loving sister to her
twenty-one siblings (R. L. Edgeworth married four times; his last marriage was to a woman born a year after Maria). There were plenty of
subjects around the house upon whom to practise educational theories,
and to whom improving stories might be told. Maria published *Practical
Education* (1798) with her father, and *Moral Tales for Young People* in 1801. In
the charming and instructive Rosamond stories originally published in
The Parent's Assistant (1796, later revised), an all-too-human child repeatedly falls from Reason – Rosamond spends her money foolishly on a
useless decorative object (a 'purple' jar that is merely clear glass filled
with coloured liquid) rather than the new shoes she needs. In 'The
Birthday Present', another tale from *The Parent's Assistant*, Rosamond
experiences the nature of true, unselfish generosity through the example
of her older sister, Laura. Called a 'little miser', Laura retains her half-
guinea given by her godmother, while the yet-impulsive Rosamond
spends hers on frippery to make a useless filigree basket for her spoiled
cousin. When a worthy cause presents itself, a poor little lace-maker who
has been ill used by a nasty footman who spoils her wares, Laura quickly
donates her money to the little girl without regard to thanks or praise.
No one cares for Rosamond's broken and impractical basket, given to
excite admiration rather than from 'really generous' motives. Laura's
rational 'purchase', however, earns the respect of adults and children
alike. Although Rosamond's parents are reasonable to a fault (her
mother rather disingenuously cannot understand why Rosamond would
like her birthday to be 'kept' as a special day), they are also physically
affectionate and actively involved in their children's upbringing. The
scenes of family life and dialogue between parent and child in
Edgeworth's tales prefigure the emphasis on the domestic found in
Victorian novels for adults and children.

DOMESTIC NOVEL

Although the best-known domestic novels by women, such as Charlotte
Brontë's *Jane Eyre* and George Eliot's *The Mill on the Floss*, for example,

feature children and childhood prominently, a young readership was not the intended audience. All three of the children's novels discussed below feature active, natural children – more akin to Brontë's passionate Jane Eyre than the anxious children found in *Oliver Twist* and *Mansfield Park* – within a supportive family setting. In the tradition of the *Bildungsroman*, women writers for both adults and children used the drama of family life as settings for their novels, often focussing on female rather than male education and development. The novels of both Charlotte Yonge and Juliana Horatia Ewing include strong, intelligent female characters as role models for female readers.

The novelist Catherine Sinclair's stories, told to amuse her niece and nephew, became *Holiday House* (1839), which perfectly enacts within one volume the hybrid nature of nineteenth-century children's literature by its combination of scenes of frivolity (through naughty child exploits that do not intend to teach moral lessons) with a tear-inducing protracted death scene worthy of Mrs Sherwood. Sinclair's professed dual purpose, to 'preserve a sort of fabulous remembrance of days long past, when young people were like wild horses on the prairies, rather than like well broken hacks on the road', as well as 'to inculcate a pleasing and permanent consciousness, that religion is the best resource in happier hours, and the only refuge in hours of affliction',[20] is difficult to sustain effectively. However, she is quite able to hold the interest of readers through good times and bad. The robust and high-spirited protagonists, Harry and Laura Graham, in contrast to their older brother Frank, a model boy, skip through the first half of the novel having fun, getting into scrapes, and being punished by their severe governess Mrs Crabtree, who finds it necessary to beat them with remarkable regularity. Laura begins to cut her hair out of boredom and in exasperation for the way it falls into her eyes: 'Laura was much diverted to see [her hair] showering down upon the floor, so she cut and cut on, while the curls fell thicker and faster, till at last the whole floor was covered with them, and scarcely a hair left upon her head.'[21] While Laura is thus occupied, Harry sets the nursery on fire. In an Evangelical tract such exploits would necessarily end badly for the children (the girl's shorn head might lead to a violent cold and eventual death, and every child who plays with fire inevitably gets burned). But Laura's only punishment for the misdeed she owns truthfully is the pain of seeing her own reflection, and she is rewarded with a sweet and a shilling for her help in putting out the fire, while the firebug Harry need spend just one night in the burned room with partially incinerated blankets as his only covering.

The novel begins to turn to more serious topics when the Graham family meets a poor boy who returns Major Graham's lost purse and whose sad life of suffering and privation gives rise to discussions of charity and duty to God. The occasion of Frank's commission as a midshipman aboard the *Thunderbolt* spurs the children to prayer and resolutions to emulate Frank's good conduct. Five years pass swiftly while Frank is at sea, Harry is at school and Laura is educated at home by a governess, until Frank is restored to the Grahams, hopelessly ill. His long, hard dying and trust in God are painful yet instructive for the once-heedless Harry and Laura:

All was changed within and around them, – sorrow had filled their hearts, and no longer merry, thoughtless young creatures, believing the world one scene of frolicsome enjoyment and careless ease; they had now witnessed its realities, – they had felt its trials, – they had experienced the importance of religion, – they had learned the frailty of all earthly joy, – and they had received, amidst tears and sorrows, the last injunction of a dying brother, to 'call upon the Lord while He is near, and to seek Him while he may yet be found'.[22]

Charlotte Yonge, like many readers since, remained unconvinced by this ending to the novel, feeling unprepared, after the larks of the first half of the book, to stand 'beside the ordinary stamp of pious death-bed'.[23]

Though she appreciated the frolicsome antics of the rascally children in *Holiday House*, Yonge's family saga *The Daisy Chain* (1856) is rather more serious throughout. *The Daisy Chain* was an important milestone in children's literature, and has been called the original children's novel.[24] It is an expansive and complex novel about a family of eleven children coping with the death of their mother and the crippling of their eldest sister from a carriage accident. A prototype for Louisa May Alcott's Jo March, Ethel May is an intelligent, competitive, awkward and earnest fifteen-year-old whose primary purpose in life is originally to keep pace with or exceed her brother Norman's progress in Latin and Greek. In fact, she is his superior in classical studies until her inattention to the younger children and to housework is brought before her and she must concede that her domestic duties allow little time for such 'masculine' pursuits. Ethel does not restrict 'home' to her father's residence, however, and while still a child she extends home duties to community effort: sponsoring the construction of a church for the poor in Cocksmoor village.

Like the hybrid *Holiday House*, Yonge's novel contains elements of moral fiction such as the deathbed scene, the primacy of the parent/child relationship, and the use of death/illness as a corrective to others. Over the seven-year course of the novel, the older children grow up and make their way in the world – with varying degrees of success. All of the older children fulfil their mother's belief in self-abnegation as the only sure thing in life. Prescient Mrs May tells her eldest daughter, "'No, Margaret, depend upon it, the only security is, not to think about ourselves at all, and not to fix our mind on any affection on earth".'[25] *The Daisy Chain* is subtitled 'Aspirations'. Each child must sacrifice something of great personal value in order to find happiness, which in Yonge's moral universe is a kind of abject self-sacrifice, an emptying of aspirations: the crippled Margaret must give up her betrothal to her worthy lover (and then die); Norman must turn from the pleasure he receives in his scholarship to become a missionary; Ethel must avoid marriage, renounce classical studies, take care of her father and become no one's best beloved; Flora's first child is sacrificed on the altar of 'neglect' as she avoids the nursery to nurture her husband's political ambitions instead of the child, with the result that the nurse doses the baby so frequently with opium that the infant expires. As Shirley Foster and Judy Simons note, Flora's physical punishment for a moral failing is 'an intrinsic element of the tract literature whose extremes Yonge herself claimed to disapprove'.[26] But Ethel's great work, the church for the 'godless' inhabitants of Cocksmoor, is finally fulfilled through steely determination and assistance from her family and community. Her vow as a teenager to build this church for others carries with it an obligation to succeed from which Ethel never flinches and, as such, Yonge creates a successful heroine.

Six to Sixteen: a Story for Girls (1875) by Juliana Horatia Ewing, a disciple of Yonge's, was first serialized in 1872 in the children's periodical *Aunt Judy's Magazine*, edited by her mother, Mrs Gatty.[27] The novel is a generic mish-mash, another 'hybrid' story, combining elements of the tear-jerker (the main character's father succumbs to cholera in an affecting deathbed scene that opens the book, and later her grandparents both die from eating a poisonous salad prepared by the senile old man), school story, fictional autobiography, and family chronicle. The book's chief pleasure is in the easy camaraderie between the orphan Margaret Vandaleur and her adoptive sister, Eleanor Arkwright, and the scenes of active family life in the Highlands. As the girls grow up together, they succumb to the charms of different 'fads', among them writing their autobiographies (Margaret's life story constitutes the entire narrative), collecting botanical specimens, sketching, dress-making and studying Italian in order to read Dante.

Margaret's ruminations on female education, intellectualism, and sturdy and independent girlhood are transparently Ewing's own.[28] For example, Margaret preaches,

> If there is a point on which Eleanor and I are quite agreed, among the many points we discuss and do not always agree upon, it is the need for a higher education for women. But ill as I think our sex is provided for in this respect, and highly as I value good teaching, I would rather. . . let [a growing girl] start in life with a sound, healthy constitution, and a reasonable set of nerves, than have her head crammed and her health neglected.[29]

In the dedication to the novel, Ewing notes that one of her aims in writing the book was to 'illustrate a belief in the joys and benefits of intellectual hobbies' as a tribute to her mother, Margaret Gatty, an amateur naturalist.[30] We learn that a year after the conclusion of Margaret's autobiography, Eleanor marries a man with whom she shares many 'rational interests'. Her husband is none other than Margaret's early friend 'Mr George', a protégé of Margaret's father and one of her trustees. Margaret is to live with her best friend and father-figure, thereby bringing the novel full circle and repairing the errors of the previous generation (Margaret's mother was a beauty who ignored her daughter, and Captain Vandaleur was mostly absent). Ewing's characters' dependence on intellectual pursuits rather than religion for happiness is in direct contrast to Yonge's earlier domestic drama where Ethel May must subordinate her intellectual ambitions to those of the affections.

POETRY

Nineteenth-century children's poetry was as wide-ranging as prose, and included both didactic or religious poems and hymns (especially early in the century), as well as the lively and imagistic verse of Juliana Ewing and Mary Howitt. Parents and educators found much to admire in Jane and Ann Taylor's charming secular as well as religious poetry. Yonge called them 'the best of the poets for children'.[31] The sisters were literary as well as domestic collaborators until Jane's marriage to Revd Joseph Gilbert in 1813 ended her career as a poet. Ann, however, continued to write and began to sign her poetry. Perhaps their best-known poems are 'My Mother' (Ann Taylor) and 'Twinkle, Twinkle Little Star' (Jane Taylor). Their *Hymns for Infant Minds* (1810) employ simple rhyme schemes and limited vocabulary so the youngest children might recite and memorize them. Each poem functions as a prayer on topics such as conduct, character traits, family relationships, illness and death, and praise of God. There is a sweetness and coaxing kindliness about these poems, even when they describe the foibles, responsibilities and dangers that beset the young. For example, the poem 'The Lily of the Valley' gently exhorts the child reader to learn humility from the example of the modest lily of the valley and thereby earn God's notice:

> Come, my love, and do not spurn
> From a little flower to learn: –
> Let your temper be as sweet,
> As the lily at your feet;
> Be as gentle, be as mild,
> Be a modest, simple child.
> 'Tis not beauty that we prize –
> Like a summer flower it dies;
> But humility will last,
> Fair and sweet when beauty's past;
> And the Saviour from above
> Views a humble child with love.[32]

The Taylors never wrote for adults, and their child-centred poetry was inspired by children conjured in their imaginations, rather than siblings or children of their acquaintance.[33]

Although Christina Rossetti's *Sing-Song, A Nursery Rhyme Book* (1872) was dedicated to a specific child – the nephew of Christina's spurned suitor Charles Cayley – in her biography of Rossetti, Jan Marsh persuasively argues that the childless Rossetti was really writing for her 'lost' children, or, more likely, for the child she had once been: 'The melodious speaking voice of the volume is that of the adult self "mothering" the child within; imaginatively, therefore, the baby to whom the book was dedicated may thus also be Christina's own infant self'.[34] Rossetti's *Sing-Song* is a volume of short, unsentimental verses appearing more than fifty years after *Hymns for Infant Minds*. Many of the poems are concerned with the conventions of childhood such as daily life (the daily post, taking medicine, childhood games), nature (especially flowers, farm animals and the seasons) and lessons (on proper conduct, addition and colours).

Unlike Robert Louis Stevenson, writing *A Child's Garden of Verses* later in the century (1885) primarily from the child's point of view, the speaker in Rossetti's children's poetry tends to be the mother. Many of the poems concern either satiation (mother-love poems) or privation. Marsh links Rossetti's *Sing-Song* to the early nineteenth-century poetry of the Taylor sisters 'which laid particular stress on the love owed to one's mother and on the duty of compassion'. Rossetti's poem about a grateful and sensitive child – 'There's snow on the fields / And cold in the cottage, / While I sit in the chimney nook / Supping hot pottage. // My clothes are soft and warm, / Fold upon fold, / But I'm so sorry for the poor / Out in the cold' – demonstrates a continuation of the moral activism found in the Taylors' verses for the very young and in tracts such as *Jessica's First Prayer*.[35] Yet these often blunt poems also confront less felicitous aspects of nineteenth-century childhood described by Ann and Jane Taylor as well – namely, early death. The solemn tone of poems such as 'A baby's cradle with no baby in it' ('A baby's cradle with no baby in it, / A baby's grave where autumn leaves drop sere; / The sweet soul gathered home to Paradise, / The body waiting here'[36]) contrasts with the playful nature of much of later nineteenth-century children's poetry written by women. For example, both Rossetti and Juliana Horatia Ewing wrote poems about the discovery of a dead song-bird and the need to mark its death by aping human conventions. In Rossetti's poem, the bird, who has died in winter, deserves funereal rites consistent with its natural status:

> Dead in the cold, a song-singing thrush,
> Dead at the foot of a snowberry bush, –
> Weave him a coffin of rush,
> Dig him a grave where the soft mosses grow,
> Raise him a tombstone of snow.[37]

Though death is permanent, the marker, of course, is not, and will melt away with the coming of the spring; the thrush makes way for new life. Ewing's sprightly 'The Burial of the Linnet', by contrast, is a comic treatment of childish delight in pet funerals. The bird's burial is a parody of the process of interring the dead:

> Bury him kindly – up in the corner;
>   Bird, beast, and goldfish are sepulchred there.
> Bid the black kitten march as chief mourner,
>   Waving her tail like a plume in the air.
>
> Bury him nobly – next to the donkey;
>   Fetch the old banner, and wave it about.
> Bury him deeply – think of the monkey,
>   Shallow his grave, and the dogs got him out.
>
> Bury him softly – white wool around him,
>   Kiss his poor feathers – the first kiss and last;
> Tell his poor widow kind friends have found him:
>   Plant his poor grave with whatever grows fast.
>
>   (Stanzas 2–4)[38]

A combination of moral instruction, pastoral delights, odes to mother love, and rather matter-of-fact assessments of harsh realities such as early death, Rossetti's poems for the very young, meant to be read aloud to pre-literate children, dispel childhood fears of death, failure and abandonment through their simplicity and frankness, and celebrate childhood delights such as the seasons, games and mothers' kisses. Sharon Smulders suggests that mothers reading the poems to their children function as another level of audience for the poetry, and that one aspect of the genius of this mid-career poetry is Rossetti's ability to capture the emotions and experiences of both child and mother: 'Speaking for as well as to nineteenth-century femininity in *Sing-Song*, Rossetti accommodates the childlike simplicity of nursery rhyme to the adult voice of duty and desire, power and passion, doubt and dependence'.[39]

FANTASY

Since nineteenth-century fantasy literature for children has long been considered the province of male writers, sketching the history of women's involvement in this genre seems a defensive act. As Nina Auerbach and U. C. Knoepflmacher argue, 'Whereas male writers encroaching on "feminine" material could be as wicked as they liked, their female contemporaries had to speak gently (like Lewis Carroll's Duchess) even when they were most enraged'.[40] The combination of fancy and realism, entertainment and moral instruction was the form that this 'gentleness' often took in fantasy literature written by women. For example, in Christina Rossetti's 'antifantasies'[41] – the stories in *Speaking Likenesses* (1873), the sewing circle frame tale where a stern aunt both superintends the charity work and tells tales at the same time – an ethos of punishment and expiation pervades the fantasy realms or dreamscapes each character enters. In the first story, eight-year-old Flora is disconsolate that her birthday party has dissolved into quarrels and complaints, until she finds herself, Alice-like, in a magical world existing parallel to her own. Flora enters a beautiful apartment filled with children where the furniture is animated and the walls and ceilings lined with mirrors. It is another birthday party, but the birthday 'queen', Flora's double, is cross and selfish and the games are a torment to Flora, who is cruelly used as their pawn. After another violent fight between all the children involving rocks and glass houses, Flora awakens from her dream resolved to reform her behaviour. The didactic spin put on her dream-experience is that through her nightmare, Flora has come to appreciate compromise, good-naturedness, and selflessness, and that

if she lives to be nine years old and give another birthday party, she is likely on that occasion to be even less like the birthday Queen of her troubled dream than was the Flora of eight years old: who, with dear friends and playmates and pretty presents, yet scarcely knew how to bear a few trifling disappointments, or how to be obliging and good-humoured under slight annoyances.[42]

Griselda, the young heroine of Mary Louisa Molesworth's *The Cuckoo Clock* (1877), learns conduct lessons resembling Flora's: the avoidance of ill-humour, idleness and losing her temper. The most important knowledge she gains, however, is metaphysical concepts promoted by the companion of her wish-fulfilment adventures, the bird from her great-aunt's beloved cuckoo clock. The bird continually admonishes Griselda that she has a 'great deal to learn' about the past, herself and how to reach 'fairyland' (one's greatest desire). For example, the cuckoo coaches Griselda on the relativity of size ('What do you mean by big? It's all a matter of fancy. Don't you know that if the world and everything in it, including yourself of course, was all made little enough to go into a walnut, you'd never find out the difference?'[43]) and time ('And what is slow, and what is quick?. . . *All* a matter of fancy! If everything that's been done since the world was made till now, was done over again in five minutes, you'd never know the difference.'[44]) during their night-time travels to the Country of the Nodding Mandarins and the Butterfly Land. After Griselda meets Phil, the younger boy who will become her playmate and her charge, she begins to mature and to understand the necessity of making her own dreams come true without the help of the cuckoo and his magic: she sagely informs Phil's mother that 'The way to the true fairy-land is hard to find, and we must each find it for ourselves, mustn't we?'[45]

In many Victorian fantasies such as *The Cuckoo Clock* that frame fanciful adventures with realistic settings as plot devices, children reach fairy-land through their dreams. Flora slumbers, worn out from her quarrels; Griselda awakens suddenly from a sound sleep at the cuckoo's soft call; and even Alice falls asleep listening to her sister read before jumping down the rabbit hole. In Ewing's short tale, 'Amelia and the Dwarfs', however, naughty Amelia is wide awake and angry when the dwarfs capture her and force her underground to an unpleasant fairy-land of her own making filled with her dirty clothes, uneaten food, objects she has destroyed and 'the broken threads of all the conversations [she had] interrupted'.[46] One of the dwarfs explains, ' "Sooner or later the mischief done by spoilt children's wilful disobedience comes back on their own hands. Up to a certain point we help them, for we love children, and we are wilful ourselves. But there are limits to everything".'[47] Amelia ultimately performs acts of penance for her prior misbehaviour, becoming homesick and yearning for her mother in the process. The dwarfs treat her kindly, yet they will not let her leave them. Amelia has reformed her character, but she retains her cleverness and appropriate wilfulness and escapes from the dwarfs (in particular from an amorous fellow who is considering making her 'partners for life'), to return home, spoiled and selfish no longer.

The need to 'ground' the fantastic realm within the realistic one for didactic purposes falls away in Jean Ingelow's complex novel *Mopsa the Fairy* (1869). As the novel opens, the reader enters the fairy world with the little boy, Jack, who climbs a hollow tree and finds a nest of fairy children. One of the children, Mopsa, becomes a main character and a queen, while Jack remains a child ultimately ejected from Fairyland and Mopsa's adult life. Mopsa the Fairy Queen outgrows her need for Jack's protection, and attains a boy-king, Jack's double, as consort. Regardless of the depth of the frame tale, in each of the fantasy stories discussed above, fairy land resolves the problems of 'real life' – character flaws, loneliness or, in the case of Jack, the struggle between masculine power (upon his return to the drawing room, Jack thinks, 'what a great thing a man was'[48]) and feminine imagination. The distinct gender identities of Jack and Mopsa reflect a greater concern for separate, gendered fiction for girls and boys found in mid-century children's literature in general, and in the school story, from an earlier period, in particular.

SCHOOL STORY

The school story breaks into gendered territory from the beginnings of the genre. Although some of the most famous school stories for children are those about male experience – Thomas Hughes's *Tom Brown's Schooldays* (1857) or Rudyard Kipling's *Stalky and Co.* (1899), for example – the earliest tales about schools were actually intended for girls. *Mrs Leicester's School: or, the History of Several Young Ladies, Related by Themselves* (1809) was for the most part written by Mary Lamb. *Mrs Leicester's School* was one of Charlotte Yonge's favourites from her own childhood: 'It is one of those books of real force and beauty that made a mark in our mind long, long ere we knew that books had authors, and that authors had different degrees of fame . . . It is a book that is nearly safe from becoming forgotten'.[49] *Mrs Leicester's School* is only nominally a 'school story', just as in Sarah Fielding's *The Governess; or, Little Female Academy* (1749), often called the first school story for children, published sixty years earlier, the boarding school exists as a frame tale only, surrounding the recitation of brief life histories by each scholar. Autobiography in Fielding's narrative has a didactic overlay: the quarrelsome pupils tell their stories as confessions of their character faults and as the first step to reforming them and achieving the rewards of virtue and happiness. The ten new arrivals at Lamb's Amwell School, by contrast, are asked to relate their brief histories for self-reflection and connection to the other lonely girls rather than as a strategy of shame-induced self-improvement. Here the school story functions as a means by which the perspectives of girls negotiating a new stage of life in isolation from the domestic circle is the central focus of the work (something L. T. Meade picks up in her school stories much later in the century). As Janet Bottoms argues, 'The narratives in *Mrs Leicester's School* are concerned both with the development of the girl child, and with the child's-eye view of the adult world around her'.[50]

Harriet Martineau's *The Crofton Boys* (1841), the fourth long tale in a series called 'The Playfellow', by contrast, is a 'cross-gendered' story: written by a woman writer about male experience at school.[51] As Claudia Nelson observes, Martineau's distance from the cruelties of boys' schools allowed her to 'present a reasonable, ordered world where violence and mutilation resulted from accident rather than malice'.[52]

Eight-year old Hugh Proctor wants nothing more than to be a 'Crofton Boy' like his older brother, and he is ecstatic when he is taken to school, though the youngest child there. Although Martineau's hero is himself an indifferent scholar at first, whose greatest wish for his manhood is to be a soldier in India, *The Crofton Boys* does not diminish the importance of intellectual activities in order to valorize cricket and other 'war-like' sports. In fact, Martineau's sceptical view of war is revealed almost immediately: Hugh's father had once himself sighed for the soldier's life until 'it was his fortune to see some soldiers from Spain, and hear from them what war really was, just when peace came and there was no more glory to be got; so that he had happily settled down to be a London shop-keeper.'[53] The manly life of the London shop-keeper would hardly have been admired in Thomas Hughes's novel promoting muscular Christianity, or Kipling's late-Victorian autobiographical account of boyhood's cruelty. Young Hugh is sorely tried, however, and proves himself to be a brave boy, though he is not afraid to shed tears on occasion, or to choose his older sister as a most precious companion. Hugh suffers a dreadful accident caused by the constant teasing of the older Crofton boys when he is pulled off a wall and a loosened rock crushes his foot. The foot must be amputated, and all of Hugh's grand plans to be a soldier are severed along with it.

School is not remade in the image of home in Martineau's text; rather, Crofton School is the locus of boy lore, companionship and scholarship. It is quite unlike home with its supportive network of mother and sisters. Hugh's fortitude, stoicism and courage enable him to overcome his disability, and his forced exclusion from many of the boys' games benefits his scholarly pursuits. This new inducement to hard work brings about Hugh's fondest wish as he and his closest friend (raised in India) are promised a trip to India to secure their fortune in the foreign service. The satisfied Hugh remarks, '"I never should have gone to India if I had not lost my foot; and I think it is well worth while losing my foot to go to India".'[54]

Though Hugh will be part of Empire-building once a man, Martineau's *The Crofton Boys* subtly reinforces feminine codes within the masculine school story. For instance, although schoolboy ethics forbid the open discussion of home and family, an older boy coaches Hugh that '"You will find, in every school in England . . . that it is not the way of boys to talk about feelings, – about anybody's feelings. That is the reason why they do not mention their sisters or their mothers, – except when two confidential friends are together, in a tree, or by themselves in the meadows".'[55] This speech indicates that, although feelings and affection are an unacknowledged part of boy life due to fears of ridicule, the gentle influences of home remain powerful. Moreover, Beverly Lyon Clark notes, the older boy's ability to discuss boy culture detaches him from it so that the reader, too, can both understand ideologies of boyhood and perhaps question them at the same time.[56]

Later in the century, L. T. Meade joins the boy life described in *The Crofton Boys* with schoolgirl ethics to create a fictional girls' culture through the literally hundreds of novels for girls she published, of which her first, *A World of Girls: the Story of a School* (1886), is the best-known. Sally Mitchell argues that 'Meade took the organizational structure of the "men's world" and grafted onto it the emotional content of the "woman's world" of friendships, feelings, and the care and development of relationships'.[57] In *A World of Girls*, some of the stock characteristics of the school story genre for boys appear for the first time in a girls' book, or are somewhat transformed according to gender: rivalry between girls,

misunderstandings and misjudgments that lead to a crisis, the beloved
teacher whose good will is necessary for the schoolgirls' happiness, grave
illness, and competition for academic prizes. As Mrs Willis, the saintly
headmistress, explains to new girl Hester Thornton, 'The great motto of
life here, Hester, is earnestness. We are earnest in our work, we are
earnest in our play. A half-hearted girl has no chance at Lavender
House'.[58] In the school story, school-life is celebrated as the 'sweetest,
brightest episode' of a girl's life.[59] When Mother is replaced by Teacher,
the transformation from home daughter to schoolgirl is complete. For
example, in *A World of Girls* the coveted award for the English
Composition competition, won by the unjustly maligned Annie Forest,
is a gold chain and a locket that held 'a miniature of the head-mistress's
much-loved face'.[60] Though the beloved headmistress watches over the
lively girls, in school fiction the girl-group dynamics are the most important and participate in the power of the 'new girl' in popular culture and
the imagination of the turn of the century.

NON-FICTION

Although fiction was queen in nineteenth-century's children's literature,
the Victorians also loved technology, facts and practical information,
and women were busy writing non-fiction for children throughout the
century in travel books, scientific studies, consolation literature and journalism, among other types of prose as well. These genres are much less
well known than the fiction of the same period, given that much of this
material was formulaic, functioned as a kind of schoolroom text or had
a very particular audience. Nevertheless, we may trace in it characteristics shared with contemporaneous fiction and poetry such as hybridity,
gender concerns and the influence of religion. Mrs Gatty published
Parables of Nature in a series from 1856 to 1861 in an effort to '[train] children to think about science in moral terms'.[61] Emily Shore, a child autobiographer as well as naturalist, was the proud author of essays on
natural science published in the *Penny Magazine* while a teenager. If she
had not died from consumption at the age of nineteen in 1839, this talented girl may well have participated in the discourse of science just
opening to women in the nineteenth century with Jane Marcet's
Conversations series.[62]

    Turning fiction to profit was the motive behind Barbara Hofland's
tales-turned-geography-lessons. Hofland was the author of numerous
books for children, including travel narratives, in the early to mid

nineteenth century. She began to publish poetry at a very young age and wrote steadily as a means to support herself and her family through two marriages and the deaths of both of her children. Hofland never willingly laid down her pen until her death at the age of seventy-four. The primary purpose of her book *Alfred Campbell, the Young Pilgrim* (1825), for example, is an extended geography lesson that describes foreign lands, people, and customs. The book opens with Mr Campbell's overwhelming grief at his wife's death. Alfred, his fourteen-year-old son, endeavours to enliven his father by suggesting that they journey through Egypt and the Holy Land as a way to accept God's will: "'[W]hy should we not follow [others who have travelled to Egypt]? Assured as we must be that the remains of antiquity, the confirmation of historic facts, the awakening of devout emotion, will not fail to rouse us from the indulgence of fruitless grief, and lead us to look more constantly to that glorious source of comfort, which can alone support us in our affliction?'"[63] This was to be an educational trip for the young Scotsman and a distraction for his father. Although intended as an introduction to the Holy Land and a review of Scripture, Hofland's work is not notable for its open-mindedness about the world beyond England. Paris is frivolous, Candia (Crete) is over-run with savages and heathen 'Mahomedans', Alexandria is full of thieves in every class, and Egypt in general is disdained for its sexism: 'Mr Campbell replied, "yes, my dear, it is to Christianity that woman owes these high and just privileges, which at once secure her own happiness, and teach her how to contribute to ours".'[64] Hofland's recitation of the patriarchal 'party line' is not surprising in a professional writer who lived by the proceeds of her pen alone and who therefore wrote within conventional boundaries. These texts have little appeal today; Dennis Butts comments in his biographical and bibliographical sketch of Mrs Hofland, 'Despite her researches, however, the second-hand experience of her travel stories gives them a faded quality'.[65]

The relatively subdued didactic tone of children's periodicals of the nineteenth century, by contrast, contributed to their popularity as leisure reading. Non-fiction and fiction writers alike published in the *Girl's Own Paper* (1880–1956), an appealing periodical companion to the *Boy's Own Paper* (1879–1967). Each number contained fiction by popular writers of the day such as Evelyn Everett Green, Mrs G. Linnaeus Banks and Rosa Nouchette Carey; poetry; articles on health and beauty; an advice column; illustrations; features on contemporary events and issues such as higher education for women, social work and fashion; drawing and

story-writing competitions; and 'How To' columns (to name only a few
of the regular offerings of the magazine). Although the tone was certainly conservative – the magazine was destined to be a 'guardian,
instructor, companion, and friend . . . preparing [girls] for the responsibilities of womanhood and for a heavenly home'[66] – the overall effect
was of a lively publication suitable for the 'new girls' of the late Victorian
period.

While the focus of the *Girl's Own Paper* was on the practical concerns
of day-to-day life – entertaining girls in the present, with their eventual
roles as wives and mothers continually in mind – consolation literature,
particularly in memoirs of child deaths, looked to the future when
parents and children would be reunited in heaven. The tragically high
infant and child mortality rate during the nineteenth century gave rise
to the genre of consolation literature, often written to comfort a dual
audience of children and adults. The death-rate for infants under one
year of age, for example, remained consistent throughout the century
at over 150 deaths per 1,000 live births, and it was the rare Victorian
family who did not have to cope with the loss of a child or children.[67]
As I have shown above, death was also a theme in nineteenth-century
children's fiction and poetry written by women. Although the scenes of
pious deaths found in children's literature might appear disturbing to
readers today, Pat Jalland argues that such books, when read within the
context of a loving family, 'could also reduce children's fears by its
emphasis on death as the entry to a happier life in heaven. Moreover, it
could teach them to cope with the likelihood of death among their own
siblings, relatives, or friends'.[68] As a record and an attempt to accept the
short illnesses and subsequent deaths from scarlet fever of five of
Archibald and Catherine Tait's seven children in March and April 1856,
the grieving parents kept detailed journals describing the deathbeds,
their prayers and their anguish.[69] In 1879, after Catherine's own death
(and that of their now-adult son, Crauford), Archibald Tait allowed the
publication of Catherine's journal as a means of solace for others.
Ewing's *The Story of a Short Life* (1885), while fiction, surely functioned as
consolation literature for children by reassuring child readers that early
death can be heroic. Six-year-old Leonard, the protagonist, becomes
gravely injured in a carriage accident, like Margaret May in Yonge's *The
Daisy Chain*, and dies about three years later, fully ensconced in a
number of affective communities that make his short life happy as well
as meaningful.[70]

CONCLUSION

Sally Mitchell's astute description of 'the story of girls' culture' at the turn of the century also holds true in a general way for children's literature of this period written by women: 'occupied by change, moving erratically toward the modern world, self-consciously "new" but still driven by powerful (and unexamined) old feelings'.[71] Early twentieth-century children's literature by women writers retained a firm grasp on inherited didactic traditions while at the same time resolutely embracing a modernist vision of a less certain and potentially more unstable world. This gradual transformation was often manifested in a change in the role of adult figures. No longer providing the essential or correct view, adult influence within children's fiction fell away, to be replaced by the independent child or children who negotiated problems best without adult interference. For example, by the turn of the century, women writers for children, such as E. Nesbit and Frances Hodgson Burnett, were reinventing the didactic tradition of their 'older' sisters. In Anglo-American Burnett's most famous novel, *The Secret Garden* (1911), the lessons in cooperation, health and happiness that Mary Lennox and Colin Craven learn within the garden are in direct contradiction to the protocols of a rarified and class-ridden adult society. As Mitzi Myers has argued, *The Secret Garden* participates in many of the same thematics as Maria Edgeworth's moral tale, 'Simple Susan' and, more importantly, similarly negotiates both the 'generic' and generic confines of literature produced within partriarchy: 'In both stories, the values associated with childish simplicity, mothering, and communal endeavor contest and transform alternative value systems, yet do not ultimately displace social codes'.[72] The Fabian E. Nesbit, for her part, playfully dismisses earlier forms of children's literature – in particular Evangelical stories of do-gooder children – in her domestic novels such as *The Wouldbegoods* (1901). Even though he and his siblings have been sent to the country to learn to behave properly, the novel's narrator, Oswald Bastable, who is well versed in the ideology of children's books, refuses to participate in any of the pious acts of charity that were so central to much nineteenth-century writing for children: '"Anyhow I'm not going to smooth the pillows of the sick, or read to the aged poor, or any rot out of *Ministering Children*".'[73] Notwithstanding this protest, however, the Bastable children, on their own and free from adult prompting, attempt to perform a number of socially responsible and commendable deeds throughout the course of the novel, such as rescuing an abandoned 'high born babe', helping a good-hearted tramp to find employment and, their most successful Golden Deed of all, assisting in the reunion between their adult friend and his long-lost sweetheart.

Though the religious and rational fever of nineteenth-century children's books had largely subsided by the *fin de siècle*, the long-held concerns over, and investment in, sentiment, didacticism and social conscience remained, albeit in frequently transformed secular and sometimes satiric forms dedicated to portrayals of the more thoroughly autonomous child stepping boldly into the new century.

NOTES

I would like to thank Howard Marchitello and Claudia Nelson for their helpful comments on this chapter.

1 Quoted in Leonore Davidoff and Catherine Hall, *Family Fortunes: Men and Women of the English Middle Class, 1780–1850* (1987; University of Chicago Press, 1989), pp. 457–8.
2 For the fascinating history of one such woman writer, see Shirley Brice Heath's essay, 'Child's Play or Finding the Ephemera of Home', on the manuscript nursery archive of Jane Johnson (1706–59), a vicar's wife and mother of four; Victor Watson's essay, 'Jane Johnson: a Very Pretty Story to Tell Children' on Johnson's unpublished story for her young children (located in the Bodleian Library); and Watson's '"Of the Spontaneous Kind"'? Women Writing Poetry for Children – from Jane Johnson to Christina Rossetti' – all in Mary Hilton, Morag Styles and Victor Watson, eds., *Opening the Nursery Door: Reading, Writing and Childhood, 1600–1900* (London: Routledge, 1997), pp. 17–30, 31–46, 142–58, respectively.
3 Davidoff and Hall, *Family Fortunes*, p. 175.
4 Ibid., p. 173.
5 Julia Briggs, 'Women Writers and Writing for Children: From Sarah Fielding to E. Nesbit', in Gillian Avery and Julia Briggs eds., *Children and Their Books: a Celebration of the Work of Iona and Peter Opie* (Oxford: Clarendon Press, 1989), pp. 221–50, 222.
6 Mitzi Myers, 'Impeccable Governesses, Rational Dames, and Moral Mothers: Mary Wollstonecraft and the Female Tradition in Georgian Children's Books', *Children's Literature* 14 (1986), pp. 31–59, 34.
7 Charlotte Yonge, 'Children's Literature of the Last Century', *Macmillan's Magazine* (1869), pp. 229–37, 302–10, 448–56, 451.
8 Richard D. Altick, *The English Common Reader: a Social History of the Mass Reading Public, 1800–1900* (2nd edn, Columbus: Ohio State University Press, 1998), pp. 2–3.
9 See Geoffrey Summerfield, *Fantasy and Reason: Children's Literature in the Eighteenth Century* (Athens: University of Georgia Press, 1984).

10 Victor Watson, 'Children's Literature and Literature's Children', in Morag Styles, Eve Bearne and Victor Watson, eds., *The Prose and the Passion: Children and Their Reading* (London: Cassell, 1994), pp. 163–75, 169.

11 Mitzi Myers, 'Romancing the Moral Tale: Maria Edgeworth and the Problematics of Pedagogy', in James Holt McGavran, Jr., ed., *Romanticism and Children's Literature in Nineteenth-Century England* (Athens: University of Georgia Press, 1991), pp. 96–128, 97.

12 Quoted in Beverly Lyon Clark, *Regendering the School Story: Sassy Sissies and Tattling Tomboys* (New York: Garland, 1996), p. 34.

13 In his avowedly 'comprehensive' (though, he admits, 'hardly all-inclusive') history of the 'so-called golden age of children's literature', narrowly defined as the early 1850s to the early 1870s, U. C. Knoepflmacher focusses on seven writers – five of them male – and all of them writing in the fantastic vein. See U. C. Knoepflmacher, *Ventures into Childland: Victorians, Fairy Tales and Femininity* (University of Chicago Press, 1998), p. xiii.

14 Ian Bradley, *The Call to Seriousness: the Evangelical Impact on the Victorians* (London: Jonathan Cape, 1976), pp. 15–16.

15 See M[argaret] Nancy Cutt's study *Mrs Sherwood and her Books for Children* (London: Oxford University Press, 1974).

16 The term 'waif romance' is J. S. Bratton's in *The Impact of Victorian Children's Fiction* (London: Croom Helm, 1981), p. 87. Margaret Nancy Cutt notes that the number of copies printed of *Jessica's First Prayer* has been said to be 2 million at the time of Stretton's death in 1911. The book was translated widely, distributed by Temperance Societies (with the sequel *Jessica's Mother* [1867] where the evils of drink are highlighted), inspired a series of coloured slides for magic lantern displays and was adapted to braille (Margaret Nancy Cutt, *Ministering Angels: a Study of Nineteenth-century Evangelical Writing for Children* (Wormley, Herts.: Five Owls Press, 1979), p. 135).

17 Hesba Stretton, *Jessica's First Prayer and Jessica's Mother* (Alberta, Canada: Inheritance Publications, 1995), p. 41.

18 The Religious Tract Society was founded in 1799 to promote the publication of specifically Evangelical works; the Society's list for children was begun early in the second decade of the nineteenth century. The RTS also published the popular magazines for juveniles, the *Boy's Own Paper* (1879–1967) and the *Girl's Own Paper* (1880–1956, in later years under different names, including its final incarnation as *Heiress*). See J. S. Bratton's *The Impact of Victorian Children's Fiction*, pp. 31–52, for an extended discussion of the RTS and its sister publishing venture, the Society for the Propagation of Christian Knowledge (SPCK).

19 Mitzi Myers, 'Canonical "Orphans" and Critical *Ennui*: Rereading Edgeworth's Cross-Writing', *Children's Literature* 25 (1997), pp. 116–36, 128.

20 Catherine Sinclair, *Holiday House* (1839; New York: Garland, 1976), pp. vii–viii, x.

21 Ibid., p. 39.

22 Ibid., pp. 353–4.

23 Yonge, 'Children's Literature of the Last Century: Didactic Fiction', p. 310. See n. 7.

24 Marghanita Laski, *Mrs Ewing, Mrs Molesworth and Mrs Hodgson Burnett* (New York: Oxford University Press, 1951), p. 17.

25 Charlotte Yonge, *The Daisy Chain: or, Aspirations* (1856; New York: Garland, 1977), p. 19.

26 Shirley Foster and Judy Simons, *What Katy Read: Feminist Re-Readings of 'Classic' Stories for Girls* (University of Iowa Press, 1995), p. 72.

27 *Aunt Judy's Magazine* (1866–85) originated under the editorship of Margaret Gatty. The magazine was highly successful and contained fiction, poetry, reviews of children's literature, and nonfiction articles on religion and natural history. After Mrs Gatty's death in 1873, Mrs Horatia Eden, Gatty's daughter, became editor.

28 See Gillian Avery's preface to Juliana Horatia Ewing, *Six to Sixteen* (1875; New York: Garland, 1976), pp. v–vii.

29 Ewing, *Six to Sixteen*, pp. 137–8.

30 Ibid., p. iii.

31 Charlotte Yonge, 'Children's Literature of the Last Century', p. 234.

32 Jane and Ann Taylor, *Hymns for Infant Minds* (1810; London: Lincoln and Edmands, 1825), pp. 43–4.

33 See the entry for Jane and Ann Taylor in Humphrey Carpenter and Mari Prichard, eds., *The Oxford Companion to Children's Literature* (Oxford University Press, 1991), pp. 516–17, 517. For a treatment of the Taylor family, see Christina Duff Stewart, *The Taylors of Ongar: an Analytical Bio-Bibliography*, 2 vols. (New York: Garland Publishers, 1975).

34 Jan Marsh, *Christina Rossetti: a Writer's Life* (New York: Viking, 1994), p. 379.

35 Ibid., p. 12.

36 *The Complete Poems of Christina Rossetti*, ed. R. W. Crump, 3 vols. (Baton Rouge: Louisiana State University Press, 1986), vol. II, p. 22.

37 Ibid., vol. II, p. 21.

38 Juliana Horatia Ewing, 'The Burial of the Linnet', in Iona and Peter Opie, eds., *The Oxford Book of Children's Verses* (Oxford University Press, 1994), pp. 254–5.

39 Sharon Smulders, *Christina Rossetti Revisited* (New York: Twayne Publishers, 1996), pp. 103–4. For a useful overview of Christina Rossetti's poetry for adults, see Antony H. Harrison, *Christina Rossetti in Context* (Chapel Hill: University of North Carolina Press, 1988).

40 Nina Auerbach and U. C. Knoepflmacher, eds., *Forbidden Journeys: Fairy Tales and Fantasies by Victorian Women Writers* (University of Chicago Press, 1992), p. 6.

41 Called thus by Auerbach and Knoepflmacher, eds., *Forbidden Journeys*, p. 317. *Speaking Likenesses* shocked John Ruskin with its unforgiving portraits of children: "'How could [Rossetti] or Arthur Hughes [illustrator of *Sing-Song*] sink so low after their pretty nursery rhymes?'" Quoted in Smulders, *Christina Rossetti Revisited*, p. 92.

42 Christina Rossetti, 'Speaking Likenesses', in Auerbach and Knoepflmacher, eds., *Forbidden Journeys*, p. 342.

43 Mary Louisa Molesworth, *The Cuckoo Clock and The Tapestry Room* (1877; New York: Macmillan, 1947), p. 40.

44 Ibid., p. 49.

45 Ibid., p. 161.

46 Juliana Horatia Ewing, 'Amelia and the Dwarfs' (1870), in Auerbach and Knoepflmacher, eds., *Forbidden Journeys*, p. 122.

47 Ibid., p. 115.

48 Jean Ingelow, 'Mopsa the Fairy' (1869), in Auerbach and Knoepflmacher, eds., *Forbidden Journeys*, p. 314.

49 Yonge, 'Children's Literature of the Last Century', p. 305.

50 Bottoms, 'In the Absence of Mrs Leicester,' in Hilton, Styles and Watson, *Opening the Nursery Door* (1997), p. 123.

51 The term is Beverly Lyon Clark's in *Regendering the School Story*, an excellent over-view of the Anglo-American school story in the nineteenth and twentieth centuries; see n. 12.

52 Claudia Nelson, *Boys Will Be Girls: the Feminine Ethic and British Children's Fiction 1857–1917* (New Brunswick: Rutgers University Press, 1991), p. 56.

53 Harriet Martineau, *The Crofton Boys: a Tale* (London: Charles Knight, 1841), p. 5.

54 Ibid., p. 335.

55 Ibid., p. 164.

56 Clark, *Regendering the School Story*, pp. 181–2.

57 Sally Mitchell, *The New Girl: Girls' Culture in England, 1880–1915* (New York: Columbia University Press, 1995), p. 17.

58 L. T. Meade, *A World of Girls: the Story of a School* (1886; Chicago: M. A. Donohue, n.d.), p. 15.

59 Ibid., p. 10.

60 Ibid., p. 160.

61 See Alan Rauch, 'Parables and Parodies: Margaret Gatty's Audiences in the *Parables from Nature*', *Children's Literature* 25 (1997), pp. 137–52, 141.

62 Mrs Marcet's *Conversations of Chemistry, intended more especially for the Female Sex* appeared in 1806, followed by *Conversations on Natural Philosophy* (1819) and others. Yonge preferred the similarly intended work of Maria Hack such as *Harry Beaufoy; or, the Pupil of Nature* (1821) to that of Marcet (Yonge, 'Children's Literature of the Last Century', p. 307).

63 Barbara Hofland, *Alfred Campbell, the Young Pilgrim* (London: John Harris, 1825), p. 8.

64 Ibid., p. 45.

65 Dennis Butts, *Mistress of Our Tears: a Literary and Bibliographical Study of Barbara Hofland* (Aldershot: Scolar Press, 1992), p. 24.

66 Quoted in Wendy Forrester, *Great-Grandmama's Weekly: a Celebration of The Girl's Own Paper, 1880–1901* (Guildford: Lutterworth Press, 1980), p. 14.

67 Pat Jalland, *Death in the Victorian Family* (Oxford University Press, 1996), p. 120.

68 Ibid., p. 133.

69 See ibid., pp. 127–39, and M. Jeanne Petersen, *Family, Love, and Work in the Lives of Victorian Gentlewomen* (Bloomington: Indiana University Press, 1989), pp. 110–15.

70 See Judith A. Plotz's essay, 'A Victorian Comfort Book: Juliana Ewing's *The Story of a Short Life*', in McGavran, ed., *Romanticism and Children's Literature*, pp. 168–89.

71 Mitchell, *The New Girl*, p. 22.

72 Myers, 'Romancing the Moral Tale' in McGavran, ed., *Romanticism and Children's Literature*, pp. 96–128, 110.

73 E. Nesbit, *The Wouldbegoods* (1901; Ware, Herts.: (Wordsworth Editions, 1995)), p. 32.

Guide to further reading

This Guide is intended as a supplement to the many primary and secondary works which are cited in the preceding chapters, references to which can be found in the end-notes to the chapters. Discussions of individual writers and texts and of particular topics can be located by using the index.

REFERENCE WORKS AND SOURCE MATERIALS

Blain, Virginia, Clements, Patricia and Grundy, Isobel, eds. *The Feminist Companion to Literature in English: Women Writers from the Middle Ages to the Present.* London: Batsford, 1990.

Helsinger, Elizabeth K., Sheets, Robin L., and Veeder, William, eds. *The Woman Question: Society and Literature in Britain and America, 1837–83.* 3 vols. University of Chicago Press, 1983.

Sage, Lorna, ed. *The Cambridge Guide to Women's Writing in English.* Cambridge University Press, 1999.

Shattock, Joanne, *The Oxford Guide to British Women Writers.* Oxford University Press, 1994.

   ed. *The Cambridge Bibliography of English Literature*, vol. IV: 1800–1900. 3rd edn. Cambridge University Press, 1999.

WOMEN'S READING AND THE CONSUMPTION OF PRINT

Beetham, Margaret, *A Magazine of Her Own? Domesticity and Desire in the Woman's Magazine, 1800–1914.* London: Routledge, 1996.

Flint, Kate, *The Woman Reader, 1837–1914,* Oxford University Press, 1993.

Gilbert, Pamela, *Disease, Desire and the Body in Victorian Women's Popular Novels.* Cambridge University Press, 1997.

Jordan, John and Patten, Robert L., *Literature in the Marketplace: Nineteenth-Century British Publishing and Reading Practices.* Cambridge University Press, 1995.

Lovell, Terry, *Consuming Fiction,* London: Verso, 1987.

Mitchell, Sally, *The Fallen Angel: Chastity, Class and Women's Reading 1835–1880.* Bowling Green University Popular Press, 1981.

Pearce, Lynne, *Feminism and the Politics of Reading,* London: Edward Arnold, 1997.

Thompson, Nicola, *Reviewing Sex: Gender and the Reception of Victorian Novels.* London: Macmillan, 1996.

Vincent, David, *Literacy and Popular Culture; England 1750–1914*. Cambridge University Press, 1989.

WOMEN WRITING POETRY

(a) Anthologies

Armstrong, Isobel, Bristow, Joseph, with Sharrock, Cath, eds., *Nineteenth-Century Women Poets: an Oxford Anthology*. Oxford University Press, 1996.
Blain, Virginia, ed., *New Annotated Anthology of Victorian Women Poets*. Basingstoke: Pearson Educational, 2001.
Breen, Jennifer, ed., *Women Romantic Poets, 1785–1832*. London: Everyman, 1992.
Feldman, Paula R., ed., *British Women Poets of the Romantic Era; an Anthology*. Baltimore: Johns Hopkins University Press, 1997.
Higgonet, Margaret Randolph, ed., *British Women Poets of the Nineteenth Century*. New York: Meridian, 1996.
Leighton, Angela, and Reynolds, Margaret, eds., *Victorian Women Poets: an Anthology*. Oxford: Blackwell, 1995.

(b) Criticism

Armstrong, Isobel, *Victorian Poetry: Poetry, Poetics and Politics*. London: Routledge, 1993.
Armstrong, Isobel and Blain, Virginia, eds., *Women's Poetry, Late Romantic to Late Victorian: Gender and Genre 1830–1900*. Basingstoke: Macmillan, 1999.
Bristow, Joseph, ed., *Victorian Women Poets: Emily Brontë, Elizabeth Barrett Browning, Christina Rossetti*. Basingstoke: Macmillan, 1995.
Cosslett, Tess, ed., *Victorian Women Poets*, London: Longman, 1996.
Homans, Margaret, *Women Poets and Poetic Identity: Dorothy Wordsworth, Emily Bronte and Emily Dickinson*. Princeton University Press, 1980.
Leighton, Angela, *Victorian Women Poets: Writing against the Heart*. London: Harvester Wheatsheaf, 1992.
    ed., *Victorian Women Poets: a Critical Reader*. Oxford: Blackwell, 1996.
Mermin, Dorothy, *Godiva's Ride: Women of Letters in England, 1830–1880*. Bloomington: Indiana University Press, 1993.
Prins, Yoppi, *Victorian Sappho*. Princeton University Press, 1999.
Ross, Marlon, *The Contours of Masculine Desire: Romanticism and the Rise of Women's Poetry*, Oxford University Press, 1989.

PROFESSIONALIZATION AND THE PUBLIC SPHERE

Bennett, Arnold, *Journalism for Women. A Practical Guide*. London: John Lane, 1898.
Caine, Barbara, *Victorian Feminists*. Oxford University Press, 1992.
    English Feminism 1780–1980. Oxford University Press, 1996.

Crosby, Christina, *The Ends of History: Victorians and 'The Woman Question'*. London: Routledge, 1991.

Gates, Barbara T. and Shteir, Ann B., *Natural Eloquence. Women Reinscribe Science*. Madison: University of Wisconsin Press, 1997.

Gleadle, Kathryn, *The Early Feminists: Radical Utilitarians and the Emergence of the Women's Rights Movements 1831–1851*. London: Macmillan, 1995.

Kavanagh, Julia, *English Women of Letters*. London, 1861.

Morgan, Thais E., ed., *Victorian Sages and Cultural Discourse: Renegotiating Gender and Power*. New Brunswick: Rutgers University Press, 1990.

Swindells, Julia, *Victorian Writing and Working Women: the Other Side of Silence*. Cambridge: Polity, 1985.

Taylor, Barbara, *Eve and the New Jerusalem: Socialism and Feminism in the Nineteenth Century*. London: Virago 1983.

Thompson, Nicola Diane, ed., *Victorian Women Writers and the Woman Question*. Cambridge University Press, 1999.

Tuchman, Gaye, with Fortin, Nina E., *Edging Women Out: Victorian Novelists, Publishers and Social Change*. London: Routledge, 1989.

WOMEN WRITERS AND RELIGION

Baker, Joseph Ellis, *The Novel and the Oxford Movement*. Princeton Studies in English 8. Princeton University Press, 1932.

Bowie, Fiona, Kirkwood, Deborah and Ardener, Shirley, eds., *Women and Missions: Past and Present*. Oxford: Berg, 1993.

Chapman, Raymond, *Faith and Revolt: Studies in the Literary Influence of the Oxford Movement*. London: Weidenfeld and Nicolson, 1970.

Cunningham, Valentine, *Everywhere Spoken Against: Dissent in the Victorian Novel*. Oxford: Clarendon Press, 1975.

Fairchild, Hoxie N., *Religious Trends in English Poetry*. 6 vols. New York: Columbia University Press, 1957.

Heeney, Brian, *The Women's Movement in the Church of England*. Oxford: Clarendon Press, 1988.

Hogan, Anne and Bradstock, Andrew, eds., *Women of Faith in Victorian Culture: Reassessing the Angel in the House*, London: Macmillan, 1998.

Jay, Elisabeth, *The Religion of the Heart: Anglican Evangelicalism and the Nineteenth-Century Novel*. Oxford: Clarendon Press, 1979.

Kreuger, Christine L., *The Reader's Repentance: Women Preachers, Women Writers, and Nineteenth-Century Social Discourse*. University of Chicago Press, 1992.

Maison, Margaret, *Search Your Soul, Eustace: A Survey of the Religious Novel in the Victorian Age*. London: Sheed and Ward, 1961.

Malmgreen, Gail, ed., *Religion in the Lives of English Women: 1760–1930*. London: Croom Helm, 1986.

O'Day, Rosemary, 'Women in Victorian Religion', in Englander, David and O'Day, Rosemary, eds., *Retrieved Riches: Social Investigations in Britain 1840–1914*. Aldershot: Scolar Press, 1995, pp. 339–63.

Owen, Alex, *The Darkened Room: Women, Power, and Spiritualism in late Nineteenth-Century England.* London: Virago Press, 1989.

Purvis, June, *Hard Lessons: the Lives and Education of Working-Class Women in Nineteenth-Century England.* Cambridge: Polity Press, 1989.

Ragussis, Michael, *Figures of Conversion: 'The Jewish Question' and English National Identity.* Durham, NC: Duke University Press, 1995.

Rowbotham, Judith, *Good Girls Make Good Wives: Guidance for Girls in Victorian Fiction.* Oxford: Basil Blackwell, 1989.

Vicinus, Martha, *Independent Women: Work and Community for Single Women 1850–1920.* University of Chicago Press, 1985.

Watson, J. R., *The English Hymn: a Critical and Historical Study.* Oxford: Clarendon Press, 1997.

Wolff, Robert L., *Gains and Losses: Novels of Faith and Doubt in Victorian England.* London: John Murray, 1977.

AUTOBIOGRAPHY, BIOGRAPHY AND SELF-WRITING

Altick, Richard D. *Lives and Letters: a History of Literary Biography in England and America.* New York: Knopf, 1966.

Amigoni, David, *Victorian Biography: Intellectuals and the Ordering of Discourse.* London: Macmillan, 1993.

Batchelor, John, ed., *The Art of Literary Biography.* Oxford University Press, 1995.

Benstock, Shari, *The Private Self: Theory and Practice of Women's Autobiographical Writings.* London: Routledge, 1988.

Corbett, Mary Jean, *Representing Femininity: Middle-Class Subjectivity in Victorian and Edwardian Women's Autobiographies,* New York: Oxford University Press, 1992.

Epstein, William H., *Recognizing Biography.* Philadelphia: University of Pennsylvania Press, 1987.

Hamilton, Ian, *Keepers of the Flame: Literary Estates and the Rise of Biography.* London: Hutchinson, 1992.

Homburger, Eric and Charmley, John, eds., *The Troubled Face of Biography.* Basingstoke: Macmillan, 1988.

Jelenik, Estelle E., *The Tradition of Women's Autobiography.* Boston: Twayne, 1986.

Marcus, Laura, *Auto/biographical Discourses: Theory, Criticism, Practice.* Manchester University Press, 1994.

Meyers, Jeffrey, ed., *The Craft of Literary Biography.* London: Macmillan, 1985.

Nadel, Ira Bruce, *Biography: Fiction, Fact and Form.* London: Macmillan, 1984.

Newey, Vincent and Shaw, Philip, *Mortal Pages, Literary Lives: Studies in Nineteenth-Century Autobiography.* Aldershot: Scolar Press, 1996.

Peterson, Linda H., *Traditions of Victorian Women's Autobiography: the Poetics and Politics of Life Writing,* Charlottesville: University Press of Virginia, 1999.

Sanders, Valerie, *The Private Lives of Victorian Women: Autobiography in Nineteenth-Century England.* London: Harvester Wheatsheaf, 1989.

Smith, Sidonie, *A Poetics of Women's Autobiography.* Bloomington: Indiana University Press, 1987.

WOMEN WRITING FOR CHILDREN

Auerbach, Nina and Knoepflmacher, U. C., eds., *Forbidden Journeys: Fairy Tales and Fantasies by Victorian Women Writers*. University of Chicago Press, 1992.
Bratton, J. S., *The Impact of Victorian Children's Fiction*. London: Croom Helm, 1981.
Clark, Beverly Lyon, *Regendering the School Story: Sassy Sissies and Tattling Tomboys*. New York: Garland, 1996.
Cutt, Margaret Nancy, *Ministering Angels: a Study of Nineteenth-Century Evangelical Writing for Children*. Wormley, Herts.: Five Owls Press, 1979.
Foster, Shirley and Simons, Judy, *What Katy Read: Feminist Re-Readings of 'Classic' Stories for Girls*. London: Macmillan 1995.
Knoepflmacher, U. C. *Ventures into Childland: Victorians, Fairy Tales and Femininity*. University of Chicago Press, 1998.
Lerner, Laurence, *Angels and Absences: Child Deaths in the Nineteenth Century*, Nashville: Vanderbilt University Press, 1997.
McGavran, James Holt, Jr, ed., *Romanticism and Children's Literature in Nineteenth-Century England*. Athens : University of Georgia Press, 1991.
Mitchell, Sally, *The New Girl: Girls' Culture in England 1880–1915*. New York: Columbia University Press, 1995.
Nelson, Claudia, *Boys will be Girls: the Feminine Ethic and British Children's Fiction 1857–1917*. New Brunswick: Rutgers University Press, 1991.
Quigley, Isabel, *The Heirs of Tom Brown: the English School Story*. London: Chatto and Windus, 1982.
Richardson, Alan, *Literature, Education and Romanticism: Reading as Social Practice, 1780–1832*. Cambridge University Press, 1994.

REPRESENTATIONS OF GENDER AND SEXUALITY

Bland, Lucy, *Banishing the Beast: English Feminism and Sexual Morality, 1885–1914*. London: Penguin, 1995.
Conway, Jill, 'Stereotypes of Femininity in a Theory of Sexual Evolution', in Vicinus, Martha, ed., *Suffer and Be Still*. Bloomington: Indiana University Press, 1976, pp. 140–54.
Cott, Nancy, 'Passionlessness: an Interpretation of Victorian Sexual Ideology, 1790–1850', *Signs* 4 (1979), pp. 219–36.
Gilman, Sander, 'Black Bodies, White Bodies: Towards an Iconography of Female Sexuality in Late Nineteenth-Century Art, Medicine and Literature', *Critical Inquiry* 12 (1985), pp. 204–42.
Jackson, Margaret, *The Real Facts of Life: Feminism and the Politics of Sexuality c. 1850–1940*. London: Taylor and Francis, 1994.
Jeffreys, Sheila, *The Spinster and her Enemies: Feminism and Sexuality, 1880–1930*. London: Pandora Press, 1985.
Levy, Anita, *Other Women: the Writing of Class, Race and Gender, 1832–1898*. Princeton University Press, 1991.
Mason, Michael, *The Making of Victorian Sexuality*. Oxford University Press, 1994. *The Making of Victorian Sexual Attitudes*. Oxford University Press, 1994.

Mort, Frank, *Dangerous Sexualities: Medico-Moral Politics in England since 1830*. London: Routledge and Kegan Paul, 1987.

Nead, Lynda, *Myths of Sexuality: Representations of Women in Victorian Britain*. Oxford: Basil Blackwell, 1988.

Pykett, Lyn, *The 'Improper' Feminine: the Women's Sensation Novel and the New Woman Writing*. London: Routledge, 1992.

Russett, Cynthia Eagle, *Sexual Science: the Victorian Construction of Womanhood*. Cambridge, MA: Harvard University Press, 1989.

Showalter, Elaine, *The Female Malady: Women, Madness and English Culture, 1830–1980*. London: Virago, 1987.

Walkowitz, Judith, *City of Dreadful Delight: Narratives of Sexual Danger in Late-Victorian London*. London: Virago, 1992.

THE DOMESTIC SPHERE

Armstrong, Nancy, *Desire and Domestic Fiction: a Political History of the Novel*. Oxford University Press, 1987.

Cohen, Monica. *Professional Domesticity in the Victorian Novel: Women, Work and Home*, Cambridge University Press, 1998.

Davidoff, Leonore, *Best Circles: Women and Society in Victorian England*. Totowa, NJ: Rowman, 1973.

Davidoff, Leonore and Hall, Catherine, *Family Fortunes: Men and Women of the English Middle Class, 1780–1850*. London: Hutchinson, 1987.

Gallagher, Catherine, *The Industrial Reformation of English Fiction: Social Discourse and Narrative Form*. University of Chicago Press, 1985.

Poovey, Mary, *Uneven Developments: the Ideological Work of Gender in Mid-Victorian England*. University of Chicago Press, 1988.

WOMEN AND THE THEATRE

Carlson, Julie, *In the Theatre of Romanticism: Coleridge, Nationalism, Women*. Cambridge University Press, 1994.

Davis, Tracy C., *Actresses as Working Women*. London: Routledge, 1991.

Davis, Tracy C. and Donkin, Ellen, eds., *Women and Playwriting in Nineteenth-Century Britain*. Cambridge University Press, 1999.

Donkin, Ellen, *Getting Into the Act: Women Playwrights in London, 1776–1829*. London: Routledge, 1995.

Marshall, Gail, *Actresses on the Victorian Stage: Feminine Performance and the Galatea Myth*. Cambridge University Press, 1998.

Poovey, Mary, *The Proper Lady and the Woman Writer: the Ideology of Style in Mary Wollstonecraft, Jane Austen, and Mary Shelley*. University of Chicago Press, 1984.

Powell, Kerry, *Women and Victorian Theatre*. Cambridge University Press, 1997.

Stowell, Sheila, *A Stage of Their Own: Feminist Playwrights of the Suffrage Era*. Manchester University Press, 1992.

Index